Unequal Allies?

*United States Security and Alliance Policy
Toward Japan, 1945–1960*

Unequal Allies?

United States Security and Alliance Policy

Toward Japan, 1945–1960

John Swenson-Wright

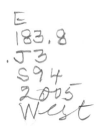
STANFORD UNIVERSITY PRESS

Stanford, California 2005

Stanford University Press
Stanford, California
© 2005 by the Board of Trustees of the
Leland Stanford Junior University

Library of Congress Cataloging-in-Publication Data

Swenson-Wright, John.
    Unequal allies? : United States security and alliance policy
toward Japan, 1945–1960 / John Swenson-Wright.
        p. cm.
    Includes bibliographical references and index.
    ISBN 0-8047-3961-7 (cloth : alk. paper)
    1. United States—Foreign relations—Japan. 2. Japan—
Foreign relations—United States. 3. United States—Foreign
relations—1945–1953. 4. United States—Foreign
relations—1953–1961. 5. National security—United
States—History—20th century. 6. National security—
Japan—History—20th century. 7. Alliances—History—20th
century. I. Title.
E183.8.J3S94 2005
327.73052'09'045—dc22

                                                  2004016215

Printed in the United States of America
Original Printing 2005
Last figure below indicates year of this printing:
14   13   12   11   10   09   08   07   06   05

Typeset at Stanford University Press in 10/13 Sabon

FOR SOFIA

Acknowledgments

In completing a project that has involved drawing on the archival re-sources of three countries, there are invariably many individuals and in-stitutions to whom I am indebted. In particular, I would like to express my deep appreciation to my dissertation supervisors, Professors Rose-mary Foot and Arthur Stockwin, for their encouragement and construc-tive criticism throughout the lengthy process of researching and writing the dissertation, as well as for their inspirational support throughout my academic career. Adam Roberts provided helpful advice at the very be-ginning of the research process, while my final examiners, Robert O'Neill and Saki Dockrill helped with critical insights and in encouraging me to pursue publication.

The Economic and Social Research Council generously funded my time as a graduate student at Oxford, while support from the Tōdai-Ox-ford exchange fellowship enabled me to spend valuable time in Tokyo, working in the Gaimushō archives. Grants from the St. Antony's College Cha Fund and an award from the Eisenhower World Affairs Institute al-lowed me to spend four critical weeks in Abilene, Kansas, examining ma-terial in the Eisenhower Presidential Library.

In Japan, I benefited from the guidance and encouragement of the late Professor Kōsaka Masataka, who first sparked my interest in the histori-cal aspects of post-war Japanese diplomacy and who was an inspiration, both in his critical and scholarly objectivity and in his enthusiasm for dis-cussing international relations. Also in Japan, I was fortunate to receive advice and assistance from a number of individuals including: Asao Shinichirō, Chiba Kazuo, Kan Hideki, Kawasaki Takeshi, Komachi

Kyōji, Muramatsu Michio, Muramatsu Yasuo, Satō Yukio, Satō Haruko, Teshima Ryūichi, Wakaizumi Kei, Watanabe Akio, Yamamoto Yoshinobu, and Yachi Shotarō. In the United States, Michael Green, George Packard, Michael Schaller, William Sherman, Nathaniel Thayer, and Robert Wampler were generous with their time, either in commenting on my work or in agreeing to be interviewed. Among archivists, I am grateful for the assistance of Wilbert Mahoney and Ken Schlessinger at the National Archives, and at the Eisenhower Library, Herbert Pankratz and David Haight were especially helpful. In the United Kingdom, Sir Hugh Cortazzi kindly commented on early drafts of the thesis, while John Gaddis, as a visiting professor in Oxford, encouraged me to consider the importance of issues of culture and identity in International Relations. The opportunity to present draft versions of aspects of the book at seminars in Boston, Ithaca, Cambridge, London, Oxford, Sheffield, Kyoto, Tokyo, and Odawara helped me sharpen the argument. Friends and colleagues across two continents, in particular Burke Burnett, Oiwa Yuri, Alan Hodges, Alison Lester, James Newton, and Maria Almeida provided hospitality, patiently tolerated my archival digressions, and in one critical instance provided late-night emergency child-care.

First books are also an opportunity to remember past teachers, and from my undergraduate days at Oxford I am especially grateful to Wendy Carlin, David Hine, and James Plaskett. I owe a special debt of thanks to the Reischauer Center at SAIS, Johns Hopkins, for enabling me to develop my interest in Japan at a critical stage in my graduate career. Inōye Meiko, in particular was vital in enabling me to come to grips with the Japanese language. In Cambridge, my students helped (and continue to help) by challenging my assertions and by forcing me to clarify my assumptions. Similarly, I thank all my colleagues at the East Asia Institute for their support and for providing a congenial and stimulating environment for both research and teaching, while the fellows of Darwin College remain a constant source of collegiality and intellectual companionship that represents the very best features of the Cambridge system. I owe particular thanks to Victor Swenson and Sarah Belchetz-Swenson for persuading me, many years ago, to embark on an academic career. I remain grateful for the patience and professionalism of everyone at Stanford University Press involved in shepherding the manuscript from submission to publication. In particular, I would like to thank Muriel Bell for supporting the proposal from the very beginning, as well as John Feneron and Carmen Borbon-Wu, and also Leo Kanner, whose copy-editing shrewdness rescued many a failing sentence and kept my unwieldly anglicisms at bay. Finally, I am most indebted to Zoe Swenson-Wright for years of encouragement and tolerant acceptance of late nights at the office and too many lost weekends. All omissions, and errors of interpretation, are naturally my own.

John Swenson-Wright
Cambridge, July 2004

Contents

Tables and Figures

Abbreviations

ABCC	Atomic Bomb Casualty Commission
AEC	Atomic Energy Commission
ANZUS	Security Treaty between Australia, New Zealand, and the United States of America
CIA	Central Intelligence Agency
CinCPAC	Commander in Chief, Pacific Command
CinCFE	Commander in Chief in the Far East
FEC	Far Eastern Commission
GARIOA	"Government and Relief in Occupied Area"
GRI	Government of the Ryukyu Islands
ICBM	intercontinental ballistic missile
JCS	Joint Chiefs of Staff
JDA	Japan Defense Agency
JSP	Japan Socialist Party
KMT	Kuomintang
LDP	Liberal Democratic Party
MITI	Ministry of International Trade and Industry
MSA	Mutual Security Act
NATO	North Atlantic Treaty Organization
NDC	National Defense Council
NSA	National Safety Agency
NPR	National Police Reserve
NSC	National Security Council
OCB	Operations Coordinating Board
OSP	offshore procurement

PACOM   Pacific Command
PARC   Policy Affairs Research Council (of LDP)
POLAD   Political Advisor
PPS   Policy Planning Staff
PRC   People's Republic of China
PSB   Psychological Strategy Board
SCAP   Supreme Commander of the Allied Powers
SDF   Self-Defense Force
USCAR   US Civil Administration of the Ryukyus
USIA   United States Information Agency

Macrons are used in the text to reflect Japanese orthography, but are dispensed with in the case of common place names such as Tokyo and Ryukyus

Unequal Allies?

United States Security and Alliance Policy
Toward Japan, 1945–1960

Introduction

Anniversaries are occasions for reflection. In 2001, the fiftieth anniversary of the signing of the San Francisco Peace Treaty of 1951 formally ending the Allied Occupation of Japan was an opportunity for sober contemplation of the strengths and weaknesses of a US-Japan relationship that has remained remarkably durable despite the vicissitudes of the intervening years.[1] From the tension of the Cold War, through the economic miracle years of the 1960s, and on to the burden-sharing debates of the late 1970s and reemerging Cold War rivalry of the 1980s, the institutional, personal, and historical ties binding Japan and the United States have successfully accommodated and adapted to a range of domestic and international pressures. There was nothing inevitable about this process. Indeed, in light of the bitterness over the Pacific War—resulting in part from the dehumanizing propaganda of the conflict and from the casualties, both men in battle and the civilians who perished in the fire-bombings and terminal nuclear devastation—it is surprising that these two countries were able to achieve a reconciliation, let alone the partnership that emerged over the course of half a century.

That the bilateral relationship should not be taken for granted began to emerge with the gradual disappearance at the end of the century of the stabilizing certainties of the Cold War. The late 1990s had been a period of major change for the security relationship between the United States and Japan. Following the end of the ideological and military stand-off between Russia and the West, the United States had gradually begun to question some of the assumptions shaping the deployment of American forces in East Asia and the various military alliances underpinning the US regional presence. An early illustration of this process was the Clinton administration's East Asian Strategic Review co-ordinated and publicized by Assistant Secretary of Defense Joseph Nye in February 1995, outlining Washington's commitment to regional stability and stipulating a continuing US presence in East Asia of approximately 100,000 uniformed personnel. Where Japan was concerned, perhaps the most dramatic development had been the issuing in September 1997 of a new set of joint guidelines, mapping out in extensive detail the basis for bilateral security cooperation between the Japanese and American governments and substantially revising the previous set of provisions agreed to in 1978. Although this had not altered the formal Security Treaty between the two countries dating from 1960, it undoubtedly represented the most far-ranging reassessment of security ties short of an actual review of the existing treaty.

Not surprisingly, interest in this new development was intense on both sides of the Pacific, generating a plethora of unofficial and official reports, think-tank studies, joint conferences, and press articles. For example, in the United States there were calls from some quarters for a withdrawal of US troops from Japan, based in part on the assumption that the Japanese could and ought to do more to meet their own defense requirements, and in part out of a sense that an arguably reduced set of threats in the region no longer required the United States to play the role of local stabilizer and security guarantor.[2] In addition, the considerable and high-profile political tensions associated with the raping of a twelve-year-old Okinawan girl by US marines in September 1995 strengthened local demands by the Japanese public that the American military presence in Japan be significantly reduced.

Pressure for a reassessment of security ties between Washington and Tokyo was not especially surprising. As Japan had steadily grown economically stronger and more confident since the mid-1960s, a bilateral relationship once dominated by strategic concerns and America's rivalry with the Communist bloc had increasingly become influenced by the debate over "fair" competition and financial and trade liberalization. During the 1980s, the US Congress singled out Japan's growing trade surplus with the United States as proof of illegitimate Japanese business practices and of a relationship between government and the business sector that was allegedly overly collusive and at odds with the free-trade principles central to the post-1945 Bretton Woods international trading regime. Over time, press and political commentary came to portray the Japanese economic challenge as more of a threat to America's national interests than the traditional military and ideological challenge posed by the Soviet Union. Moreover, the first Gulf War of 1991 and a series of drawn-out and often acrimonious discussions between the American and Japanese governments over the size of Japan's financial contribution to the Allied coalition reinforced US congressional criticisms that Japan was insufficiently committed to its alliance relationship with the United States, either ideologically or in simple practical terms. Outspoken and inflammatory statements by politicians in Washington provoked equally emotional responses from Diet representatives in Tokyo, and a relationship frequently hailed, in the famous phrase of Senator (and former ambassador to Japan) Mike Mansfield, as "America's most important bilateral relationship bar none" seemed to be becoming poisoned by mutual mistrust and even, at times, racial antipathy.

As Japan's economy slowed down in the early 1990s in the face of a series of financial crises, and particularly following the collapse of the ruling Liberal Democratic Party (LDP) government in 1993 (the first defeat for Japan's conservatives in 38 years), American popular and political preoccupation with rivalry with Japan diminished in intensity. Nevertheless, the sense of distrust and conflict persisted in some quarters, casting a shadow over the signs of recent security cooperation. In assessing the likely success of the new security guidelines, most analysis focused understandably on contemporary developments. However, surprisingly absent from the debate was much in the way of an informed discussion of the historical background to the bilateral relationship.[3] Constrained by bureaucratic schedules and time pressures, policy professionals are rarely free to take a long-term view, but it is questionable whether decision-makers can be confident of choosing the right course of action without a full and accurate understanding of the past.[4]

This tendency toward historical myopia appeared to change at the turn of the century. In October 2000, in the midst of the presidential transition from Clinton to George W. Bush, a cross-party group of American policy-makers and security specialists, led by two distinguished Washington Japan-hands (Richard Armitage[5] for the Republicans and Joseph Nye for the Democrats), released a report arguing vigorously for a more "mature partnership" between the United States and Japan and stressing that the 1997 defense guidelines should be seen as a floor rather than a ceiling for future bilateral defense cooperation. Past US-Japan policy was criticized for being too episodic and betraying a lack of leadership. In its place, the report called for a strengthened and expanded US commitment to the defense of Japan, enhanced bilateral military cooperation, and a more mobile and flexible US-Japan defense structure; wider sharing of defense technology and intelligence; and the removal of Japan's long-standing prohibition on its participation in collective security initiatives. Most important of all, the report stressed that a more self-consciously independent Japanese foreign policy need not be at odds with America's diplomatic priorities.

> U.S. policy must consider Japan's goals, even as it strives to ensure that our agenda is well understood and actively supported by Tokyo. Washington must recognize that multilateral efforts are important to Tokyo. The Japanese Government regards such initiatives as expressions of national identity, not as attempts to undermine U.S. leadership. . . . The search for an independent Japanese identity in foreign affairs is not in conflict with American diplomacy. Indeed, the United States and Japan largely share the same overall diplomatic goals. The two countries have many common interests.[6]

This acknowledgment of the importance of Japan's foreign policy-making autonomy almost certainly reflected an American awareness that, alongside the stress on multilateralism, Japan was injecting a more pronounced sense of realism into its security and defense policies. During the second half of the 1990s, newly emerging regional threats (whether current or potential) in the form of China's rapidly expanding defense budgets and the challenge posed by North Korea's biological, chemical, and possibly nuclear weapons, as well as its expanding ballistic missile capabilities, encouraged an incremental but nonetheless distinct shift in attitudes, both among Japanese policy-makers and, significantly, among the Japanese public.[7] Against such a backdrop of perceived security vulnerability, it was reasonable for US policy-makers to assume that the policy of their Japanese counterparts would increasingly dovetail, albeit not always perfectly, with American strategic priorities.

In terms of the following analysis, the importance of the Nye-Armitage report is the resonance it has with the views of American policy-makers dealing with Japan during the early Cold War. For individuals such as John Foster Dulles, George Kennan, Joseph Grew, Dean Rusk, John Allison, and Douglas MacArthur II, managing the post-war relationship with Japan involved much more than merely using the security relationship with Tokyo to advance US strategic interests. Central to their vision of the post-war partnership was the concept of an active alliance, one in which the common interests of Washington and Tokyo would be advanced by both sides of the relationship, and in a manner that would be in accordance with Japan's own security and diplomatic policy priorities. On the American side, this did not imply an identity of foreign policy interests, but the understanding, or at least the expectation, was that there were enough common points of interests to ensure a mutually beneficial security partnership. Periodically, and over time, this hope would be tempered by the realization that domestic and institutional weaknesses in Japan undercut the ability to foster an active partnership. Nonetheless, these positive expectations remained a critically important aspect of American thinking on Japan from the late 1940s through the 1950s.

Stressing the importance of mutuality as a policy objective helps also in refining our understanding of the historiographical debate among diplomatic historians and political scientists who have looked closely at the post-war bilateral relationship. American writers, such as Edwin Reischauer and Robert Ward, in assessing the nature of US-Japan relations in the early post-war period, tended to accentuate the positive dimension, by highlighting, for example, the achievements of the US Occupation as an instance of enlightened social engineering, or by stressing that post-war Japan's political and economic development was converging on a Western-oriented model of modernization.[8] By contrast, later revisionist writers, such as John Dower and Chalmers Johnson, have been far more critical of American policy, seeing it, in its most extreme form, as inherently exploitative rather than enlightened, intent on subordinating legitimate Japanese interests and aspirations to US wishes and fostering ultimately a debilitating and dependent relationship between the weaker and the stronger power.[9] The following analysis takes issue with both these opposing schools of thought and advances a post-revisionist interpretation which acknowledges the practical limitations and, in certain instances, shortcomings of US policy but which nonetheless recognizes the attempt to devise an active and mutually beneficial partnership with Japan.

The Historiographical Background

Detailed and scholarly English-language historical studies of the post-war US-Japan security relationship are relatively rare, especially by comparison with examinations of the US relationship with China and other aspects of American Cold War policy toward East Asia.[10] Among the existing studies, there has been a tendency to focus on specific events or issues,[11] or more commonly to adopt a chronological or thematic approach extending over a broad time period, but not necessarily relying extensively on primary source materials in addressing historical questions.[12] A common approach has also been to discuss the security relationship from a narrowly contemporary viewpoint.[13] Recent years have seen the first attempts to fill the gap in the historical literature. For example, Roger Buckley's work is an interesting and provocative early attempt to examine the bilateral relationship, drawing on both American and British diplomatic sources as well as much of the English-language secondary literature on US-Japan relations.[14] However, it is probably fair to argue that Buckley's analysis represents a preliminary foray into the accessible archival records—a body of material which, with the passage of time, has grown extensively in terms of both documents in the National Archives in Washington, DC, and in the various Presidential libraries and the published *Foreign Relations of the United States (FRUS)* series.

Toward the end of the 1990s Walter LaFeber published a valuable and detailed assessment of the entire US-Japan relationship, from its beginning in the mid-nineteenth century until the present.[15] His book is a major piece of imaginative and scholarly synthesis and interpretation and will doubtless stand as the definitive one-volume history of the overall relationship for many years to come. It is particularly noteworthy in drawing on the work of Japanese, American, and British scholars. LaFeber, although not formally a Japan specialist, was able to cite from a body of translated Japanese secondary material which enabled him to provide one of the first attempts at a genuinely cross-cultural analysis of the post-war relationship.

The most detailed examination of the post-war US-Japan relationship to date is to be found in Michael Schaller's book *Altered States*.[16] An extensively researched analysis, the study focuses on the period from 1945 to 1974. Besides examining material in the National Archives, it relies on a large number of manuscript collections, including the Truman and Eisenhower Presidential libraries, as well as (albeit to a lesser extent) the Kennedy and Johnson archives. The volume builds on Schaller's past examination of the American Occupation of Japan and his critical biography of General Douglas MacArthur,[17] and is particularly valuable for its careful examination of a range of issues encompassing the political, economic, and security aspects of the relationship.[18]

While these recent works signify the start of a long overdue historiographical debate on the character of the Cold War US-Japan relationship, none of them concentrate exclusively on security issues. The few diplomatic histories that examine this aspect of the relationship tend to be limited to the period of the Occupation, before Japan regained formal sovereignty.[19] Marc Gallicchio has written about the early post-war security relationship, and has outlined American East Asian security policy in a volume edited by Cohen and Iriye.[20] However, there has been no systematic effort by diplomatic historians or by historians of international relations to examine the role of Japan in US strategic policy toward East Asia beyond the Occupation and especially during the 1950s—a period when arguably the bilateral security relationship was most fraught with tensions and at its most vulnerable. The analysis in the following pages attempts to address this gap and also, in the process, to re-examine some of the central assumptions which have shaped past and contemporary views of the overall US-Japan relationship.

In present-day Japan, preoccupation with issues of equality and the country's apparent subordination to the United States remains intense.[21] During the 1950s these feelings were, if anything, more pronounced. At a time when Japan was still recovering from the material and psychological devastation of World War II, there was no mistaking the enormous difference in power and global influence between the United States, a "preponderant power"[22] on the world stage, and Japan, a pale shadow of its pre-war self in terms of both its economic and industrial strength and its international and, especially, regional influence. Actual power disparities were quickly translated into a perception on the part of many Japanese that American politicians in Washington were inclined to treat Japan as a pawn within its wider foreign policy agenda.[23] The United States, during both the Truman and the Eisenhower administrations, was assumed to be dismissive of legitimate Japanese aspirations and overly inclined to place US Cold War objectives ahead of Japan's policy priorities.[24] Japan, in short, was forced, whether it liked it or not, to play the role of submissive and accommodating follower of American global interests. Although both countries were formally aligned on one side of the East-West divide by virtue of the Peace and Security treaties signed in San Francisco in 1951, the alliance was, in this interpretation, at best a tenuous and one-sided relationship in which Japanese sovereignty and national ambitions received only passing acknowledgment from the United States. The clearest symbol of this imbalance in the minds of many contemporary observers was the Security Treaty of 1951, allowing the United States to station American forces in Japan for an indefinite period, to be used not only in defending Japan against a possible attack from the Soviet Union or the People's Republic of China, but also in promoting and enhancing America's strategic presence in East Asia.

To say that this perceived inequality rankled in the minds of critics on both the left and the right of the political spectrum in Japan would be an understatement. Japanese popular dissatisfaction grew in intensity, especially during the later stages of the 1950s (particularly after 1957), and the imbalance was only adjusted in 1960 with the agreement between the administrations of Dwight Eisenhower and Kishi Nobusuke on a new Mutual Security Treaty. This change appeared to represent a shift to a more balanced relationship, and after 1960, during the Kennedy and Ikeda administrations, with attention much more focused on economic matters, Japanese grievances and criticism became much less pronounced. Nonetheless, the climate of the times quickly came to shape later scholarly analysis of bilateral relations and it became almost a truism to argue that the United States had been willing during the 1950s to discount legitimate Japanese national aspirations and inclined to take its security and overall relationship with Japan for granted.[25]

The following analysis re-assesses this claim by reconstructing the policy-making process in the United States as it related to US-Japan security issues,[26] and also by examining the diplomatic relationship between Japanese and American government officials in both countries. The central question considers how and with what degree of success the US government developed its post-war security relationship with Japan from 1945 to 1960 and the extent to which issues of equality and mutuality may have shaped America's Japan policy. The impetus for this investigation was the suspicion that the US view of the emerging security relationship might be more complex than traditional, critical interpretations had suggested—that from the perspective of Washington there might have been self-interested, pragmatic reasons for accommodating Japanese national interests which have been insufficiently examined in the existing literature. Equality and mutuality, in this context, imply more than simple formal acknowledgment of Japan's sovereignty and independence. The US government's ability to establish and develop a sustainable alliance relationship with Japan may have rested critically on American policy-makers' recognition of the importance of psychological and emotive factors, as well as more conventional material interests—either economic advantages in the form of direct assistance and trading opportunities, or the military protection afforded by US conventional and nuclear capabilities.

These psychological concerns were reflected in Japanese early post-war preoccupation with questions of cultural legitimacy and national identity,[27] often centered on the country's constitution. My intention has been to consider the extent to which recognition of the importance of these issues shaped the views and actions of American policy-makers in dealing with Japan.

Responding to Japanese concerns over sovereignty could potentially generate a sense of mutuality in the bilateral relationship which in turn might provide a basis for an effective and lasting long-term security partnership. Such a perspective could go some way to explaining the longevity of US-Japanese post-war security cooperation, despite later economic tensions and historical and cultural differences (not least of which were the tensions associated with the Pacific War), which might have been expected to divide rather than unite the former wartime opponents. However, while attention to psychological and cultural issues is likely to have been a necessary requirement for a durable and effective alliance, it may not have been sufficient to generate active and vigorous bilateral cooperation. Domestic politics and internal faction tension, mainly among Japan's conservative leaders, may have seriously undercut US efforts to work with Japan—a theme that runs throughout the chapters which follow.

The investigation does not purport to be an exhaustive analysis of the views of all the principal actors on both sides of the relationship. Rather, it focuses on the perceptions and motivations of those US policy-makers central to the security relationship with Japan, in an attempt to consider how important a role the concept of mutuality played in the Japan policy of the Truman and Eisenhower administrations. In addition, the analysis examines the reasons why Japan was judged by the United States to be important in terms of security and how these altered over time. It considers, in particular, how and why the focus on rearmament changed during the 1950s, setting the issue in the context of America's wider strategic policy in the early Cold War, while also examining incidents and controversies which threatened to destabilize the security relationship. Japanese views on security and alliance ties with the United States are assessed, principally by focusing on the policies of prime ministers Yoshida Shigeru, Hatoyama Ichirō, and Kishi Nobusuke, and also by highlighting the responses of individuals within the Gaimushō (Japan's Foreign Ministry) and Japan's defense community to US security and alliance initiatives.

Each chapter deals with issues that are central to the security relationship[28] during the period under study. Chapter one examines the early stages in the development of the bilateral relationship from 1945 to 1950, and focuses on the tensions between US policy-makers in Washington and officials in the American-dominated Occupation in Japan, drawing on some of the new scholarship on this critically important period that has recently appeared in both Japan and the United States. Chapter two extends this analysis beyond 1950, with the Korean War as the principal turning point, and also considers in detail the debate over rearmament within the Japanese government as well as a wider set of controversies relating to the new American-sponsored Constitution of 1947. The constitutional issue, while somewhat separate from conventional security concerns, is significant both because of specific provisions in the document limiting Japan's rearmament (Article 9—the famous "no-war clause") and because of the important political tensions it generated within Japan. These tensions continued throughout the 1950s, involving questions of legitimacy and nationalism, and arguably explain in part the difficulties encountered by the United States in developing an effective security partnership with Japan.

Chapter three examines some of the important practical elements of the early security relationship, mainly the drafting of an Administrative Agreement governing the stationing of US forces in Japan, as well as highlighting the multilateral context in which these talks took place by examining the early debate over Japan's post-war relationship with China. As with the constitutional question, the Sino-Japanese topic ranges beyond narrowly defined security issues, but is important in illustrating the major differences between the United States and its allies (principally the United Kingdom) over how best to develop a cooperative post-Occupation relationship with Japan.

Chapter four considers the role of Japan within US strategic policy in East Asia by concentrating on the issue of Okinawa and the Ryukyu and Ogasawara islands mainly during the two Eisenhower administrations from 1953 to 1960. Okinawa was important not only because it served as the central and most important base in America's Far Eastern perimeter defense strategy, but also because of the clear challenge it posed to the State Department–supported policy of accommodating and harmonizing as far as possible US security objectives and Japanese concerns over national sovereignty and territorial integrity.

Chapter five narrows the focus of the analysis to the *Lucky Dragon* crisis of 1954—an incident which represented the most serious challenge to the bilateral relationship since the Occupation. The crisis revolved around US hydrogen bomb tests in the Pacific and reveals the tension between America's broad Cold War strategic choices and developing effective alliance relations. The chapter, in highlighting Japanese domestic political instability, at the same time reveals that US security concerns in relation to Japan involved not only the problem of external aggression, but also American worries over the risk of internal subversion in Japan—concerns which may or may not have been justified but are nonetheless vitally important in understanding the development of the bilateral relationship.

Finally, chapter six examines perhaps the most immediate and obvious security controversy between Japan and the United States during the 1950s—the debate over rearmament and the renegotiation of the Security Treaty, beginning with the visit to Washington of Foreign Minister Shigemitsu in 1955, and culminating in the Kishi administration's agreement to a new Mutual Security Treaty in 1960. The chapter also, by focusing on the Japan-Soviet normalization talks of 1955–56, further explores the theme of Japanese domestic political instability introduced in chapter five and its importance in explaining the difficulties faced by the United States in promoting a worthwhile security partnership with Japan.

Each of the chapters either challenges, questions, or qualifies existing interpretations of the US-Japan relationship during the period under examination. As a diplomatic history, the study attempts a fresh assessment, offering a new perspective, and drawing on a considerable body of archival material that has received limited attention to date.[29] It is based heavily on US diplomatic (and where relevant, British Foreign Office) records, but there remains a considerable body of documentation that has yet to be declassified, leaving room, therefore, at some point for new interpretations. Moreover, on the Japanese side there is a striking shortage of comparable primary material. The early part of the analysis draws on available records in the Japanese Foreign Ministry archives in Tokyo, but for the period beyond 1953 the available material becomes much thinner. Consequently, for the later part of the period, I rely on the secondary accounts of Japanese scholars (both in English and in Japanese), as well as press and journal articles from the period. Japanese diplomatic historians have traditionally dug deeply into the American and British archives in analyzing the bilateral relationship,[30] and increasingly younger scholars are developing new and original interpretations based on these

sources, as well as on interviews with some of the Japanese protago-
nists.[31] However, until the Japanese government decides to join the rest of
the developed world in opening its post-war archives to extensive, independent scholarly scrutiny, Japanese historians interested in understanding the US-Japan relationship will continue to have to rely on US archival
collections for much of their source material.

As well as addressing specific questions central to the US-Japan relationship, the analysis, by closely scrutinizing US diplomatic records, attempts to cast light on a wider historiographical debate among scholars
of US Cold War diplomacy. Studies of both President Eisenhower and his
secretary of state, John Foster Dulles, have increasingly built up a complex and variegated picture of both men as foreign policy practitioners.
The interpretive dialogue among academics has moved a considerable
distance away from the earlier orthodoxy that tended to view Dulles as a
rigid, ideologically doctrinaire and unsophisticated secretary of state and
Eisenhower as a disengaged chief executive with little appreciation of the
subtleties of international relations.[32] My intention (in contrast with the
latest works on the US-Japan relationship by LaFeber and Schaller, which
do not directly address this debate) has been to assess the validity of the
more positive revisionist studies by examining Dulles and Eisenhower's
policy-making in the context of America's security relationship with Japan.

There are some aspects of the overall relationship from 1945 to 1960
that I have intentionally chosen not to address. In order to concentrate on
the security dimension, the analysis has not scrutinized the economic
character of the relationship. It has not, for example, examined the role
of Japan's developing trade and investment connections with Southeast
Asia—an area where US and Japanese leaders at times cooperated and
disagreed over policy. Nor has it pursued in any great detail, beyond considering Japan's treaty with Taiwan in 1952, the complicated political
and economic issues associated with post-war Sino-Japanese relations.[33]
It is perhaps also important to stress that what follows is primarily a
study of the diplomatic relationship and therefore focuses on elite-level
interaction. It concentrates on the conflicts and agreements between the
governments and leaders in both countries and consequently considers
the views of opposition parties, interest groups, and public opinion in
America and Japan only to the extent that they cast light on this relationship.

Theoretical Observations

All writers approach their material under the influence—either conscious or unconscious—of preconceptions, assumptions, and biases. Historians tend, as has often been remarked, to leave such assumptions buried, hidden often from their own view as well as that of their audience. By contrast, their colleagues in the social sciences are trained to highlight from the outset the key issues and intellectual certainties that underpin their research. In this spirit, it might be helpful, in examining the security relationship, to identify a number of central theoretical propositions from the international relations literature—although, since my approach is fundamentally historical, it must be emphasized that such observations are tentative rather than conclusive. With this caveat, there are a number of questions and issues which immediately come to mind.

Competing Typologies

Where does Japan stand in existing alliance typologies? While Arnold Wolfers, in his succinct definition, has stressed the military dimension of alliances,[34] other writers, such as Robert Osgood, have offered a broader characterization in which an important distinction is drawn between stated goals and actual intentions. According to Osgood:

> There are four principal functions of alliances and they are not necessarily mutually exclusive: accretion of external power, internal security, restraint of allies, and international order. . . . Internal security is sometimes a more important function of alliance for a weak state than accretion of external power. In recognition of the international significance of internal threats and developments which are often supported covertly from outside, alliances may be intended principally to enhance the security or stability of an ally's government or regime, often by legitimizing material assistance or military intervention against internal opposition. This purpose is usually not made explicit, however, since intervention in the domestic affairs of another state, even at that state's invitation, has acquired a stigma in the age of popular national governments.[35]

It is possible that internal security considerations may have been a decisive factor in the development of the US-Japan security relationship and therefore Osgood's description (rather than Wolfer's) may be the more accurate of the two accounts.

Realism versus Culture

Perhaps the most well-known attempt by international relations theorists to make sense of alliance behavior is to be found in the work of

Stephen Walt. Writing from a neorealist perspective (with its stress on "system-level" explanations and the materialist, rational, and power-based motivations of competing nation-states in an anarchic world), Walt argues that alliance decisions can best be explained by the concept of "balance of threat." In a bipolar environment, typified by the Cold War competition between the United States and the Soviet Union, individual countries choose to ally with one another to offset and protect themselves against those rival states which are judged, in terms of power, geographical proximity, offensive capabilities, and hostile intentions to be the most threatening. This is in contrast to the traditional theory of balance of power, which says little if anything about motivation, focusing instead on the raw strength of individual states, measured in terms of population, economic and military strength, technical sophistication, and political stability.[36] Factors such as ideology, foreign assistance, or political similarities between states are of relatively limited importance in explaining specific alliances, and, confronted with the choice between aligning with a threatening opponent ("bandwagoning") and joining a countervailing coalition ("balancing"), states will, for the most part, "balance" rather than "bandwagon."[37] Walt's analysis deals mainly with alliance behavior in the Middle East during the Cold War, but purports also to be a general theory, valid in a variety of contexts and, therefore, arguably of use in explaining US-Japan security relations in the late 1940s and 1950s.[38]

In recent years, and particularly since the end of the Cold War, the neorealist approach has been challenged from a number of directions. Historians, particularly those specializing in diplomatic history, have criticized international relations theory in general on methodological grounds. Neorealist theorists, according to this view, in their effort to devise generalizable propositions with strong predictive value have been too eager to simplify and to devise abstract models which are of little value in understanding inherently complex and often unique historical events. This does not mean that there is no room for identifying particular trends or speculating about "long-term forces" in human history.[39] It does, however, require a recognition that human behavior, at the level of either the individual or the nation-state, involves a degree of indeterminacy and chance, together with a variety of motivating factors (either implicit or explicit) and background conditions which make narrowly defined predictions unhelpful and often inaccurate. International relations (IR) theorists in general (and neorealists in particular), in their stress on rationality, in their enthusiasm for "parsimony" or simplicity in proposing theories, and also in modeling their work on a mistaken view of the scientific process as practiced by physicists and chemists, have become hemmed in by an investigative approach that appears to leave no room for the genuinely social dimension of human activity. Repeatable laboratory experiments, involving quantifiable reagents, of the type favored by practitioners of natural science are of little value in making sense of the role of individual personalities, mass movements, or nonrational behavior so often important in shaping historical events. Moreover, scientific research (as new developments in the field of chaos and complexity illustrate) has itself increasingly come to recognize the importance of apparently random or at least unpredictable events in shaping outcomes in the physical world, while still acknowledging that scientific "laws" or regularities shape the environment which scientists seek to understand. In this regard, scientists, historians, and social scientists stand on common ground. This is particularly true of scientists who work in what John Lewis Gaddis has characterized as the "semi-hard" sciences of biology and geology—fields of investigation which share with history and international relations the challenge of devising coherent and comprehensive explanations of past events from which one can draw generalizable observations of value in loosely anticipating (albeit not predicting in a precise sense) future developments. Underlying this common approach are familiar analytical tools—the use, for example, of reason, logic, imagination, metaphor, and analogy, as well as the application of well-established principles for judging the reliability and coherence of individual theories and the accuracy of data in a given field—either, for example, the fossil collections of paleontologists, the opinion-polls of political scientists, or the archival records of diplomatic historians.[40]

This is not the place to examine in detail the arguments of historians and IR theorists, although it is perhaps important to reiterate that the approach adopted here favors the historical perspective.[41] It should also be stressed that many IR specialists (in part in direct response to Gaddis's criticism) have begun to re-examine their own long-standing theoretical assumptions. This is perhaps reflected most strikingly where questions of culture and national identity are concerned. Samuel Huntington, for example, has been at the forefront of the movement among American social scientists to challenge the neorealist stress on power, arguing that cultural factors expressed through competing forms of "civilization identities" are increasingly central in understanding post–Cold War international relations.[42] In the process, there has been a steady chipping away at the assumption of rationality underpinning IR theory. Promoters of "reflec-tivist" or "constructivist" theory, such as Alexander Wendt, have drawn on sociological arguments to argue for an explicit effort to address issues of culture and identity, while some writers have returned to the ambi-tious, large-canvas works of Arnold Toynbee and C. W. Manning in crit-icizing the work of neorealists and neoliberals.[43] Most striking of all, per-haps, has been the sign that neorealists themselves are inching away from their earlier commitment to rationalist theories, although in the process they appear to be advancing propositions which most historians would accept as self-evident, if not banal.[44]

Where alliance theory is concerned, interest in culture has led to new theoretical work challenging the neorealist position.[45] Michael Barnett, for example, has argued that the concept of state identity rather than bal-ance of threat is of more use in explaining alliance behavior in the Mid-dle East during the Cold War. Similarly, Thomas Risse-Kappen, in ana-lyzing the durability of the NATO alliance during the Cold War, has emphasized the importance of the development of a security community (based on shared norms and common democratic and cultural values) rather than neorealist approaches, which fail, in his assessment, to ex-plain adequately why variations in power between the superpowers ap-pear to have had little impact on alliance choices.[46] Even Walt himself, in his most recent writing, attempting to explain both the durability and the disintegration of alliances, has apparently departed considerably from a systems-level, rationality-based account of state behavior. He now recog-nizes that domestic politics, misperceptions, irrational factors such as personal pique, and demographic and social trends which incorporate ethnic and cultural factors can all have an important role in shaping al-liances.[47] Parsimony seems to be yielding to the diversity and complexity of historical analysis.

In light of these developments, it is appropriate to consider what value the new stress on culture might have in understanding the US-Japan se-curity relationship in the 1940s and 1950s. Peter Katzenstein, for exam-ple, has argued that where security issues are concerned Japan has a "col-lective identity," first established in the 1950s, that involves a consensus on the virtues of anti-militarism, a preference for economic development over rearmament, and a bias in favor of defining national security in non-military terms.[48] At first sight, this claim might not seem especially con-tentious. Certainly, as the Gulf War of 1991 demonstrated, Japan's reluc-tance to engage in military action is well documented, while the Japanese state's focus on economic development is a central feature in the literature of international political economy. The difficulty lies in making the leap from specific policy choices to the notion of national or collective identity expressed in terms of cultural norms. As Ōtake Hideo has pointed out, much of the discussion over Japanese security policy in the 1950s can be explained in terms of political choices as well as the cognitive frameworks of individual Japanese leaders.[49] Moreover, detailed analysis of intellectual and political debates in Japan throughout the post-war period reveals that there has been little if any agreement on the nature of the state or nation since 1945.[50] If anything, the intensity of the debate over this issue (together with institutional obstacles—such as the difficulty of constitutional reform—has constrained policy options (particularly in the security field), creating in the process the illusion of consensus, rather than genuine collective agreement.[51]

The difficulty with the approach favored by Katzenstein and others is two-fold. First, the concepts of culture and identity are notoriously slippery and hard to define. Certainly, sociologists and anthropologists have spent considerable time and energy arguing over terminology, and some writers have criticized the tendency to view identity as a "social fact."[52] Yet this hardly seems a basis for ignoring the concept altogether. Much useful work has been carried out by scholars who recognize that cultures "are not static entities" but who are also frustrated by the failure of existing theories (particularly those stressing the importance of international structures) to explain state behavior.[53] This type of cultural approach draws, at its best, on a range of analytical tools and source materials, combining intellectual, political, and social history, but without carrying out the detailed investigation of bureaucratic decision-making favored by diplomatic historians. Here lies the second shortcoming in Katzenstein's work. The key challenge involved in incorporating cultural analysis in studies of relations between nations is (as Akira Iriye has recently pointed out[54]) the need to combine both approaches—the detailed study of policy-making as well as the thematic, comprehensive investigation of the role of emotion, mood, affect, and ideas (frequently expressed symbolically) in creating an "imagined community" at the level of the nation-state.[55] Any such study would clearly be an ambitious and lengthy undertaking, requiring detailed multidisciplinary training as well as familiarity with a diverse body of primary and secondary sources. The approach here is much more modest in scope and falls clearly within the tradition of diplomatic history. Nevertheless, accepting the importance of culture helps to highlight features that have tended to be ignored or at least underemphasized in existing studies of the US-Japan relationship. This is particularly true of the late 1940s and early 1950s when it was clear that US State Department officials, in seeking to develop a stable and effective working partnership with Japan, were particularly concerned about issues of Japanese culture and identity (even if the language used in describing such concepts was far removed from the traditional vocabulary of social scientists). Just as focusing on culture is valuable, it is also important to stress that a detailed study of archival sources can raise legitimate doubts regarding some of the assumptions of the cultural and political science studies of Japanese security policy.[56]

Small versus Large Powers

Finally, in addition to the role of culture and national distinctiveness, the question of state size, in particular the distinction between small and great powers, may have an impact on alliance formation—a point argued by Robert L. Rothstein. Rothstein suggests that small powers are inclined, because of their relative vulnerability, to focus on short-term rather than long-term goals[57]—a strategy that seems, in the field of international relations, somewhat analogous to the behavioral economists' notion of "satisficing"—the idea that in an uncertain world, firms (or in this case states) sacrifice their rationally desirable goal of profit maximization (the promotion of the national interest) in favor of more limited objectives.[58] Rothstein also argues that uncertainty encourages small powers to focus on foreign rather than domestic policy, while also demanding from their alliance partners that they be accorded "formal equality in all situations." These three points—the stress on short-term goals, the primacy of foreign policy, and the emphasis on equality—all seem at odds with the conventional view of Japan, which often depicts the country as a state dominated by domestic political concerns, unwilling to articulate forcefully its foreign policy goals, and resigned to a subordinate rather than a leading role.[59] At the same time, some Japanese scholars have suggested that Japan's leaders, especially during the 1950s, have thought in terms of long-term strategic objectives—albeit objectives which have been defined in economic rather than military terms.[60] A detailed examination of the bilateral security relationship may help in assessing the theoretical validity of Rothstein's claims regarding small powers, as well as the degree to which Japan's alleged cultural and political distinctiveness may have influenced its ties with the United States. It would be overly ambitious to expect the analysis in the following pages to resolve the differences between these theories of alliance behavior. Nonetheless, there is surely a case for making our assumptions as transparent as possible in the expectation that the findings from the archival record will allow, in the concluding chapter, some assessment of the strengths and weaknesses of these competing arguments.

CHAPTER ONE

"Neither Victors nor Vanquished"

Establishing the US-Japan Alliance, 1945–50

On September 4, 1951, President Harry S. Truman, speaking in the opulent surroundings of the San Francisco Opera House, attempted to characterize the Peace Treaty heralding the official end to hostilities between Japan and the Allied Powers. The Treaty and the process that had led up to it could be likened, in the President's words, to an "intercontinental cable"[1]—an interwoven collection of strands representing the political, military, economic, and cultural ties that would in time bind Japan and the nations of the world into a mutually supportive international partnership. With allowance for the rhetorical hyperbole that such dignified occasions often demand, the President's words accurately summarized the important elements in the emerging alliance relationship between the United States and Japan. Traditional interpretations of relations between Washington and Tokyo have tended to focus on a limited number of these elements—one or two of the strands that were to link the two countries together over the coming years. Economic and military issues have understandably (given the prominence of these themes during the Cold War) received much attention, with a number of scholars finding in the relatively unbalanced power relationship between Washington and Tokyo evidence to support their claim that the US-Japan alliance relationship was inequitable. The United States has often been depicted as a coercive power, dictating terms and compelling Japan to subordinate its interests to America's wider Cold War priorities in the struggle with the Soviet Union.[2] Such arguments are mistaken or at the very least overstated. By neglecting the cultural, emotive, and psychological aspects of the alliance in favor of its power political features, critics of the United

States have risked presenting a distorted picture of the US-Japan relationship in 1951. They have also, perhaps, fallen into the trap of imposing the future on the past, assuming that the Japanese disgruntlement over the alliance that emerged in the later part of the 1950s was equally present at the beginning of the decade.

In reality, influential American policy-makers (particularly in the State Department), in laying the foundation for a long-term cooperative relationship with Japan, were acutely sensitive to Japanese concerns for equality, sovereignty, and independence. Paying heed to these concerns often meant recognizing the limits to the promotion of distinctly American political and ideological norms, in favor of alternative cultural and national traditions. Washington recognized, from the vantage point of American national self-interest, that a secure sense of Japanese national identity (often expressed in cultural terms) was as important as a healthy economy and military preparedness in ensuring a strong and durable alliance partnership. Accounts of the evolution of the US-Japan relationship from 1945 to 1951, even when interpreting Washington's policy sympathetically, have often avoided explicitly addressing this issue.[3] Consequently, the continuities underlying America's early post-war Japan policy have been concealed, along with the constructive role played by a small but influential number of American decision-makers based in Tokyo and Washington. Rather than attributing the success of the San Francisco Peace Treaty process to one or two individuals as has sometimes been the case,[4] it is perhaps more helpful to view the outcome as a long-term, collective initiative—a case of enlightened teamwork. This initiative did not pass unchallenged. It faced opposition not only from other groups within the Washington bureaucracy (most notably the Department of Defense and the Joint Chiefs of Staff), but also from some of America's Allied partners (in particular Australia, New Zealand, and the United Kingdom). Examining the role of culture and identity in alliance building highlights this international dimension to the San Francisco Treaty process as well as the importance of questions of "self" and nation in post-war Japan.

MacArthur Pre-eminent, 1945–47

Early US thinking on Japan at the beginning of the post-war period was, in some respects, haphazard and uncoordinated, subject to departmental and personal tensions and often overshadowed by Washington's priorities in other regions of the globe, most notably Europe and the Asian mainland. During the Pacific War, planning naturally focused on the practical issue of winning the war, while still leaving room for consideration of how best to secure and manage a post-conflict Japan. However, both issues quickly became subject to the complexities of bureaucratic decision-making and overlapping jurisdictions, and the un-coordinated involvement of many individuals from both the military and the diplomatic wings of the US government frequently prevented the emergence of clear and coherent policy prescriptions.[5] Within the State Department policy-making responsibility for Japan had been concen-trated in the hands of a relatively small group of individuals. Figures such as Joseph Grew, former ambassador to Japan during the 1930s, Eugene Dooman (who served with Grew in Tokyo), and Joseph Ballantine be-longed to a small coterie of experts who had had considerable exposure to Japan, and whose expertise occasionally gave them important policy-making influence in a Washington where understanding of things Japa-nese was often shallow and impressionistic.[6] However, this influence was tempered by rivalry with the State Department's "China Hands," men such as Owen Lattimore and Andrew Ross, who envisaged an American post-war Asian policy focused on China rather than Japan and who, as the war drew to a close, advocated a tough, relatively punitive policy to-ward Japan. With the appointment, in January 1944, of Stanley Horn-beck as the head of the newly established Office of Far Eastern Affairs[7] within the State Department, it appeared as if the "China Crowd" was to be the dominant voice. However, barely three and a half months later Grew had replaced Hornbeck and the pendulum of bureaucratic influ-ence had swung back in the direction of the Japan specialists.[8] It would be simplistic and misleading to view this tension as the pre-eminent, po-larizing fault line within the government.[9] Japan-related policy-making reflected a range of competing interests, including the War and Navy De-partments, their separate, at times competing divisions, and the cabinet-level principles and their various assistant secretaries—formally second-tier players but often important participants in the policy process, such as Dean Acheson (assistant, in turn undersecretary, and ultimately secretary of state), Archibald MacLeish (also at State), and John McCloy (from the War Department). This wider, more general discord over policy, as well as the internal State Department debate is important in understanding the difficulties of Washington's professional foreign policy specialists in devising a coherent blueprint for post-war relations with Japan.

Grew's influence in shaping America's early post-war Japan policy was felt most decisively in the question of the post-war status of the Japanese Emperor and the discussion of how best to secure the surrender of Japan. As is well known, opinion in Washington in the summer of 1945 was divided. In drafting the Potsdam Declaration of July 26, calling for Japan's unconditional surrender, President Truman and his secretary of state, James Byrnes, had been reluctant to provide a clear guarantee to the Japanese that the Emperor system could be maintained following a Japanese capitulation. By contrast, Grew (by now Undersecretary of State) and Secretary of War Henry Stimson pointed out that some reassurance to Japan might strengthen the hands of moderates in the Japanese cabinet in favor of surrender, thus obviating the need for a difficult and, in terms of human life, costly Allied invasion of Japan's principal islands. Based on his pre-war experience in Japan, Grew recognized the symbolic significance of the imperial institution as a source of national unity and widespread popular loyalty. His advice was instrumental in persuading the American government to dispatch a letter to Tokyo on August 11 indicating that Japan's future form of government would be decided in accordance with the wishes of the Japanese people. The letter, in effect, was a restatement rather than a modification of the Potsdam Declaration. Nonetheless it was interpreted in Tokyo as implicitly guaranteeing Japan's national traditions and was used to overcome opposition from militarists and conservative voices in the Japanese cabinet who, despite the destruction wrought by two atomic bomb attacks, still advocated a policy of no surrender and virtual national suicide.[10] As Hata Ikuhiko has observed:

> If the allied nations, in their demand for unconditional surrender, had not recognized the importance of Japan's "kokutai" (or national polity), then the pre-arranged plan for death with honor for a hundred million Japanese and a final battle for the homeland would, most likely, have been considerably strengthened.[11]

In the immediate aftermath of the war, despite Grew's earlier recognition of the importance of tradition as a stabilizing force, consideration for Japan's cultural sensibilities was largely absent from American policymaking on Japan, although on key issues such as the importance of maintaining the imperial institution as a source of domestic political stability there were a number of State department officials who shared Grew's stress on continuity, at least for the office if not the man himself.[12] Washington turned its gaze away from the complicated issue of political re-

construction and focused instead on dismantling the Japanese war ma-
chine, preventing a recurrence of Japanese militarism, and ensuring peace
in the Far East. In the words of the US Initial Post-Surrender Policy for
Japan (SWNCC 150, a document drafted on September 2 by the State-
War-Navy Coordinating Council, a forerunner of the National Security
Council), "Japan was the principal if not the only, threat to the tranquil-
ity of the Far East," and "if Japan's military power were destroyed, Japan
and its neighbours would live in peace."[13]

A change of personalities after August 1945 signified a diminished role
for the State Department's Japan specialists. Grew (along with Eugene
Dooman) had retired at the end of the war and was replaced as Undersecretary by Dean Acheson.[14] Acheson felt that the Potsdam Declaration
had been too lenient and, together with Byrnes, believed that a harsh,
albeit not necessarily punitive approach should be adopted toward Japan.[15] He appointed George Atcheson, a China specialist, to serve as de
facto State Department representative and the first Political Advisor (or
POLAD) to General MacArthur's Occupation regime in Japan. Atcheson,
and his deputy John Stewart Service (another China hand) had little sympathy for Japan and reinforced Washington's view that post-surrender
policy should be geared to the country's demilitarization and pacifica-
tion.[16] Such an approach required stern measures, and although the
American government recognized the need to avoid the repetition of Ver-
sailles-style draconian sanctions, many of its recommendations (such as
those of the Pauley Mission of December 1945, calling for major reduc-
tions in Japan's aircraft industry, iron and steel production, ship-building,
and machine-tool capacity) were judged to be very severe.[17]

For the first two years of the post-war Occupation, American policy-
making on Japan was dominated by the figure of General MacArthur, the
Supreme Commander of the Allied Powers (or SCAP as both he and the
Occupation bureaucracy were often referred to). Japan during this period
was in many ways MacArthur's personal domain—a country he administered as if it were an independent fiefdom, with scant regard for the
views of either Washington or the other Allied powers that he nominally
represented.[18] In Moscow in December 1945, the Allies had agreed to establish a Far Eastern Commission (FEC, an eleven-member body, based
in Washington and representing the Allied powers involved in the war
against Japan), together with a smaller Allied Council for Japan in
Tokyo, composed of one representative each from the United States, the
Soviet Union, China, and the British Commonwealth, and designed to

function as an advisory body to MacArthur. Neither organization ever exerted much practical influence. From the very beginning of the Occupation, MacArthur defined and implemented policy almost entirely independently. The rewriting of the Japanese Constitution, dissolution of the zaibatsu (Japan's large industrial combines), and SCAPIN 555, the purge directive of January 1946 that swept away some 418,000 Japanese from public life, were all SCAP initiatives, sometimes introduced secretly and with limited consultation (this was true of the new Constitution) and often (as was the case with the purge) criticized by officials back in Washington.[19] Indeed, despite his dual status as both SCAP and the US Commander in Chief in the Far East (CinCFE), MacArthur deeply resented and resisted any notion of deferring to policy-makers back home in the United States. For much of the Occupation, he refused to acknowledge the authority and independent status of POLAD, the State Department representative in Tokyo, even going so far as to intercept diplomatic cables passing between it and the government in Washington.[20] In the initial years of the Occupation, friction over these issues was relatively limited, largely because of Washington's preoccupation with non-Japan-related issues. In later years, however, as the Cold War intensified and Japan became much more important to Truman and his advisors, MacArthur's independent and imperious style of governing became a major source of tension between Washington and Tokyo.

MacArthur and the wider SCAP bureaucracy cast themselves in the role of reformers, striving, as they implemented a process of demilitarization and democratization, to transform Japanese society almost overnight. Influenced heavily by the interventionist philosophy of the New Deal, and steeped in the proactive, can-do thinking of the modern social sciences, many of SCAP's youthful and enthusiastic social engineers sought to remake Japan in America's own image. However, what this initiative gained from the enthusiasm and conviction of its practitioners, it tended to lose through lack of understanding of the cultural and national context in which these reforms were taking place. Few members of the Occupation had much knowledge of Japan's traditions and language,[21] and in their eagerness to prove that Japan could be made to change—to slough off its allegedly reactionary, "feudal" past—they occasionally overstepped the mark, creating tensions and divisions in Japanese society that would complicate Japan's domestic politics and foreign relations in later years. MacArthur prided himself on understanding "Oriental psychology," and his decision to support the maintenance of the Emperor system and to avoid the trial of the Emperor as a war criminal in 1946 is often hailed as proof of his cultural sensitivity. However, his frequently expressed intention to "Christianize" Japan, the insensitive way in which much of the Occupation was conducted, and MacArthur's extremely limited contact with his Japanese "subjects"[22] raise legitimate doubts about the true extent to which he comprehended events and conditions within Japan.

General MacArthur's ability, from 1945 to early 1947, to run the Occupation largely free from the influence of Washington policy-makers can be explained by MacArthur's personality, by the State Department's relative detachment from events on the ground in Tokyo,[23] and also in terms of the wider international situation and the character of American foreign policy at this time. Harry Truman, after suddenly inheriting the Presidency following the death of Franklin Roosevelt in 1945, found himself confronting a bewildering and complex set of foreign policy challenges. With little experience in foreign affairs, he was often compelled to defer to the advice of his cabinet advisors, and in his first few months in office focused on the immediate task of ending the war with Japan. Japan's surrender in September temporarily eased it out of the President's field of vision, and Truman's attention shifted to Europe and the Middle East, where there was growing concern over the expanding influence of the Soviet Union.[24] Both during World War II and in its immediate aftermath, American policy-makers had had serious reservations about the durability of the wartime alliance between Moscow and Washington. Consequently, the months following the end of the war represented a period of considerable uncertainty and change. There were few clear, unambiguous guides to Soviet intentions and although officials in Washington nervously suspected that Moscow was attempting to carve out spheres of influence on its borders, the Cold War adversarial relationship that was to define international relations for the next forty-five years had not yet fully crystallized.

In the Far East, China much more than Japan was the subject of American concern. Since the latter half of the nineteenth century and John Hay's "Open Door" notes, the United States had increasingly come to think of itself as a Pacific power. The national "frontier" had shifted westward, and for some Americans, especially those active in the Christian missionary movement, America's "Manifest Destiny" had been extended to the Asian continent, most notably to China. It was here, rather than in Japan, that American policy-makers worried about a possible in-

trusion of Soviet influence. Indeed, Truman's decision to use the atomic
bomb at the end of World War II reflected not only a wish to spare Allied
casualties and bring the war to a speedy conclusion, but also a desire to
limit Communist expansion on the Asian mainland.[25]

Moscow's interest in Japan in 1945, by contrast with its involvement
in China, seemed relatively muted. Stalin had, it is true, suggested to Truman that Soviet troops receive the surrender from Japanese forces in
Hokkaido, but after being rebuffed by the President, had declined to pursue the issue. The Russians seemed willing to accept a balancing of interests, implicitly acknowledging America's predominant position in Japan
in return for Washington's recognition of a Soviet sphere of interest in
Romania, Bulgaria, and Hungary.[26] Against such a background, there
was little need or incentive to think in terms of recruiting Japan as a partner in America's wider foreign policy goals—goals which at this stage remained vague and ill-defined. Moreover, even by early 1946, as the rift
between Moscow and Washington widened, Truman was largely preoccupied with domestic matters,[27] hoping to accelerate troop demobilization and reduce the massive military expenditures of the wartime years.
Only by February 1946, and the appearance of George Kennan's "Long
Telegram," advocating a strategy of containment, did Washington begin
to shift gradually toward a policy of "patience and firmness" in confronting Soviet influence.[28] Even then, the East-West conflict was con-
ceived of in economic and political rather than military terms. A national
security ideology had yet to emerge[29] and Japan was viewed largely in isolation. General Charles Willoughby, the head of SCAP's G-2 intelligence
section, suggested at the time that Japan might prove to be a valuable
partner in an American-Soviet conflict,[30] but this remained a minority
view and no attempts were made to develop an active alliance relationship with Japan.[31]

Cold War Tensions and the "Reverse Course," 1947–48

The first signs of a possible change in Japan's status emerged in early
1947. General MacArthur, in a March 17 press conference, dramatically
and unexpectedly called for an end to the Occupation, the rapid conclusion of a Peace Treaty, and the withdrawal of US troops from Japan.
SCAP's announcement set off alarm bells in Washington. The Far Eastern
General had a history of periodically antagonizing the Truman adminis-

tration (as early as 1945, he had annoyed both the President and Acheson by independently authorizing the demobilization of some 200,000 troops based in Japan), and many in Washington were irritated by this latest unsolicited proposal, suspecting that his actions were a deliberate attempt to undermine the government.[32] Indeed, there was evidence to suggest that MacArthur harbored presidential ambitions. As early as 1944, although he was absent from the United States, his name had been submitted in the Wisconsin presidential primaries, and despite suffering a major defeat he privately continued in later years to support the efforts of his backers at home to establish a presidential campaign on his behalf.

Despite the surprise nature of MacArthur's initiative, the Truman administration decided to test the waters for an early Peace Treaty. Early in 1947, Secretary of State George Marshall urged the four-power Council of Foreign Ministers (comprising the principal wartime Allies—Britain, France, the USSR, and the United States) to address the Peace Treaty question, and in July 1947 America officially proposed convening an eleven-nation peace conference in San Francisco on August 19, 1947. This initiative failed largely due to Soviet insistence that peace with Japan should be decided exclusively by the Council of Ministers rather than via a general conference. At the same time, disagreement over the location of the conference, together with Nationalist China's preference for the maintenance of veto rights rather than the two-thirds majority voting principle advocated by the United States, helped to bury any hope of an early agreement.[33]

Although temporarily stymied, MacArthur's peace initiative, necessarily prompted Washington policy-makers to devote greater attention to Japan. In the summer of 1947, the Policy Planning Staff (PPS), set up at the beginning of the year by George Marshall to give more coherence and focus to the policy-making process, began to address the question of Japan—an issue which had been largely overshadowed by preoccupation with European matters. George Kennan, the PPS director, assisted by John P. Davies, his principal advisor on Asian matters, sought to place Japan in a wider geopolitical context than earlier administration studies had done. He challenged the assumption that China should be the focus of America's Asia policy, arguing that China was industrially weak and lacked any significant military or amphibious-based capability to project its influence beyond the Asian mainland. Even should the Chinese Communists come to power, their tenure of office was likely to be brief, while China's powerful nationalism would, in Kennan's view, discourage Mao and his followers from remaining subservient to Moscow.[34] Most important of all, both Kennan and Davies were appalled at the apparent lack of any serious examination of Japan's strategic importance to the United States. Hugh Borton of Columbia University, as Special Assistant to the State Department's Office of Far Eastern Affairs, by August 1947 had prepared a draft treaty of peace with Japan. However, the proposal echoed the demilitarization rhetoric of Potsdam and made no provision for either American or Japanese security interests. For a twenty-five-year period, Japan's government was to be denied the right to possess any military forces, and was to be prohibited from manufacturing either military or civil aircraft. Nor was it to be allowed to stockpile strategic resources or to conduct research into fissionable materials.[35] No attempt was made to relate the terms of a Peace Treaty to America's likely strategic interests in the region.

In the face of a policy-making vacuum on Japan, Kennan and his advisors set about developing new plans. Relying on the advice of the State Department's former Japan specialists—in particular, Grew, Ballantine, and Dooman—Kennan and his associates had, by October, drafted PPS 10, a first attempt to think systematically and broadly about Japan.[36] Kennan was deeply critical of MacArthur's demand for an early Peace Treaty, as well as of the way in which he had administered the Occupation. Two years of SCAP control had failed to create a stable environment in Japan, and in the context of persistent American-Soviet rivalry (the Greek civil war and the Truman Doctrine of March 1947 had highlighted the continuing tension between the superpowers), Japan remained strikingly vulnerable, both politically and economically, to hostile Soviet actions. Such a threat was assumed to take the form of internal subversion rather than direct military aggression or a conventional electoral challenge by Japan's Communists, but, nonetheless, Kennan felt it was sufficiently serious to rule out any possibility of an early peace at this stage. As he pointed out later in his memoirs, Japan

> had no effective means of combating the Communist penetration and political pressure that was already vigorously asserting itself under the occupation and could be depended upon to increase greatly if the occupation was removed and American forces withdrawn. In the face of this situation, the nature of the occupation policies pursued up to this time by General MacArthur's headquarters seemed, on cursory examination, to be such that if they had been devised for the specific purpose of rendering Japanese society vulnerable to Communist political pressures and paving the way for a Communist takeover, they could scarcely have been other than what they were.[37]

As might have been expected in the aftermath of war, the political situation in Japan in the early years of the Occupation had been fluid and highly unpredictable. In late 1945, the country's political forces had regrouped into three main parties—on the left, the Socialists made up of activists and intellectuals reveling in the newly emerging political freedoms that contrasted with the authoritarian wartime regime; and on the right, the Progressives and Liberals who were in essence the direct descendants of the pre-war conservative Seiyūkai and Minseitō. SCAP's Purge Directive of January 4, 1946, by targeting anyone associated with the wartime establishment, swept away the political veterans and established members of these last two groups, leaving in place a relatively inexperienced and politically untested leadership and contributing to the mood of political uncertainty.[38]

The first electoral focal point for these nascent parties came with the elections of April 10, 1946, which effectively unseated the caretaker government of Shidehara Kijūrō, replacing it with a Liberal-Progressive coalition headed by Yoshida Shigeru as prime minister.[39] The new government was in power for just over a year and was dogged from the beginning by internal differences, poor organization, and disaffection among the rank and file of the two partner parties. The government's policy program was vague and unfocused, with many of its members preoccupied with past Seiyūkai-Minseitō rivalries and ensuring their own political advancement. Public opinion quickly turned against a government that appeared unable to combat inflation and the acute shortage of food and commodities that dominated Japan in this early period. In particular, Yoshida's penchant for prescribing harsh economic medicine in the form of mass lay-offs and regular government interference in settling labor disputes added to the government's unpopularity, particularly after MacArthur's order suspending the General Strike of February 1947.

The election of April 25, 1947, heralded an important realignment of political forces. In March, the Progressives has reconstituted themselves as the Democratic Party, drawing into their ranks a splinter group from Yoshida's Liberals led by Ashida Hitoshi, a former diplomat turned politician. The election had delivered a finely balanced outcome, with the Socialists winning 141 seats, the Liberals 132, and the Democrats 126. Teaming up with the Democrats, the Socialists were able, under the leadership of Katayama Tetsu, to capitalize on their ideological distinctiveness and relative novelty in post-war Japanese political life and form a new government. However, here too inter- and intra-party differences in the coalition were soon to prove a problem. Policy-making quickly became bogged down over measures to introduce state control over the country's coal industry—an issue which ultimately prompted 28 Democrats to withdraw from the government, undermining the government's position although not its overall majority in the House of Representatives. Internal divisions were compounded by growing criticism from organized labor (particularly its more radicalized ranks), increasingly irritated by the government's persistent efforts to hold down wages (a source of considerable discontent in a context of spiraling black-market prices), and its seeming inability to address the country's worsening food situation.[40]

Ultimately these policy frustrations prompted an internal adjustment of coalition forces, with Democrats trading places with their Socialist colleagues in the cabinet hierarchy and Ashida assuming the premiership in March 1948. Such adjustments were, however, of limited benefit. Policy and personal differences persisted and were compounded by scandals, including a bribery controversy in which Ashida was himself implicated. Most damaging of all was the controversy in July 1948 over the implementation of the National Public Service Bill—a MacArthur-inspired initiative intended to outlaw strikes in the public sector. The issue split the coalition, encouraging some Democrats (led this time by Shidehara Kijūrō) to regroup a second time, pairing with Yoshida's Liberals to form a new Democratic Liberal Party and ultimately constituting a conservative cabinet in October 1948 under Yoshida's leadership. Such persistent electoral uncertainty—three changes of administration in as many years—highlighted the volatile nature of the times and suggested that the electorate had yet to find its political feet. Under such circumstances, it is hardly surprising that many American government officials, in both Washington and Tokyo, as well as prominent Japanese politicians, worried about the country's long-term stability.[41]

By early 1948, concern over Japan policy had reached the point where Kennan felt the need to fly to Tokyo to meet with MacArthur and examine actual conditions within Japan—a visit he anticipated would not be easy. MacArthur, like many military commanders, jealously guarded his authority, while also harboring a "violent prejudice" toward the State Department. Relations between MacArthur and Marshall were tense, largely on account of earlier disagreements over the importance of Europe and Asia as theaters of operations during World War II, and this, together with MacArthur's general reluctance to defer to Washington, led Kennan to characterize his visit as comparable to talks with a "hostile, foreign power."[42]

Kennan's discoveries during his visit confirmed his earlier belief that a Peace Treaty would be premature. Japan was clearly unready for independence. It lacked its own defense facilities, and the absence of a centralized and organized police force raised serious doubts about the country's ability to maintain internal security. Economically, Japan was still very weak (industrial production in 1947 was only 15 percent of its 1941 level),[43] while the continuation of the zaibatsu deconcentration campaign and the provision of reparations to China and the Philippines were a continuing impediment to long-term recovery. Equally important, Kennan encountered a population resentful of American tutelage and a regime of control that was "parasitical" and oppressive. The costs of the Occupation absorbed as much as a third of the Japanese annual budget, while the policy of requisitioning Japanese houses for Americans as well as the tendency for some Occupation personnel to enrich themselves at the expense of the local population were clearly a source of legitimate Japanese resentment. Moreover, the purge of Japanese officials—a policy which Kennan felt had been carried out "with a dogmatic, impersonal vindictiveness for which there were few examples outside the totalitarian countries themselves"—disproportionately affected individuals predisposed to be sympathetic to the United States and as a result potentially jeopardized long-term US-Japanese relations.[44]

Disturbed by what he had found, Kennan returned to the United States and proposed a detailed set of policy changes. He recommended an end to the reform process of the early Occupation years and emphasized the need to take immediate steps to promote economic recovery. Occupation costs were to be reduced, reparations halted, and the purge program discontinued. To provide for Japan's security from external attack, US tactical forces were to remain in Japan, but only until a peace agreement had been reached. In order to improve internal security, the Japanese police were to be re-equipped and strengthened and a coast-guard and fledgling maritime force established. A long-term US presence in Okinawa would allow America to protect its strategic interests in the region, and, in the meantime, Kennan recommended postponing to the post-treaty period the question of whether the US should continue to have bases on the main Japanese islands. The eventual Peace Treaty ought, in Kennan's view, to be "brief, general and non-punitive."[45]

Perhaps the most significant aspect of Kennan's recommendations was his emphasis on the psychological dimension of the relationship between Japan and the United States. While recognizing that an immediate Peace

Treaty was inappropriate, Kennan was quick to stress the need to encourage Japanese independent responsibility, to return decision-making
authority to the Japanese government, and to minimize the Occupation
presence. This was clear from his proposals for the stationing of American troops in Japan, in which he emphasized the need to be sensitive to
potential slights to Japan's national pride and independence. Locating US
forces away from major population centers and restricting interaction between American troops and ordinary Japanese would "reduce to a minimum the psychological impact of the presence of occupational forces on
the Japanese population."[46] Similarly, promoting cultural exchange between Japan and America and ending press censorship could also be seen
as measures intended to correct the earlier impression that Western political and social customs were being foisted on Japan at the expense of Japanese traditions.

Kennan's recognition of the importance of issues of face and prestige in
the case of Japan was in accordance with his general outlook on American
security policy. As John Lewis Gaddis has pointed out, Kennan, in proposing a strategy of containment vis-à-vis the Soviet Union, rejected a "uni-
versalist" campaign to promote US values and institutions worldwide.
Direct intervention in the affairs of other states could prove counterproductive. He advocated, instead, a more "particularist" approach that relied on support for nationalism as a means of creating points of strength
to resist Soviet expansion and ideological blandishments.[47] Containment,
at this stage, assumed that the Soviet threat was psychological in nature,
heightening the risk of internal subversion in Western Europe and Japan,[48]
rather than military. In this, Kennan displayed an intuitive awareness that,
in thinking about US national security policy, ideology, and national identity, the affective, nonmaterial (and therefore hard to define) factors shaping individual and national behavior might prove as important as
economic growth rates, munitions, and troop numbers—the straightfor-
wardly quantifiable and traditional ingredients of power politics. As he
pointed out in a talk in June 1947, "it is the shadows rather than the substance of things that move the hearts, and sway the deeds of statesmen."[49]

Kennan's recommendations for Japan eventually formed the basis for
NSC 13/2, approved by President Truman on October 9, 1948. It represented a significant shift in thinking and can be seen as the first major re-
definition of America's Japan policy since 1945. Kennan himself regarded
his role in shaping this new policy (with the exception of his involvement
with the Marshall Plan) as his most significant achievement during his

time in government.[50] By contrast, in later years, some Japanese writers have been critical of this change of direction (often referred to as the "Reverse Course"), arguing that it represented a subordination of popular left-wing sentiment in Japan to a narrowly defined American goal of coopting Japan into the Cold War struggle with the Soviet Union.[51] Such criticisms, while perhaps understandable from the vantage point of the 1990s given the tensions in US-Japan relations, can be challenged on a number of grounds. First, they ignore Japanese government and bureaucratic support for the new approach[52] as well as mischaracterizing Japanese sentiment at the time, overlooking the eagerness with which a people that had endured three years of Occupation would have actively welcomed Kennan's initiative.[53] Second, they exaggerate the scope of the change. NSC 13/2 envisaged a gradual restoration of authority to the Japanese government, rather than the emasculation and overturning of earlier reforms. As the document made clear:

> SCAP should be advised to relax pressure steadily but unobtrusively on the Japanese government in connection with these reforms and should intervene only if the Japanese authorities revoke or compromise the fundamentals of the reforms as they proceed in their own way with the process of implementation and adjustment.[54]

Third, they seriously misrepresent US strategic thinking at the time. The militarization of American security policy was a future development, and Washington had not yet embarked on a conscious alliance-building strategy. Despite the undoubted tension between the superpowers, the American government's perspective was limited rather than global in scope. The Truman Doctrine and the Marshall Plan, rhetoric notwithstanding, were attempts to bolster the confidence and position of the Europeans via economic aid and political support rather than the start of a worldwide struggle against international communism.[55] Even following the Czech coup of early 1948, Washington emphasized reassurance for Europe rather than retaliation against a Soviet threat which American intelligence reports suggested was unlikely to develop into military aggression.[56] Moreover, the American Congress rejected military (as opposed to economic) aid to Europe and resisted the establishment of a formal alliance with the West Europeans.[57] Against such a background, Kennan's immediate goal involved simply denying Japan to the Soviet Union—preventing Asia's potentially most powerful industrial country from drifting into the Communist orbit—rather than enlisting an active ally in the defense of the Free World. Kennan's thinking at this stage echoed the balance-of-power philosophy of the nineteenth century, and involved creating separate, independent power centers rather than the division of the world into two ideologically opposed, super-power–dominated spheres of interest.[58] A neutral Japan would not constitute, in Kennan's view, a threat to American interests, and Washington, in 1948, was willing to see a middle-of-the-road government in Tokyo centered on the Socialist Party, rather than a more explicitly conservative, right-wing administration.[59] Even as late as February 1949, Secretary of the Army Kenneth Royall, by publicly questioning, on a visit to Japan, the strategic importance of maintaining US troops in Japan, confirmed that there was no firm agreement in Washington on the precise role that Japan should occupy in American foreign policy.[60]

While Kennan was the critical figure in redefining America's Japan policy at this time, he was not the only person who recognized the need for a change of approach. Paul Nitze, deputy director of the State Department's Office of International Trade, as early as February 1947 was concerned about Japan's economic weakness. Analyzing the global economic situation, Nitze concluded that the world dollar gap was a potentially serious threat to post-war stability. US exports amounting to $16.2 billion far outstripped its $8.7 billion worth of imports from the rest of the world, and the resulting massive short-fall in demand ran the risk of plunging the world into a major recession.[61] In the case of Japan, the loss of pre-war markets on the Asian mainland made the dollar-gap problem particularly severe, while low levels of industrial production, the threat of starvation in 1946, and the loss of some 90 percent of the country's merchant shipping fleet undercut any hope of economic recovery via trade expansion. Nitze approached Acheson and, stressing the dangers of the current policy, persuaded him to take steps to have America ease unilaterally the existing Occupation limits on industrial recovery.[62] In a keynote speech in May 1947, Acheson advocated the rehabilitation of Japan as the "workshop" of Asia (balancing his speech with a call for a similar role for Germany in Europe)—an approach that not only envisaged an economically strong Japan, but also involved linking Japan's trade with the economies of Asia (particularly Southeast Asia), as a way of promoting both political and economic stability in the region.[63]

Acheson's speech marked an increase in awareness in Washington of the importance of Japan in America's foreign policy. However, in the late spring–early summer of 1947, the Truman administration still had its eyes set on Europe rather than Asia as it sought to persuade Congress of the merits of the Marshall Plan. Acheson himself left the State Department in June 1947 (returning only in early 1949),[64] and as a result Nitze's Japan proposal made little immediate headway through the Washington bureaucracy. However, by late 1948, doubtless in part because of the efforts of the PPS, interest in Japan had increased. In particular, Undersecretary of the Army William Draper (prompted by a report critical of SCAP written by James Lee Kaufmann and Harry Kern—two principal figures in the American Council on Japan, a private body of Japan specialists[65]) joined Nitze in drafting a proposal—"Economic stabilization in Japan"—for strengthening the Japanese economy. Following the visit to Japan in May 1948 of the Deconcentration Review Board (a Draper-sponsored measure to halt the process of zaibatsu dissolution), this initiative culminated in early 1949 in the selection (at Nitze's suggestion) of Joseph Dodge to head a mission to Tokyo to restore stability to the Japanese economy. Dodge, a fiscally orthodox Wall Street banker who had cut his policy-making teeth in reforming the post-war German economy, advocated a stringent set of reforms—a nine-point stabilization plan intended to squeeze inflation out of the Japanese economy via a combination of sharp restriction of the money supply, measures to balance the budget and stabilize the exchange rate, and the introduction of modern accounting techniques. The "Dodge Line" (as this policy was subsequently referred to) proved in the long run remarkably effective. After a brief recession, economic growth rates improved and by 1950, industrial output, which in 1948 had been 54.6 percent of the pre-war level, had increased to 83.6 percent. Trade figures also recovered, although not as quickly or as dramatically as output levels.[66]

State and Defense Department Tensions

Despite the efforts by Kennan and Draper to correct some of the political and economic deficiencies of the Occupation, by the early part of 1949 American officials in Washington and in Tokyo were becoming increasingly concerned about the state of US-Japanese relations. In January 1949, Yoshida Shigeru's Democratic Liberal Party, through campaign proposals of tax cuts, increased national independence, and reduced foreign interference in domestic affairs, had won a dramatic victory in Japan's Lower House elections (the first to be held under the new constitution), securing an absolute majority of 264 out of 466 seats.[67] To some observers, this "Yoshida Boom" was a sign of growing Japanese disaffec-

TABLE I

A Comparison of the Japanese Lower House Elections of 1947 and 1949

Popular Vote by Party

Party	1947 No. of votes (thousands)	1947 Percentage of total	1949 No. of votes (thousands)	1949 Percentage of total
Liberal (Democratic Liberal)	7,235	26.5	13,382	43.8
Socialist	7,169	26.2	4,130	13.5
Democratic	6,857	25.1	4,836	15.8
People's Cooperative	1,863	6.8	1,042	3.4
Communist	1,003	3.6	2,985	9.6
Independents	1,614	5.9	2,007	6.6
Minor parties	1,561	5.7	2,209	7.2
TOTAL	27,303		30,590	
Registered voters	40,896		42,091	
Percentage voting		66.7		72.9

Number of Seats by Party

Party	1947 election No. of seats	1947 election Percentage of total	December 1948 No. of seats	December 1948 Percentage of total	1949 election No. of seats	1949 election Percentage of total
Liberal (Democratic Liberal)	132	28.3	152	32.6	264	56.7
Socialist	143	30.7	111	23.8	49	10.5
Democratic	126	27.0	90	19.3	68	14.6
People's Cooperative	31	6.7	29	6.2	14	3.0
Communist	4	0.9	4	0.9	35	7.5
Independents	13	2.8	3	0.6	12	2.6
Minor Parties	17	3.6	58	12.5	24	5.2
TOTAL	466		466		466	

SOURCE: "An Interpretation of the Japanese Lower House Election of January 1949," Feb. 4, 1949, OIR Report, No. 4894, NA-II

tion with the Occupation as well as widespread irritation with the economic hardships associated with the Dodge Line.[68] Yoshida had been able to capitalize on the unpopularity of the coalition cabinets of Katayama and Ashida, while also presenting himself to the electorate as independent-minded and ready to confront the authority of MacArthur and the SCAP administration. As one US report noted in early February, "the general public and the press in Japan have begun to show grudging admiration for the 'stubborn little Tory' who so boldly stood up to the attacks of the Democrats, Socialists, and Communists, on the one hand, and the displeasure of the Occupation officials on the other."[69] However,

Yoshida was not the only beneficiary of public discontent. The Communists also did surprisingly well, exploiting the unpopularity of the Socialists and relying on their tightly organized structure, support within the union movement, and the high-profile successes of the Communists on the Chinese mainland to raise their profile with the Japanese electorate. Dramatically this translated into an increase in their representation in the Lower House from 4 to 35 seats, raising fears both in SCAP and back in Washington of a polarization of political life that might provoke anti-American sentiment.[70]

In order to offset this discontent, and in keeping with NSC 13/2, the Truman administration in the spring of 1949 unexpectedly announced its opposition to any further FEC-sanctioned attempts to extract war reparations from the Japanese government, while stressing the importance of integrating Japan into the international community.[71] However, this initiative received a luke-warm reception from those among America's Allies, most notably the Philippines government, who wished to extract compensation from Japan for the depredations of the war. Wartime memories were vivid and bitter and there was precious little sign of any nascent spirit of reconciliation or compromise.

By August, there were signs that America might be willing to relax further the Occupation regime of control. In Washington, George Kennan, along with W. Walton Butterworth of the State Department's Office of Far Eastern Affairs, favored an early Peace Treaty, while from Tokyo, William Sebald warned that continuation of the Occupation threatened long-term US-Japan relations and recommended the return of sovereignty to the Japanese government.[72] Moreover, Dean Acheson, in his new position as secretary of state, had, since the summer of 1949, been trying to develop a more unified State Department approach to Asian matters through the establishment of a small group of Asia specialists known as the Far Eastern consultants.[73] General recognition that Japan was the most valuable industrial resource in the Far East, as well as a belief in Washington that the Russians were gaining the initiative in the Cold War—a feeling heightened by the Soviet detonation of its first atomic bomb in August 1949—persuaded Acheson that it was time to begin planning for the end of the Occupation.[74] In September, he met with his British counterpart, Ernest Bevin, in Washington, and the two men decided to set the Peace Treaty process in motion. Bevin was scheduled to attend the Commonwealth conference in Canberra in November, and he agreed to sound out the other members of the Far Eastern Commission on the likelihood of their agreeing to a Peace Treaty.[75]

Despite these first steps toward a Peace Treaty, rapid progress toward reaching an agreement with Japan was hampered by bureaucratic tension between the State and Defense departments. While Acheson and the State Department emphasized the negative psychological consequences of delaying a settlement and the risk of heightening anti-American sentiment in Japan, Secretary of Defense Louis Johnson and Omar Bradley, Chairman of the Joint Chiefs of Staff (JCS), argued that international instability militated against an early peace. The Pentagon set out its objections in NSC 60 in December 1949. Largely a reaffirmation of earlier JCS decisions (in particular, NSC 13/3 of May 1949 and NSC 49 of June 1949), the document advanced three central justifications for a delay: first, the continuing unstable political and military situation on the Asian mainland, as well as in Taiwan and Southeast Asia; second, the assumption that any treaty signed without the participation of the Soviet Union and Communist China would jeopardize America's exclusive right to continue stationing military forces in Japan; and third, and perhaps most important, the belief that a Peace Treaty in accordance with the surrender terms of the Potsdam Proclamation of 1945 would offer no assurance of a continuing close relationship between the United States and Japan. As the report made clear, "a treaty consistent with the terms of the armistice by which Japan surrendered could not at this time assure the denial of Japan's ultimate exploitation by the USSR or assure her orientation toward the Western powers."[76]

State Department personnel responsible for Japan policy railed against what they viewed as impractical and overly rigid Defense Department thinking. John Howard, the principal official responsible for Peace Treaty matters, drafted a January memo to Walton Butterworth, assistant secretary of state for far eastern affairs, warning that postponing a settlement ran the risk of undermining any long-term alliance relationship between Washington and Tokyo. "Failure to obtain a peace treaty would seriously disappoint the Japanese in their desire for a treaty, with unfortunate consequences for the continuance of Japan's pro-Western orientation and for Japan's economic recovery."[77] While acknowledging the uncertain security climate in Asia, Howard criticized the Defense and JCS attitude as unrealistic and excessively literal in its interpretation of earlier decisions and in assuming that an agreement with Japan would either require the US military to withdraw from Japan or necessitate "joint-action"— namely, some form of Soviet participation in a future Peace Treaty. Rejecting the notion that the absence of a firm guarantee of Japan's commitment to the United States should be taken as grounds for rejecting a Peace Treaty, Howard emphasized that it was precisely because no such guarantee was attainable that it was imperative to seek an early resolution of the impasse.[78] In this regard, State Department thinking was more imaginative and psychologically astute than Pentagon plans and echoed Kennan's earlier emphasis on the need for a constructive approach in fostering America's long-term alliance relationship with Japan.

> The inaction recommended by the JCS takes no cognizance of the underlying political problem which confronts the United States because of these adverse consequences of inaction. This problem is to determine a course of action which will preserve the security position of the United States in the Far East but will at the same time create a new set of relationships with respect to Japan which will be more stable than present relationships during the foreseeable future under foreseeable conditions.[79]

State Department irritation with the Pentagon was also exacerbated by JCS reluctance to indicate whether or not it was necessary to maintain long-term US bases on Japan's four main islands as well as on the smaller Ryukyu and Bonin island chains to the south. US strategic thinking on Japan had not advanced significantly since 1948 and the discussions associated with NSC 13/2. At that time, Kennan, visiting Tokyo, had written to Secretary of State George Marshall recommending an American Far Eastern security posture centered on bases in Okinawa and the Ryukyus. These bases would form

> the central and most advanced point of a U-shaped security zone embracing the Aleutians, the Ryukyus, the former Japanese mandated islands, and of course Guam. We would then rely on Okinawa-based air power, plus our advance naval power, to prevent the assembling and launching any [sic] amphibious force from any mainland port in the east-central or northeast Asia.[80]

Kennan was very critical of the absence of any clear thinking on America's security policy in the region.

> Today, as far as I can learn, we are operating without any overall strategic concept for the entire western Pacific area . . . We are remaining in Japan principally because we have no international mandate to leave . . . We have formulated no definite objectives with respect to the military security of Japan in the post-treaty period.[81]

Two years later, the position seemed little changed—a sign of bureaucratic inertia and a puzzling reluctance on the part of the US military to give serious thought to Japan.[82] Confronted by bureaucratic deadlock, State Department officials pressed for a clearer statement of JCS views and, in the meantime, were restricted to a gradual, piecemeal restoration of Japanese sovereignty (in December 1949, for example, General MacArthur announced a Christmas amnesty for forty-nine Japanese war criminals[83]), while making periodic statements emphasizing America's commitment to the national independence of its Asian allies.[84]

It would be wrong to assume that Defense Department intransigence was the sole obstacle to an early peace. Acheson, it is true, did claim that the Pentagon, much more than Allied or Communist objections, constituted the chief stumbling block.[85] However, domestic political conditions in the United States also had a role to play. By late 1949, bipartisan consensus on foreign policy had begun to unravel. The Republicans, smarting after the surprise defeat of Thomas Dewey in the 1948 Presidential race and frustrated by their long absence from the White House, were increasingly critical of the Truman administration. An aging Senator Vandenberg was no longer able to play a conciliatory role, and influence was shifting to figures such as Senators Robert Taft, William Knowland, and H. Alexander Smith and former President Herbert Hoover—men who were little inclined to view Truman sympathetically.[86] Republican critics directed their fire against the administration's Asia policy, particularly its refusal to give unconditional support to Taiwan.[87] At the same time the conviction of Alger Hiss on perjury charges in late January 1950 and Joseph McCarthy's launch of his witch-hunt against alleged Communists in the State Department in February forced Acheson and company onto the defensive. The administration had been slowly extending its containment strategy to Asia, but in the face of such fierce Republican attacks was inclined to play safe and retreat from controversial Asian matters—limiting policy to rhetorical pronouncements rather than concrete initiatives. Acheson, in particular, in the spring of 1950, still remained more focused on Europe, often at the expense of US Far Eastern policy.[88]

By March 1950, the Peace Treaty process was gathering momentum again. Since postponing an agreement potentially jeopardized America's long-term relationship with Japan and Washington was now facing added pressure from its allies for an early settlement, some in the State Department felt that further delay might undermine US prestige in the Far East. Since the meeting between Bevin and Acheson in September, Britain had been pressing for a change of direction and, following the Colombo conference of January 1950, the Commonwealth countries, especially Australia and New Zealand, were anxious to see more attention given to Asia and especially to Japan-related peace and security issues. In addition, there were growing fears in Washington that the Soviet Union might exploit the delay by making its own appeal for an early treaty, thereby seizing the initiative from the United States—a fear which may have been heightened by growing Soviet involvement in Asia following its February 14 signing of a treaty of "Friendship, Alliance and Mutual Security" with the People's Republic of China (PRC).[89]

Despite these fresh concerns, the Defense Department continued to drag its feet. Tracy Voorhees, who replaced Draper in March 1949 as the Undersecretary of the Army, sought to delay the Peace Treaty by advocating a "stand-by-SCAP" proposal—an incomplete peace arrangement in which a treaty would be drawn up to deal with economic and political matters leaving other aspects of the Occupation, such as the stationing of US troops in Japan, unchanged. Acheson angrily rejected the Defense proposal, arguing that it was a deliberate attempt to sabotage any hope of an early peace. In the face of continuing Pentagon recalcitrance, State and Defense both agreed that a new decision would be delayed until after Johnson and Bradley had returned from a planned visit to Tokyo to consult with General MacArthur.[90]

The sudden and unexpected outbreak of the Korean War on June 25, 1950, dramatically altered the international and regional context in which America's leaders would have to decide future policy for Japan. There was no doubt in Washington that Moscow was behind North Korea's attack across the 38th parallel, and that a swift Western response was necessary.[91] Uncomfortable memories of the disaster of appeasement at Munich in 1938, as well as the need to preserve American prestige and reassure allies, persuaded the Truman administration to respond swiftly and decisively to the crisis.[92] As North Korean forces swept southward, US troops were rapidly dispatched from Japan into the Pusan enclave at the southeastern tip of Korea to resist the Communist assault and maintain an American toe-hold on the peninsula. The sudden nature of the attack and the need to respond quickly meant that the 8th Army contingents stationed in Japan to police the Occupation were soon drastically undermanned. To compensate for this short-fall and reinforce Japan's internal security in a highly unstable and unpredictable international environment, MacArthur, on July 8, authorized the creation of a National Police Reserve (NPR) of 75,000 men and the addition of 8,000 troops to Japan's existing coastal protection force—the Maritime Safety Board (MSB). This increase, when added to the existing 125,000-strong police force and separate rural police organization of 30,000 men, meant that

Japan now had a 200,000-strong domestic security force. However, it was not clear that this would be an adequate safeguard against future unrest. Although some writers have written approvingly of the speed and firmness with which MacArthur responded in setting up the NPR,[93] policy-makers in Washington were concerned about the Japanese government's ability to maintain domestic security. Even before the outbreak of the war, John Foster Dulles, President Truman's recently appointed special consultant on Japan, and John Allison, the Director of the State Department's office of Northeast Asian Affairs,[94] on a June visit to Tokyo, discovered serious weaknesses in the readiness of the Japanese police force. As Allison pointed out on returning to Washington:

> We were informed by various Japanese, including a member of the National Rural Police, that as presently organized the police system in Japan would be completely ineffective against Communist activities if it were not backed up by American military force and American counterintelligence units. With a large portion of our troops being diverted to Korea, it is extremely doubtful whether or not Japanese police will be able to carry on should any real internal trouble begin.[95]

This was doubtless frustrating to policy-makers in Washington, not only because of the immediate danger resulting from the Korean crisis, but also in light of earlier, long-standing efforts to persuade MacArthur to improve Japan's internal security. Despite repeated requests from the State Department, MacArthur had resisted implementing many of the provisions of NSC 13/2 including those measures intended to strengthen the Japanese police.[96] Even with the setting up of the NPR, the new organization was poorly equipped (armed only with pistols), and MacArthur appears to have concentrated mainly on increasing manpower, with no provision for an improvement in training or equipment. SCAP's contribution to Japan's defense, therefore, may have been exaggerated and (without faulting him for failing to anticipate the Korean attack—Washington after all had also overlooked this possibility), MacArthur can perhaps be legitimately criticized for misreading the international situation and for exaggerating the degree of domestic stability within Japan.

Not only was Japan internally vulnerable, but in Dulles's judgment, the possibility had to be considered that the Soviet-endorsed North Korean aggression was an attempt to disrupt the Peace Treaty process and possibly was the prelude to a more far-reaching attack on key Allied positions worldwide.[97] State and Defense department personnel agreed on the need to strengthen Japan's police force, although they recognized that such a course of action would be difficult in light of both the peace clause (Article 9) of the Japanese Constitution and sections of the FEC's 1947 Basic Surrender Policy for Japan expressly prohibiting rearmament or the creation of a Japanese paramilitary force.

Fundamental changes in American strategic thinking during 1950 might also have been expected to have encouraged a greater emphasis on a distinctly military contribution by Japan to US foreign policy goals. With Paul Nitze replacing George Kennan as head of the PPS in January 1950, the political and economic character of America's containment strategy was increasingly overshadowed by an emphasis on a military response to the Soviet threat. This shift (culminating in April 1950 in a major new statement of US security policy—NSC 68) represented the world as divided into two ideologically opposing camps (the Free and Slave Worlds), and replaced Kennan's selective strategy of strongpoint defense with a much more wide-ranging and ultimately undiscriminating policy of resisting Soviet expansion wherever it might occur. The new policy called for a major US rearmament campaign, eschewing Kennan's psychological subtlety in favor of the rhetoric of bipolar conflict and representing the Soviet threat in terms of readily quantifiable Soviet military capabilities rather than the hard-to-define but nonetheless crucially important intentions of the men in the Kremlin. Universalism, in effect, replaced particularism.[98]

Despite NSC 68's stress on military preparedness and the immediate threat posed by the North Korean attack, US policy-makers proposed only a moderate rearmament strategy for Japan. NSC 68 itself avoided any call for Japanese rearmament, merely indicating that neutrality was no longer a viable option for the Japanese,[99] a point which Acheson, during his talks with Bevin, had already recognized in advocating stronger, positive links between the West and Japan. Although Dulles had raised the specter of a major Soviet worldwide campaign, opinion in Washington was more muted and less concerned about Japan's immediate security. A meeting of the NSC consultants four days after the North Korean attack omitted Japan from its list of critical danger spots comprising Yugoslavia, Iran, and East Germany.[100] Similarly, in NSC 73, an attempt to anticipate Soviet behavior, the National Security Council characterized the North Korean attack as a probing action—a grab for control over Korea and a test of US resolve rather than the beginning of World War III. A direct Soviet attack on Japan was considered improbable.[101] Southeast Asia, if anywhere, was felt to be a more likely target.[102]

Washington planners, fearing that Moscow might attempt to infiltrate
and subvert Japan by using the considerable numbers of World War II
Japanese POWs (some 370,000) still under Soviet control, emphasized
the need to bolster Japan's internal rather than external security.[103] Again,
the political as opposed to the strictly military aspects of the US-Japan relationship were especially important. George Kennan, despite having left
the Policy Planning Staff, continued to play a role in Japan-related matters,[104] warning of the dangers of continuing bureaucratic deadlock over
an early Peace Treaty and emphasizing that the Korean crisis made a
rapid agreement more rather than less important. There was a pressing
need to avoid a lengthy, overly technical document—"the text of the
treaty should be regarded as an instrument in political warfare, and not
as a legal document," and the final agreement should, he argued, contain
no clauses binding the Japanese government to preserve the social and
economic reforms of the Occupation.[105] In language reminiscent of his
earlier criticism of MacArthur, and reflecting a keen sensitivity and pragmatic understanding of the Japanese point of view, Kennan pointed out
the impossibility and undesirability of dictating terms to Tokyo:

> I am against binding the Japanese to anything in the field of domestic policy. I
> think our reform program in Japan, taken in its entirety, has been of dubious
> wisdom and see no reason for trying to perpetuate the memory of something
> which has been at least partially a mistake . . . [W]e are not able to compel
> their obedience. In general, I have a feeling that we have permitted ourselves
> to become confused in our thinking by traditional concepts about Peace Treaty
> problems. Normally a peace treaty was a contract between victor and van-
> quished, defining the terms on which a state of war would be terminated. In
> the present instance, however, we have had five years of actual US administra-
> tion of the country in question. This has given us ample opportunity to estab-
> lish by fiat all the initial conditions of the peace. All that remains is to termi-
> nate the state of war, define the future military arrangements governing the
> protection of Japanese territory, and give the Japanese the best possible psy-
> chological boost for their entry upon the new era. Anything more than that,
> and particularly anything reflecting a continuation of the school-masterish and
> smug attitude which has detracted so much from the excellent achievements of
> our occupation, can only be unhelpful.[106]

Kennan was not alone in recognizing the need for an early peace.
Dulles also pushed for an agreement and urged Acheson not to allow preoccupation with the military dimensions of the Korean situation to undermine the political relationship with Japan.[107] However, progress was
complicated by the continuing intransigence of the Defense Department,

which was now talking loudly about the need to preserve US base rights in Japan. According to some interpretations, much of the success in overcoming Pentagon resistance can be attributed to General MacArthur. In particular, it has been suggested that MacArthur's willingness (during the June visits to Tokyo of Bradley, Johnson, and Dulles) to abandon his opposition to US bases in Japan and to accept the possibility of a Japan closely allied with the United States (he had previously advocated neutrality for Japan) had a mediating effect, bridging the gap between State and Defense and removing Pentagon opposition to an early peace.[108] However, this argument appears to have been overstated. As Michael Schaller has pointed out, Bradley and Johnson, following their June trip, while pleased by MacArthur's concessions, were still unwilling to commit themselves to an early peace, and as late as August 14, the Defense Department remained opposed to the State Department position.[109] The final breakthrough may have had less to do with MacArthur's compromise and more with pressure from Dulles and perhaps most importantly the President, acting in his role as bureaucratic arbiter. Truman had a knack for simplifying complicated arguments, pulling "out of the pile that jackstraw which seemed to be the crucial element."[110] Intervening in the interdepartmental debate, he pushed aside the more detailed objections, argued instead for a simple, brief non-punitive Peace Treaty with Japan, and by September 14 was able to announce the beginning of informal, exploratory Peace Treaty talks with the FEC countries and the appointment of John Foster Dulles as principal American negotiator.[111]

CHAPTER TWO

Negotiating the Peace and Security
Treaties, 1950–51

Dulles's appointment as negotiator in the exploratory treaty talks in September 1950 opened up the route to a settlement, but in the process multiple actors in both Japan and the United States would need to be accommodated and their often conflicting views reconciled. At the same time, the special consultant and his State Department colleagues would have to manage a very diverse international constituency, offsetting calls for a punitive, retributive settlement in favor of a more pragmatic, enlightened Peace Treaty establishing a foundation for Japan's reengagement with the international community. As part of this process, US officials would not only have to address the easily identifiable, concrete demands of competing national interests, they would also have to make sense of mixed and, at times, intentionally confusing messages coming out of Tokyo. During this period and in fact throughout the 1950s, the Americans would find it difficult to separate Japan's true intentions from the "background noise" that intruded as Japanese politicians sought to placate a volatile and at times confused public opinion at home. The national mood in Japan remained ambivalent, balanced—seemingly precariously—between the traditionalism of the past and the new ideals of the 1947 Constitution. Monitoring and responding astutely to this uncertainty would prove a challenging task for Dulles and his colleagues but one which arguably they managed surprisingly well.

Early Japanese Views on Peace and Rearmament

The Korean War, representing a further militarization of Cold War relations, was a defining moment less for Japan than for the United States.

From the start of the post-war period in 1945, the Gaimushō (the Japanese Foreign Ministry) had given serious thought to questions of peace and security.[1] Despite suffering a disproportionately higher cut in personnel than other Japanese government ministries at the start of the Occupation, the Foreign Ministry (or Central Liaison Agency as it was officially known under SCAP), while harboring no illusions about Japan's ability to significantly influence the terms of a future Peace Treaty, worked energetically to restore Japan's independence and to preserve the country's sense of national identity in the wake of its bitter and demoralizing defeat. In January 1946, Gaimushō officials argued that Japan was entitled to build up its military forces in order to protect against external attack and advocated a policy of "defensive and peaceful armament" (bōeiteki heiwateki gunbi). Such an approach would, in the Gaimushō's somewhat optimistic estimation, remove the need and ultimately the right of Allied governments to station troops in Japan.[2]

Against the backdrop of the Potsdam Proclamation and America's Basic Post Surrender policy with its emphasis on democratization and demilitarization, the Japanese rearmament proposal was a non-starter. It was soon replaced in May 1946 by a second Gaimushō policy envisaging permanent neutrality for Japan with security guaranteed via the establishment of a regional collective security system.[3] As a practical measure, this new suggestion carried little weight in light of developing tensions with the Soviet Union and Washington's unwillingness to approve an end to the Occupation. Thus for a period of approximately half a year the Gaimushō devoted little attention to security planning.[4]

MacArthur's surprise call for an early Peace Treaty in March 1947 prompted a more urgent and structured approach from the Japanese government, and two groups within the Foreign Ministry—a Peace Treaty Deliberation Office (Kōwa jōyaku shingi shitsu) and the ministry's Research Secretariat (Kenkyu kanji kai)—were assigned responsibility for drawing up Peace Treaty proposals. SCAP was aware of this bureaucratic development, but in agreement with the Japanese government concealed it from public attention to offset any possible negative Allied response. In light of the continuing bitterness of wartime memories, it was judged important and politic at this stage to avoid any hint that the Japanese government might be playing an active role in the Peace Treaty process.[5]

Significant progress in developing a well-defined Japanese security policy only occurred through the intervention of Ashida Hitoshi. Ashida, a former diplomat, founder of Japan's post-war Progressive Party, and, in 1947, foreign minister in the Socialist coalition cabinet of Prime Minister

Katayama Tetsu, was a conservative politician with little sympathy for notions of permanent neutrality and disarmament.[6] In 1946, as chairman of the Japanese Diet's Lower House subcommittee set up to review SCAP's draft Constitution, he had played the central role in rewriting Article 9—the no-war "peace clause" of the Constitution—subtly reinterpreting the clause in a fashion that would allow Japan to use military force defensively.[7] Ashida, like many conservative politicians, and in keeping with the views of his Foreign Ministry colleagues, was unenthusiastic about the stationing of foreign troops in Japan, especially if their presence was for the purpose of monitoring and supervising Japan as well as protecting it from external attack. However, he recognized that for the immediate future Japan would not be in a position to guarantee its own security independently. During late 1947, he attempted in a series of memoranda to present a new draft Gaimushō security proposal to the Truman administration. Ashida's view of Japan's security choices embraced two scenarios. If US-Soviet relations remained relatively stable and harmonious, external security would be met via the United Nations, while Japan would assume responsibility for its own internal security. In the more likely event of a widening rift between Washington and Moscow, the United States would be entitled to maintain bases in Japan to protect Japan and to enhance security in the Pacific, while Japan would build up its land and maritime police organizations in order to enhance security at home. Under the bases arrangement, US forces would be stationed on Japan's four main islands only in times of crisis. At other times they would be situated on Japan's smaller, outlying territories.[8]

Ashida's security initiative failed to bear fruit in the context of 1947 largely because of bureaucratic disagreements in the US administration and the lack of international tensions grave enough to persuade Washington that ending the Occupation was essential. Nevertheless, his proposal was an important turning-point in Japanese thinking about security and post-war foreign policy. It was a clear sign that Tokyo was prepared to align itself explicitly with the United States and to embark on a program of modest rearmament for the purpose of enhancing the country's internal security. Moreover, Ashida's initiative demonstrated that Japan, even during the Occupation, was able to draft its own independent proposals and, in its essentials, it foreshadowed the security arrangement that Prime Minister Yoshida eventually signed with the United States in September 1951.

Following the failure of Ashida's initiative and the fall of the Katayama coalition government in the summer of 1948, the Foreign Ministry lost some of its assertiveness in formulating security policy. Under Yoshida's premiership, it was generally less adept diplomatically and found it harder to generate internal consensus.[9] Nevertheless, it maintained a realistic awareness of the challenges associated with the peace process. Gaimushō personnel, for example, quickly recognized the difficulties the United States would experience in persuading the Allied countries to accept a relatively lenient or "soft" Peace Treaty.[10] Similarly, the Foreign Ministry warned of a rise in domestic opposition and anti-Americanism if a high-profile US military presence continued on Japan's main islands.[11] At times, the Gaimushō's thinking paralleled the views of the State Department, as in May 1950, when both acknowledged that a comprehensive Peace Treaty including both the Soviet Union and Communist China was unrealistic, and recognized that the key threat to Japan's security was the risk of subversion ("miezaru shinryaku"—an unseen attack), rather than a direct, external assault by the Soviet Union.[12]

Despite the realism of the post-Ashida Gaimushō, a climate of hesitancy clouded the thoughts of the Foreign Ministry bureaucrats in Kasumigaseki, Japan's Whitehall, and it was only because of pressure and decisiveness from Prime Minister Yoshida that significant steps were taken to build a foundation for close cooperation with the United States. Yoshida's policy activism led him to establish two separate research groups within the ministry, one dealing with the Peace Treaty and all related security matters and a second focusing more narrowly on strictly military matters. These two bodies produced a considerable number of reports in the final years of the Occupation dealing with Peace Treaty questions.[13]

The prime minister, who acted as his own foreign minister, was very much a pragmatist, believing that by skillful and active diplomacy Japan could recover from its wartime defeat.[14] Despite having served as a diplomat in the pre-war period, he would often act separately from the Gaimushō, launching major initiatives without informing the Foreign Ministry, for example, sending two of his closest advisors—Ikeda Hayato and Shirasu Jirō—to Washington in April 1950 to inform the Americans privately that he would welcome the stationing of US troops in Japan.[15] This independent style and a tendency to keep close counsel has made it difficult to interpret his thinking on certain critical diplomatic issues, a problem compounded by the Japanese government's reluctance to open its diplomatic records. Much has been written about Yoshida's antipathy to rearmament, and some have gone so far as to posit the existence of a

"Yoshida Doctrine"—a single-minded avoidance of military expenditure in the interests of promoting Japan's economic recovery. Certainly, there is no doubting Yoshida's reluctance to embark on a major program of rearmament in 1950–51. The bitter experience of the Pacific War, as well as Yoshida's own clashes with Japanese militarists during the 1930s, made him wary of doing anything that might enhance the position of his former political rivals.[16] Moreover, during his talks with John Foster Dulles in early 1951, the prime minister made clear his opposition to immediate rearmament, citing as justification Japan's economic weakness and lack of raw materials, hostile public opinion, the risk of handing a propaganda advantage to the Soviet Union, and the danger of potentially strengthening Japan's militarists.[17] However, one should be careful not to confuse short-term considerations with a long-term strategy. Yoshida appears to have been reacting to the immediate situation, and indirect evidence suggests that he may have been willing to entertain the possibility of a rearmed Japan in the near future. Shirasu Jirō, perhaps one of Yoshida's closest confidants, in a January meeting with State Department representatives, informed the Americans that Article 9 of the Japanese Constitution should be changed to allow Japanese rearmament. Similarly, Ichimada Hisato, the governor of the Bank of Japan, on a visit to Washington in early 1951 made clear that Japan was prepared to rearm, while Admiral Nomura Kichisaburō (former ambassador to the United States in 1941 and in the days preceding the attack on Pearl Harbor), who had close links with the prime minister, handed US Admiral Arleigh Burke, on January 29 a detailed rearmament plan.[18] It does not seem far-fetched to assume that some, if not all of these individuals, were reflecting Yoshida's point of view, although, of course, the intended timetable for any future rearmament remains uncertain.[19]

Even if Yoshida had wanted to rearm in 1951, domestic politics would have presented a major obstacle. The prime minister was caught between two political extremes—on the one hand, socialist and left-wing intellectual sentiment unreservedly opposed to rearmament and demanding an overall peace arrangement, including the Soviet Union and the PRC, rather than a close alignment with the United States; and on the other, those conservative politicians centered on Yoshida's principal political rivals such as Hatoyama Ichirō, Shigemitsu Mamoru, and Ashida Hitoshi who advocated a major increase in rearmament as well as a foreign policy position independent from Washington.[20] By positioning himself between these two political camps, Yoshida was able to preserve his electoral distinctiveness while also avoiding the risk of antagonizing public opinion, which remained for the most part wary of any major rearmament initiative.[21]

If Yoshida can be said to have been motivated by any doctrinal considerations, then these are more likely to have been linked to questions of cultural and national identity than to the rearmament debate. In the immediate aftermath of the war, Japan was, in the words of the distinguished political philosopher Maruyama Masao, a "spiritual vacuum." Defeat had discredited Japanese religious and national traditions, but the Occupation values of democracy, constitutionalism, and pacifism had not acquired any "compelling attraction for the people." The ideological foundation of society represented by the Emperor system or tennōsei, which had been immensely important to ordinary people and not merely a product of the authoritarianism of the 1930s, had been severely undermined. The country had lost its sense of mission—a sense of purpose which was associated with the expression and realization of unconscious drives and motivations as much as with the material goals of modernization.[22]

In the face of this cultural crisis, post-war politics and intellectual debate became preoccupied with questions of individuality, identity, selfhood, and independence—a set of issues best captured perhaps by the Japanese term shutaisei.[23] The Japanese remained both a "very practical [and] at the same time an intensely spiritual people," and many individuals, while welcoming the economic lifestyle improvements associated with the Occupation, had serious misgivings about the apparent erosion of the country's national traditions.[24] This sentiment found expression in a number of ways—in criticism of SCAP and MacArthur,[25] in efforts to interpret the new 1947 Constitution in ways that were consistent with Japanese values,[26] and above all in the defense of the Emperor system. Support for the imperial institution cut across all levels in society and could be found both in the government bureaucracy and among ordinary people.[27] For Yoshida, the Emperor was crucially important and represented a compelling and emotionally charged national symbol—a source of social stability and, through the reinforcement of Japan's political traditions, a basis for the recovery of national independence. Yoshida's commitment to these values manifested itself in a number of contexts—both in the marginal notes requesting greater emphasis on the legitimate role of the Emperor that he scribbled on Gaimushō documents, and in his repeated requests to American officials to avoid including guarantees of Occupation reforms in the various drafts of the San Francisco Peace Treaty.[28]

Concern over questions of national identity extended widely into the political sphere, creating divisions which would seriously complicate US efforts to develop a coherent and stable partnership with Japan. As Charles Spinks, a perceptive embassy official, observed from Tokyo in 1951, there existed widespread support at the end of the Occupation for moderate conservative views, among both the political elite and the general public. This sentiment did not exist in rigid isolation and covered a broad range of political opinion, overlapping at times with more extreme right-wing positions:

> It would be a mistake to attempt to divorce the ultra-rightist elements of Japan from the general conservative trend of the times and deal with them as a separate phenomenon to which special criteria or measures can be applied . . . Japanese conservatism today covers a wide range of thought and activity. Even its ultra-right has interlocking relationships and affinities with the more moderate aspects of Japanese conservatism. It is essentially an attitude and way of life premised upon Japan's traditional mores and generally hostile to the importation and adoption of what are considered unpalatable, if not disruptive foreign ways and philosophies, whether of Communist or democratic origin. Japanese conservatism is not necessarily reactionary in the customary meaning of the term. Nor is it necessarily static in its insistence on the merits of Japan's traditional concepts. It has frequently displayed a remarkable degree of progressiveness, but has always insisted that progress or the betterment of life be achieved within the framework of Japan's traditional mores. It is largely for this reason that there has been a basic conflict between Japanese conservatism and so-called foreign innovations.[29]

As the Occupation drew to a close, moderate conservatism increasingly became linked to the re-emergence of a commitment to nationalist ideals as well as criticism of the Occupation and the Constitution, a trend which Spinks recognized, with considerable foresight, would develop into powerful pressure for constitutional revision:

> The Occupation in fact brought little new to Japan, but instead built its reforms upon the political, economic, and social foundations which had already been laid. Its mistake has been the attempt to build a completely western edifice upon a foundation which was designed through the process of absorption and adaptation to meet Japanese requirements. What we may witness in the future, will not be the tearing down of this edifice but the remodeling of it.[30]

This growing resentment of the imposition of foreign concepts and practices also influenced and was capitalized on by the Left, and by 1951 the Japanese Communists had "already attempted to exploit the alien, un-Japanese character of American life and its utter irreconcilability with Japan's native culture and traditions."[31] Moreover, this pattern was prominently reflected in ideological debates among Japan's left-wing intellectuals as many Marxist academics and commentators increasingly sought to replace class-based analysis and criticisms of modernity defined in Western and European terms with a more distinctly Japanese, nativist tradition.[32] Indeed, a wide body of opinion throughout Japan appears to have been increasingly predisposed either to question the legacy of the Occupation or to try to find some legitimate means of reconnecting with or reasserting a coherent sense of national identity (for example, by supporting neutralism[33] or looking to China as an Asian and therefore culturally familiar model)—a trend which was likely to complicate the development of post-Occupation alliance relations. As Spinks noted:

> Many Japanese are discontented and frustrated because ideals and traditions of a lifetime have been rudely brushed aside. Others are irked by specific Occupation reforms and controls. Some are alarmed by the way the Occupation has set organized labor and other liberal forces into motion. Thousands were purged and regardless of their present re-instatement will never forget or forgive the humiliation of their pariah-like disqualification. A few, but perhaps a very important few, have bitterly resented the war crimes trials and the execution of Japan's former top leaders. . . . It is most essential, therefore, that we recognize that the post-Peace Treaty position of the United States in Japan will be vulnerable at many points to anti-American agitation on the part of rightist as well as leftist elements.[34]

Here, in Spinks's analysis, was an echo of the recommendations of Kennan following his visit to Japan in 1948 and a reminder of the importance of cultural factors in shaping political behavior. For the Americans, addressing this situation involved a basic difficulty. Endorsing either the Communists or Socialists was clearly not a viable option, given the former's hostility to the United States and the latter's support for neutrality. At the same time, backing moderate conservative opinion (represented in 1951 by Yoshida's Liberals) ran the risk of making the United States appear unprincipled and self-serving, in the eyes of both the Left and, it should be emphasized, the Right. In the ideologically charged environment of post-war Japan, an American endorsement of constitutional revision could easily seem like political opportunism, given the parallels between the 1947 Constitution and the ideals of America's own Founding Fathers. As a result, MacArthur's provision of a new Constitution—both the manner in which it was introduced and the foreign tenor of some of its political terminology—had, to some degree, created a policymaking straitjacket for post-war US administrations in their dealings with Japan. Stable and strong government in Japan arguably required the creation of an effective consensus on national political values. However, nationalism extended across the political spectrum and was expressed in different forms, and both the Left and the Right could bolster their claim to be promoting Japanese interests by criticizing the United States.

For the Japanese government, the mirror-image of Japan's concern for cultural integrity and legitimacy was the country's strong desire for national independence and equality—a leitmotif that dominated the postwar policy proposals of the Foreign Ministry. As one Gaimushō document put it, equality was the "preeminent consideration" (senketsu mondai). "In order to substantially strengthen Japan as a member of the democratic camp, complete independence must be restored to Japan."[35] It is this powerful sentiment which Kennan, Grew, Howard, and others in the State Department were responding to, not altruistically, but for reasons of American national self-interest—promoting domestic stability in Japan in 1945, and encouraging Japan in 1951 to be an active rather than a passive ally in the Cold War struggle with the Soviet Union.

Yoshida's desire for national independence did not prevent him from promoting Japan's alliance with the United States. From the prime minister's perspective, as he later revealed in his memoirs, a close relationship with Washington, in itself, did not imply that Japan was being treated unequally and was no more a threat to Japan's sovereignty than earlier diplomatic agreements such as the pre-war Anglo-Japanese alliance.[36] Japan entered into its partnership with the United States freely, without any coercion from Washington, and on the basis of its own assessment of long-term national interests.[37] Moreover, Yoshida played an active role in promoting ties between Washington and Tokyo and did not simply respond passively to Washington initiatives. This was well demonstrated by Japan's vigorous enforcement of the unpopular Dodge Line,[38] and also by the Ikeda and Shirasu mission of April 1950, when Yoshida, aware of tension between the State and Defense departments, sought to break the bureaucratic deadlock by proposing the establishment of American bases in Japan. Similarly, during Dulles's early 1951 visit to Japan, Yoshida made clear to the American envoy his desire to contribute actively to the Western camp and to establish good relations with Washington.[39] That these statements were more than diplomatic politesse was already clear from the constructive way in which Japan had responded to the Korean crisis—providing, on its own initiative, minesweepers and stevedores, as well as men, materiel, and training areas for US forces still in Japan.[40]

Despite Yoshida's proactive policy-making style, the prime minister suffered from one major weakness in attempting to align Japan with the United States. Yoshida was very poor at mobilizing public opinion, in building political coalitions, and in creating anything resembling a genuine suprapartisan foreign policy.[41] He could be caustically dismissive of his political opponents and did not encourage a genuine Left-Right consensus in the months leading up to the San Francisco Peace Treaty conference. As a result, the prime minister often found himself having to assume two different and often contradictory political stances—publicly rejecting moderate rearmament for internal security as well as any notion of long-term US bases in Japan, while in private trying, via intermediaries, to reassure the Americans that there existed a secure foundation for security cooperation between Washington and Tokyo. Inevitably, this produced confusion and occasionally frustration in America and added to the difficulties of building an alliance between the two countries.

Toward San Francisco: Bilateral and Multilateral Talks

President Truman's decision to begin preliminary Peace Treaty talks in September 1950 suggested that a settlement would be reached before long between Japan and the United States. However, within barely three months, unpredictable and dramatic events once again (as had been the case the previous June) disturbed Washington's diplomatic agenda. After the enormous September success of the American Inchon landings in the southwest of Seoul, General MacArthur, in his role as Allied Commander-in-Chief and with the backing of Truman, the JCS, and the NSC,[42] had vigorously extended the war to the north of the peninsula across the 38th parallel. In late November, discounting indications of small-scale Chinese involvement in the war (until this stage the enemy, although equipped with Soviet arms, had been predominantly North Korean), and confidently boasting of bringing American troops home by Christmas, MacArthur launched a final, end-the-war offensive. However, the General's confidence was misplaced. The American-led UN attempt to unite Korea and to roll back Communist influence unexpectedly triggered a massive intervention by Chinese troops resulting in thousands of US casualties and a complete reversal in the tide of battle. Almost overnight, the whole character of the war changed. Washington and Allied capitals were gripped by a sense of crisis and the Korean War, until then an apparently limited conflict, was now seen as the possible prelude to World War III.[43]

In the face of impending disaster, US policy-makers were forced to re-think their plans for Japan. In particular, the Pentagon firmly recom-mended that any future Peace Treaty be delayed and that priority be given to rearming Japan. There were no US combat troops in Japan, and with all of America's Far Eastern naval and air power focused on Korea, Japan was, in effect, "a military vacuum." At the same time, in light of the prevailing international uncertainty, with the JCS not knowing whether a possible second Communist attack might occur in Europe or in the Far East, the American military was unwilling to make any formal commitment to the defense of Asia's off-shore islands. Ending the Occu-pation in such a situation would, in the Pentagon's estimation, prove highly destabilizing since there was no firm guarantee that Japan would remain free from Soviet influence or control.[44]

In early January, Truman agreed, on the advice of Acheson and George Marshall (who had replaced Louis Johnson as secretary of defense), to send a mission to the Far East headed by John Foster Dulles. Its purpose was to explore with America's regional allies the possible establishment of a regional security arrangement or Pacific Pact, as well as to engage in talks with the Japanese to strengthen bilateral ties and defense arrange-ments and to lay the foundation for a future, if delayed, Peace Treaty. The Defense Department, in the face of State Department warnings that im-mediate militarization would violate existing FEC regulations and antag-onize America's Far Eastern allies, had agreed to the postponement of Japanese rearmament until after the Occupation. For its part, the State Department had acknowledged that a peace arrangement would need to wait until the situation in Korea had stabilized.[45]

Some writers have argued that Dulles's principal purpose in visiting Tokyo in early 1951 was to pressure Japan into making a firm post-Oc-cupation military commitment to the American-led struggle against the Soviet Union.[46] Certainly, rearmament was a central topic in the discus-sions between the Japanese and the Americans in January and February, and Dulles was by all accounts eager to persuade Yoshida to agree to build up Japanese armed forces (especially ground troops) over the me-dium to long term. However, this objective had to be set against the more pressing goal of ensuring that Japan remained firmly part of the Western alliance. "Commitment" in this sense was primarily political in character and only secondarily a strategic concern. A mood of panic dominated Ja-pan following the Chinese intervention, and however much rational cal-culation might have recommended a close alignment with Washington, the country's loyalties seemed uncertain. As Dulles pointed out in early December:

> Recent developments in Korea make it doubtful whether Japan can be relied upon to form a dependable part of the non-Communist world. It is important to seek to resolve that doubt in our favour. . . . There should be a prompt effort definitely to commit Japan, spiritually and politically, to the cause of the free world. In this respect, time is of the essence. The United States still possesses prestige in Japan and the full political and military implications of the Korean defeat are not yet apparent. There is probably more chance of mobilizing Japanese public opinion and getting a Japanese commitment now than in a month or two. Delay and inaction may count heavily against us.[47]

Similarly, as Sir Alvary Gascoigne (the head of the UK Liaison Mission in Tokyo) observed, Japan was "a land situated in the middle of a cyclone. . . . The Japanese have not shown their hand as regards their future affiliations, but it is probable that they will continue to remain within the allied fold so long as it is to their advantage to do so."[48] It was vital, therefore, to convince the Japanese that it was in their interest to side with the Americans, and questions of equality and sovereignty became important once again. Dictating terms was not a viable approach. As Robert Fearey in the State Department's Office of North East Asian Affairs pointed out in early December 1950, "Chinese aggression in Korea . . . renders the establishment [of] a *genuinely cooperative relationship* between the United States security forces and the Japanese of even greater importance than before" (emphasis added).[49]

To reassure Japan and reach an early arrangement guaranteeing America's long-term security interests in the region, the Truman administration, in keeping with George Kennan's advice from the previous July, envisaged a simple non-punitive Peace Treaty and a brief, broadly defined bilateral security agreement with Tokyo. However, Washington's freedom to woo Japan through relatively generous and mutually acceptable terms faced a major constraint in the form of the American Congress. Although the Democrats controlled both of the legislative chambers, the Republicans had done well in the November mid-term elections, gaining 28 seats in the House of Representatives and 5 in the Senate,[50] and congressional and public opinion as a whole was critical of the administration's foreign policy. For example, in the debate over NATO and in a resolution sponsored by Senator Kenneth Wherry of Nebraska, Congress had sought to limit the President's freedom to dispatch troops overseas. Ultimately a compromise was reached and the administration's plan to send four extra divisions to Europe was approved on the understanding that no additional forces would be sent.[51] However, in this climate, and especially in light of the 1948 Vandenberg Resolution, requiring reciprocal aid from countries participating in security arrangements with the United States, there were potential obstacles to a generous settlement with Japan.

Both before and after traveling to Japan, Dulles was forced to spend a considerable amount of time drumming up congressional support for the administration's proposals by testifying before the House Foreign Affairs committee and the Foreign Relations committee of the Senate. Indeed, Dulles had been brought into the White House largely on the strength of his impeccable conservative credentials and his links with senior Republicans,[52] and his track-record as a successful "lawyer and an accomplished negotiator."[53] However, congressional arm-twisting and coalition-building were not, in themselves, sufficient. If, in accordance with Pentagon thinking, American forces were to continue after the Occupation to be stationed in Japan, the Japanese government would have to provide something in return. This turned out to be a Japanese general undertaking (included in the US-Japan security agreement) to build up Japan's defensive capabilities once its sovereignty was restored. The need to secure such an agreement explains, in part, the vigor with which Dulles during his early 1951 visit to Tokyo urged the Japanese to rearm. Dulles was anxious both to boost Japan's long-term military preparedness and to obtain a "token" contribution that would satisfy congressional critics and pave the way to a smooth ratification of the Peace and Security treaties.[54]

Taken as a whole, the 1951 talks appear to have been a success. Both sides wanted to reach a mutually satisfactory agreement and the US negotiators appear to have been sincere in respecting Japanese sovereignty and avoiding punitive measures. Those restrictions that were eventually included in the final agreement appear to have been intended more often than not to pacify hostile Allied and US public opinion rather than to advance a particular policy. As the American side pointed out in commenting on the February discussions:

> There is very considerable difference of opinion as between the Allies and there is within the United States a considerable body of opinion which questions the desirability of the kind of peace which is here outlined. It may be that public opinion either within the United States or within the Allied Powers may render it necessary, *in order to get peace*, to add certain restrictions and burdens not enumerated in the above outline of projected treaty and it is suggested that the Japanese government, in dealing with the people of Japan, should avoid giving any impression that it can be now be taken for granted

that the final treaty will be free of restrictions and burdens of the character mentioned in these general observations. [Emphasis added][55]

Dulles's own character and actions provide powerful evidence of the Truman administration's desire for a just peace. Dulles had been present at Versailles following the end of the First World War and was conscious of the dangers and undesirability of imposing terms on a defeated enemy.[56] A draconian peace would undermine any hope of long-term cooperation with Japan, stirring up resentment among the Japanese and providing a basis for the possible revival of xenophobic, militaristic sentiment. At the same time, Dulles recognized the inappropriateness of trying to achieve the wholesale Westernization of Japan. Dulles's public language was often colored by a powerful religiosity, with frequent references to the significance of spiritual concerns in the lives of nations and individuals. This, together with his pre-war active involvement with the International Council of Churches, might have prompted Dulles to view Christianity as a suitable means of filling Japan's post-war moral vacuum. However, his recognition of the importance of non-material concerns appears to have embraced a range of beliefs rather than a single doctrine—a tolerant attitude which may have been shaped by his earlier study of philosophy with Woodrow Wilson at Princeton and Henri Bergson at the Sorbonne.[57] Certainly, in the case of Japan, he was aware of the limited appeal of Western ideals. Returning from his first official visit to Tokyo in June 1950, Dulles cited the advice of Christian missionaries that keeping Japan on the side of the West required a more liberal attitude to racial and cultural differences—something which could be achieved, perhaps, by easing restrictions on Japanese immigration to the United States. It was important to avoid anything suggestive of a white, Western sense of superiority.[58]

Dulles's private thinking on Japan was also dominated by his belief that a Peace Treaty with Japan was only the first step in developing a partnership with Japan, and while he recognized the importance of ensuring that Japan did not fall into the Soviet camp, it was clear that this could only be secured through genuine cooperation between Washington and Tokyo. This would require not only a just peace, but measures and a cooperative frame of mind on both sides of the Pacific that extended well beyond the formal terms of the Peace Treaty itself. Perhaps the clearest exposition of this point of view can be found in the minutes of the Council on Foreign Relations. On October 23, 1950, the Council's Study Group on Japanese Peace Treaty Problems met with Dulles for four hours of confidential discussion on the emerging relationship with Japan. Present at the meeting were some of Washington's pre-eminent Japan-watch-ers—State Department "Japan hands" past and present such as Eugene Dooman, Hugh Borton, and John Allison; former key members of the Occupation such as Charles Kades; and individuals with a long associa-tion with Japan and East-Asia related issues, either professional or acad-emically, including Everett Case (previously one of Dean Acheson's Far Eastern consultants), William Draper, and Edwin O. Reischauer. Other notable members of the group (unable to attend) included Joseph Grew, Bernard Brodie, and Harold Stassen.

Japan's importance, Dulles underlined, had to be seen in the wider context:

> The Japanese peace treaty is not an isolated problem. It must be considered within the framework of a larger problem, namely, the prevention of the over-powering of the free world by the Soviet world. The treaty is not merely a problem between Japan and the Allies; it is also a part of this much greater world problem. The future of the world depends largely on whether the Soviet Union will be able to get control over Western Germany and Japan by means short of war.[59]

Moreover, Japan remained acutely vulnerable to external shocks and there was no certainty, in Dulles's judgment, that it would necessarily ally itself with the United States.

> Had Korea been conquered Japan would have fallen without an open struggle. The reaction of Japanese public opinion to the Communist attack in Korea was ominous. It was Mr. Dulles' opinion that if the aggression had succeeded the Japanese would have been so impressed by Soviet power and by the phys-ical and moral weakness of the United States that they would not have felt it worth while to resist.[60]

In such a situation, the United States and its Allies needed to choose be-tween either a "very rigorous and strictly enforced" treaty or a "very lib-eral" one. The Allies, warned Dulles, had to avoid repeating the mistakes of Versailles when, by choosing neither of these options, they had put in place the conditions that eventually proved so fateful for Germany and the rest of the world. Dulles was unambiguously committed to the second option:

> The United States view is that aside from territorial clauses, which will restrict the Japanese to the four main islands of Japan and which in fact have already been executed, the treaty should contain no restrictions on the freedom of ac-tion of the Japanese. The United States does not expect to insist on repara-tions, or to impose economic limitation of any kind on the Japanese. Nor will any restrictions be placed on Japanese rearmament or on the recreation of a

navy or an air force. Subject only to the views of its Allies, the United States intends to restore to Japan complete and untrammeled sovereignty.[61]

Even allowing for this commitment, Dulles continued, there were no guarantees that Japan would align itself with the West:

> It will not be possible to coerce Japan into remaining within the free world. Japan is a nation of 85 million people. The United States, with all its far-flung responsibilities, cannot maintain sufficient power within Japan to control its development, especially in view of the fact that Japan is several thousand miles away from us and very close indeed to the Soviet Union. It must be assumed that if the Japanese do not fall into the Soviet orbit, it is because they do not want to. Certainly the United States cannot prevent them from doing so. . . . [T]he peace treaty, no matter how intelligent its provisions, cannot of itself assure that Japan will remain within the orbit of the free world. The most that the treaty can do is to give to the Japanese the freedom and opportunity that they desire, and to avoid placing them under such restrictions as will tend to make them restive and discontented. There are other grave problems that the treaty alone cannot possibly resolve. For one thing, the Japanese must be made to feel that they are equals of the people of the West. If we persist in treating them as inferiors, if, for example, we continue our discriminatory immigration policies toward the Japanese and thus deny to them that sense of equality which they so ardently desire, the treaty will have been useless. Any failure of ours in this respect will only serve to drive the Japanese into the arms of the Soviets; for the Russians will offer equality.[62]

Equality implied, therefore, a minimalist strategy of denying Japan to the enemy rather than linking it inextricably to the West, a position that echoed the balance-of-power perspective of George Kennan rather than NSC 68's Manichean division of the world in two uncompromisingly antagonistic rival blocs. Dulles indicated that:

> He had not meant to imply that it was American policy to keep Japan within the orbit of the United States. What we wish to do is to keep it within the free world, in much the same way as India and Indonesia are within the free world but not the American orbit. It is not vital to the United States that any of these countries should be assimilated to us, but only that they do not become satellites of the Soviet Union. So long as this is assured, whatever other attitudes or policies they maintain is of no vital concern to the United States.[63]

From a practical point of view, denying Japan to the Soviets rested, in Dulles's judgment on three key requirements, namely:

> The provision of a peace treaty that avoids irritating the Japanese and yet provides for a certain measure of security . . .
> The assurance to Japan of that sense of social and cultural equality which is so vital to its self-respect . . .

The opportunity for achieving a decent standard of living without undue dependence on Communist-held Asia.[64]

Security, for example, could only be ensured through "mutual agreement," with the United States retaining its forces in Japan along the same lines as American forces in the UK and without any continuation, either direct or implied, of a "military occupation."

Where cultural issues were concerned, Dulles would soon take steps to create a personalized "bridge" between the two former wartime opponents, choosing on his second visit to Japan, in early 1951, to include John Rockefeller III in his party of advisors. Rockefeller's limited assignment was to promote cultural exchange between Japan and the United States—encouraging genuine dialogue between two sovereign states rather than the dominance of one country's values over another. This initiative implied that Washington recognized at some level that building a durable, active alliance with Japan would require more than guns and butter.[65] The Truman administration, in contrast to the self-righteous overconfidence of the Occupation, had apparently grasped that American national interest was (at least in the case of Japan) best served by tolerating if not actively encouraging national distinctiveness. Kennan's particularism still, apparently, had a role to play. As George Clutton, the British chargé d'affaires commented following his meeting with Rockefeller:

> Mr. Rockefeller gave me the impression of being a thoroughly civilized person alive to the extremely delicate nature of the work with which he was concerned, fully aware of the slaphappy methods which perforce had had to be employed to date and indeed conscious of the combination of ignorance and arrogance of some of their exponents. He seemed to be aware also of the need in the future to take into greater account Japanese traditions and achievements and to grasp that the essence of the problem to which he is addressing himself is that of bringing the Japanese elite in all fields into the main stream of world democratic culture.[66]

According to Yoshida, Dulles, despite not being an Asia specialist, demonstrated a good understanding of conditions in Japan during his visit to Tokyo in early 1951, and the Japanese side appears to have welcomed the American side's initiatives.[67] As the prime minister himself remarked in February 1951 at the time of Dulles's departure from Japan:

> By treating Japanese, not as vanquished people, but as equals, he [Dulles] has shown special consideration to our national sentiments and sensibilities. He has taken pains to see leaders of political parties, Diet members, representatives of the press, business and labor, and numerous other private individuals

and listened to what they had to say. Such a chivalrous attitude on the part of the ambassador should go far to clear the ground for the rebuilding of the ruined citadel of Japanese-American friendship.[68]

The US envoy took seriously the importance of treating Japan as an equal partner and (as William Sebald pointed out) "insisted throughout the Peace Treaty negotiations, both privately and publicly, that Japan was free to make its choice: to join the West, remain politically neutral, or join the Communist bloc."[69] Dulles's overriding objective was to ensure Japan's long-term alignment with the United States.[70] His success in this task appears to have had much to do with his diplomatic agility and his sensitivity to Japan's legitimate national interests and its concern to have its sovereignty—what Yoshida referred to as Japan's "amour propre"—adequately respected. Certainly, there were disagreements between Japan and the United States, particularly over the question of rearmament and Japan's post-treaty territorial rights. However, these do not appear to have tarnished the negotiations, which remained, on balance, positive and mutually satisfying. In the words of George Clutton:

> In sum it may be said that Mr. Dulles's visit to Japan has been a very considerable success. . . . [T]he press almost universally has sung Mr. Dulles's praises. . . . [T]here is probably a general belief that at any rate on essentials Japan and the United States see eye to eye. The visit has also been a personal triumph for Mr. Dulles. In his contacts with the Japanese and the representatives of foreign ministries here, he showed a geniality, charm and understanding which established at once a basis of confidence. As one newspaper put it on the morrow of his departure: "Mr. Dulles sold himself and his program to the Japanese people."[71]

Earl Johnson, a member of the US delegation, summed up the bilateral talks as follows:

> As Kipling once said "East is East and West is West and never the twain shall meet." However, in these discussions, I am happy to say that East and West—two nations, America and Japan, that were once at war with one another, have reached a meeting of minds.[72]

Multiple Actors

Although Dulles was given considerable decision-making discretion and was very important in smoothing the path to a final agreement in San Francisco, it is important not to exaggerate his contribution or to view it in isolation from the efforts of other US government officials.[73] In particular, the constructive and in many ways decisive role of Dean Rusk (assistant secretary of state for far eastern affairs after May 1950) has been overlooked in many of the standard accounts of the Peace Treaty negotiations. Although Rusk, like many of the senior Washington officials involved with Japan policy, was not formally trained as a Japan specialist, he developed, in the course of his government service an extensive knowledge of Japan and the Far East.[74] He was also a firm supporter of the United Nations and displayed a keen sensitivity to the interests and rights of the new post-colonial nation-states that emerged following World War II. In this respect he was perhaps more of a moralist than Kennan and Acheson, who were inclined to emphasize pragmatism as a basis for promoting American national self-interest.[75] However, in the case of Japan policy and the importance of Japanese sovereignty, Kennan's particularism and Rusk's aversion to aggressive interventionism embraced a common agenda. As Rusk declared in a speech early in 1951:

> We want to see the people of Asia organised and governed by institutions of their own making and by men of their own choice, their relations with other peoples and governments resting solidly on mutual consent. We want to see the new nations of Asia actively participating as full and equal members of the international community on the basis of agreed principles set forth in such government documents as the Charter of the United Nations. . . . We must accept the proposition that the problems of Asia are to be worked out by the governments and peoples of Asia, not because of any lack of interest on our part but because the peoples of Asia themselves will insist on it. We must remember that we have relations with other people, not control over them. We can help but we cannot take over.[76]

Rusk's first exposure to Japan-related issues came early in his Washington career. In the final stages of the Pacific War, he had served in the Operations Planning Division (OPD) of the War Department. Based in Washington, this group had helped in planning the Occupation of Japan and, as Rusk recounts in his memoirs, played a major role in advocating the retention of the Japanese Emperor—a decision which he felt was instrumental in saving the lives of large numbers of American soldiers. Early on it seems, Rusk had recognized (along with Grew and others) the emotive power and stabilizing influence of Japan's cultural and national traditions. Later on, while acting as assistant secretary to Robert Patterson, the secretary of war, Rusk was responsible for providing food supplies for Germany and Japan and served as US representative on the FEC. After George Marshall became secretary of state in January 1947, Rusk moved to the State Department and as Undersecretary of State was often responsible for briefing the President on Asian matters.[77]

Rusk's movement to center stage in Washington's Japan policy occurred in May 1950. In the face of fierce Republican criticism of the Truman administration's Asian policy, Butterworth had stepped down as assistant secretary of state for far eastern affairs, creating an awkward bureaucratic vacancy within the State Department. Recognizing this difficulty, Rusk approached Acheson and volunteered for the new position, effectively demoting himself in the State Department's chain of command (in Washington's official hierarchy assistant secretaries are ranked below the Undersecretary) to take on what was probably at that stage the least appealing and most demanding job in the department. The assistant secretary's position was seen as a lightning rod for Republican attacks on the beleaguered administration and, in light of Congress's partisan combativeness, an almost certain graveyard for the career prospects of an ambitious and promising bureaucrat.[78] It was perhaps this act of self-sacrifice, together with his effectiveness in handling Republican criticism, that enabled Rusk to assume such an influential role in the Peace Treaty preparations. Certainly, his action appears to have impressed Acheson and would almost certainly have bolstered his standing within the State Department even while exposing him to unsettling attacks from Congress. By the autumn of 1951 he was regarded by many as the unofficial number two in the department[79] and was deeply involved in steering and promoting the administration's Japan policy. As Thomas Schoenbaum has pointed out:

> A mark of Rusk's success was that journalists and historians have generally given Dulles all the credit for the Japanese Peace Treaty. Dulles was the up-front negotiator and performed admirably, but insiders at State knew that Rusk was calling most of the shots. The Japanese settlement was one of his most notable accomplishments.[80]

Rusk's success rested on a number of factors. As someone who had felt that MacArthur's 1947 call for an early peace was mistaken and who believed in the importance of quiet diplomacy in laying the groundwork for an adequate agreement, Rusk had been instrumental in persuading both Truman and Acheson, despite initial reservations, to agree to the appointment of John Foster Dulles as the government's special consultant on Japan.[81] Similarly, he had advised that Philip Jessup (one of Acheson's Far Eastern consultants) should be appointed Ambassador-at-Large and sent on a fact-finding tour of the Far East—a trip which included Japan and involved a number of important meetings with MacArthur in Tokyo in January 1950.[82] During Dulles's various visits to Japan, Rusk was responsible for compiling the US envoy's instructions as well as acting as his "blocking back" at home in Washington, fending off hostile opinion (especially from the Pentagon) and preventing the insertion of unnecessary trivia and excessive detail into the various drafts of the Peace and Security treaties. All of this was in keeping with Truman's desire for a simple, non-punitive treaty of reconciliation with Japan.[83] It also reflected Rusk's personal skills—his low-key persuasiveness and his ability to avoid antagonizing people. Acheson viewed Rusk as the chief liaison between the State and Defense departments and the new assistant secretary had good links also with leading Republicans in Congress, such as Senators William Knowland and H. Alexander Smith, as well as Harold Stassen, a widely tipped future contender for the Republican presidential primaries of 1952.[84] Rusk was good at working behind the scenes—maintaining a low public profile but nonetheless often playing a vital role in cajoling and persuading others to reach agreement, a pattern that was exemplified by his actions during the San Francisco peace conference.[85] This quality—what Ronald McGlothlen has referred to as his "catalytic charm"—was also important in the late 1951–early 1952 Administrative Agreement talks with Japan setting out the detailed conditions governing the stationing of US forces in the country.[86] Above all, perhaps, it enabled the Truman administration to function in a unified fashion, overcoming bureaucratic differences, placating powerful personalities, and enabling Acheson, Dulles, and John Allison to work together as a "formidable team."[87]

Recognizing that Dulles was one among a number of individuals instrumental in promoting the peace settlement with Japan should not detract from his contribution as a negotiator—in particular the skillful manner with which he persuaded America's Allied partners to accept the Truman administration's treaty terms. Washington was not in a position to act unilaterally. American officials had no expectation that either the Soviets or the Chinese Communists would endorse their proposals, and were concerned to ensure a united front among the Western Allied powers. This was particularly true in the case of Australia and New Zealand. Both countries remained deeply suspicious of Japan and, as the Occupation drew to a close, viewed the prospect of a Peace Treaty with considerable unease and misgiving. Both informed and popular opinion in the two countries questioned Japan's commitment to peaceful, democratic values, and against a backdrop of fear that Japan might once again prove an aggressive military threat in the region there were calls for an extension of the Occupation—with some individuals advocating the maintenance of a fifteen- or twenty-year-long regime of control.[88]

Not everyone was fearful of the future. The Conservative Australian prime minister, Robert Menzies, as early as the summer of 1950 and in the wake of the start of the Korean War, explained to both the British and MacArthur in Tokyo that he favored the rearmament of Japan.[89] However, his was a minority opinion and Menzies faced opposition within his cabinet and throughout Australia. In particular, Percy Spender, the minister for External Relations, was enthusiastically promoting the merits of a Pacific Pact, in effect an Asian NATO—an idea Menzies had little confidence in and referred to disparagingly as an "effort to erect a superstructure on a foundation of jelly."[90] By involving the United States, a future pact would, in Spender's overconfident estimation, provide a cast-iron guarantee of Australia's security. At the same time, public opinion remained firmly opposed to any notion of either rearming Japan or forming an alliance relationship with the government in Tokyo.[91]

Given Australia and New Zealand's fears, the US government found itself confronting an urgent dilemma. Establishing a long-term cooperative relationship with Japan involved reaching an early peace agreement, laying a foundation for later rearmament, and avoiding punitive policies. However, winning Canberra's and Wellington's acquiescence to the terms of the proposed Peace Treaty required explicit limits on Japan's rearmament and the imposition of precisely those sorts of sanctions and punitive measures (such as war-guilt clauses, reparation requests, and ceilings on Japan's industrial output) best calculated to antagonize Tokyo and to discourage it from aligning with the West. The Truman administration's attempted solution was to propose a regional security agreement of its own—not modeled on Spender's idea, but instead a looser arrangement centered on the Asian off-shore island chain.

Even before the outbreak of the Korean War, John Howard, in drafting proposals for a Japanese Peace Treaty, had suggested a new regional security structure which might function as a Far Eastern parallel to NATO. Such an arrangement would have had a broad membership, including the United States, Canada, Japan, New Zealand, Australia, and the Philippines, with the possibility of expansion at a later date. However, Howard's suggestion had made little headway through the American bureaucracy. Dulles had rejected it on the grounds that the need to omit countries on the Asian mainland would have left some countries vulnerable to a possible Communist attack, and also because it would have been difficult to win Senate approval for such a wide-ranging proposal.[92] Moreover, by late 1950 the JCS remained firmly opposed to tying American forces into any explicit security agreement in Asia. In a volatile and unpredictable world, American military planners emphasized the importance of flexibility. Rather than establishing a formal collective security agreement involving specific, reciprocal military commitments, Washington favored an Asian "Monroe doctrine"—possibly including the creation of a regional defense council—which could reassure America's allies in the Pacific while permitting the eventual rearmament of Japan.[93] However, even such a loose arrangement presented major difficulties. Washington, sensitive to any charge that it might be resurrecting colonialism in Asia, was anxious to avoid anything suggestive of a white-man's pact in the region and therefore wanted to exclude the British and French except in a purely consultative role. Britain, not surprisingly, felt that this would be a slight to its prestige in the region (already much diminished through its humiliating defeats during the Pacific War). It opposed the American initiative also on grounds that it might prevent Australia and New Zealand from fulfilling their existing pledges to provide manpower and material support for UK and Commonwealth security interests in the Middle East.[94]

In the face of British opposition to a Pacific Defense Council, Dulles, during his trip to the Far East in early 1951, was obliged to change tactics. After his negotiations in Tokyo he traveled as planned (via the Philippines) to Canberra and then on to Wellington. In preparation for his visit, Australian military and civilian officials had drawn up a series of measures restricting the types of weapons Japan could possess, limiting the importation and stockpiling of military provisions, freezing Japan's shipbuilding capacity at a peacetime level, delaying most-favored-nation status for Japan, and requiring the inclusion of a war-guilt clause in the Japanese Peace Treaty. In response, Dulles highlighted the Soviet security threat and stressed the need to avoid any restrictions which would undermine Japan's sovereignty and consequently jeopardize Tokyo's willingness to side with the West. Most important, instead of an overarching regional security arrangement, Dulles proposed a trilateral Security Treaty between Australia, New Zealand, and the United States (ANZUS).[95]

Dulles's talks with the Australian and New Zealand officials proved successful. In the months that followed, both governments, despite periodic attempts to reintroduce formal limits on Japan's rearmament, gradually softened their opposition to America's Japanese peace and security proposals. In New Zealand, the ANZUS arrangement helped to calm public anxieties regarding Japan. In Australia, where the fear of Japanese militarism was more pronounced, the situation was more finely balanced. In particular, Menzies had to contend with H. Evatt's Labor Party and its persistent demands for a restrictive Peace Treaty[96]—a particularly worrying situation for Washington during the Australian General Election at the end of April. However, Labor lost the election, and by August both Australia and New Zealand were reconciled (albeit somewhat apprehensively and grudgingly), to the American-sponsored Peace and Security treaties.

Dulles's shuttle diplomacy and mediating skills were important both in overcoming Australia's and New Zealand's opposition and in persuading Britain to accept America's Peace Treaty plans. Despite the September 1949 agreement between Bevin and Acheson to push ahead with plans for a peace settlement, in private senior British government officials grew increasingly irritated with the Truman administration during 1950 for what they viewed as unnecessary and potentially harmful delays in ending the Allied Occupation. In the eyes of Sir Esler Dening (the senior Foreign Office official responsible for Japan), Washington was guilty of failing to develop an adequate Asian policy and was therefore contributing to instability in the Pacific. Moreover, by refusing to move quickly on the Peace Treaty issue there was a real risk of allowing Japan to be drawn into the Soviet camp. "The fact of the matter is that the United States have [sic] neglected and are neglecting the Far East, and that unless and until they can be moved from their inertia, the rest of us will be in great danger."[97] British criticism not only reflected London's frustration with delays in the policy-making process in Washington. It was also rooted in broader disagreements over Asian policy, most notably over the treatment of Communist China, as well as Britain's instinctive belief that its long historical involvement with the Far East made it better qualified than the American newcomer to pronounce on Asian matters. Ernest Bevin pointed out in a speech to the United Nations in September 1950, "For more than two centuries the British people were responsible for the administration of vast areas of Asia, and we believe that that long association has given us some insight into the affairs of that great continent."[98]

In the case of Japan, the Foreign Office echoed the thinking of the State Department, stressing the importance (especially following the Chinese intervention in the Korean War) of securing an early peace agreement and restoring sovereignty to the Japanese government. However, this emphasis on Japan's independence was tempered by the British government's reluctance to agree to a brief, non-punitive Peace Treaty. Whitehall's apparent broadmindedness was, on closer examination, often clouded by narrow self-interest. Concern over a revival of Japanese economic competitiveness, especially in low-wage sectors such as the textile industry, encouraged the Labour government (anxious about the electoral consequences of undermining a traditional industry) to resist America's proposal for the restoration of most-favored-nation status to Japan.[99] For similar reasons, it lobbied for the inclusion in the peace settlement of specific limits on Japan's shipbuilding capacity and sought the abrogation of Japan's preferential trading rights in Africa under the Congo Basin Treaties.[100] Britain was especially concerned by Japan's economic challenge in the Far East—a region where the UK hoped to earn export revenue to offset its huge World War II–generated dollar debt.[101] Sensitivity to critical British public opinion also encouraged the Attlee administration to propose the inclusion of a war-guilt clause in the preamble to the Peace Treaty as well as formal limits on Japan's right to rearm—despite the Foreign Office's recognition in early 1951 that the worsening security situation in the Far East necessitated a build-up of Japan's military capabilities.[102] Drawing up its own Peace Treaty drafts as part of the consultation process with the Americans during the spring of 1951, the British government proposed a lengthy, legally precise, and well-defined albeit somewhat pedantic Peace Treaty.[103]

American government officials responded to the British position by repeatedly emphasizing the need for a quick solution to the Peace Treaty problem and the importance of avoiding coercive measures when dealing with the Japanese government. Acheson and Dulles, in their various discussions during 1951 with the London government and with Sir Oliver Franks, the British ambassador in Washington, replayed the arguments that the State Department had previously used in trying to persuade the Pentagon to agree to an early peace.[104] Building a constructive post-treaty relationship with Japan was in some respects a gamble. It was not possible, via detailed treaty obligations, to guarantee an iron-clad Japanese commitment to the West. Instead, it was important to trust Tokyo and to avoid any "pin-pricks" which might run the risk of inciting Japan to use its future strength against the West.[105] Of importance here are the clear indications that Washington did not take Japan for granted. Despite the rise in Cold War tensions with the Soviet Union, the Truman administration was under no illusion that the Japanese would simply line up alongside the Western Allies. Building an alliance depended critically on psychological as well as material considerations. Japan's formal and actual sovereignty and independence had to be respected, and it was not enough to provide Tokyo with economic and military assistance.

Dulles, in persuading the British to agree to Washington's position, skillfully combined firmness with flattery—making clear that the Americans, given their preponderant role in the Pacific War, could legitimately assume the leading position in shaping Peace Treaty terms, while also taking pains (despite the reservations of less accommodating voices in the State Department) to build a cooperative relationship with the British.[106] Part of his success in this regard rested on his personal friendships gained through earlier diplomatic experience in the United Nations. As George Clutton pointed out following Dulles's third visit to Japan in April 1951:

> Dulles, who left on the 23rd April, was as friendly and forthcoming as on his previous visit. He is an old friend of mine from Lake Success and I don't find him difficult to talk to. . . . What struck me most of all was his anxiety for Anglo-American cooperation as regards the peace treaty and all matters connected with it. This he repeated more than once to me was why he particularly wished to wed the United States and United Kingdom [treaty] drafts and issue the result as a joint Anglo-American document. In contrast with Dulles, his staff quite clearly did not like our draft at all and if they had their own way I am inclined to think that they would not pay much attention to it.[107]

A series of meetings between Foreign Office and State Department officials in Washington at the end of April 1951 helped to iron out some of the more technical differences separating the British and the Americans, and on June 4 Dulles visited London for a week of talks aimed at reaching a final agreement. In his conversations with Herbert Morrison (Bevin's successor as foreign secretary), Dulles stressed the importance of avoiding a Carthaginian peace and anything reminiscent of the Versailles settlement.[108] Formal arms limits were, he argued, unenforceable, and any likely Japanese military threat could best be prevented by incorporating Japan in a wider collective security arrangement—a reference presumably both to the nascent ANZUS pact and to the bilateral US-Japan and US-Philippines security agreements. Dulles pointed out that the economic challenge posed by Japan was a long-term rather than immediate issue and cited JCS concerns about protecting Japanese supply lines against possible Soviet submarine attacks in a future war, going on to argue against setting limits on Japan's ship-building capacity. For their part, the British dropped their request for formal arms restrictions, agreed not to demand Japanese gold stocks as a form of reparations, and accepted that the waiting period before Japan received most-favored-nation status after the ratification of the Peace Treaty could be reduced from five to three years.[109] In general, the talks were successful and Dulles returned to Washington very satisfied. In the time remaining before the opening of the peace conference in September, the Americans continued to woo the British, stressing the importance of high-level consultation and the symbolic significance of their joint sponsorship of the peace process.[110] By the time the Allies met in San Francisco, the British had accepted virtually all of Washington's points, agreeing to a peace treaty that was brief, non-technical, and remarkably free of punitive restrictions.[111]

The Truman administration's successful conclusion of its negotiations with the Japanese government and its success in persuading its key Western Allies to accept the American Peace Treaty proposals opened the door to the San Francisco peace conference. During 1951 a number of issues intervened to complicate the process of reaching a final agreement. These included General MacArthur's sudden recall in early April 1951 and his replacement by General Matthew B. Ridgway,[112] continuing Pentagon misgivings about the timing of the peace settlement, and the Japanese government's efforts to persuade Washington explicitly to commit itself to the defense of Japan. However, these issues were of minor importance in relation to the overall settlement. Opening the Peace Conference in early September heralded, in effect, the end to a year-long period of informal treaty negotiations that had started with President Truman's announcement of the appointment of John Foster Dulles in September 1950. The conference itself was an occasion for confirming the decisions of the Western Allies rather than an opportunity for active debate on the Peace Treaty. Through calculated and self-serving handling of the conference agenda and rules of procedure, Acheson as chairman of the proceedings was able to prevent the Soviet Union and any of the Eastern bloc nations attending the conference from challenging or modifying the already agreed upon Peace Treaty draft.[113]

Both Yoshida and Dulles viewed the San Francisco settlement as crowning achievements in their professional lives,[114] and for both the United States and Japan the Peace Treaty itself and the process leading up to it can, on balance, be judged a success. In the context of the times and against the backdrop of the residual bitterness associated with the Pacific War, the treaty could be judged to have been fair to both sides. By avoiding the punitive or restrictive measures favored by America's wartime Allies, it was a settlement designed to ensure that the former wartime opponents would, in Truman's words, "be neither victors nor vanquished . . . but only equals in the partnership of peace."[115] The Americans, through an extended collective effort involving the actions and foresight of a number of leading figures in the State Department, had overcome the objections of their Western Allies. By paying attention to Japan's cultural and psychological concerns, the Truman administration had avoided provoking major irritation and anti-US sentiment in Japan and had laid the foundation for a potentially long-term alliance relationship with Tokyo. Certainly, there were some disappointments. Japan had, via the bilateral Security Treaty that was signed alongside the Peace Treaty, made a general rather than explicit commitment to rearm and Washington had not formally defined its strategic policy in the region, indicating at most a willingness in principle to act to defend Japan in the event of an attack, but not providing a formal, binding guarantee. However, these concerns were more than offset by Japan's willingness and intention to permit the stationing of US troops in Japan as well as by the strong indication that Tokyo had renounced neutrality and was willing to commit itself to the Western side in the Cold War. From the perspective of the Treaties Bureau of the Japanese Foreign Ministry, the United States, in keeping with its inherent right to self-defense (underpinned by Article 51 of the United Nations Charter) would defend its own forces stationed in Japan if they were attacked and, therefore, would indirectly provide for the defense of Japan. In other words, US forces were not providing a cast-iron assurance of security associated with collective security arrangements such as NATO, where an attack against one contracting party was seen as an attack against all. Yet by their very presence in Japan they would act as a trip-wire, ensuring that Japanese and US security interests would be jointly secured.[116]

In Japan, the San Francisco Peace Treaty provided vital US economic and military assistance at a time of great international instability. It signified the end to a long and, by 1951, debilitating Occupation and ensured, most importantly, the restoration of sovereignty and national independence. Its shortcomings were perhaps more long-term than immediate. Territorial issues, particularly Japan's claims to the Kurile, Ryukyu, and Bonin island chains had, from Tokyo's vantage point, not yet been adequately settled. Moreover, while Prime Minister Yoshida had positioned himself relatively safely between Left and Right on the Peace Treaty issue, security questions remained in the public mind at least a point of dispute domestically. Public opinion broadly welcomed the security pact with the United States but remained divided on the question of how long it should remain in place and on the timing of any future Japanese rearmament.[117] Unlike the case with the Peace Treaty, Yoshida alone among the various Japanese party representatives present in San Francisco had signed the US-Japan bilateral Security Treaty. By failing to secure an open and unambiguous commitment by the Japanese public to future rearmament he had perhaps made his biggest mistake,[118] leaving open a sensitive and controversial issue which would continue to complicate both Japanese politics and the relationship with the United States in the years to come.

It is worth emphasizing that the San Francisco settlement was very much provisional in nature. (There was no formal time limit, for example, to the bilateral Security Treaty.) In the unstable and unpredictable context of the Cold War, and confronted by pressures both at home and abroad, American and Japanese leaders recognized the importance of compromise and flexibility in reaching an early and satisfactory agreement. Sustaining this cooperation and developing it into a strong alliance relationship in the months and years to come would demand continuing imagination and resourcefulness on the part of both governments.

CHAPTER THREE

Foreign and Domestic Pressures

China Policy and the Administrative Agreement, 1951–52

With the signing of the Peace and Security treaties in San Francisco, Japan, symbolically at least, made the transition from occupied, defeated power to independent, sovereign state. In reality, however, the process was incomplete. Japan had certainly reached the final stretch in its race to secure independence, but it had yet to cross the finish line. In order to give substance and permanence to the San Francisco agreement, the national parliaments of the signatory powers needed to formally ratify the two treaties. Although this was not an especially drawn-out process, taking some seven months in total, two key issues—the question of Japan's future relations with China, and negotiations between Washington and Tokyo over the terms of the Administrative Agreement governing the stationing of US forces in post-Occupation Japan—threatened to delay if not jeopardize a final settlement. Both issues were significant not only because of their impact on ratification but also because they highlighted tensions between alliance partners, old and new, bureaucratic disagreements within national governments, and the persistent entanglement of domestic politics with diplomacy.

Where Sino-Japanese relations were concerned, John Foster Dulles and others in the US government worked energetically and determinedly to establish a treaty relationship between Japan and the Chinese Nationalist government in Taiwan. Dulles's efforts were largely an effort to offset potential opposition from Republican senators who threatened to vote against ratification unless Japan demonstrated a willingness to identify explicitly with America's Far Eastern policy by extending some form of diplomatic recognition to Chiang Kai-shek's regime. In the process of creating consensus at home, Dulles clashed with America's allies abroad, in particular with Britain (which for its own political and economic reasons disapproved of a policy of favoring the Nationalist Chinese over the Communist Chinese), and also, it has often been argued, with Japan. While the disagreement between Britain and United States is well documented, that between Japan and the United States is less clear-cut. US scholarship, in particular the work of "New Left" revisionist writers such as John Dower and Howard Schonberger, has portrayed Dulles as dictating terms to the Japanese, effectively compelling the government in Tokyo, against its better judgment, to align with the Nationalists at the expense of a more extensive, and from Japan's perspective, more desirable, economically rational, and culturally legitimate relationship with the PRC.[1] Similarly, in Japan, a number of prominent historians, most notably Hosoya Chihiro, have long endorsed a conventional interpretation of Dulles as a practitioner of heavy-handed and coercive diplomacy vis-à-vis Japan (Kōatsu shudan to kyōatsu tekina gaikō shuhō).[2] However, unambiguous archival evidence to support this claim is strikingly absent, as will be demonstrated below.

Setting the issue of Japan's future relations with China alongside the Administrative Agreement negotiations raises legitimate questions about the extent to which US and Japanese leaders disagreed with one another over early Cold War alliance policy. Certainly, popular sentiment in Japan opposed America's lead on certain issues, but it is possible that the putative clash of elite-level opinion has been exaggerated by later commentators. At the very least, US diplomats, including Dulles, appear to have felt that there was broad agreement between the Japanese and American governments over the political desirability of a Peace Treaty between Japan and the Kuomintang (KMT) leadership. Moreover, given the State Department's meticulous attention during the Administrative Agreement talks to Japanese concerns regarding sovereignty and equal treatment, both formally and substantively, it is unlikely that Washington would intentionally have risked pressuring Tokyo and unsettling if not fatally undermining the fledgling bilateral partnership.

US-Japanese Relations and the Recognition of Nationalist China

Although the debate over China policy was a source of bitter disagreement among the Western Allies during the Cold War, with the United States adopting an apparently unremittingly hostile stance toward the PRC, it is important to emphasize, as many scholars have done, that America's China policy betrayed signs of flexibility, especially during the early post-1945 period. Initially, America had in fact attempted to play a mediating role, seeking at the end of World War II to reconcile the warring Nationalist and Communist factions in the Chinese civil war. However, the failure of the Marshall Mission in late autumn 1946 soon indicated the limits to a strategy of accommodation.[3] High-profile disagreements between the Truman administration and Mao's Communists, in particular the diplomatic war of words brought on by the detention in November 1948 of Angus Ward, the American Consul General in Mukden, Manchuria, signaled a deteriorating relationship.[4] US public opinion grew increasingly critical of the Chinese Communists as the Cold War with the Soviet Union gathered pace and as the American domestic political climate became more vehemently anti-Communist following the trials of Klaus Fuchs and Alger Hiss and the launch of Senator Joseph McCarthy anti-Communist crusade in February 1950.[5] Prior to the outbreak of the Korean War, although neither Truman nor Acheson was inclined to view the PRC as part of a monolithic, Soviet-directed Communist bloc, internal administration differences complicated the process of developing a clear position toward China. Policy options were spread out on a spectrum. Some in the State Department favored a Titoist strategy involving eventual political recognition and normal economic ties as a way of seducing Beijing away from any close relationship with Moscow. Others were more critical, believing that non-recognition and economic sanctions might, by forcing Beijing to depend on Moscow for economic assistance, exacerbate rivalries and tension between the two Communist states and ultimately discredit and bring down Mao's government.[6]

Hostile public opinion and congressional opposition acted as the most powerful break on the development of a flexible China policy. Republican critics of the administration, centered on figures such as Senator William Knowland and Congressman Walter Judd, were fervent supporters of the Nationalists and Chiang Kai-shek and fiercely opposed any accommodation with Beijing. Their arguments were amplified by the supporting voices of prominent media figures such as Henry and Clare Booth Luce, the editors of *Time-Life*, and by the leading syndicated-columnists, Joseph and Stewart Alsop. This "China Lobby" was not especially tightly organized and coherent, but in the absence of any countervailing interest group or body of opinion it was able to put severe limits on the administration's freedom of action.[7]

Despite the political pressures and bureaucratic differences standing in the way of any significant political accommodation with the Chinese Communists, where trade was concerned the Truman administration had some room for compromise. NSC 41, passed in February 1949, essentially endorsed a Titoist strategy and envisaged the eventual restoration of economic ties with the Chinese mainland.[8] In this context there was scope for the development of a trading relationship between Japan and China. In the pre-war period, some 25 percent of Japan's overseas trade had been with China and, political differences aside, China was still in many ways Japan's natural market.[9] State Department officials recognized that limiting such trade might cause disaffection within Japan and, despite opposition from the Pentagon and CIA, favored encouraging non-strategic trade even following the passage of NSC 48/2 in June 1949, which limited the export of oil and railway sleepers to China, and even after the Communists came to power in late 1949.[10] Such trade was viewed as a way of boosting Japan's economic independence while minimizing the costs of post-war recovery and the American Occupation. Traditionally, Japan relied heavily on China for much-needed food and raw material imports, particularly coking coal and iron ore. As early as May 1946, it had begun importing salt from China; in April 1950, it had received some 15,000 tons of Chinese soybeans and had made arrangements to receive coal from China.[11]

Some measure of the open-ended quality of the China question as it related to Japan, and as seen from the vantage point of the State Department at this stage, can be gleaned from a Tokyo mission report prepared by Charles Spinks and his fellow foreign service officer Cabot Coville in December 1949. The report was a strikingly undoctrinaire and dispassionate assessment of the pros and cons of recognition of the PRC as the sole government of China not only by the international community but specifically by the United States and, implicitly, by Japan. It acknowledged the historical and cultural affinities between mainland China and Japan and the "strong economic arguments" which had an "understandable appeal to the Japanese businessman."[12] Against all this had to be balanced the risk that recognition and the establishment of a Chinese diplomatic mission in Japan might, either directly or indirectly, bolster the position of subversive, Communist groups among both Chinese and Korean residents in Japan. However, more important was the counterintuitive observation that recognition of the PRC might weaken US-Japanese relations, not by allowing Japan to be lured into the Communist camp, but by undermining Japanese confidence in the strength and reliability of its emerging partnership with Washington. Coville and Spinks were afraid, not of Tokyo intentionally leaning toward Beijing, but of a crisis of confidence in Washington-Tokyo relations: "Any indication that recognition of communist China in any way signifies acquiescence by the United States in a communist Asia would be disastrous. . . . Japan is . . . profoundly concerned that she might be left isolated among communist neighbors, and if the conviction sweeps over her that she faces that possibility the situation will deteriorate with rapidity."[13]

The corollary of this sober assessment was that the United States would itself have to conduct a campaign to win the hearts and minds of the Japanese and to convince them that the PRC should be viewed as evolving eventually into a normal power—a modernizing, emerging nation-state rather than a subversive source of revolutionary contagion.

> This program might place emphasis on the fact that China has been only half a nation; that even the rudimentary adjuncts of modern government are absent in China; that the process of her development must be long and arduous; that, in the confusion and lack of enlightenment which have been inseparable from the basic urge for reform in China, communism and the self-interested advocates of communism have seen and exploited an unusual opportunity for their purposes; and that with the responsibilities and practical necessities of adequate government facing them hereafter, the Chinese people must assuredly develop sound political and economic practices, with the inevitable attenuation of their pro-communistic acceptances.[14]

Ultimately, the mission—or rather its head, William Sebald, in his capacity as POLAD—recommended against recognition on grounds that: "On balance . . . no definite good can accrue to American interests in Japan through American recognition of the communist regime in China, either in terms of really significant trade advantages or in the form of political benefit."[15] Of note here, and somewhat at odds with the conventional wisdom articulated by later historians, is the notion that a political accommodation with Mao's regime had to be sold to the Japanese rather than being something that Tokyo would embrace of its own volition. As Spinks and Coville emphasized in their concluding summary:

> Recognition itself raises no insoluble problems in United States relations with Japan provided Japan's consequent apprehensions with regard to security are adequately met. Suggested means to removal of such apprehensions are (1) assurances that post-recognition Chinese Mission in Japan would be precluded from internal political activity and communist propaganda; (2) an educational campaign showing that the long-range significance of current change in China

is not communism but her dire need of betterment; (3) appropriate proof that there is no relaxation of United States interest and position in the Far East and Japan; and (4) support for the strengthening of Japan's internal security (in the face of communist neighbors) and the maintenance of the integrity of her frontiers against illegal entry.[16]

Notwithstanding such examples of policy flexibly, the outbreak of the Korean War, for obvious reasons, imposed severe constraints on the Truman administration's freedom of action toward China. Despite the State Department's inclination to distinguish subtly between Moscow and Beijing, the need to avoid any hint of appeasement of aggression and maintain a solid Allied coalition militated against accommodation with the Chinese Communists. The Korean War confirmed in the minds of the American public the image of international Communism as a threatening and monolithic force.[17] Although Acheson was still inclined to differentiate between trade with China and that with other Communist bloc countries,[18] China's intervention in the war in late 1950 signaled the demise of the earlier trade initiatives and by December 6, 1950, SCAP was instructing the Japanese government to suspend the export of all controlled items to the Chinese mainland.[19]

Policy toward the Chinese Communists was not only a contentious issue in US domestic politics, it also complicated relations between America and its Allies. Britain, in particular, took issue with the Truman administration's Asian policy. Whereas the Americans were inclined to stress the global ideological and security challenge to the West posed by an expansionist Communist movement, the British adopted a more traditional view of international relations. From London's perspective, not only could the Soviet Union be viewed essentially as a "normal" state that would eventually, on the basis of self-interested power-political calculations, compromise and reach a modus vivendi with the West, but also, in Asia, major superpower confrontation was an unlikely prospect.[20]

By early January 1950, London had formally recognized the Beijing government—an initiative based in part on political motivations (the Foreign Office felt that diplomatic recognition might loosen Sino-Soviet ties), but also on economic self-interest. Britain sought to protect its financial interests on the Chinese mainland as well as to guarantee the future of Hong Kong.[21] Indeed, economic considerations were soon to play an important role in the debate between London and Washington over Japan's future relations with China. The British remained preoccupied (as was clear from their negotiations with the United States over the precise terms of the San Francisco Peace Treaty) with the likely threat to Britain's economic interests of a revived Japan. Such a threat was not limited to the challenge posed by Japanese textile exports to Britain. Japan was also a competitor with Britain's trading interests in Southeast Asia.[22] This rivalry could best be dealt with by encouraging a trading relationship between Japan and mainland China—continuing in effect Japan's pre-war pattern of trade and obviating any need for Japan to expand into new markets. Clearly, America's strategy of embargoing trade with the PRC was at odds with such an approach. So too, according to London's calculations, was any tendency to favor Nationalist China politically over the Communists. If Japan, either independently or at American urging, reached some form of political accommodation with Taiwan, Communist China would be unlikely to favor a close trading relationship with Japan and Japanese business would be forced to turn to the Southeast Asian market, in turn exacerbating Britain's economic difficulties.[23]

Early on in the Peace Treaty proceedings, Sino-Japanese relations became a point of contention between Washington and London. In the spring of 1951, the British government made clear to American representatives that it opposed the inclusion of Nationalist China as a signatory of the Peace Treaty, in part because this could create resentment among the Japanese who ultimately wished to establish close ties with the mainland. Similarly, in Washington, Sir Oliver Franks, the British ambassador, informed Dulles that Britain favored Communist China's participation in San Francisco. Including the PRC would, in Britain's view, leave the door open to future Sino-Japanese trade and eventually enable Japan to become economically self-sustaining.[24]

The Truman administration remained firmly opposed to the British proposal. Distrust of China brought on by the Korean War, and Republican opposition, ruled out any inclusion of Beijing. Although the Americans recognized the significance of the Chinese market to Japan, they felt that a combination of US aid, access to the American market, and the development of trading links with Southeast Asia (precisely the strategy the British were opposed to) could compensate for the loss of China.[25] Increasingly, Dulles and his assistant, John Allison, grew irritated with the British for failing to appreciate the political obstacles faced by Washington and for refusing, despite a number of American concessions, to be flexible in negotiating the terms for the Japanese Peace Treaty. As Allison noted in an April 5 memo to Dulles: "While the United States has made an honest and sincere effort to meet the British point of view wherever possible, I cannot readily recall to mind any case in which the United Kingdom had made any effort to accommodate itself to the United States position."[26] In the face of this bilateral tension, Dulles and Allison apparently agreed to try to minimize further disagreements with the British. Shortly before his departure for London for talks in June with the Attlee government, Dulles briefed Truman on the state of the Treaty negotiations and recommended the deferment of any attempt to resolve the China issue.[27] Inviting the PRC would be at odds with the administration's agreed position of not recognizing Mao's regime as a legitimate representative of the Chinese people. At the same time, inclusion of the KMT made little sense in light of the Nationalists' much-reduced political influence. Despite his public remarks and subsequent support for Taiwan, Dulles clearly recognized that Chiang's claim to speak for China had, for the time being at least, little basis in fact. As he pointed out in a telegram to William Sebald, SCAP's political advisor in Tokyo, inviting KMT representatives to San Francisco would "involve apparent treatment of the National Government as authorized to speak for and bind the hundreds and millions of Chinese over which it has lost, at least temporarily, de facto authority."[28] To avoid further controversy with the British, Dulles suggested that neither of the two Chinas be invited to the Peace Conference.

Initially, the London talks proceeded fairly smoothly. Morrison, the British foreign secretary, seemed willing to accept Dulles's non-invitation formula. However, Attlee took issue with Morrison's position. The British prime minister was concerned that under the terms proposed by Dulles, Japan would eventually recognize the Nationalists—an outcome that would prejudice the position of the British government and produce a hostile reaction from the British public.[29] Rather than leave the issue open-ended, Attlee suggested entrusting the decision over Japan's future relations with China to the Far Eastern Commission in Washington. A final decision would be postponed until two-thirds or more of the FEC countries had voted in favor of one of the two Chinas, at which point Japan would recognize the China endorsed by the FEC majority.[30] Dulles rejected the new British suggestion, criticizing it for violating Japan's sovereignty and undermining the entire basis of the Peace Treaty.[31] Once again, as with the other proposed provisions of the Peace Treaty governing reparations, rearmament, war-guilt clauses, and Japan's future trading relations, there appears to have been a major gap between Britain's rhetorical defense of Japan's independence and the Labour government's

somewhat clumsy efforts to protect its own political and economic interests. At no point in the June discussions do the British appear to have reiterated their earlier suggestion that Japan would oppose the establishment of ties with the Nationalists. If anything, both sides assumed (as
Dulles himself later pointed out) that Japan would naturally identify with
Taiwan, without necessarily jeopardizing future contacts with the mainland. Moreover, Dulles's rejection of Attlee's proposal as a violation of Japan's sovereignty would presumably have cut little ice with the British
had they believed that the Americans were actively pressuring Japan to
recognize Chiang's government. The record does not suggest a clash of
interests between Japan and the United States. If anything the focal point
of disagreement lay between Britain and the United States, and to a lesser
extent between Britain and Japan. There is nothing to suggest that Dulles
was contemplating limiting Japan's freedom of action as a means of winning over critical political opinion at home. By contrast with the more restrictive British approach, Dulles was apparently at this stage committed
to preserving Japan's diplomatic discretion, even entertaining the possibility of future Japanese ties with mainland China. As the Foreign Office
minutes of Dulles's June 8 meeting with Morrison reveal:

> Mr. Dulles replied that there was considerable objection to a Treaty which did
> not fully restore Japanese sovereignty. The proposal to leave in the hands of a
> group of the Allied powers control of a major question of Japanese foreign
> policy would restrict Japanese sovereignty. Japan would in any case have rela-
> tions with the island of Formosa, if only because of the economic interdepen-
> dence of the two territories. He thought it inconceivable however that Japan
> would make Treaty arrangements with the Government of Formosa as though
> the latter were able to commit the whole of China. *He personally would be
> pleased if Japan could also make some arrangements with the Government on
> the mainland of China.* He did not think it wise to inject into this problem the
> opinions of a group of Allied Powers. It was much better to leave Japan as the
> controller of her own foreign policy. Any mistakes the Japanese made would
> then be their own and not those of the Allied Powers. It was also important to
> prevent anyone from being able to argue that the Allied Powers had prejudiced
> Japan's chance of developing relations with the mainland. [Emphasis added][32]

Similarly, Attlee's own record of his conversation with the US envoy indicates:

> In my talk with Mr. Dulles the question turned almost entirely on the giving of
> absolute sovereignty to Japan. He was not prepared to consider any restriction
> on the freedom of Japan to recognise either Communist China or Nationalist
> China.[33]

Despite their differences, Dulles and the British eventually agreed on the earlier strategy of inviting neither China to San Francisco while recognizing that Japan should be permitted to make up its own mind which of the two Chinas it would later establish relations with. Dulles returned to Washington happy to have avoided a falling out with the British, which might have delayed the Peace Treaty, and also reassured to discover that leading Senate Republicans, in particular William Knowland and Robert Taft, approved of his approach.[34]

However, Dulles's China compromise did not satisfy everyone. Unsurprisingly, the Nationalists were annoyed to have been excluded from the Peace Treaty proceedings. Wellington Koo, the KMT official representative in Washington, made clear to Dulles his government's dissatisfaction and suggested that if Taiwan were unable to sign the multilateral Peace Treaty in San Francisco, it should be permitted to sign a separate agreement with Japan before the September conference. Dulles firmly rejected Koo's suggestion, pointing out its impracticalities and warning that KMT objections might jeopardize the overall peace process. At the same time, as if to offset this disappointing news, Dulles went out of his way to reassure Koo that Japan was intent on establishing close ties with Taiwan, including eventually a formal treaty relationship. As Dulles pointed out to Koo:

> I know that the Japanese government is very favourably disposed towards your government. It wants to develop extensive commercial ties between Taiwan and Japan and certainly wishes to conclude a treaty with you. At the same time, the Japanese government is opposed to any effort to force it to establish a relationship with Communist China.[35]

Dean Rusk, who was also present at this meeting, interceded at this point, and impressed on Koo the importance of secrecy, enjoining him "not to divulge this understanding."[36] This brief exchange, apparently unrecorded in the American archives, is interesting since it strongly suggests that Japan was already, at this early stage, committed to recognizing Nationalist China. Although Dulles would have had his own reasons for wanting to reassure Koo, his words hint at an early understanding between Japan and the United States and provide grounds for questioning the traditional assumption that America pressured the Yoshida cabinet to align with Taiwan.

The successful convening of the San Francisco Peace Conference and, in particular, the prevention of Soviet obstructionist tactics boosted the political fortunes of the Truman administration and temporarily eased Republican partisan criticisms of Acheson and the State Department.

However, China issues continued to act as an irritant between the executive and legislative branches of the government. During August and September, rumors had been circulating in Congress that the Japanese government was preparing to sign an agreement with the Communist Chinese. Japan had, as early as June 1951, indicated an intention to establish an Overseas Agency in Taibei, but by the time of the Peace Conference the Agency had not yet been established—a delay which Republican supporters of Chiang attributed to a change of heart by the Yoshida government and a reluctance to establish ties with the Nationalists. According to William Sebald, Tokyo's caution reflected an unwillingness to antagonize the British rather than coolness toward Taiwan. In fact, it was American advice—John Allison had cautioned Nishimura Kumao, the head of the Gaimushō's Treaties Bureau, against overly hasty initiatives when he had first proposed establishing an agency—that had initially delayed Japan's proposal.[37] Moreover, Yoshida, despite delaying the opening of the overseas agency, had already agreed to dispatch to Taibei a senior-ranking Gaimushō official, Kawada Isao, to act as financial advisor to the Nationalist government.[38]

Whatever the motivations behind Japanese actions, congressional supporters of Chiang Kai-shek remained eager for reassurance that Japan identified with Taiwan. On September 13, 56 senators sent a joint letter to Truman opposing any recognition of Communist China by Japan or the establishment of any treaty between the two countries.[39] Increasingly, Dulles recognized that Republican skepticism might pose a risk to ratification of both the Peace and Security treaties. During the San Francisco Peace Conference, Yoshida had proposed making a speech severely critical of Communist China, but had been politely discouraged by Acheson who wanted to avoid generating any unnecessary controversy during the conference.[40] Dulles was more anxious to mollify senatorial concerns and hastily arranged a meeting between Yoshida and a prominent Republican senator, H. Alexander Smith. During the meeting, Yoshida, without making an explicit commitment to Taiwan, suggested that Japan was genuinely interested in signing a Peace Treaty with the Nationalists and had no intention of reaching any sort of agreement with the PRC.[41] However, despite Dulles's best efforts, Smith was not fully convinced by the Japanese prime minister's assurances. Moreover, by the late autumn, statements by Yoshida in the Japanese Diet supporting Japanese trade with the PRC and raising the possibility of the establishment of a trade office in Shanghai once again stimulated American congressional concern.[42]

Anxious to alleviate Republican anxieties, Dulles on November 7 wrote to Acheson informing him of his plans to visit Tokyo, with John Sparkman and H. Alexander Smith, both leading figures on the Far Eastern subcommittee of the Senate's Foreign Relations Committee.[43] The trip would be an opportunity to offset any potential partisan obstacles to Treaty ratification by demonstrating to the senators Japan's close alignment with US Asian policy. Shortly after arriving in Tokyo on December 13, Dulles met with Yoshida and Iguchi Sadao, the vice-minister for foreign affairs, and set out his thinking on China policy. Congressional concern over Japan's future relations with China meant that it was imperative for Japan to demonstrate tangibly its opposition to Communist China and its willingness to identify in some way with the Nationalists. Dulles proposed that Japan could advance its interests by agreeing to enter into negotiations with Taiwan regarding a future treaty relationship between the two countries. Such a treaty would recognize only the de facto authority of the Nationalists (thereby minimizing any damage to Tokyo's future relations with Beijing), and would only be signed once the San Francisco Peace and Security treaties had come into effect following ratification. Explicitly opening channels with the Nationalists would, according to Dulles, be beneficial to Japan not merely because it would calm senatorial anxieties and reduce any risk of delay to Peace Treaty ratification, but Taiwan's strategic importance as a part of America's offshore island defense network, its role as a trading partner with Japan, and its United Nations seat and associated authority to influence Japan's future membership of the international organization all argued in favor of some sort of formal relationship between Tokyo and Taibei.[44]

Dulles's initiative eventually developed into the "Yoshida Letter"—a formal document, ostensibly written by the Japanese prime minister, but in fact the product of deliberations between Yoshida and Dulles, indicating Japan's intention to conclude a treaty with Taiwan and its opposition to any treaty with the PRC. Yoshida endorsed the letter on December 18—in fact, Yoshida inserted a statement in Dulles's original draft attacking the Sino-Soviet Treaty of Friendship as a military alliance explicitly directed against Japan[45]—and Dulles indicated that he had already shown the text to Senators Sparkman and Smith, who had accepted it as the minimum measure necessary to guarantee Senate ratification of the Peace Treaty. The letter would be released at a later date, but only after being made known to the Japanese government.[46]

Critical commentary has suggested that the letter provides clear proof of American pressure on Japan. However, the evidence to suggest any major divergence in American and Japanese thinking regarding Japan's relations with Taiwan is limited and at best equivocal. Dulles, in his own mind, was certain that he had not pressured or coerced Japan,[47] and the Japanese government made clear that it had no objections in principle to Dulles's proposal. Yoshida's main concern was over possible British retaliation against Japan once the text of the letter was made public. In particular, he feared that it might jeopardize Japan's commercial opportunities in the sterling-based trading regions of Africa and Southeast Asia. Dulles was quick to reassure Yoshida, pointing out that, even if the British remained hostile to a Japanese alignment with Taiwan, "the United States would take the 'blame,' so that Japan would not be subject to counteraction on the part of the British."[48] In effect, Dulles appears to have been suggesting that the United States would, if need be, make clear to London that the Sino-Japanese rapprochement was an American initiative, thereby exonerating Japan in the eyes of the British.

The argument that Japan was pushed against its wishes into treaty negotiations with Taiwan requires clear evidence of Japanese resentment at the American proposal. In contrast, the American diplomatic record, although not fully conclusive on the matter, suggests agreement rather than disagreement between Yoshida and Dulles. In endorsing Dulles's draft letter, Iguchi characterized it as a "Christmas present" from the Americans[49]—an unusually positive phrase to use if Japan had in fact opposed the initiative.

John Dower has criticized Yoshida for setting Japan on an "abject and acquiescent course" in following the US lead over China policy.[50] He accuses the prime minister of passiveness and irresolution in failing to stand up to America and of clumsy diplomacy and inconsistency because of his willingness to agree privately to Washington's demands while also issuing Diet statements at odds with Washington's China strategy. Such criticisms are only valid if based on clear evidence that Yoshida disagreed fundamentally with the American position. Moreover, they fail to take into account the powerful domestic, political forces that constrained Yoshida's freedom of action. Certainly, it is fair to point out, as much of the primary and secondary literature reveals, that Yoshida was eager to develop economic ties with the Chinese mainland. It is also clear that Yoshida prided himself on his long experience and understanding of Chinese affairs, and believed that this provided him with an insight into the Chinese situation that the Americans possibly lacked. However, agreeing to enter into negotiations with the Nationalists was a limited strategy, based on political calculation and the need to secure an early peace settlement (both Dulles's and Yoshida's primary objective) rather than a grand effort to contain mainland China economically. A treaty with Taibei, while undoubtedly unpopular in Beijing and unlikely to foster close relations between the PRC and Japan, need not necessarily have precluded future ties between the two countries, especially since Dulles had already made clear that the Treaty would only acknowledge Taiwan's de facto authority.[51] As Dulles observed in conversation with Herbert Morrison in September 1951: "We assumed the Japanese would want quickly to put trade, diplomatic and consular relations with Formosa on a normal peace time basis. None of this, however, necessarily implied Japanese acceptance of the Chinese Nationalist Government as empowered to speak for, and to bind, all of China."[52] Indeed, for Japan, the benefits of close links with Taiwan were not limited to securing US congressional support for Treaty ratification. As the sitting representative of China in the United Nations, Taiwan could also in the future prove valuable voting support for Japanese membership in UN agencies. Dower's criticism of Yoshida's stance on the China issue underplays the significance of the competing national interests of Japan, both the political, economic, and strategic backing it received from the United States and its long-term interest in engaging with the United Nations. Yoshida's alignment with the United States on the China issue seems, therefore, to have been the product of a shrewd calculation of Japan's strategic priorities rather than a case of abject acquiescence.[53]

It is important to recognize also, as Kitaoka Shin'ichi has pointed out, that Yoshida was staunchly anti-Communist.[54] Any nostalgic sympathy Yoshida may have had for China based on his lengthy pre-war experience as a Foreign Office official in Manchuria needs to be set against his intense fear of Communism as a revolutionary force capable of bringing chaos to Japan.[55] While hoping to trade with mainland China, he recognized that trade would not neutralize the Communist threat. Also, aligning Tokyo firmly with Washington was more of a priority than establishing Japanese links with China.[56] Unlike his successors as prime minister, Yoshida saw the alliance with the United States as a means of actively opposing Communism rather than merely providing protection to Japan. Indeed, in later years, Yoshida criticized prime ministers Hatoyama Ichirō and Kishi Nobusuke for adopting too passive a relationship with the United States.[57] From Yoshida's point of view, economic involvement with the PRC did not require a political rapprochement with Beijing, nor any distancing of Japan from Nationalist China. Yoshida's personal letters reveal that in the early 1960s when the question of China recognition was again being debated, he firmly supported Chiang Kai-shek and opposed any abandonment of Taiwan.[58] Similarly, in late 1958, in a discussion with Harry Kern, the editor of *Newsweek*, Yoshida vehemently denounced the PRC, arguing that it was aiming, together with the Soviet Union, to communize Asia and warning that the United States "should never recognize Communist China."[59]

Yoshida's anxieties regarding the potential threat posed by Communist China explain the prime minister's willingness to endorse US China policy during his discussions with American officials. His eagerness to criticize the PRC in San Francisco and his efforts to strengthen the anti-Communist language of the Yoshida Letter were apparently in keeping with his personal convictions. However, whatever may have been Yoshida's private beliefs, his ability to publicly defend a close alignment with the Americans was severely circumscribed by fear that identification with Washington might invite an unfavorable response from other Western powers at a critical juncture in the Peace Treaty ratification process and by pro-PRC sentiment at home.[60] Early on during the post-war period, it was clear that a significant body of opinion in Japan favored a close relationship with mainland China. In part this was in direct reaction to the experience of the 1930s. Guilt over Japanese activity in China was a major preoccupation of the media in the aftermath of the war, and the press and academic journals of the time were filled with Chinese writings, many of which were very critical of Japanese traditions and the Emperor system.[61] In such a context, friendly relations with Beijing were a way of partially atoning for past misdeeds. At the same time, China still represented a major economic market, and a substantial majority of the members of Keidanren, the leading business organization, according to a survey of 1949–50 were in favor of trade with Communist China.[62]

Politically and in an organized context, there was considerable activity in Japan in support of Communist China. In October 1949 the "Sino-Japanese Friendship Association" (Nitchū Yūkō Kyōkai), a diverse and at times influential organization favoring close links with the mainland, was established.[63] In May of the same year, the "China-Japan Trade Promotion Association" (Chū-Nichi bōeki sokushin kai) was formed, while in the Japanese Diet the "Parliamentary League for China-Japan Trade Promotion" (Chū-Nichi bōeki sokushin giin renmei) provided a context for cross-party support for close ties with the mainland. By December 1952, the League included more than half the members of both houses of the Diet.[64] Support for links with the PRC existed on both the left and right of the political spectrum, and some of Yoshida's principal political rivals, such as Ishibashi Tanzan (finance minister in the first Yoshida cabinet and a later prime minister), actively campaigned in favor of close (especially economic) relations with Beijing.[65] Similarly, the Ryokufūkai ("Green Breeze Society"), on which Yoshida's Liberal Party depended critically for support in the Diet's Upper House prior to the elections of June 1950, backed parliamentary resolutions favoring the establishment of formal trade links with the PRC.[66]

In such a charged political environment, Yoshida had to tread warily. Moreover, after the San Francisco Peace Conference, the position of the Liberal government became increasingly precarious. Yoshida's popularity declined significantly once the Peace Treaty had been signed, and the cabinet was viewed as having no fixed policies. As Sebald reported from Tokyo, by January 1952 there was a risk of an early dissolution of parliament and the possibility that the government would not see out its full term, scheduled to run until January of 1953.[67] It is easy to appreciate why Yoshida would have felt the need to issue parliamentary statements hinting at possible Japanese ties with the PRC and calculated to reassure both domestic political opinion and overseas governments such as the United Kingdom.[68]

Against the backdrop of domestic political uncertainty associated with disagreements over rearmament and China policy, it is perhaps legitimate to view the Yoshida Letter as an early example of what later writers have referred to as gaiatsu (foreign pressure) politics. In its most basic form, gaiatsu refers to attempts by American trade negotiators in the 1980s and 1990s to force a reluctant Japanese government to remove structural and bureaucratic barriers to American exports to the Japanese market.[69] A more subtle interpretation views gaiatsu as a tool for justifying the pursuit of government policy unpopular with Japanese mass opinion, but which Japanese bureaucrats and politicians consider genuinely desirable. Foreign pressure, in effect, legitimizes or excuses initiatives which would otherwise fail because of domestic opposition. Yoshida may have welcomed Dulles's letter as a means of promoting policy which, if independently endorsed, would have undermined his political position at home. Though the letter was officially written by Yoshida, its content and the manner in which it was publicized (by Dulles in mid-January) would almost certainly have suggested to popular opinion in Japan that it was the result of some form of "understanding" between the two governments.[70] Nor is it likely that either Yoshida and Dulles would have failed to appreciate this. As a diplomatic device, the letter could play differently to different audiences. In the United States, where Senate opinion was little concerned about Japanese sensibilities, politicians merely needed to receive formal confirmation that Japan was aligning with America's Asian policy. In Japan, the letter may have allowed Yoshida to disingenuously suggest that unpopular decisions were the result of foreign pressure rather than his own actions, thereby mollifying or at least blunting domestic opposition and helping to avoid a hostile British reaction. Where Britain was concerned, Yoshida could rely on Dulles's diplomatic support; by interceding with the government in London as well as its representatives in Japan, Dulles could act in some ways as a diplomatic lightning rod, deflecting criticism from Tokyo.

Since his talks with the Attlee government in June 1951, Dulles had attempted to keep the British notified of developments regarding Japan's future relations with China. In early August, he had informed F. S. Tomlinson of the British embassy in Washington that nothing should be done to prevent Japan from voluntarily improving relations with Taiwan—a suggestion which Tomlinson appeared to view as reasonable.[71] Similarly, flying back from San Francisco after the Peace Conference, Dulles had pointed out to Morrison that Japan wished to establish ties with the Chinese Nationalists and that failure to promote such ties might endanger ratification of the Peace Treaty. The British foreign secretary made clear his wish that no action be taken until the San Francisco treaties had been formally ratified, but at the same time indicated that he was not opposed ultimately to some sort of arrangement between Japan and Taiwan, provided it only involved recognition of the Nationalists' de facto authority, rather than any extended claims to represent the whole of China.[72] For the moment, it seemed as if China was unlikely to be an especially divisive issue between London and Tokyo.

A change of government in Britain, with the election of the Churchill cabinet in October, offered a sign of further progress. Officials in Washington hoped that the new Conservative government would not be bound by the decisions of its predecessor, including the political and economic constraints militating against a Japanese alignment with Taiwan. Moreover, Anthony Eden, the new foreign secretary, was a long-standing friend of Acheson's—further indication of a possible meeting of minds between the two Anglo-Saxon powers.[73] Prior to traveling to Tokyo for his talk with Yoshida, Dulles recommended that Livingstone Merchant, the State Department's deputy assistant secretary for far eastern affairs, be sent to London to confer with the British. In talks in November with R. H. Scott of the Foreign Office's Far Eastern department, Merchant reached a tentative understanding that talks could go ahead between Japan and Taiwan, with the assumption that neither Britain nor the United States would exert any influence on Japan to recognize either of the two Chinas and on the basis that no agreement would be signed before the implementation of the San Francisco Peace Treaty.[74] Scott, it seems, had no reason to assume that the United States was planning to exert pressure on the Japanese, and he recognized the political difficulties faced by the Americans because of Senate reluctance to proceed with ratification.

Scott's accommodating position was not shared by his more senior colleagues. Both Dening and, most significantly, Eden himself, rejected the agreement reached with Merchant. The British opposed the US initiative on the grounds, in part, that Japan was unwilling to align with the Nationalists and would resent American pressure. However, from Washington's vantage point, British economic self-interest and the need to avoid political embarrassment at home, rather than London's professed wish to safeguard Japanese sovereignty and independence, were responsible for Britain's opposition. Protecting Britain's commercial interests in Southeast Asia from Japanese competition still appeared to be a powerful motivation in resisting any alignment between Taiwan and Japan. As Senator Smith observed following a meeting with the Japanese prime minister in Tokyo in December, Yoshida "pointed out that Britain recognised Communist China and wanted Japan to ultimately do the same, and Britain also desired to keep some of East Asia as its own hunting ground for trade and therefore wanted the Japanese to trade with Communist China and not interfere with the British in southeast Asia."[75] British protestations of concern for Japan's independence were at odds with the powerful evidence that Dening had been actively pressuring Japan to recognize Communist rather than Nationalist China. As Merchant pointed out in late November: "I believe Dening is the real fly in the ointment and that he has been actively attempting to influence the Japanese, not to a position of choice on their part of which China, but actually to an ultimate choice of the Peiping government."[76] Eden insisted that the terms of the Dulles-Morrison agreement of the previous June ruled out any peace treaty talks between Japan and Taiwan prior to the ratification of the San Francisco agreements.

The deadlock between Britain and the United States was only resolved when Churchill and Eden flew to Washington for talks with their American counterparts in early January. Although the Yoshida Letter was not formally presented to either Churchill or Eden, the substance of the letter was discussed. Moreover, Dulles, prior to his meeting with Eden, did show a copy of the letter to Oliver Franks, the British ambassador, who registered little criticism of the American proposal.[77] Eventually, Eden reluctantly agreed that Japan should be permitted to enter into talks with Taiwan, and the British and the Americans agreed that a letter should be sent to Dening in Tokyo instructing him to inform the Japanese that they would not incur British displeasure if they were to negotiate with the Nationalists.[78] Dulles and the Americans had acted, as Yoshida would have expected, to forestall any possible retaliatory pressure from Britain.

After the conference and the departure of Churchill and Eden, Dulles on January 16 publicized Yoshida's Letter for the first time. Back in Britain, Eden reacted with shock and indignation, claiming that he had been misled by the Americans. It is clear that the British foreign secretary's irritation was largely prompted by the public embarrassment of appearing to have acceded to a US initiative inimical to Britain's Far Eastern interests. As Franks's earlier meeting with Dulles had demonstrated, the British were aware of Washington's position on the China question. America could be faulted, as Acheson revealed in his memoirs, for the timing of the release of the Yoshida Letter—but not for failing to inform the British or for violating the terms of the Morrison-Dulles agreement. The main source of the Churchill government's embarrassment was less United States unilateral action than the Foreign Office's own "fumbling and error."[79]

With British opposition no longer an issue, the road was now free for Japan to enter into negotiations with Taiwan. Talks between the two sides lasted some two months, throughout March and April, and involved thirteen detailed bargaining sessions and three formal conferences.[80] The principal issue of contention involved the treaty's territorial scope, with the Nationalists attempting to leave the door open for Japan's future recognition of Taiwan's claim to speak for the whole of China. The Japanese resisted these efforts, while the Americans avoided any temptation to intervene to accelerate the negotiation process. However, as the talks dragged on and the US Senate's scheduled ratification vote on the San Francisco treaties approached in mid-March, Republican senators again began to question Japan's commitment to a treaty with the Nationalists, fearing that once ratification had taken place in Washington Tokyo might back-pedal on its earlier commitment and seek an excuse to abort its talks with the Nationalists. However, Yoshida, in conversation with Sebald, laughingly reassured the Americans that such anxieties were unfounded.[81] As State Department reporting from Tokyo made clear, the Japanese prime minister remained, throughout the negotiations with Taiwan, firmly committed to his earlier agreement with Dulles. As Niles Bond reported on April 7, the US mission believed that the:

> [The] Yoshida government [is] sincere in its expressed desire conclude peace treaty with Chinese Nationalists on basis Yoshida letter. Iguchi has told me his government strongly resents implication, which he attributes to "China lobby" that with US Senate ratification San Francisco Peace Treaty Japanese have ceased to care whether or not bilateral with [sic] Chinese Nationalists concluded.[82]

By April 28, despite some last-minute disagreements between Tokyo and Taibei over the wording of the final agreement and with some prompting by the Americans, a Peace Treaty was signed. Japan established diplomatic relations with Taiwan while avoiding any suggestion that it recognized the Nationalists as representing the whole of China.

The Administrative Agreement

During the period when China policy was being debated, American and Japanese officials were also involved in discussions to determine the precise terms of post-Occupation security cooperation between their two countries. During Dulles's visit to Tokyo in February 1951, the Japanese government indicated its desire to have details regarding troop stationing, military facilities and expenses, and the status of American forces based in Japan excluded from the bilateral Security Treaty. In the midst of the Korean War, withdrawing Allied troops from Japan was clearly both undesirable and impractical, and both sets of officials recognized that in order to avoid any suggestion in Japan that the Occupation was continuing following the signing of the Peace Treaty, it would be appropriate to include the details on security cooperation in a separate agreement. Moreover, characterizing this understanding as an "administrative agreement" would remove any need for formal Diet or Senate approval associated with a treaty, and thereby minimize the risk that the final arrangement might become a hostage to political fortune. During the February talks, the Japanese and American negotiators drew up a rough draft agreement intended to form the basis for discussion between the two countries once the Peace and Security treaties had been signed.[83]

Early progress in preparing a formal US version of a possible Administrative Agreement was held up by bureaucratic delay and disagreement in Washington. The JCS, despite having received a copy of the Dulles Mission's February draft shortly after it had been endorsed by the Japanese, did not respond until August when they were highly critical and recommended its complete revision. In particular, the JCS objected to the Dulles draft on two grounds. The first was their wish to assign civil and military jurisdiction over American forces based in Japan exclusively to the United States. Unfettered jurisdiction was necessary, argued the JCS, since the different Japanese legal system might otherwise undermine US troop morale and because Japan, as a "conquered" and "oriental" nation, was different from the NATO nations with which the United States had made comparable administrative arrangements.[84] The second objection was based on a JCS desire to ensure that, during actual or imminent hostilities, the US military commander in Japan would have complete authority over all American and Japanese forces, without any formal requirement to consult with or seek the approval of the Japanese government. At most, the American commander would only be obliged to "advise" the Japanese cabinet of his actions.

Not surprisingly, State Department officials, in light of their concern while preparing the Peace and Security treaties to respect Japan's sovereignty and desire for national independence, were fiercely opposed to the US military's proposals. John Allison condemned the JCS for their historical ignorance and insensitivity in recommending measures strikingly reminiscent of the extraterritoriality provisions imposed by the West on Japan during the nineteenth century. Arguing that genuine and equal cooperation represented the only basis on which to build a secure and lasting, long-term alliance with Japan, he firmly resisted any suggestion that Japan's cultural differences or its status as a defeated power justified providing American authorities with sweeping jurisdiction rights. Allison was uncompromising in defending existing State Department policy and hinted strongly that he might resign if the JCS proposals were accepted.

> As one who has been designated to serve in a responsible position in Japan in the post-treaty period, I can only say that should this Joint Chiefs of Staff phi-

losophy be accepted, directly or indirectly, as the philosophy underlying United States Government policy toward Japan, I should have to consider seriously requesting a different assignment.[85]

Allison's views matched those of his State Department colleagues in Washington and in Japan. For example, U. Alexis Johnson, the director of the Office of Northeast Asian Affairs, stressed the importance of treating Japan as a genuine equal and the need (in order to ensure maximum Japanese cooperation and support for American policy) to involve it as a "real partner" in the defense-planning process. Failure to respect these principles risked, in light of Japan's "hypersensitivity to real or imagined discrimination," provoking a revival of Japanese nationalism and an anti-American reaction.[86] Similarly, Dean Rusk criticized the JCS for placing excessive reliance on paper guarantees of US military interests and for undermining American-Japanese cooperation by attempting to treat Japan differently from America's NATO partners: "Our own future relations with [Japan] will not be regulated merely by formal arrangements; to be workable such agreements must reflect a continuing recognition by our two nations of our mutual interest and free association in a common cause."[87]

While still attempting to resolve bureaucratic tensions, senior State Department and military officials met in the late autumn of 1951 and agreed to dispatch a joint State-Pentagon mission to Tokyo to negotiate the final terms of the Administrative Agreement with Japan.[88] Dean Rusk, the senior State Department representative, and Earl Johnson, assistant secretary of defense for far eastern affairs, left for Tokyo in January for four weeks of detailed talks with the Japanese government. Japan's reaction both before and during this period demonstrated that the State Department's earlier reservations regarding the JCS position had been justified. The principal Japanese negotiators, Okazaki Katsuo (informally Japan's foreign minister but officially minister without portfolio in the Yoshida cabinet) and Nishimura Kumao, made clear that they favored a jurisdiction arrangement comparable to that proposed for the NATO powers[89]—i.e., one that would still leave US service personnel and their dependents subject to Japanese law for crimes (both civil and military) committed outside American bases. In the case of Article XXII of the draft Administrative Agreement, dealing with the prerogatives of the US commander in Japan, the Japanese officials did not, in substance, object to the US position. They recognized that, in a crisis situation, the Americans would consult with Japan and that for practical reasons the United

States needed to be able to exercise a combined command over both Japanese and American forces. However, Okazaki and Kumao expressed considerable concern over the wording of the US proposal, which they felt failed to demonstrate a willingness on the Americans' part to consult with Japan and would consequently provoke considerable hostile public opinion that might not only encourage the Diet to call for a full legislative review of the Administrative Agreement but also, warned Okazaki and Nishimura, bring down Yoshida's Liberal government.[90] Once again, as was the case with China policy, the divergence between popular and senior government-level thinking within Japan was a source of tension in US-Japanese relations.

In order to reconcile these differences, both governments agreed to compromise on the Administrative Agreement. On the jurisdiction issue, the Japanese agreed that the United States would continue to enjoy exclusive jurisdiction rights until the NATO Status of Forces Agreement came into effect, after which Japan would be free to adopt the NATO formula if it desired. In the case of Article XXII, the Americans accepted a general statement that avoided any mention of a combined command and enjoined the two governments to "immediately consult" in a crisis situation.[91]

The successful resolution of the Administrative Agreement talks can in some ways be attributed to a process of bureaucratic accommodation and adjustment in the United States government. By late 1951, most of the principal figures in the Truman administration, including the President himself,[92] were keenly aware of the need to treat Japan as an equal and trusted partner. Dulles, although only partially involved in the Administrative Agreement talks, was highly critical of the JCS position and advocated a major and immediate effort to change Pentagon thinking.[93] Together with Truman, he recognized the importance of not allowing military considerations to overshadow the vital, political side of the US-Japan relationship. The stationing of large numbers of US troops in Japanese territory was a reminder of earlier conflicts and a potential source of bilateral tension, especially given the average soldier's limited experience as a goodwill ambassador.[94] As Dulles pointed out to the President in early October, in building an equal partnership with Japan the key issue was "getting the colonels out of the Japanese villas." Truman agreed with Dulles's assessment, and the internal administration debate, where it mattered most (at the pinnacle of government), seemed weighted in favor of the State Department rather than the Pentagon. According to Dulles, "the President said he was fully aware of the problem that there would be need of a strong civilian in Japan who could stand up to the military and the President said with obvious feeling, 'I'll back him up.'"[95]

The State Department's increasing ability to shape America's Japan policy was not merely the result of straightforward, internal bureaucratic victories. Its position was also enhanced by its ability to overcome differences by building alliances and winning converts among members of the military and within the Pentagon. Dean Rusk, perhaps in part because of his earlier experience in the War Department, was especially adept at administrative fence-mending. Particularly in his working relationship with Earl Johnson, he appears to have won a useful ally. Johnson had a high regard for Rusk, and his reports from Tokyo during the Administrative Agreement talks reveal a sensitivitiy to the possible counterproductiveness of pressuring the Japanese.[96]

Another figure of importance in explaining the State Department's increasing ability to prevail in bureaucratic battles with the Pentagon was Matthew Ridgway. In some respects, Ridgway, after taking over from MacArthur as SCAP and Commander in Chief in the Far East (CinCFE) in April 1951, continued to express a traditional, conservative military viewpoint. He initially favored the JCS position on jurisdiction questions, resisted (ultimately unsuccessfully) State Department pressures to have SCAP headquarters moved away from the Dai-Ichi Building in Tokyo's center, and campaigned aggressively (and successfully) to maintain the right to appoint the American members of the US-Japan Joint Committee—the body set up to put into practice the Administrative Agreement and of particular importance where military matters were concerned.[97] However, in other respects, Ridgway's position was close to that of the State Department. Many of his reports from Tokyo betray a sympathetic understanding of the Japanese position, and he frequently emphasized the need to reassure the Japanese government of America's long-term commitment to Japan while also building an equal and genuinely cooperative relationship between Washington and Tokyo.[98] Ridgway's tenure in Japan was relatively brief, but unlike his predecessor he made a point of traveling extensively throughout the country in order to better understand the land and its people. He recognized the political importance of lowering the US military profile in post-Occupation Japan, and supported the State Department's initiative to have all US military garrisons (with the exception of his own, Tokyo headquarters) withdrawn from urban areas.[99] Similarly, Ridgway aligned himself with the State Department in advocating the return of sovereignty over Okinawa and the Ryukyu islands to the Japanese government—a position the Pentagon ultimately rejected.[100]

In terms of influencing the Administrative Agreement talks, Ridgway played an important role in persuading the JCS to agree to the general version of Article XXII,[101] allowing (subject to consultation with the Japanese authorities) US command over combined American and Japanese forces in the event of a crisis. Perhaps most significantly, he enjoyed (as his memoirs reveal) a close, if not friendly, relationship with Yoshida.[102] During the few months while the Administrative Agreement was being negotiated, the American general showed a broadly sympathetic understanding of the prime minister's political difficulties, particularly those associated with rearmament.[103] In keeping with the principles laid down by the bilateral Security Treaty, American military plans called, at this stage, for a gradual build-up of Japan's defensive capabilities—an expansion of the National Police Reserve from 75,000 to between 150,000 and 180,000 men in the 1952 calendar year.[104] Ridgway accepted at face value Yoshida's assurances that he intended to commit Japan to rearm once Japanese public opinion accepted such a strategy, and he showed a patient understanding of the economic obstacles preventing full-scale rearmament.[105] In later months Ridgway would be more critical of the prime minister, but their agreement during the Administrative Agreement negotiations helped moderate State-Pentagon tensions. There was no major disagreement between Japan and the United States over the pace of rearmament during this period. As James Auer has demonstrated, close collaboration was occurring between military representatives of the two countries, especially in the creation of the Coastal Security Force, an organization established in late 1951 within the Maritime Security Agency to provide the nucleus for a future Japanese navy.[106] However, despite this cooperation before Japan's return to full independence, US military planning for Japan remained ill-defined.[107] US Intelligence estimates and JCS reports acknowledged the significant capabilities of the Soviet Union in the Far East, but there was little expectation of a direct Communist attack on Japan. It was important to rearm for the future, but an invasion was not judged to be imminent. Rather, the Soviets were expected to concentrate on propaganda and subversion as a way of undermining Japan and weakening its ties with the West.[108] These factors—the absence of an immediate foreign threat, the lack of a well-defined US strategic policy for Japan, Japan's relative economic weakness, and Ridgway's positive assessment of Yoshida—may have tempered any instinct on the part of the US military to pressure the Japanese to accelerate their rearmament program. Such a combination of factors would have smoothed the path to an agreement between the State Department and the Pentagon.

By the end of February an agreement broadly satisfactory to both sides had been finalized and signed. For Rusk and Dulles the process represented a success. The American military's more provocative proposals had been either eliminated or significantly toned down, the Japanese side had not been visibly antagonized, and neither had the talks significantly interfered with or delayed Senate ratification of the Peace and Security treaties on March 20. The Agreement was also positive from the Japanese government's point of view. As Yoshida remarked later in his memoirs, the talks had been carried out in "an atmosphere of friendliness and goodwill,"[109] and Japan had been able to negotiate vigorously and in a manner reflecting its gradual return to independence and sovereign status. Even before the January talks, the Americans had recognized (on the basis of an earlier set of fishery negotiations) the considerable patience and bargaining skills of their Japanese counterparts.[110] Nishimura Kumao was optimistic that the Agreement provided a good basis for subsequent bilateral relations and felt that with the establishment of a US-Japan Joint Committee the Japanese public would view the outcome favorably.[111]

Both the China talks and the Administrative Agreement negotiations demonstrated the ability of the two governments to cooperate in the face of a common international threat, while also addressing potentially disruptive domestic political and bureaucratic challenges in either country. Despite the two countries' differences in power, the talks suggested the emergence of a genuine alliance relationship providing mutual benefits to each, rather than a situation in which the United States unilaterally imposed terms on Japan. Through elite-level cooperation, the US government secured its primary goal of early ratification of the Peace and Security treaties. Similarly, Yoshida was able to take comfort from the formal confirmation of the end of the Occupation and the reduced risk of British retaliation against current and future Japanese trading interests in Southeast Asia.

The argument that Japan resented American pressure tactics is based largely on retrospective historical interpretations colored by later Japanese-American disagreements over China, or on contemporaneous British criticism of US Asian policy—criticism which, since it was self-serving and intended to undercut American policy, is of questionable value as an unbiased guide to Japanese perceptions. The impression of Japanese-American tension over China in 1951–52 can perhaps more plausibly be seen as the product of domestic political calculation and of disagreement principally between Tokyo and London rather than between Tokyo and Washington. Prime Minister Yoshida was concerned about possible British economic retaliation if Japan chose to openly favor Chiang over the Communists and therefore needed (as Dulles himself recognized) the appearance of irresistible American "pressure" to excuse his actions, as well as to pacify critical Japanese public opinion and voices in his own party more in favor of a close relationship with Communist China. In other words, interpretations critical of America have mistaken a somewhat overstated, synthetic diplomatic clash of opinions for a genuine, substantive historical disagreement. In addition, recent Japanese Yoshida scholarship has questioned some of the traditional assumptions concerning the prime minister's desire for a close relationship with the PRC and his alleged preference for an Asia-focused rather than America-focused foreign policy.[112] Such new interpretations indicate that Japanese-American differences, at least between national leaders, may not have been as significant or as divisive as American revisionist historians have suggested.

Not only is the evidence of Japanese resentment questionable (particularly given the limited access to Japan's diplomatic records), but the image of coercive, insensitive American diplomacy is also open to reinterpretation. The release of new archival material in the United States has encouraged some diplomatic historians specializing in the 1950s to question the traditional view of Dulles as a dogmatic and inflexible foreign policy practitioner, replacing it with an analysis that emphasizes his pragmatism and foresight.[113] Moreover, where China is concerned, Dulles is no longer judged to have been the staunch supporter of the Nationalist government that his public statements at one point suggested[114]—a reinterpretation which sits well alongside a more nuanced, less critical view of his role in encouraging Japan to negotiate with the Chinese Nationalists. This is particularly true if Dulles's actions are viewed in a wider context. The Administrative Agreement negotiations illustrate, as was the case in the months leading up to San Francisco, the State Department's belief in the importance of promoting long-term US national interests by recognizing and respecting Japan's concerns over issues of state sovereignty and equality.[115] Dulles repeatedly (together with key figures such as Dean Rusk and John Allison), in planning discussions with other administration figures—particularly military personnel—emphasized the importance of according Japan genuinely equal treatment. Against such a background, it would have been counterproductive to have ridden roughshod over Japan's China sensibilities.

Setting an analysis of the Administrative Agreement talks alongside a discussion of the China question usefully illustrates not only America's keen interest in promoting a genuinely cooperative relationship with Japan but also the diminishing salience of State-Defense tensions over Japan policy and the important role played by key individuals in promoting interdepartmental and bilateral international cooperation. Dean Rusk was especially important in bridging differences between State and Defense, and Matthew Ridgway's replacement of General MacArthur as SCAP in the spring of 1951 helped soften tensions that hindered Japanese-American relations while promoting greater bureaucratic consensus within the American government. The Administrative Agreement negotiations also revealed an increasingly assertive and diplomatically agile Gaimushō, indicating a growing maturity in the alliance relationship and casting doubts on those arguments that stress the inequalities of the US-Japan partnership.

Despite the evidence of a meeting of minds between senior government officials from both countries, the treaty with Taiwan and the Administrative Agreement would in subsequent months and years create further tensions and complications in the emerging alliance relationship. As was the case in San Francisco, Yoshida's views diverged from those of his colleagues—both bureaucrats and professional politicians. More important, Japanese popular opinion (encouraged by a radical, sometimes naive and often uncompromisingly hostile, anti-government mass media) was much less inclined than the Yoshida cabinet to view the relationship with the United States in a favorable light. Fear of being embroiled in a future East-West conflict, residual resentment toward Japan's former occupiers, and idealized notions of the viability of a neutral stance in international affairs encouraged a vocal, albeit minority, section of public opinion to criticize the Yoshida government for toadying to the United States. In effect, Yoshida's gaiatsu strategy eventually backfired. While the Americans can perhaps be faulted for underestimating the strength and durability of this critical sentiment, they share some of the blame with the Japanese government, which may also have misread some of the early warning signs. Moreover, in this instance, the strength of Japanese popular sentiment had to be set against critical opinion in the US Senate—a body which posed a more immediate treat to a long-term bilateral relationship. Failure to reach an early end to the Occupation would presumably have damaged ties between Washington and Tokyo much more than a debate over future China policy. Consequently, it was necessary to compromise. Despite broad agreement between Japanese and US government leaders, the desire to present Japan as a sovereign, independent country had to be offset against the more immediate priority of creating a viable and mutually beneficial security and alliance partnership. In striving for such a partnership, and against the backdrop of the intensifying tensions of the Cold War, both the Truman and Yoshida governments recognized the inescapable consequences of cooperating in a complex environment of limited means and global requirements. In this respect, the alliance reflected a basic feature of interdependence and a principle that Dulles endorsed— namely, a willingness to sacrifice aspects of formal sovereignty in order to preserve if not enhance independence.[116] Whether such a trade-off would be viable in the future remained to be seen.

CHAPTER FOUR

Strategic Goals versus Local Interests

Okinawa, Nuclear Weapons, and the
Article III Territories, 1953–60

With the ending of the Occupation in the spring of 1952, Japan seemed once more master of its own destiny. As an editorial cartoon in the *Dallas Morning News* of April 29 suggested, the hand of history was poised over a blank page with the country's imperial traditions, symbolized by a tattered Rising Sun flag, firmly relegated to the pages of the past.[1] Ostensibly, the country's future development and its relationship with the United States were based on a new foundation, free from the troubling and corrupting influences of the pre-war era. Japan, in other words (at least in the minds of some contemporary journalists), had changed.[2] In analyzing the immediate post-war US-Japan relationship, it is worth bearing in mind that in certain respects America too had changed, although clearly by no means as dramatically as Japan. Barely half a year after the ratification of the Peace and Security treaties, a presidential election signaled the end of some twenty years of Democratic control of the executive branch of government, and with the inauguration of Dwight D. Eisenhower as President in January 1953, the Republican Party recaptured the White House. In light of the bitter criticisms leveled against the Truman administration for its allegedly flawed Far Eastern policies (congressional Republicans, for example, had berated Truman and Acheson for "losing China," while Dulles, during the campaign, had cynically attacked his former employers for treating Asians as "second-class expendables"[3]), it would be natural to expect some change in America's Japan policy following the change of government. By 1952, the bipartisanship that had characterized the early years of the Cold War had disappeared, and with Dulles aggressively advocating an anti-Communist policy of "roll-back" and "liberation" rather than the "containment" strategy associated with George Kennan, foreign policy appeared to be moving in a more self-consciously assertive direction.[4] Where Asia policy was concerned, Eisenhower demonstrated his seriousness by quickly honoring his campaign pledge to "go to Korea" to assess strategic conditions on the ground. Partly as a result of this visit, he selected Admiral Arthur Radford, the Commander in Chief, Pacific Command (CinCPAC), to succeed General Omar Bradley as Chairman of the Joint Chiefs of Staff—a decision calculated to please Congress's most outspoken "Asia-firsters" such as Senator William Knowland.[5]

Despite the powerful rhetoric of the election campaign, one should be careful not to exaggerate the magnitude of these changes. Eisenhower emphasized in his first State of the Union Address in early 1953 that his foreign policy would be global in scope rather than focused exclusively on one particular region,[6] and continuities in terms of personnel (most notably John Allison, assistant secretary of state for far eastern affairs and, from May 1953, ambassador to Japan), as well as the appointment of John Foster Dulles as secretary of state, indicated that, in the case of Japan policy, the break from the Truman administration might not be as sharp as first appeared. Nevertheless, it soon became apparent that conditions in Japan might themselves impose new strains on the fledgling trans-Pacific partnership. Ending the Occupation had removed the most immediate source of bilateral friction, but as newspaper headlines[7] and contemporary academic commentators[8] frequently pointed out, the continuing presence of large numbers of American troops on Japanese soil threatened to generate a new set of difficulties. Most important of all were a series of unresolved territorial questions, in particular those relating to the post-war status of Okinawa and the collection of islands to the south of Japan.

Examining this issue provides a convenient starting point for considering the degree to which the Eisenhower administration was able to maintain and build on the achievements of its predecessor. In particular, it is a basis for gauging the success of the United States in managing its emerging alliance relationship with Japan from 1953 through 1960 and the durability of, arguably, the leitmotif of the San Francisco Treaty process—namely the emphasis, for self-interested, pragmatic reasons, on treating Japan as a sovereign, independent state. America's handling of the Okinawa question during the 1950s, while partially flawed, illustrates that this emphasis persisted, not only within the State Department,

Fig. 1. Political cartoon describing the end of the Allied Occupation of Japan. "Japan—a Sovereign State." Source: *The Dallas Morning News*, April 29, 1952. Reprinted with the permission of the *Dallas Morning News*.

but also in the White House and in Eisenhower's own decisions regarding Japan. The Okinawa issue (together with a related, but generally overlooked event in US-Japan relations during the 1950s—the Girard incident of 1957) sheds light on the wider question of Eisenhower's presidential style, largely supporting the revisionist view of the President as an engaged and activist chief executive. In turn, these two case-studies can be revealingly set against another important bilateral controversy—the

Lucky Dragon incident of 1954—an event that in many ways represents the low point in US-Japanese relations during the 1950s. These diverse examples illustrate America's occasional willingness to subordinate alliance relations to larger Cold War priorities as well as the enduring importance of contingency or chance in international history. The Okinawa issue is addressed below, while the *Lucky Dragon* and Girard controversies are treated in chapters five and six respectively.

Early Thoughts on Okinawa and the Return of Amami

US interest in Okinawa and the whole Ryukyu island chain as a site for post-war military bases predated the San Francisco Peace Treaty process.[9] Although the territory itself had been conquered in bitter fighting at the end of World War II,[10] it was only in 1948, during Kennan's visit to the Far East, that America's policy-makers began to think systematically about the importance of the Ryukyus. Kennan was quick to recognize that the close proximity of the islands to Asia made them particularly valuable as air and naval bases from which to project America's forward defense strategy in the Pacific while resisting amphibious encroachments from the mainland. Okinawa itself was to form "the center of . . . a U-shaped, US security zone embracing the Aleutians, the Ryukyus, the former Japanese mandated islands, and . . . Guam," with the United States committed to developing and maintaining a naval base on the island.[11] Kennan's advice was soon incorporated in NSC 13/1, an early expression of America's post-war Japan policy, and by the middle of 1949, Congress had appropriated $50 million for the construction of permanent facilities on the island.[12]

In light of the subsequent political tension associated with the reversionist campaign both on Okinawa and in Japan to reunite the island with Japan, Kennan's recommendations are interesting not only in terms of US Asian strategy, but also because of his view of local sentiment on the island. Kennan clearly felt that the islanders had no desire to reunite. Likening the Okinawans to another recently liberated people—the inhabitants of the Philippines—Kennan viewed them as victims rather than as perpetrators of aggression, and eager to shelter under America's protective wing.[13] In the context of the time, the assessment is perhaps not all that surprising. Historically, Okinawans had a somewhat ambivalent identity, having had strong cultural and economic ties with China (via the tribute system) since as early as 1372, and only having been formally in-

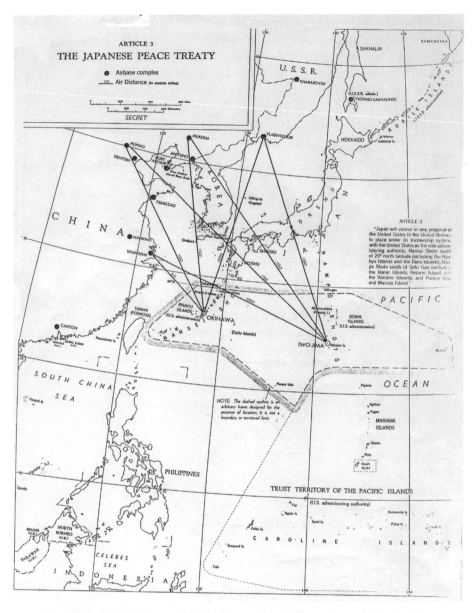

Fig. 2. Map of Okinawa's strategic significance following World War II. Source: National Archives, Washington, DC.

corporated in the Japanese state in 1871.[14] Moreover, Okinawans had suffered disproportionately by comparison with other Japanese during the war, and certainly for the early part of the post-war period resented the apparent willingness of mainland Japan (the four principal islands of Honshu, Kyushu, Hokkaido, and Shikoku) to overlook Okinawan interests. In the early post-war period, majority sentiment on the island favored a separate Okinawa under US protection, and the Okinawan press, as late as 1949, gave serious attention to the possibility of independence for the island. It was only in the middle of 1951 that the first signs of a serious reversion movement began to appear on the island.[15]

Despite Kennan's early analysis, by the time the San Francisco Peace Treaty process was under way, policy-makers in Washington were aware that the territorial issue might develop into a source of future tension. Dulles, in particular, partially at the prompting of William Sebald, the State Department's political advisor in Tokyo, recognized the importance of balancing America's strategic objectives against Japanese irredentist claims. His solution was to base Washington's right to administer the Ryukyus on Article III of the Peace Treaty (under which Japan acknowledged that the United States might elect to administer the territory as a UN trusteeship), while acknowledging that Japan enjoyed "residual sovereignty" over the islands and that they would ultimately be returned to Japanese jurisdiction.[16] In a sense, this compromise constituted a diplomatic sleight of hand. Dulles had chosen to avoid assuming explicit responsibility for the territories either as a UN trusteeship or as a strategic trusteeship since both options potentially exposed the US authorities to external interference—either from the United Nations General Assembly, in the case of a regular trusteeship, or from a Soviet veto in the Security Council in the case of a strategic trusteeship. At the same time, "residual sovereignty" served as a face-saving formula for the Japanese leadership. Yoshida, although by most accounts disappointed not to have had the territory returned, was relatively restrained in lobbying the Americans on the territorial issue.[17] The Gaimushō took a pragmatic view of the issue, which had yet, at the time of the San Francisco Peace Conference, to develop into a pressing, divisive issue in domestic politics.[18]

Surprisingly, one of the early voices in favor of a restoration of full Japanese sovereignty over the Ryukyus came from the US side. Matthew Ridgway, still serving as Commander in Chief in the Far East (CinCFE) in December 1951, argued vigorously for the return of political control to Japan in anticipation of the sympathetic and generally flexible position he would adopt during the Administrative Agreement talks of 1952.[19] Provided the US maintained exclusive jurisdiction over the military facilities on the islands, such a decision, argued Ridgway, would strengthen US-Japan relations and avoid undermining the strong political, economic, and cultural ties between the mainland and the islands, while remaining consistent with the principle of self-determination as well as with America's overall strategic objectives. Indeed, the strategic and political considerations were, in Ridgway's assessment, complementary. As he pointed out, "the achievement of the long-range US strategic objectives in the Far East is inseparably interlocked with the concept of a revivified and self-reliant Japan, friendly to the US and capable of maintaining internal security and defense against external aggression and contributing to the security of the Far East."[20] However, Ridgway's superiors in the JCS in Washington took a less sanguine view of the situation. In the context of the continuing war on the Korean peninsula and China's rapid modernization of its air force, US strategic requirements in the region were simply too important to risk losing control over the territory. Moreover, the Chiefs questioned the degree to which sovereignty was a sensitive issue for the public either in Okinawa or in Japan, and pointed to the heavy toll in human casualties suffered by American forces when capturing the islands in 1945 as an oblique justification for maintaining the existing system of control.[21]

The Pentagon's conservative approach was ultimately endorsed and reinforced in the conclusions to NSC 125/1. Japan, it was assumed, would not necessarily align with the United States for a period longer than two years. Anticipating the growth of right-wing nationalism and possibly neutralism or explicit anti-Western sentiment in Japan, the NSC paper erred on the side of caution and, highlighting the possibility that a future Japanese government might severely restrict US freedom to use its military facilities in Japan, recommended America's long-term retention of the Ryukyus.[22] The State Department, by contrast, recognized the fragility of the US-Japan relationship and argued for a more proactive approach, reinforcing and strengthening the alliance by enhancing mutuality rather than hedging against an uncertain future by rejecting Japanese claims out of hand. US intelligence reports in early 1952 had pointed out that a cooperative relationship with the government in Tokyo rested not only on the creation of a favorable trade and security environment for Japan, but also on a belief on the part of the Japanese that they were being treated as a "sovereign equal."[23] Similarly, officials in the State Department's Office of Northeast Asian Affairs criticized the Defense Department's inflexibility and argued that "failure to take into account Japanese political and psychological interests in the Ryukyus will keep alive a touchy issue in United States–Japanese relationships."[24] Once again, Defense and State department policy-makers, as had been the case during the Peace Treaty negotiations, lined up on opposite sides of a line demarcating cautious from activist policy options—a tension which high-level government policy papers seemed unable to resolve. As NSC 125/2 noted, somewhat unhelpfully, in August 1952, achieving US security objectives in East Asia involved both the "maintenance of a strong United States power position in the Pacific" and "respect for Japan's Status as a sovereign independent state."[25]

Shortly after the beginning of the Eisenhower presidency, the controversy over Okinawa developed in a fashion that would test the contrasting opinions of the State and Defense departments. The key issue centered on the island of Amami Ōshima, one of the principal territories which, together with Okinawa and the Ryukyus, made up the southwestern chain of islands (or nansei shotō) held and administered by the Americans under Article III of the Peace Treaty. Amami, one of the northernmost of these islands, enjoyed a somewhat special status through its long-standing association with Kyūshū's Kagoshima prefecture rather than with Okinawa. Partly for this reason, the Washington-based Japan policy-maker Hugh Borton had recommended, as early as the spring of 1946, that it not be made into a trusteeship and should in fact be returned to Japan.[26] Borton's advice went unheeded, but by early 1953 developments in Japanese politics forced the issue back onto the policy-making agenda. Prime Minister Yoshida, since the ending of the Occupation, had been experiencing a steady decline in popular approval. Despite careful efforts by Dean Rusk and Allison to ensure a fair and even-handed treatment of Japan during the negotiations over the Administrative Agreement, Yoshida's involvement in the talks and his close association with the Americans had exposed his government to criticism from the Japanese public. Against this background, the opposition Left and Right Socialist Parties had performed well in the elections of October 1952, increasing their seats in the Diet.[27] Mindful of this reversal, and anticipating further setbacks for his Liberal Party in the forthcoming elections of April 1953, Yoshida had sent an unsigned letter[28] to Ambassador Robert Murphy (Allison's predecessor) arguing for the return of Okinawa and Amami as well as for the freeing of war criminals and the provision of World Bank financial support for Japan. Araki Eikichi, the Japanese ambassador in Washington, reinforced this request in an April 9 meeting with Walter Robertson (the recently appointed assistant secretary for far eastern affairs), suggesting that the return of Amami would help to secure a victory for the Liberals in the forthcoming election—an outcome beneficial for US-Japan relations.[29]

Matters came to a head in the US government in June of 1953 when, in preparation for a meeting of the National Security Council, Defense and State department representatives debated their contrasting responses to the Japanese government request. The State Department adopted a characteristically flexible position. Returning Amami, it argued, would greatly allay political differences with Japan, bolster the Yoshida government, eliminate possible Communist propaganda advantages, provide the US with bargaining leverage in other negotiations with Japan, and materially enhance cooperation between the Japanese and US governments. The problem was, in general, "to keep Japan friendly." State representatives were quick to point out not only the close ties between Amami and Japan (citing the island's sixty-year-long association with Kagoshima prefecture), but also the overwhelming strength of local opinion in favor of reversion (99 percent of all residents of Amami supported a return to Japanese jurisdiction). Such opinion was neither "synthetic nor communist-inspired," nor could it be offset by improved land policy and labor relations or by simply strengthening economic relations between the islands and Japan. Moreover, Amami's strategic value was considerably less than that of other islands in the nansei group—as the Japanese government was well aware. The island lacked any major army or navy bases, and its single aircraft control and warning installation was mainly a site for monitoring and communication facilities. Access to these facilities was already guaranteed under the terms of the existing Administrative Agreement and did not require exclusive US jurisdiction over the entire island.[30]

Not surprisingly, the US military's characterization of the situation was more conservative. Emphasizing the deterioration in the Far Eastern security situation since late 1950, the Defense Department and the JCS rejected the suggestion that political benefits outweighed the strategic risks associated with returning the island. Japanese reversionist pressure, they claimed, would be stimulated rather than sated by the return of Amami and there was no guarantee that the possible psychological advantage of a return of territory would extend beyond a single Japanese administration. At a practical level, Defense suggested (somewhat implausibly given the past record of largely autonomous US policy in Japan) that any reversion agreement would require the cooperation of the other signatories to the San Francisco Peace Treaty, as well as pointing out that the return of Amami would remove six out of seventeen pro-US legislators in the Ryukyuan legislature, thus tilting the local political balance in the remaining islands away from the United States.[31]

A June 25 meeting of the NSC provided an opportunity to resolve the State-Defense disagreement. Dulles rejected the Defense argument, claiming that US strategic interests were compatible with a restoration of civilian authority over Amami to Japan. In keeping with the accommodating posture he had adopted in San Francisco, the secretary of state emphasized the importance of conscious efforts to win the allegiance of America's Japanese partners, pointing out that "the extraordinary legal rights" secured by the United States in the Peace Treaty would "eventually prove quite worthless" if America lost the loyalty of Japan.[32] The President, for his part, firmly endorsed this view and stressed the importance of a broad, long-term perspective on the emerging US-Japan relationship:

> To insist on controlling this little group of islands, which obviously meant a lot to Japan, amounted to risking the loss of our main objective, which was to assure ourselves of Japan's friendship and loyalty over the long-run. This seemed to him, said the President, silly and he felt that the Army was taking a little too narrow view if its opposition to the return of these islands was only to secure a radar station. . . . The President . . . stated emphatically that it was a "must" to return these islands to Japan.[33]

Eisenhower, as a former military commander, was fully aware of the tensions and resentment generated by occupying armies. "He pointed out that in almost every case the people of the occupied areas had come to hate our soldiers, for one thing because they were comparatively rich," as well as noting "the inevitable hostility which occupation status involved US in" and that Americans "would feel very much the same way if any foreign forces were long stationed on our soil."[34] The meeting decided to endorse the State Department's recommendation to return Amami, with the proviso that a final decision be delayed for ninety days to allow time for a review of the security situation in the Far East.

International political developments limited Washington's freedom to delay action on the Amami issue. CIA and State Department reporting suggested that the Soviet Union might be preparing to launch a major political and propaganda offensive against Japan, intended perhaps to loosen its ties with the United States. While there was no reason to assume any common ground between the Russians and the Yoshida administration, a series of Soviet initiatives, including the return to Japan of a large number of Japanese fishermen and their vessels in April, the provision of $10,000 worth of food assistance in July, and statements by Molotov, the Soviet foreign minister, describing steps that the USSR was planning to take to re-establish normal relations with Japan and promote economic and cultural ties, all indicated the possible start of a new Soviet initiative.[35] In Japan, Allison was sufficiently concerned to write in early August to Dulles, then visiting Korea, highlighting this issue and recommending that Dulles act before the waiting period was over and travel to Japan to inform Yoshida that the United States was willing to return Amami.[36] Dulles duly accepted Allison's suggestion, and after meeting with Yoshida, publicly announced in Tokyo on August 8 the US intention to return Amami to Japanese jurisdiction. The announcement was well received at first, generating an immediate positive reaction among the Japanese public. However, literally overnight, the success was tarnished by a report in the *Asahi Shinbun* citing Dulles's intense dissatisfaction with the Japanese government for failing to adopt a more active Asian defense policy. Dulles had held an off-the-record interview with a group of journalists in which he commented on Japan's relatively passive rearmament position, and one of the journalists, James Reston of the *New York Times*, had publicized the secretary's views in an article which formed the basis for the *Asahi* report.[37] Allison had at the time been concerned that critical press reports would generate a negative public reaction, allowing Japan's opposition parties to attack the Japanese government and Yoshida in particular (a point he relayed to his superiors in Washington),[38] and when the Reston piece appeared, he recommended that a strong protest be lodged with the *New York Times* for a breach of off-the-record principles.[39] In his memoirs, Allison criticized Dulles for publicly discussing rearmament without first consulting with the embassy in Tokyo or considering the implications for Washington's Japan policy as a whole. He also denied, at the time, the suggestion that territorial concessions might be linked to Japanese rearmament efforts and a more active defense posture. From the vantage point of the Tokyo embassy, policy-makers in Washington, and in particular the secretary of state, were overly eager to use public fora to exert diplomatic pressure on Japan over the rearmament issue.[40] In later years, Allison criticized Dulles for ignoring Japanese sensibilities and for impatience in expecting a swift response over defense matters. Dulles, according to Allison, "had little real understanding of how the Japanese or any other Oriental people thought and assumed that they would automatically respond to ideas in the same way as Westerners."[41] This criticism seems at odds with Dulles's performance during the San Francisco Peace Treaty process, which Allison acknowledges was a success.[42] There is little evidence in the diplomatic cables of the time to suggest a sharp difference of opinion between the ambassador and the secretary of state,[43] and it is possible that Allison's recollections were colored by hindsight, as often happens in the writing of memoirs. Indeed, from contemporary documents, the two men appear to have been in firm agreement over the need to establish a genuinely cooperative and mutually beneficial alliance relationship. As Allison pointed out to Dulles on one occasion, commenting on the position of the Yoshida administration at the end of 1953:

> In my opinion, Yoshida and his government offer the best hope for the immediate and mid-term future. Yoshida is getting stronger—to some extent he gets stronger as people believe he is not an American puppet. *My understanding of your policy, with which I heartily agree, is that we want allies not satellites.* The fact that the Japanese are talking back and not immediately saying "yes" to every American request is indicative of a resurgence of the old Japanese spirit—if we can continue to work with that and guide it, in the right direction, which I believe we are now doing—we will have an ally with spirit, and eventually strength, on whom we can rely. [Emphasis added][44]

The difference, then, between Allison and Dulles may have been more one of tactics than of goals. It is also worth bearing in mind that, from Tokyo, the ambassador often witnessed the results and final expressions of policy, rather than the internal debates within the White House and State Department, many of which, as the following analysis reveals, reflected an awareness of the importance of Japanese concerns. Nevertheless, for much of the decade and certainly while Allison was ambassador (between 1953 and 1957), there were occasional differences of opinion between Washington and Tokyo over how best to promote US interests in Japan. This marked a change from the Occupation years, when disagreements arose most frequently between SCAP and the State Department representatives in Tokyo. After 1952, the principal clash of opinion was often between the Pentagon and the JCS on one side and on the other the embassy in Tokyo, which, depending on the issue and timing, received more or less support from the State Department in Washington. Interestingly, US civil-military relations within Japan appear to have been relatively harmonious, again in contrast to MacArthur's era. For example, General Mark Clark (Ridgway's successor) favored returning Amami to Japan (though because of JCS opposition was constrained from saying so openly) and displayed a political sensitivity that Allison felt was often lacking among America's military leaders at home.[45] In general, although his interaction with them was not always trouble-free, Allison appears to have been happy in his working relations with his US military counterparts in Japan.[46] At the same time, the ambassador and former assistant secretary was, given his long involvement in Japan-related matters, well placed to develop a close and effective relationship with officials in the Japanese government. In particular, he appears to have been on good terms with Okazaki Katsuo, Yoshida's foreign minister. This was partly due to common experiences (the two men had first met in 1937, when Allison was running the US consulate in Nanjing), and also to temperament. Okazaki was an easy individual to deal with, comfortable in expressing his own or his government's reasons for disagreeing with the United States on a particular issue, while appreciating the diplomatic environment shaping the decisions of US negotiators.[47]

Notwithstanding the reservations of the JCS, by late December of 1953 the Eisenhower administration had taken all the steps necessary to return Amami to Japan and on Christmas Eve, in a signing ceremony in Tokyo, both countries formally agreed to the transfer of the territory. Dulles, who had traveled to Japan to sign the agreement, publicly announced the reversion of the territory in a statement which was well received by Japanese public opinion.[48] At the same time, he was careful to emphasize that the status of the remaining Ryukyus and Article III territories would not change and that, given the strategic importance of the islands in the defense of the Pacific, the United States would continue to act as "custodian" of the territory "for the foreseeable future."[49] This position (subsequently characterized in the 1960s as the "blue-skies" condition[50]) was hardly calculated to win much support within Japan, but it hinted at some flexibility. In the thinking of America's most senior policymakers there was certainly the expectation that things would have to change at some point. Dulles was well aware that failure to return the remaining territory might provoke strong reaction in Japan (and the United Nations) potentially sufficient to offset the immediate strategic advantages of maintaining an exclusive US presence on the islands. Eisenhower himself, during the December 23 NSC meeting authorizing Dulles's announcement, had suggested modifying the draft statement to emphasize the reasons for America's presence in Okinawa and its intention to with-draw once these factors no longer applied—a suggestion which, because of pressures of time, does not appear to have been carried out.[51]

Land Controversies and Political Representation

While the return of Amami can be viewed as a qualified success for the United States, other aspects of the Okinawa problem threatened to complicate and undermine the relationship with Japan. Perhaps most significant of all during the 1950s was the often bitterly contentious land issue. During fierce fighting at the end of the Pacific War, the Ryukyus suffered considerable devastation, with approximately 20 percent of the population killed and 95 percent of all housing destroyed.[52] The US military (first the Navy, and subsequently the Army) immediately occupied the territory and proceeded to establish bases that would form part of America's strategic front line in the Far East. Initially, the land required for these bases (much of it, in the case of Okinawa, situated in the island's fertile lowlands) was forcibly appropriated as territory seized during conflict. No compensation was paid to the former owners. By 1952, at the end of the Occupation, the US authorities had altered their position and were attempting to introduce a system of retroactive rental payments, in an effort to compensate landowners. This policy suffered from a number of shortcomings. To begin with, the war had destroyed most of the land records in the territory so that it was often difficult to establish rights of ownership and the precise value of the land in question. In determining an appropriate annual rental payment (assessed at 6 percent of the fee value of the land), the US authorities based their calculations on tax assessments rather than the true market value of the land. The average displaced Okinawan landowner could expect to receive less than $20 a year for one acre of his former property, and with few individuals willing to part with their land for such meager compensation, much of the land still had to be acquired under duress and held under implicit leases (formal contracts not signed by the original landowners), with rental payments deposited with the islands' Japanese administrative authorities. In addition, the geography of the islands added its own set of strains. Although Okinawa's total territory amounts to some 290,000 acres, much of it is mountainous and only 80,000 acres were considered arable following the Occupation. By the mid-1950s the American military was using 40,000 acres in total, 16,000 of which were arable—in effect, 20 percent of all farm land on the island—and in the process had displaced approximately 50,000 families, or a total of 250,000 individuals.[53]

In the face of considerable local disaffection with the rental policy, the Army proposed shifting to a policy of lump-sum payments in return for an acknowledged long-term claim over the occupied land. At the same time it recommended the creation of a US funded small-scale public works program, providing roads, schools, and hospitals, as a means of injecting capital into the economy to compensate for the lost farming revenue and generally to improve economic conditions on the islands.[54] In the early post-war period, in the absence of a vocal reversionist movement in the Ryukyus, US authorities believed that generating economic growth rates higher than the rest of Japan might discourage efforts to renew links with Tokyo and strengthen ties with the United States. This strategy was largely ineffective. To begin with, land had great emotional significance among the Okinawans, who viewed the continuous possession of family territory as an important way of venerating one's ancestors,[55] and therefore financial compensation (even if it had been generous) was at best a partial solution. Second, US strategic interests in the Far East, and the competing requirements of the various branches of the US military, meant that the American demand for land continued to grow rather than remaining static. All four branches of the military (Army, Navy, Air Force, and Marines) viewed Okinawa as a viable base site, and in 1955, for example, the Marines hoped to acquire some 48,000 acres in the north of the island—which would have more than doubled the amount of expropriated land.[56]

Against this background of persistent grievances, it is hardly surprising that eventually local opinion in Okinawa would attempt to communicate its discontent directly to the US authorities. In June 1955, Higa Shūhei, the chief executive of the Japanese administration in the Ryukyus, traveled to Washington and presented a formal complaint and set of demands to the US Armed Services Committee. The Okinawans rejected the lump-sum payment system and demanded an increase in rental rates to seven times the estimated value of the land. In addition, they argued against any further land acquisition, demanding the return of any unnecessary land acquisitions, and the introduction of a system providing a one-off payment equivalent to five years' worth of rental payments to compensate for the loss of livelihood resulting from land acquisitions.[57]

The US authorities had not been entirely oblivious of Okinawan concerns. In early 1955, a meeting of the Operations Coordinating Board

(OCB, part of the NSC structure involved mainly in the implementation and interdepartmental coordination of national security decisions[58]) acknowledged that the land issue represented a problem, that residents of the territory had not received adequate compensation, and that their grievances were legitimate. However, this sympathetic acknowledgment of local problems was qualified by the OCB's readiness to label Okinawan grievances partly the product of Communist agitation—"a concerted anti-American propaganda program under the sponsorship and direction of international communism."[59]

US concern regarding the situation in the Ryukyus had been prompted not only by Higa's mission to Washington, but also by the increasing internationalization of problems associated with the Article III territories. As early as March 1954, the Japan Civil Liberties Union (JCLU), partly at the prompting of its parallel organization in the United States—the American Civil Liberties Union (ACLU)—had begun to investigate alleged human rights abuses in the islands and, in particular, whether the United States was requisitioning land at unfairly low prices. This initiative was reinforced by the International Confederation of Free Trade Unions (ICFTU), which sent a delegation of American and Japanese trades unionists to investigate labor conditions on the island and to publish a report outlining their findings.[60] By 1955, the issue of human rights' violations in Okinawa had taken on an international character and in January, the JCLU had presented its case to the Asian Lawyers' Conference in Calcutta.[61] It was clearly in the interest of the United States to prevent the issue getting out of hand and to avoid handing a propaganda advantage to the Soviet Union.

Congress responded by holding hearings in Washington and by sending a delegation from a special subcommittee of the House Armed Services Committee, under the chairmanship of Representative Melvin Price, to inspect conditions on the island between October 14 and November 23, 1955. In diagnosing the sources and nature of local discontent, the report of the subcommittee (issued in June 1956) was reasonably accurate, although its eager characterization of the system of government on the island as a "showcase of democracy" was an unfortunate overstatement. Moreover, in its proposed solution to the problems of the territory, the report provoked both disappointment and irritation in Okinawa and Japan. It rejected Higa's request for new annual rents and compensatory payments (costing approximately $23 million in total) as prohibitively expensive and likely to create a new "landed gentry" on the island.[62] It also advocated the continuation of the existing lump-sum payment system, while highlighting the collateral benefits of the US Occupation, most notably infrastructure investment and the employment opportunities associated with the presence of US forces on the islands.[63] It suggested, condescendingly, that the average Okinawan was poor at handling money and that any payments should be set aside for a dedicated government fund and used for a variety of beneficial projects. Moreover, the report betrayed a similar lack of sensitivity to Japanese and local concerns in proposing the establishment of nuclear power plants on the islands in order to meet the electrical needs of the islands' inhabitants.[64] The memory of Hiroshima and Nagasaki, not to mention the unforeseen and unfortunate consequences of nuclear weapons testing in the Pacific in 1954,[65] appears to have had little or no impact in shaping the report's recommendations.

Popular reaction to the report in both Japan and the Ryukyus was swift and dramatic. The press, in particular, responded very critically to what appeared to be an uncompromising US stance, citing statements by Lyman Lemnitzer, the US CinCFE, suggesting that the Japanese would have no role in the land requisitioning problem.[66] In the words of an OCB assessment, "the current Okinawa situation is potentially the most serious threat to Japanese-US relations since . . . 1954" and "the Japanese press, which has been handling the matter with restraint, has now reached a pitch of 'near hysteria' over the alleged sufferings of the Okinawans."[67] The land controversy suddenly became a point of contention in Japanese domestic politics. For the Liberal Democratic Party (LDP) administration of Hatoyama Ichirō (who had succeeded Yoshida as prime minister in late 1954), the Okinawa question was to some extent a distraction from efforts to develop a more independent foreign policy through negotiations (ultimately abortive) to sign a peace treaty with the Soviet Union.[68] However, the principal opposition party, the Japan Socialist Party (JSP), seized upon the issue as a public rallying point and source of discontent, criticizing both the United States and the LDP administration in an effort to strengthen its own position in the run-up to the Diet Upper House July elections.

Opinion within the LDP remained divided, with Hatoyama's foreign minister, Shigemitsu Mamoru, arguing at a June 19 cabinet meeting that overt conflict over Okinawa was not in the interests of either Japan or the United States and that the matter should be left in the hands of the Americans.[69] Nonetheless, the LDP felt obliged to respond to the problem, if only symbolically, and agreed to participate in a cross-party rally with the JSP and Sōhyō (the leading union organization) on condition that there be no mention of military bases, no Communist participation, and no red flags on display.[70] In Okinawa itself, the report had dramatic political consequences and in December 1956 the capital Naha, for the first time in its history, elected as its mayor a member of the far-left Okinawa People's Party (OPP), one Senaga Kamejirō.[71]

The damaging repercussions of the Price Report and continuing difficulties over the land issue generated much anti-American sentiment. The US authorities nevertheless did not respond immediately, and Congress merely commissioned a study of US overseas assistance programs dealing in part with conditions in Okinawa. Failure to resolve this problem would, in the words of one US government study, "continue to hand an issue to the Communists on a silver platter and to supply Japanese politicians with ready made anti-American propaganda."[72] By April 1958, General James E. Moore, the head of the US military authorities in the Ryukyus, had informed the Okinawans that further long-term land acquisitions would be suspended to allow time for a review of existing land compensation programs—a process of investigation that was further encouraged in July by the second visit to Washington of a Ryukyuan chief executive—Thōma Jūgō. The Army, Defense Department, and State Department all agreed that a new, simple, and readily understandable land policy needed to be introduced based on consultation with local Ryukyuan leaders both in Washington and in Naha.[73] Eventually, this review process led to the abandonment of the former lump-sum payment system and the introduction of rents at approximately twice the previous level—a change that was well received both in Japan and in Okinawa, where the settlement was viewed as satisfactory by the main political parties.[74] Political stability re-emerged in the Article III territories and there was a "marked decrease in leftist strength in the Ryukyus." The land controversy had lost, at least for the immediate future, some of its emotional intensity, and pressure for immediate reversion had been reduced both locally and in Japan.[75]

While disagreements over land policy provoked the strongest reaction from the inhabitants of the Ryukyus, these were not the only source of conflict with the US authorities. The formal structure of government was also a point of contention, both between the United States and the inhabitants of Okinawa and within the Eisenhower administration. Initially, control over the Article III territories was in the hands of the US military, which throughout the Occupation generally received a free hand from Washington. Officially, full administrative authority rested with the US CinCFE in his capacity as governor of the islands. In practice, since the governor was based in Tokyo and preoccupied with his other responsibilities, decision-making rested with the deputy governor, appointed by the CinCFE, locally based, and invariably a military official.[76] In 1946, an 86-person advisory council was established, made up of leading Ryukyuan officials, charged with the responsibility of nominating an individual who, once approved by the deputy governor, served as the official leader of the local community. In April 1952, this system was more formally defined. A 31-member locally elected legislature was created to form the basis for the new Government of the Ryukyu Islands (GRI) and the office of chief executive was established—a position again determined by nomination from the legislature, subject to the approval of the deputy governor. Establishment of a legislature provided a context for a degree of partisan politics and some semblance of popular accountability.[77]

In this context there was very little room for State Department and nonmilitary participation in either administration or long-term planning for the islands, although periodically officials in Washington and Tokyo sought to increase their involvement in Okinawan affairs. In early 1954, for example, a first attempt was made to qualify the independence of the local military authorities, with a proposal from the State Department that the governor of the Ryukyus be appointed directly by the President rather than by the secretary of defense, and that a civilian rather than military official be chosen to fill the position. The State Department proposal was part of a larger initiative to reduce US direct involvement in the islands while increasing the status and responsibilities of the GRI. While the American authorities would retain sweeping veto powers, enabling them to overturn legislation and court decisions and remove officials from office, in principle the newly designated US Civil Administration of the Ryukyus (USCAR) was an attempt to limit direct intervention in local affairs while promoting greater cooperation with the Ryukyus government.[78]

Eisenhower's reaction to the State Department proposal was cautious and measured. While acknowledging that strategic considerations necessitated a military representative in the islands, the President accepted that a civilian might be preferable as governor. At the same time, he alluded to the importance of avoiding jurisdictional disputes between civilians and the military, citing as a salutary warning the clash between Douglas

MacArthur and William Taft in the administration of the Philippines in 1908, and suggesting (no doubt accurately) that the problem of local discontent was unlikely to be resolved simply by changing the individuals in charge of the US administration. As for the appointment of a governor, the President maintained that the decision was already his own, whether or not he chose to delegate immediate responsibility to the secretary of defense,[79] and in the end the State Department proposal for a civilian governor failed, even though it had the strong backing of Dulles and Walter Robertson.

Despite this setback, the State Department continued to test the limits of military authority within the Article III territories. In 1954, it proposed appointing a Foreign Service Officer to act as a political advisor on the staff of the deputy governor of the islands, and by 1956 John Steeves was regularly sending reports to the Tokyo embassy on conditions in Okinawa.[80] Nonetheless, the Pentagon jealously guarded its command prerogatives and rejected any attempts to limit its authority, arguing that the military were competent administrators and that any effort to meet Japanese or local grievances would jeopardize America's wider strategic interests in the Far East.[81] Frequently, the military characterized all local opposition as Communist-inspired and calculated to subvert American control. Citing the continuing threat posed by Communism, USCAR rejected a 1954 resolution of the Ryukyuan legislature calling for the direct election of the chief executive of the GRI,[82] and used electoral redistricting and direct pressure to undermine politically undesirable local officials. Following the election of Senaga, the radical mayor of Naha, General Moore, the head of the military administration, sanctioned a series of crass and heavy-handed measures to undercut his position. The US-controlled Ryukyu Bank suspended payments to and froze the deposits of the city government, and Moore issued ordinances modifying the Local Government Act and Local Election Act in order to reduce the required quorum for a no-confidence vote for the mayor. Senaga was ultimately forced out of office by conservative city officials in June 1957,[83] while US-inspired rule changes prevented him from standing for election for a second time.[84]

It would be an exaggeration to argue that the US military always had the final word over local administration of the islands. Both Dulles and Eisenhower, in the wake of the land controversy of the mid-1950s, were aware of the long-term political problem of continuing local discontent. In June 1957, against the wishes of the Defense Department and Army but with Dulles's prompting and State Department support, Eisenhower issued Executive Order 10173 modifying the structure of military government. The deputy governor was replaced by a high commissioner—admittedly still a military official—but now appointed with the President's approval in Washington rather than locally, and on the basis of both State and Defense department recommendations. The order was an extension of the original State Department proposal of 1954, and made clear that respect should be paid to the principle of local autonomy. The military government was expected to respect the decision of the government of the Ryukyu Islands and to avoid interfering in local court decisions, only acting when the larger security concerns and overall objectives of the US military presence were jeopardized. Nonetheless, this guidance was loosely defined, and while it signaled a change of emphasis and an attempt by Washington to compensate for heavy-handed local Army rule, the underlying principle of military authority remained unchanged.[85]

Psychological and Symbolic Issues

Despite the mistakes and compromises associated with the US handling of the land and government issues in the Ryukyus, it would be wrong to assume that American officials in Washington and Tokyo trivialized or took for granted the Okinawa issue or the overall relationship with Japan. The State Department remained anxious about the relationship throughout the decade, and there is evidence that in certain instances such concern influenced the views and actions of senior officials, including both Dulles and the President. During the middle of the decade, in particular, steps were taken to reappraise the overall alliance relationship in a fashion that reflected the continuing legacy of the San Francisco Treaty process.

As early as August 1954, a US intelligence report predicted that the Japanese government would at some point before 1957 seek to develop a more independent foreign policy and that neutralism, nationalism, and a critical view of US policy were likely to persist.[86] This was not an isolated opinion. At a meeting of the NSC in August 1954, Dulles himself highlighted the importance and fragility of the relationship with Japan, noting that "Japan was the heart and soul of the situation in the Far East. If Japan is not on our side our whole Far Eastern position will become untenable."[87] Similarly, the State Department's Far Eastern specialists continued to emphasize the need to avoid making unreasonable demands on

Japan and the importance of paying careful attention to Japanese sensibilities:

> Overemphasis by US on Japanese defense measures could easily be self-defeating. *The United States should continue its policy of negotiating on the basis of what the Japanese themselves propose in the way of defense measures*, attempting of course to expand our Japanese effort where feasible but without going so far as to strain our relations. . . . Japanese reluctance to take stronger internal security measures should not be underestimated. Pressure by US on the Japanese to do more about internal leftism and anti-Americanism could be self-defeating. [Emphasis added][88]

In Japan, Allison echoed this analysis, noting the growing perception gap between the two countries and the readiness of both Japanese government officials and the media to mistakenly interpret US initiatives as attempts to dictate terms or to use Japan exclusively for America's own interests.[89]

US concern at a possible deterioration in bilateral relations resulted in the drafting of an entirely new NSC paper dealing with Japan—NSC 5516/1—approved by the President on April 9, 1955. Considerable time had elapsed since the previous formal assessment of policy toward Japan (NSC 125/2, approved in August 1952 and then reconfirmed in largely unmodified form as NSC 125/6 in June 1953), and the new document represented a "major change in emphasis and approach." It acknowledged the developing strains in relations with Japan and made clear that the United States should avoid pressing Japan to rearm since this would risk jeopardizing the country's political and economic stability. At the same time, it emphasized the importance of equality, recommending that the administration "consult with the Japanese government as an equal on matters of mutual interest." Similarly, where the Article III territories were concerned, the paper, while noting that the United States would maintain control and authority, advised acceding "to Japanese requests for fuller relations, consistent with US security interests."[90]

This formal expression of administration policy did not exist in a vacuum. Outside the structure of the NSC there were, and continued to be, a number of initiatives that focused on developing an alliance with Japan based on equality and mutual advantage. In June 1955, Nelson Rockefeller, with Eisenhower's approval, assembled a group of eleven distinguished academics and defense specialists at the Marine base in Quantico, Virginia, to consider ways to enhance America's position vis-à-vis the Soviet Union.[91] The group prepared a number of detailed reports taking as their central theme the importance of the psychological dimension of the Cold War. It was not enough merely to consider the military and economic means of resisting the challenge of international Communism. Of equal importance were the symbolic aspects of national security policy:

> Success or failure in this struggle may turn in considerable part on which side captures the symbols that express man's aspirations and thereby influence political behavior. These include peace, self-government, economic advancement, security, freedom and cultural progress. All policy must therefore be examined not only for its substantive but also for its symbolic impact.[92]

Where alliance strategy was concerned, such an approach required policies calculated to appeal genuinely to the interests of the citizens of America's partner nations. "Foreign grass-root support for US policies can be obtained only if people at the grass-roots understand our endeavours and benefit from them."[93] Given Japan's critical importance as the only "operational" Great Power in Asia,[94] it logically followed that US foreign policy needed to concentrate on treating Japan as an equal and sovereign partner—something, which, according to the Quantico participants, had not been sufficiently emphasized.

> Japan will not become an effective partner unless Japanese spiritual and political factors develop in a way that keeps Japan firmly attached as a member of our community of states. This requires that Japan be given a position of honor and respect among nations and that we help Japan become strong and stable. Unless we are successful in this effort there is danger that Japanese opposition to continued alliance with the Free World will increase to a degree damaging to our interests.[95]

Similarly:

> The Japanese have never done well as a satellite nation. They must be treated with real honor and seriousness as a principle if they are to perform well, not with a feigned or psywar deference. . . . The American-Japanese alliance already exists in all but name. The missing essential is to make it actual by treating the Japanese as a great power, not as a mercenary dependent of the US forces in the Western Pacific.[96]

It is difficult to determine how much influence the Quantico studies ultimately had on America's Japan policy. At a purely circumstantial level, there were clearly very close similarities with general State Department thinking. The documentary record indicates that the findings were favorably endorsed by leading policy-makers responsible for Far Eastern affairs. For example, Robert McClurkin, the director of the Office of

Northeast Asian Affairs, wrote to Jeff Parsons in the embassy in Tokyo, pointing out that the group's work on Asia was "pretty much in line with our current policy objectives."[97] At the very least, specialized and administration thinking worked in tandem, and US policy on Japan reflected the importance of developing an astute and mutually beneficial alliance strategy.

Developments in domestic Japanese politics underlined the need for a more openly responsive and accommodating US position. Since early 1955 the Hatoyama government had indicated its intention to distance itself from Washington, raising fears in the American military that restrictions might be imposed on its use of US military bases.[98] Where Okinawa was concerned, differences of opinion were emerging among Japanese bureaucrats and politicians over how to respond to the United States while accommodating increasingly vocal public opinion and a more active opposition movement. Officials in Hōmushō, the Japanese Justice Ministry, were critical of the Foreign Ministry for what they felt was an unnecessarily weak stance over the territorial issues.[99] Popular disquiet regarding Okinawa was on the rise—in November 1955, a National Movement for the Return of Okinawa (Okinawa henkan kokumin undō kyōgikai) was launched—and senior LDP officials began to actively involve themselves in the issue because it was politically charged and in order to deny the JSP an electoral advantage. In 1956, a special Okinawa committee was established in the Policy Affairs Research Council (PARC—the main formal policy-making body of the LDP),[100] and its head, Kishi Nobusuke, a leading conservative politician and LDP secretary general, approached the US CinCFE to discuss the Okinawa problem on a number of occasions.[101] Similarly, in the Prime Minister's Office, Yoshida Tsugunobu, a senior official, proposed a series of recommendations to strengthen coordination of Okinawa policy-making issues. His suggestions included the establishment of a full-time bureaucracy with extra-ministerial jurisdiction over matters relating to Okinawa; the setting-up of a permanent Upper House Diet Committee on Okinawa; and the creation of a semi-private, supra-partisan body with close links to the government to provide aid to Okinawa and to handle issues of particular diplomatic and international sensitivity. While Yoshida's proposals were positively received by the LDP leadership, only a few were actually implemented. Senior figures were wary of strengthening progressive political forces in the Diet and therefore rejected the idea of a joint standing committee in the Upper House. Similarly, while the benefits of providing economic assistance were acknowledged, existing ministerial interests blocked the setting up of a new bureaucratic mechanism to coordinate Okinawa issues. Instead, it was recommended that a Foreign Ministry official be seconded to the Prime Minister's Office to deal exclusively with Okinawa issues. Aid was provided via a semi-government relief organization, the Southern Compatriots Aid Council (nanpō dōhō engokai—established in November 1956), and through the existing Southern Liaison Bureau (nanpō renraku jimukyoku) in the Prime Minister's Office.[102]

It is important to consider the responses of America's leadership, and in particular the attitude of the President, to this continuing disquiet. During and for at least ten years after the end of his administration, Eisenhower had an average and undistinguished reputation as a chief executive among both popular and scholarly commentators. He was regarded as a relatively passive leader, disengaged from the intricacies of decision-making (apparently spending more time on the golf course than in cabinet meetings), and, where foreign policy was concerned, inclined to delegate most responsibilities to his secretary of state. Over time, this conventional view has been persuasively challenged by an extensive body of revisionist scholarship. Fred Greenstein, in advancing the notion of a "hidden-hand" presidency,[103] is perhaps the earliest and most well-known exponent of the notion that Eisenhower was in fact closely involved in decision-making and remained securely in charge of the Executive Branch, while recently Richard Bissell (from the perspective of an involved policy-maker in the 1950s) has presented fresh evidence of the President's active leadership style.[104]

The President's approach did not require close scrutiny or micro-management of all decisions. Eisenhower's military experience (particularly the leadership example of General George Marshall) had early on impressed on him the importance of delegating policy-making where possible to trusted and skilled subordinates. Ideally this allowed him to retain a broad perspective and to intervene only in situations of particular importance. Aspects of the Okinawa controversy reflect this decision-making pattern. For example, in the summer of 1958, a proposal was mooted within the administration to reform the currency system within the Article III territories. Since the Occupation, financial transactions within the Ryukyus had been carried out using military-regulated B-Yen. By the late 1950s, this medium of exchange was obsolete, and Defense Department officials, together with Treasury and Bureau of the Budget officials, recommended converting the outdated currency into dollars—a decision endorsed by Dulles. However, in June, Eisenhower intervened in the process, overturning the recommendations on the grounds that they smacked of "annexation":

> I am sure that use of American currency in the islands would be interpreted in Japan as an unexpressed but nevertheless latent ambition of this country to annex those islands. The mutual friendship and trust that have been built up between our country and Japan are extremely valuable and I do not see why we should chance damaging them in the effort to achieve a greater administrative efficiency.[105]

Despite Eisenhower's initial objection, ultimately the decision to change the currency went ahead. Economically there were strong reasons for change and it transpired that Ryukyuan businessmen were lobbying on behalf of the dollar.[106] Nevertheless, Eisenhower, in response to a request from Kishi Nobusuke (now serving as prime minister), chose to delay the formal announcement of the new policy until the dissolution of the Japanese Diet and the enactment of constructive land reforms affecting Okinawa. The delay intentionally softened the impact of the US decision and, importantly, shielded the Japanese prime minister (viewed by the State Department as a conservative friend and valuable US ally) from domestic criticism.[107] Kishi was especially grateful to Eisenhower for understanding his position and acceding to his request,[108] and the close personal relations between the two men added a positive dimension to US-Japan relations during this period. Although the currency issue might have seemed relatively insignificant, Eisenhower gave it serious consideration and (in keeping with the prescriptions of the Quantico participants) attempted to handle the symbolic aspects of bilateral relations sensitively.

The military bases question similarly reflects Eisenhower's proactive decision-making style and the emphasis he placed on positive alliance relations. At the conceptual level of foreign policy, Eisenhower regularly acknowledged the importance of treating allies as equal partners and recognized that sovereign states should not be coerced into taking sides in the Cold War. One reflection of this was his opposition to colonialism and his belief that the growth of nationalism worldwide after 1945 might encourage some countries to opt for neutrality rather than aligning with either the West or the Communist bloc. His anti-colonialism was evident in his rejection of Churchill's proposal at the Bermuda Conference of December 1953 for a two-power condominium between the United States and Britain,[109] and also in his emphasis on courting Third World opinion, reflected for example, in his effort to persuade the French to devolve power in Vietnam and in his opposition to the British-French-Israeli combined seizure of the Suez Canal in 1956.[110] Where Japan was concerned, Eisenhower sought to apply these principles by minimizing the presence of American troops on Japanese soil. As early as 1954, according to one contemporary account, he appears to have considered the possibility of completely withdrawing US troops from Japan for both psychological and economic reasons, although strategic necessity and the Japanese inability to fill the security vacuum left by American forces prevented him from taking such action.[111]

The President recognized that the benefits the United States enjoyed from its network of overseas bases could easily be jeopardized if it failed to pay due attention to local sensibilities. In a 1957 letter, formally commissioning a Defense Department review of America's bases worldwide, Eisenhower noted:

> We must develop the feeling that the US military facilities, far from being a derogation of local sovereignty, are a part of the security system of the host countries, and in reality are an expression of their national sovereignty. We must explore possibilities where, without sacrifice of essential military utility, there can be an increased sense of participation by the host country.[112]

The impact of this pattern of thinking had been evident in Eisenhower's agreement to the return of Amami in 1953. In April 1958, the President initiated investigations into the possibility of reorganizing US bases on Okinawa to create a single enclave allowing jurisdiction and administrative authority over the Ryukyus to be returned to Japan, while limiting America's authority to the base areas on the islands.[113] Eisenhower felt that such an approach would strengthen relations with Kishi and the Japanese government, without risking an explosion of irredentist sentiment comparable to anti-occupation popular movements in Cyprus or Algeria. Dulles, more so than Eisenhower, appears to have been preoccupied with this risk,[114] but both men saw the enclave strategy as a way of reinforcing alliance relations. Ultimately, the proposal failed because of predictable opposition from the Defense Department and unexpected resistance from MacArthur in Japan. There were too many disparate bases on the islands to allow an effective concentration of resources in one area, and in the ambassador's view, political pressures in Japan might limit America's freedom to use the bases at some point in the future.[115] Despite the inability to put this plan into action, it is interesting to note the strong expectation of Dulles and Eisenhower, that within three to five years it might be possible to return the island territories fully to Japan, a belief which explains why Eisenhower a year later again considered the adoption of an enclave strategy. Once more, the plan appears to have failed because of opposition from the Pentagon,[116] but the President was clearly committed to a flexible solution and aware of the need to assess the relationship with Japan on a regular basis. As he remarked at an earlier stage to Senator Styles Bridges: "I'm not concerned about 'buying friends' or purchasing satellite countries or any other thing—that is all false. As a free country, the only ally we can have is a free ally, one who wants to be with us—that is what we are trying to develop."[117]

Regional Security and the Nuclear Question

Notwithstanding Eisenhower's concern to construct alliance relations on a basis of genuine mutual self-interest, compromises were inevitably required in resolving conflicting national ambitions. In the case of Japan, US security interests in the global struggle with international Communism—particularly the need to preserve an effective system of nuclear deterrence—demanded that America retain its monopoly of administrative control over Okinawa and the Article III territories. Kennan's prescient recognition of the strategic importance of the Ryukyus was reflected in US planning throughout the 1950s, and from the very beginning of the Eisenhower administration it was clear that American military planners in the Far East were seriously contemplating employing nuclear weapons, possibly in a first-use scenario, in any future conflict in the region.[118] As General John Hull, CinCFE, pointed out from Tokyo in a memorandum to the Joint Chiefs of Staff in December 1953 commenting on the military situation in Korea:

> [The] concept of ground operations is to seek a fluid situation wherein atomic weapons and superior UNC [United Nations Command] mobility will be used to inflict maximum destruction on enemy forces and mat[eriel]. Plan does not repeat not contemplate securing any fixed line, and the success of the plan will depend to a large degree on effectiveness and el[e]m[ent] of surprise in use of atomic weapons.[119]

Okinawa rapidly became a significant base for America's strategic and tactical nuclear weapons in East Asia. Some 500 miles east of mainland China, and 825 miles from Tokyo and Manila, the islands were ideally situated on America's Pacific Defense perimeter, providing both a forward position for the Strategic Air Command (SAC) and bases for Army ground forces armed with nuclear weapons. Conventionally, the territo-

ries were also especially valuable, controlling the approaches to the Yellow and Japan seas as well as exit points for Soviet bases in the Far East.
The Navy relied on the islands as a location from which battle-ready
forces could quickly move to any potential site of conflict in the Western
Pacific, and also as a base from which land and sea planes could engage
in reconnaissance and anti-submarine warfare.[120]

While the strategic importance of the islands would be difficult to
overestimate, Okinawa by itself had certain limitations. Air Force planners in 1956, for example, worried that excessive concentration of resources on the main island air base at Kadena would leave the US position exposed to a single missile strike from the South China coast,[121] and
therefore over time the American bases (and presumably the nuclear
weapon sites) became more widely dispersed throughout the Ryukyus
archipelago. Throughout the 1950s, even following the development of
intercontinental ballistic missiles (ICBMs), US overseas bases remained
vitally important—part of what the American nuclear strategist Albert
Wohlstetter referred to as a "delicate balance of terror."[122] Contending
with the Soviet Union demanded that America's global strategic and tactical nuclear forces be carefully balanced and widely dispersed to avoid
provoking Soviet miscalculation and a violent, potentially uncontainable
reaction. Dispersion was necessary, in particular, to prevent Soviet and
Communist Chinese forces from crippling US retaliatory forces in a "single massive assault."[123] A network of worldwide bases and varied arse-
nals provided such an assurance, and Okinawa, despite its vulnerability
to air and submarine attack, was regarded by US military planners as
part of a group of bases which both separately and collectively were critically important. As one particularly important report noted in 1957:
"Our base system is key to our survival as a nation. If this system is so organized as to demonstrate our strength and our readiness to meet all
types of military action, there is solid reason to believe that our policy of
containment will succeed, that total war will be avoided, and that limited
aggression can be smothered."[124]

From Eisenhower's perspective, a future US withdrawal from Okinawa and the return of full administrative authority to Japan could only
be seriously contemplated once the situation in the Far East was no
longer threatening, even though efforts might be made in the meantime
to minimize the disruption to the lives of the inhabitants of the islands.
As the US-Japan Communiqué of 1957, following the visit of Prime Minister Kishi to Washington, made clear in language that would prove a fa-

miliar feature in subsequent negotiations over Okinawa:

> The Prime Minister emphasized the strong desire of the Japanese people for the return of administrative control over the Ryukyus and Bonin Islands to Japan. The President reaffirmed the United States position that Japan possesses residual sovereignty over these islands. He pointed out, however, that so long as the conditions of threat and tension exist in the Far East the United States will find it necessary to continue the present status. He stated that the United States will continue its policy of improving the welfare and well-being of the inhabitants of the islands and of promoting their economic and cultural advancement.[125]

At the end of the decade, despite further progress in ICBM technology and the development of the sea-launched intermediate-range Polaris missile, bases remained a key component in America's global strategy, although Okinawa's importance as a site for nuclear weapons now seemed limited to tactical rather than strategic forces.[126] By 1958 all US Army combat forces had been withdrawn from Japan, and all branches of the American military continued to rely on the Ryukyus as a critical base in the Western Pacific. The Army in 1960 was in the process of deploying an airborne battle-group to Okinawa; the Air Force maintained two bases there, with another six in the Japanese homeland; while the Navy and the Marines had concentrated their forces on the territories, possessing nine installations in Okinawa by comparison with five in Japan proper.[127] Emphasis was still placed on a flexible system of deterrence and the use of forward-deployed forces. At the very end of the second Eisenhower administration in January 1961, it was clear that the US military in the Far East was planning for a worst-case scenario and expected no substantive easing of tension with Communist forces in the region. Despite earlier talk of détente and peaceful coexistence, Moscow, at least in the judgment of the Pacific Command, was implacably hostile:

> The principal political objectives of the Soviets are:
>   1. to achieve world-wide domination of Communism,
>   2. to resolve, to Soviet benefit, intrabloc disharmony,
>   3. to achieve economic penetration in non-Bloc countries and to secure their ultimate economic dependence on the USSR; and
>   4. to neutralize or negate US and Western influence in all non-bloc countries.[128]

Moreover, in spite of political tensions between the USSR and PRC, it was assumed that the Communist alliance in Asia remained cohesive, with all of the bloc's members (apart from the Soviet Union) directly "engaged in outright military aggression."[129] The absence of any unambiguous evidence of Soviet offensive military action was counterbalanced by Moscow's earlier support for Chinese and North Korean war-fighting activities and by the clear signs of an expansion of Soviet military capabilities in East Asia.

According to US military assessments, the Russians were actively developing and diversifying their nuclear armaments, both low- and high-yield weapons, employed on a variety of delivery systems, including missiles, aircraft, and naval vessels. The Soviet Navy was an effective force, including a fleet of modernized, long-range submarines as well as a naval air arm of one hundred "Badger" bombers deployed in the Far East. Moreover, the Soviet Air Force presented "a formidable threat to the US and its allies in the Pacific," and its long-range bombers, equipped with medium-range ballistic missile, were able to deliver nuclear weapons against the continental United States and targets in the northern Pacific. Similarly, the PRC (although there were no signs that Beijing had acquired nuclear weapons[130]) was viewed as a major regional threat. With two and half-million men under arms, it enjoyed a great advantage in terms of manpower, and according to US strategists was in a position to attack Southeast Asia, Taiwan, and South Korea simultaneously.[131]

In the face of this daunting combination of hostile military hardware and personnel, it is hardly surprising that America's Far Eastern military planners remained committed to a nuclear war–fighting strategy, in both the early and later stages of any future regional conflict:

> The initial operation will probably be characterized by an intensive exchange of nuclear blows and the initiation of operations and deployment by all forces designed to achieve strategic advantage. During the initial operations, PACOM [Pacific Command] nuclear capability will be exploited fully. . . . The governing principle in the employment of nuclear weapons for the initial phase is that the United States must emerge from an initial exchange with the greatest possible over-all advantage.[132]

Subsequent operations would involve PACOM using its nuclear capabilities to destroy or neutralize essential enemy war resources. Such pressing and threatening security concerns made it difficult for any responsible US Commander in Chief to contemplate a withdrawal from Okinawa, and one can understand why Eisenhower, despite his concern for alliance harmony, felt the need to maintain the existing administrative system in the Article III territories.[133]

While Okinawa was clearly important, its central role in American military planning in the Far East raises the question of what concrete benefits the territories provided which Japan itself was not able to offer. At the most immediate level, Japan's shortcomings were linked to public opinion. Pronounced and widespread fear of becoming involved in a future conflict, as well as local and sometimes fierce opposition to the presence of American military personnel, threatened to tie the hands of the US military and destabilize the political authorities in Japan. Perhaps one of the most dramatic illustrations of Japanese concerns was an extended and vigorous campaign by a coalition of protest groups (including farmers, labor unions, and members of the Japan Communist Party) against a planned runway extension at the Tachikawa air base in the autumn of 1955. Such demonstrations were by no means isolated incidents, and it was clear that public opposition to runway extensions and other aspects of the American military presence could seriously limit the flexible deployment of US forces in the Far East. Popular anxiety that Japan might be used as a base for American nuclear weapons frequently flared up into vocal protests whenever there was any suggestion that such weapons might be introduced into the country. For example, in July 1955 an announcement from Washington, DC, that "Honest John" missile units would be deployed in Japan provoked immediate public protest. Tension was eventually alleviated, albeit only partially, following the resignation of the head of the Japan Defense Agency, Sugihara Arata, and US Army assurances that no atomic weapons had accompanied the missile units.[134]

Lyman Lemnitzer, CinCFE in 1957, was scathing about Japan's security preparedness and deeply suspicious of trends that in his view indicated a growing neutralist sentiment within Japan. Many of the government's defense-related proposals were, in Lemnitzer's view, "unreasonable and militarily unacceptable." The country was unwilling to "face military reality at home" and was "moving steadily towards further subordination of national security to political expediency."[135] Under such conditions there were, according to Lemnitzer, powerful reasons to maintain full American jurisdiction over Okinawa. A system of bilateral cooperation in which US military forces were subject to the constraints operating in the rest of Japan would involve a range of practical and potentially crucial difficulties. It would not be possible to obtain airfield extensions; US military authorities would have to adjudicate constant labor disputes; there would be constant pressure for the relinquishment of facilities; disagreements would arise over which facilities and maneuver areas could be used; and (most important) there would be "limitations on the introduction and storage of modern [that is, nuclear] weapons."[136]

Lemnitzer's concerns reflect a pronounced lack of confidence in Japan on the part of the American armed forces—sentiment which, in light of the frequency of popular agitation against bases and nuclear weapons and the unstable domestic political climate and internal tensions on the right and left of the political spectrum, may well have been justified. US military planners, both in Washington and in the Far East, were eager to maintain an enviable degree of operational and administrative freedom, especially in the latter part of the decade. This concern became increasingly important after 1957, when the Japanese government began to push more vigorously for a revision of the 1952 US-Japan Security Treaty. Under the terms of the original Security Treaty, the United States had the freedom to deploy its forces in Japan and to operate from Japanese bases without consulting the Japanese government, and without any explicit obligation to assist in Japan's defense. The revised Security Treaty, enacted in 1960, was more narrowly defined, establishing a basis for joint consultation in the event of a security crisis (Article IV), and making it clear that America was committed to defending Japan (Article V).[137] These changes, while important in strengthening alliance cooperation, also, paradoxically, enhanced the value of Okinawa in the eyes of US military personnel, undercutting arguments for an early reversion. Okinawa now was one of a handful of strategically placed major island bases in the Pacific from which America could count on being able to deploy nuclear weapons without having to consult with its allies.

Reliance on Okinawa as a base for nuclear weapons (either tactical or strategic) did not necessarily mean that the remainder of Japan was entirely free of nuclear weapons during this period. Given the public's aversion to nuclear weapons, Japan's leaders were compelled, in their public statements and responses to questions in the Diet, to deny the existence of nuclear weapons on Japanese soil. In the spring of 1955, for example, both Prime Minister Hatoyama, and his foreign minister, Shigemitsu Mamoru, in testimony to the Diet, clearly stated that neither the Security Treaty nor the Administrative Agreement of 1952 allowed nuclear weapons to be positioned in Japan and that, in the unlikely event of the United States requesting the introduction of such weapons, Japan would refuse to accept them. Similarly, Shigemitsu pointed out that, if a war were to occur in the Far East, the United States would not use Japan as a base for atomic and hydrogen bombs.[138] Two years later, Prime Minister Kishi, in comparable language, emphasized that America would not introduce nuclear weapons into Japan against the wishes of the Japanese people.

The official Japanese position was that Japan's Self-Defense Forces would not be equipped with nuclear weapons and nuclear-capable foreign troops would not be stationed in Japan.[139] However, these apparently clear-cut statements were at odds with a situation which, in reality, was much more ambiguous. Despite Hatoyama's assurances, for example, no public formal written agreement between the two countries explicitly ruled out nuclear weapons on Japanese soil. Indeed, we now know, thanks to recently declassified US intelligence reports, that the LDP leadership was prepared to mislead public opinion in order to insulate itself from public criticism and maintain the fiction that the government was unreservedly opposed to the introduction of American nuclear weapons into Japan. Shigemitsu's May 1955 Diet statement that he had secured an "understanding" from John Allison that US forces in Japan did not have nuclear weapons and that America would seek Japanese consent if it wished to change this policy prompted a secret exchange of revealing letters between the ambassador and the foreign minister.

> On July 7, 1955, the foreign minister was officially informed by the embassy that the ambassador "made no commitments on May 31 regarding the storage of atomic weapons in Japan" and that "the US Government does not consider itself committed to any particular course of action." In reply, a letter from the foreign minister of July 13, 1955, gave assurances that "nothing in the discussions in the Diet commits the US Government to any particular course of action."[140]

With dramatic understatement, the report noted dryly: "The tenor of the reply suggests that the government secretly did not share, at least to a decisive degree, the objections of the Japanese public to nuclear weapons storage." Yet the Shigemitsu-Allison correspondence remained secret, and public opinion continued to believe that an understanding had been provided—a problem compounded by Kishi's subsequent Diet announcement, against the recommendations of his diplomatic advisors, that the Americans had indeed provided such assurances.

A close reading of the diplomatic record reveals that, toward the end of the 1950s, the US authorities seriously contemplated the possibility of working with the Japanese authorities to introducing nuclear arms covertly into Japan. There was little doubt that the Japanese public would not agree to the reintroduction of nuclear weapons. Felix Stump, as CinCPAC, noted in a cable in early 1958:

> Regardless of the need and desire to have atomic weapons placed around the
> world where they will be immediately available to the forces which will use
> them, with the political situation as it now is in Japan and will be for a long
> time to come, it would be a fatal mistake to think of any negotiations now, or
> in the near future, leading to the introduction of atomic weapons into Japan.
> To do so at this time would not only accomplish nothing, but might jeopardize
> the possibility at some future date.[141]

However, the absence of public support did not preclude a secret arrangement. Less than five months after having pointed out the difficulty of openly introducing nuclear weapons into Japan, Stump (in considering how best to revise the Security Treaty) was willing to entertain the possibility of a covert understanding on nuclear matters: "For political purposes, concurrent oral assurances concerning the non-entry of atomic weapons might be made, provided that a secret protocol between President Eisenhower and Prime Minister Kishi authorized the secret introduction of these weapons at such time as the United States considers them essential to the defense of Japan."[142]

Whether such an agreement existed is hard to determine with any certainty. A close study by J-5 (the International Policy Branch of the Joint Chiefs) of the possibility of a secret arrangement warned of the practical dangers of such action: "Secret introduction is feasible, but the political and ethical risks which this would involve and the consequences of discovery, not only with relation to Japan, but with the rest of the world, as well, are so formidable that its consideration becomes impracticable."[143] However, it is not clear to what extent this advice shaped subsequent policy decisions. The weight of circumstantial evidence is not decisive, but there are indications that a secret arrangement between the Kishi and Eisenhower administrations might not have been out of the question. Certainly, in 1958, the Operations Coordinating Board (OCB) felt that an agreement might eventually be workable, despite Kishi's public statements ruling out the possibility of nuclear weapons on Japanese soil:

> There are strong indications that the present Japanese government will change
> its position opposing the introduction of nuclear weapons as Japanese public
> opinion grows to accept equipping Japanese forces with modern weapons having
> a dual capacity. A preliminary step in this direction was acceptance of the
> US offer of December 1957 to supply Sidewinders, an air-to-air non-nuclear
> missile, to the fledgling Japanese air force. Further steps can be expected
> within the next year.[144]

Even Japanese public opinion, according to one cautious (and, as it

Fig. 3. Political cartoon illustrating the disposition of nuclear weapons in Asia. "Soviet Government says this threatens the peace of the Far East." Source: *Asahi Shinbun*, June 1958. Reprinted with permission of the *Asahi Shinbun*.

turned out, overoptimistic) report from the embassy in Tokyo, might swing round in favor of a more flexible position. For example, a June 1958 editorial cartoon in the progressive *Asahi Shinbun* portrayed an American soldier, looking remarkably like President Eisenhower, handing a nuclear weapon to Prime Minister Kishi standing in the foothills of Mt. Fuji and overlooked ominously in the background by a long row of guided missiles on Russia's Asiatic coast. As the embassy noted, "This remarkable cartoon speaks more eloquently than words of the changing climate of Japanese public opinion regarding the general subject of nuclear weapons," suggesting a growing wariness of the Soviet nuclear threat in the Far East and a willingness to view more tolerantly the American military (and potentially nuclear) presence in Japan.[145]

Recent scholarship, in both Japan and the United States, has examined the question of possible secret agreements between the United States and Japan concerning nuclear weapons—not, it should be emphasized, dealing directly with the 1950s, but nonetheless demonstrating persuasively that there was frequently a striking discrepancy between the public statements and private positions of Japan's leaders on the issue. For example, it is now clear that during the negotiations over the reversion of Okinawa which took place during the late 1960s between the administrations of Richard Nixon and Satō Eisakau, Prime Minister Satō (despite having clearly committed Japan to a policy—the so-called "three non-nuclear principles"—of neither possessing, manufacturing, nor introducing nuclear weapons into Japan) had signed a secret document (binding on his successors) allowing the United States to station nuclear weapons on Japanese territory in the event of a crisis in the Far East.

Details of this agreement were provided by Wakaizumi Kei, a university academic who acted as Satō's personal emissary during the negotiations with the Nixon administration, and in particular with Henry Kissinger (at that time the President's national security advisor). Wakaizumi's memoirs are interesting not only because they reveal how few individuals from either government were aware of the secret agreement (in Japan's case—probably only Wakaizumi and the prime minister), but also because they hint, albeit rather obliquely, at the possibility of a similar arrangement on nuclear weapons having been made prior to the Satō administration. Satō was Kishi Nobusuke's younger brother,[146] and in a conversation with Wakaizumi, the prime minister suggested that a similar secret deal might at one point have been reached with the United States during Kishi's premiership.[147] Even if one cannot point to a document that conclusively supports this suggestion,[148] it is clear that among senior politicians and bureaucrats in post-war Japan, the "nuclear allergy" so conspicuous among the general public was much less in evidence. Indeed, it is possible to discern what might loosely be described as a strong strand of "realist" sentiment on security issues, including the nuclear question. For example, in August 1955, Sunada Shigemasa (Sugihara Arata's replacement as head of the Japan Defense Agency) issued a series of statements that suggested a much more assertive Japanese stance on security issues. According to Sunada, the Self-Defense Forces should learn to use atomic weapon launchers, the Japan Defense Agency (JDA) should become a full-fledged ministry, and the Japanese government should begin research into manufacturing hydrogen and cobalt bombs, while receiving guidance in the use of nuclear weapons.[149] Not surprisingly, Sunada's recommendations generated considerable controversy and negative press commentary, and under questioning in the Diet, he was forced to admit that his statements had been "reckless" and without cabinet approval.[150]

Notwithstanding this public change of heart, successive conservative administrations in Japan remained focused on the possibility of acquiring an independent Japanese nuclear weapons capability and continued cautiously to test and push against the wider public's aversion to nuclear weapons. Indeed, US intelligence analysts in August 1957 felt there was strong reason to believe that elite sentiment in Japan was much more unambiguously open to the nuclear option.[151] The Kishi administration was enthusiastically committed to developing Japan's civilian nuclear energy program; it was actively working with Japanese scientists to find ways of extracting uranium from low-grade ores; and it was involved in surveys to determine the location of uranium deposits throughout Southeast Asia. Within the Japanese defense community, hawkish LDP politicians and JDA bureaucrats were apparently aiming at "ultimately equipping Japan's forces with nuclear weapons" and assumed that "nuclear weapons would be a standard condition of future warfare."[152] Kishi himself, in May 1957, had sought to test the limits of the public's nuclear tolerance by publicly "asserting that the 'acquisition' of tactical nuclear weapons by Japan's defense force would not be unconstitutional, and that he could envisage a future situation in which such weapons would be necessary for effective defense of the nation."[153] Kishi—like so many officials before and since—was forced to issue a retraction in the face of a public outcry. Nonetheless, from America's perspective, the nuclear issue at this juncture remained finely balanced. Stable conservative government, continuing economic growth, and the possible re-election of Kishi at the end of the decade, argued US analysts, would be enough to allow Japan to develop a nuclear navy within ten years.

Kishi's nuclear ambitions—real or imagined—never came to fruition, closed off in part by the political instability that gripped Japan in the late 1950s. However, much later, in 1967, Prime Minister Satō revisited the issues when he convened a secret study group on nuclear policy which concluded that there were no technical obstacles to Japan developing its own nuclear weapons, although anxiety on the part of Japan's neighbors and the cost of such a program rendered it unfeasible.[154] At various stages in the post-war period, individuals within both the Gaimushō and the JDA have argued in favor of Japan possessing nuclear weapons, and in 1970, Nakasone Yasuhiro, then head of the JDA (and later prime minister), publicly pointed out that there were no constitutional reasons why

Japan could not possess defensive tactical nuclear weapons.[155] As far as relations with the United States were concerned, it became clear in 1981, following a highly publicized interview between a Japanese journalist and Edwin O. Reischauer (US ambassador to Japan from 1961 to 1966) that the Japanese government had implicitly recognized the right of US ships carrying nuclear weapons to enter Japanese waters. The United States, for understandable security reasons, maintained a policy of neither confirming nor denying whether its naval vessels were equipped with nuclear arms, but it was clear that this arrangement was at odds with Satō's "three non-nuclear principles."[156]

Even if there are doubts over the extent to which US and Japanese officials colluded over nuclear matters, the "realist" perspective of Japanese government officials clearly carried weight in the case of Okinawa and explains in part why tensions between the governments in Tokyo and Washington over the territorial issue were relatively muted. Even as early as September 1947, during the American Occupation, the Emperor, Hirohito, had, according to one interesting account, sent a special envoy to William Sebald, the State Department's political advisor in Japan, to relay his concern that Japan might become Communist and suggesting that the United States should temporarily occupy Okinawa and use it as a strategic base to resist the Soviet Union and the Chinese Communists.[157]

Even when Japan's leaders did make a public issue out of the territorial question, they may have been more concerned to accommodate domestic political pressures than to dislodge the Americans—a motivation which US officials appear to have been well aware of. For example, in October 1955, Tokyo embassy personnel, following a meeting with Prime Minister Hatoyama, reported that the prime minister stated that "Japan would make a *political* gesture for the return of the Ryukyus but did not intend to press the request in view of the United States involvement in Okinawa and protection afforded Japan by bases maintained by the United States in the Ryukyus" (emphasis added).[158]

A similar pragmatism is evident in the US-Japan Mutual Security Treaty negotiations beginning in 1957. Originally, Prime Minister Kishi had suggested that the Article III treaty islands should be included in the territorial scope of the new treaty. Japan and the United States would cooperate in the defense not only of the main islands of Japan but also of the Ryukyus and Bonins. Including the treaty islands would, from Kishi's perspective, be politically convenient since it would force the Opposition parties, which had long called for the return of the islands, to accept the wider, reformulated security relationship with the United States. However, the political gambit failed for two principal reasons. First, Socialist Diet members were afraid that the Ryukyu islands would be used by the Americans in the event of a clash between Taiwan and Communist China and would therefore inevitably suck Japan into a wider regional conflict that did not involve an immediate threat to Japanese security, narrowly defined. Second, and most important, realist strategic thinkers within Kishi's own party argued against inclusion of the treaty islands, on the grounds of military flexibility. Both former Prime Minister Ashida Hitoshi and Admiral Nomura Kichisaburō, the head of the LDP's Okinawa policy committee, argued that maintaining both US bases and nuclear weapons on the Ryukyus was a vital part of Japan's defense.[159] Including the islands in the terms of the new Security Treaty would expose the nuclear issue once more to public and political debate and jeopardize not only Japan's overall security but also the reversion of administrative authority over the islands.[160]

Missed Opportunities

Powerful security considerations, acknowledged by leaders in both Japan and the United States, meant that Okinawa and the Ryukyus island chain remained under US jurisdiction. Nonetheless, more could have been done to reduce tensions over the territories[161] and there were a number of what might be termed "missed-opportunities" in the context of America's Okinawa policy during the 1950s. Wage-rates, for instance, for Okinawan workers were for a long time noticeably lower than those paid to US and Filipino laborers employed in the construction of American bases on Okinawa—an economic and symbolic slight that could have been easily and inexpensively avoided.[162] State Department proposals for an explicit role for US diplomats in the administration of the Ryukyus were largely blocked by the Pentagon, although a diplomatic presence would have helped the government in Washington to anticipate and respond to political problems in the Article III territories. Even a simple request to allow the flying of the Japanese flag over public buildings in the Ryukyus was rejected on the grounds that this would stimulate reversionist pressure and jeopardize American strategic interests in the Far East.[163]

US policy toward the Bonin or Ogasawara islands (also governed by Article III of the San Francisco Peace Treaty) was the most striking illustration of a failure of diplomatic imagination. Part of the problem here predated the Eisenhower administration. During the Pacific War, Japan had evacuated the inhabitants of this collection of small, rocky islands situated to the southeast of Japan, and in 1946 the Occupation authorities had agreed to the repatriation of some 127 residents who were able to claim descent from early occidental settlers who had landed on the islands in the late nineteenth century.[164] The decision was a curious one and the source of much frustration for the Japanese government, popular opinion, and, most important, the 5,000 to 7,000 other islanders (not of occidental extraction) who wanted to return to the islands.

As early as 1947, the former inhabitants had established a pressure group—the Ogasawara Return Home Promotion League (Ogasawara kikyō sokushin renmei), a body which continuously petitioned both the Japanese and the American authorities to allow the previous residents to return.[165] In September 1952, Yoshida sent a personal message to Admiral Radford, the US CinPAC, urging him to give the issue a favorable hearing,[166] and in October of the same year Okazaki Katsuo met both Radford and Robert Murphy (the US ambassador to Japan) in a further effort to persuade the Americans to allow the islanders to return. Radford and Murphy had recently returned from an inspection visit to the islands, and the US naval commander firmly turned down the Japanese request, arguing that, since Japan lacked adequate naval power, the United States would have to shoulder the responsibility for defending Japan and for organizing naval convoys. Since the islands were a part of this system and would need to be used exclusively for military purposes, the islanders could not be permitted to return. Okazaki reinforced his request by arguing that the earlier US decision to allow a select number of "occidental" islanders to return was unfair and smacked of racism. However, Radford refused to compromise, suggesting only that the United States would provide compensation to the dispossessed islanders.[167]

Throughout the 1950s, the Japanese continued to raise the issue with the United States,[168] but their requests were repeatedly turned down. Within the US government, the military privately admitted that it had been a mistake to permit the return of Bonin islanders of non-Japanese extraction, but the Pentagon continued to argue rigidly that any accommodation of Japanese requests would pose a security threat and stimulate reversionist pressure over both the Bonin and the Ryukyu islands.[169] It is hard to see the logic of these arguments. Tokyo offered, on a number of occasions, to meet the relocation and support costs of the islanders.

Moreover, the requests associated with the Bonins were not for reversion but simply for a physical return home—that is, that the Bonin islanders be accorded the same treatment shown to the Ryukyuans allowed to return to Okinawa. Failing this, the Bonin residents hoped to receive some sort of financial compensation—but even in this instance, when Washington could have made an early and symbolically significant gesture that would have helped to soothe bruised feelings, the United States failed to act, agreeing to compensation only in 1958.[170] Even the strategic argument is open to question. The Bonin islands were much smaller than the Ryukyus, farther removed from the Asian mainland, and at best capable of providing submarine bases rather than the extensive network that the United States enjoyed in Okinawa.[171] Defense reports in the late 1950s talked about the possible value of the Bonins should America be forced to leave Japan, the Philippines, and Okinawa, but this was not an especially likely outcome and consequently the strategic importance of the islands remained much more potential than actual. Perhaps a partial key to understanding US intransigence on this issue is emotional rather than practical considerations. Iwo Jima was part of the Bonin chain, and the tremendous cost in lives associated with the American campaign for the island during the closing stages of World War II may have been a major obstacle to a change of policy by the US military.

Clearly America's handling of the territorial issue could have been improved. Moreover, US officials were at times inclined simply to manage the problem instead of pushing energetically to resolve it. On at least two occasions during the 1950s, the State Department sponsored a major emigration program to address the land-shortage problem in the Ryukyus, enabling thousands of Okinawans to emigrate to Bolivia.[172] Similarly, economic resources and refinancing arrangements were made to improve the lot of local residents, and by the late 1950s the Japanese government was permitted to provide financial support and economic and educational development assistance to the islands. Such changes hardly constituted bold gestures. However, the Okinawa controversy has to be set within the larger context of the Cold War and the immediate security requirements of the 1950s—constraints which were accepted by senior decision-makers both in Washington and in Tokyo. In addition, it is worth keeping in mind, as Kōno Yasuko has emphasized, that the Japanese and American governments approached the territorial issue from similar perspectives—Japan "within the basic framework of constructing a cooperative relationship with the United States,"[173] and the Eisenhower administration from a viewpoint that stressed both cooperation with Japan and the need to avoid thinking of security exclusively in military terms, in favor of a relationship based on a normalized system of American administration in the territories—focusing on encouraging stability and public welfare.[174]

Whatever the difficulties the Eisenhower administration may have encountered in handling the Okinawa issue, it does not seem fair to argue, as Roger Buckley has done, that Washington took Tokyo for granted and that "for the United States in the 1950s, Japan was rarely a nation of any particular import."[175] Where the territorial question was concerned, a partial explanation of America's actions may be the absence of any pronounced sense of urgency or imminent crisis regarding the territories—a state of affairs which both the Japanese authorities and, at times, public opinion in Japan may have contributed to. It is well known that during the crisis over the renewal of the Security Treaty in 1960, Eisenhower was forced to abandon his visit to Japan—part of a scheduled trip to the Far East—due to violent demonstrations in Tokyo against the Kishi administration. However, it is rarely noted that during this trip, the President did in fact visit Okinawa, albeit briefly. Eisenhower did encounter demonstrators during his visit to the capital, Naha, but they were outnumbered by the far larger welcoming and enthusiastic crowds.[176] Local Okinawan press editorials of the time were uniformly in favor of the President's visit since he, if not overall US policy, was popular,[177] and Okinawan opinion seemed anxious to make amends for the riots in Tokyo (particularly the attack on the car of James Hagerty, Eisenhower's press secretary[178]), viewing them as a source of national shame and an inexcusable slight to the visiting President.[179]

In this context, the concerns of the islanders, while substantive, would not have appeared destabilizing or likely to generate popular unrest and certainly not sufficiently serious to offset wider strategic considerations. Consequently, America's Okinawa policy during the two Eisenhower administrations (despite its shortcomings) demonstrates that the US government was seeking to develop an effective and cooperative alliance relationship with Japan within the context of an international environment and an adversarial relationship with the Communists that imposed serious and unavoidable constraints on America's freedom to maneuver. Such constraints should not be overlooked when assessing the record of Eisenhower's policy toward Japan, nor should the President's own views on alliance relations and his low-key but revealing involvement in executive-level decisions affecting Japan be ignored. Nonetheless, Okinawa during the 1950s, as a bilateral issue, never reached crisis proportions. A comprehensive examination of US policy toward Japan during this period also needs to consider the manner in which moments of potentially acute tension and emergency were handled—a question which is addressed in the following chapter.

CHAPTER FIVE

The *Lucky Dragon* Incident of 1954

A Failure of Crisis Management?

International crises rarely, if ever, happen in isolation. Certainly there are few instances in which a country's policy-makers, at the moment of an unforeseen catastrophe or diplomatic disaster, are able to respond instantaneously and with complete attention, undistracted by competing issues of comparable importance. The *Lucky Dragon* incident of 1954, in which the twenty-three crew members of a Japanese fishing vessel were exposed to radioactive fallout from the test detonation of a US hydrogen bomb in the Pacific, was, at the time it occurred, a major disruption to relations between Washington and Tokyo, imposing "the most serious strain on Japanese-American relations since 1945."[1] Public reaction in Japan was one of anger at the US government and its apparent failure to give adequate consideration to Japanese grievances, and subsequent scholarly analysis has often been sharply critical of American actions.[2]

However, there are grounds for arguing that this criticism may have been overstated. The emotional intensity of the Japanese reaction to the incident is readily understandable in light of the psychological and physical scars left by the bombing of Hiroshima and Nagasaki, but to view it at face value would be to neglect the various efforts within the Eisenhower administration, both in Washington and in Tokyo, to handle the crisis constructively. Moreover, studies of the incident may have been drawn on too narrow a canvas, missing, or at least giving insufficient attention to, the wider context. Historians have perhaps assumed too readily that policy-makers could or should have viewed events with the same degree of dispassionate clarity that access to the archives and the benefit of hindsight provides.

In the context of 1954, the broader policy considerations associated with nuclear weapons testing, the reliability of existing scientific knowledge relating to nuclear technology as a whole, concern for adequate security cooperation between allies, and the overall conflict between international Communism and the Western alliance, all influenced the decisions and judgment of the Eisenhower administration in dealing with Japan. Stressing these factors is not a basis for exonerating or excusing US actions. Mistakes occurred, and in certain respects the crisis could have been handled more effectively and sensitively and with less disruption to alliance relations. Nevertheless, explicitly taking these factors into account, while extending the analysis both before and beyond 1954, provides a more complete picture of events. It also reveals the importance of psychological and propaganda techniques in America's Japan policy at this time, as well as the recognition by US officials that Japanese domestic political instability (itself, in part, the product of American actions stemming from the Occupation) and the threat of Communist subversion, seriously constrained the United States in developing a strong alliance with Japan. Japanese internal bureaucratic tensions as well as the lack of effective Japanese security legislation undercut efforts to promote an active security partnership. This issue has generally been neglected in existing work on post-war US-Japan relations, and examining it in detail reveals the important role played by inter-agency institutions, most notably the Operations Coordinating Board, in influencing the Eisenhower administration's Japan policy at this time.

Viewing the *Lucky Dragon* incident more broadly also reveals an interesting ambivalence in Japan's attitude to nuclear issues. Japan's nuclear allergy was highly selective, based on a widespread aversion to the testing of nuclear weapons, but at the same time official and, at times, public opinion was enthusiastically in favor of the development of the peaceful use of nuclear energy and Japan's own nuclear power industry. This sentiment gave US officials a tool with which to limit the political damage associated with the *Lucky Dragon* incident, and developments in the latter half of the 1950s suggest that the Americans had learned important lessons from the earlier crisis, enabling them to prevent similar tensions in the future. This adaptive capacity suggests that in any balanced assessment of US-Japan policy, it is important to consider, in addition to points of unmistakable bilateral tension, those crises which did not occur. The absence of conflict can sometimes be just as significant as instances of disagreement.

The Outline of the Crisis

The broad sequence of events surrounding the crisis of 1954 can be set out quite simply. In certain respects, the year should have been a promising one for relations between America and Japan. Just over one hundred years previously, in 1853, Commodore Matthew Perry had arrived in Japan as the first official representative of the United States, carrying a letter from President Fillmore to the Japanese Emperor. A year later, Perry returned and concluded the Treaty of Kanagawa, laying the basis for formal relations between the two countries. In 1954, government and private organizations were involved in planning various commemorative events, in particular a US-Japan Centennial Celebration covering the period from April to June that might have been expected to stress common interests and mutual cooperation.[3] However, expectations of positive dialogue and fruitful exchange were soon dramatically and abruptly overshadowed by unanticipated events in the Pacific.

On March 1, a small private fishing vessel—the *Daigo Fukuryū Maru* (or *Lucky Dragon, No. 5*)—was situated some eighty-two miles east of Bikini Island,[4] a coral atoll that formed part of the Marshall Island chain in the Western Pacific. The ship was far from Japan and fishing in a relatively unfamiliar area. Traditionally, Japanese fishing vessels preferred the waters closer to Indonesia, but both the boat's owner and captain had felt that the usual fishing grounds had been over-fished and that a less conventional site would provide a larger catch, despite the risks involved in navigating an area of ocean where the seas were often rough and unpredictable.[5] However, such dangers were entirely natural, and nothing could have prepared the crew members for the events of that day. Early in the morning, the crew was startled by a bright flash of light, followed some seven minutes later, by an enormous explosion. Two hours later, a fine, white powder had started to rain down on the boat and its crew, adding to the puzzlement and anxiety of the men. It was not immediately clear what had happened. Some of the fishermen could recall that the Marshall Islands had been the site for earlier nuclear testing by the United States in 1946 and that as recently as 1952, Japan's Maritime Safety Board, responding to information provided by the US government, had warned vessels to stay away from Bikini.[6] However, the *Lucky Dragon* was well outside the official exclusion zone (some fourteen miles according to later reports[7]), and in theory the crew had no reason to be concerned.

In reality, the situation was much more serious. The United States had resumed its nuclear testing program in the Pacific, and the March 1 explosion, or "BRAVO shot" as it was officially known, was the first detonation in the "Operation CASTLE" series of nuclear tests planned for an area that included Bikini as well as the populated atolls of Ailinginae, Rongelap, and Utirik. However, unlike the tests of 1946, which had involved atomic weapons, the CASTLE series was designed to test the latest developments in hydrogen bomb technology and represented a major and dramatic increase in destructive power. Defined in strictly scientific terms, BRAVO was hugely successful. The anticipated size of the explosion (a fission reaction which in turn triggered a much larger fusion explosion[8]) had been five megatons. However, the US nuclear scientists who had designed the bomb overlooked an important stage in the lithium-based chain reaction and seriously underestimated the final yield—a massive 15 megatons—unquestionably at that stage the world's largest ever nuclear explosion.[9] In an instant, a vast crater, 250 feet deep and 6,500 feet wide was carved out of Bikini and the coral remnants sucked into the atmosphere,[10] soon to be deposited as atomic rain, or as the Japanese media would later describe it, "Ashes of Death." In effect, chance or contingency, rather than conscious planning,[11] had intervened abruptly, catching the unsuspecting and hapless fishermen in a radioactive downpour and in the process creating the basis for intense bilateral tension.

Confused by what they had witnessed, the Japanese fishermen decided to return home. Distrustful of the Americans and fearing that their vessel might be seized in light of its proximity to the tests, they chose not to relay any details of their experience by radio, preferring to wait until returning to their home port of Yaizu, in Shizuoka prefecture, before reporting the incident. En route to Japan, it gradually became clear to the men that the experience had not left them unscathed, as each of them, in varying degrees, began to display the characteristic symptoms of radiation exposure, including hair loss, sores, loss of appetite, and diarrhea.[12] Returning home by March 14, the men reported to a local physician who downplayed the extent of their condition, suggesting that they would have displayed more serious symptoms if their exposure had been severe. Indeed, such was the doctor's confidence that he reassured the men that they could safely sell their catch to the local market.[13] There was, apparently, no danger of contamination. However, by March 16, an enterprising local *Yomiuri Shinbun* newspaper reporter had managed to tease out the details of the story, which, once published, rapidly transformed a local incident into a major international event.[14]

News of the event prompted an immediate response from Washington, where the Atomic Energy Commission (AEC), the government agency with overall responsibility for the civilian and testing aspects of the nuclear program, ordered the dispatch to Tokyo of Dr. John Morton, the director of the Atomic Bomb Casualty Commission (ABCC[15]), together with a group of US Air Force radiation physicists, to examine the affected fishermen—two of whom, with their conditions deteriorating, had already been sent to Tokyo University hospital.[16] Morton, on the basis of his visit with the two men (and before heading off to Yaizu to see the other twenty-one crew members) issued a public statement that the men were in better condition than he had anticipated and that he expected them to recover within two to three weeks.[17]

Any hopes that the Americans might have had of a rapid resolution of the problem were dashed by reports from private Japanese researchers that the hull of the *Lucky Dragon* registered high levels of radiation and, most significantly, that recently caught fish stocks in Osaka, including the latest shipment from Yaizu (some of which had already been sold and consumed), were heavily contaminated.[18] Not surprisingly, the news caused an immediate panic, closing markets not only in Osaka but also in Tokyo and throughout the country—a trend which was exacerbated when it was learned that fish had been removed from the Emperor's diet.[19] However, restoring market confidence was the least of the Americans' problems. Far more serious was the widespread press criticism of the United States for allowing testing to take place in the first place, for revisiting (intentionally, according to some reports) the horrors of radiation exposure on a vulnerable and defenseless Japan, and for American alleged indifference to the fate of the twenty-three fishermen. Some of this criticism was overstated and some, it turns out, clearly inaccurate. However, Japanese grievances (at least at the level of public opinion) were reinforced by public relations blunders and crass insensitivity on the part of certain US government officials, and were also compounded by news of the death of the oldest of the crew members, Kuboyama Aikichi, in September 1954.[20] In addition, extended government negotiations over the issue of financial compensation for the fishermen and their relatives further increased tension between the two countries, delaying a final settlement until January 1955, ten months after the original incident. Understanding the causes of this tension and the manner in which the issue was resolved provides a basis for assessing alliance relations between the United States and its junior partner and is important in examining the degree to which the perceptions which had shaped the State Department's Japan policy at the end of the Occupation were still operative by the middle of the 1950s.

Testing and Nuclear Strategy

In order to make sense of US actions in 1954, it is necessary to explore the context and overall rationale behind America's nuclear testing program. At the start of the Eisenhower administration, there were superficial signs that East-West relations might be on the point of improving. With a new President in the White House and, since early March (following Stalin's death), a new Soviet leader—Prime Minister Georgi Malenkov—some in the West anticipated a movement away from the tense adversarial relations that had existed since the advent of the Cold War in 1946–47. Certainly, the succession process within the Soviet leadership indicated that Moscow might be more preoccupied with internal rather than foreign matters and Malenkov's public statements suggested some moderating of direct ideological conflict with the West.[21] The US leadership nevertheless remained deeply suspicious of Soviet intentions. The "Solarium Project"—the Eisenhower administration's early re-examination of policy toward the USSR—had reaffirmed Kennan's 1947 analysis that the struggle with the Soviet Union would involve a political and ideological offensive as well as a military challenge from Moscow.[22] Moreover, with the successful testing of thermonuclear devices by the United States and Soviet Union in 1952 and 1953, respectively, there was little reason to assume any easing of the arms race between the superpowers, and the Joint Chiefs of Staff remained preoccupied with the risk of being overtaken by the Soviets militarily.[23] Such fears in turn stimulated an extensive strategic review, ultimately leading to the administration's "New Look" (formally expressed in NSC 162/2, issued on October 30, 1953)—a conscious endorsement of nuclear deterrence as a means of minimizing the enormous economic burden associated with a conventional arms race.

Criticisms and Misperceptions

Much of the criticism of the US reaction to the *Lucky Dragon* affair, both at the time of the incident and subsequently, was focused on a number of issues. The Americans, it was argued, were slow in responding to the crisis and in issuing a formal apology to the Japanese government.[28] They had refused to disclose information on the effects of the explosion and had therefore demonstrated little concern for the fishermen's well-being. Moreover, according to the more critical Japanese press reports, the Americans had deliberately and callously triggered an explosion likely to inflict damage on Japan: contrary to official US statements, Washington, it was suggested, had been fully aware of the power of the bomb and may well have been testing a cobalt-bomb intended to spread radiation over a wide area.[29] In effect, the Japanese were being used as human guinea-pigs in American radiation experiments.[30] In general, America, in the eyes of the Japanese press, could be attacked for not taking Japan's views and interests seriously and for placing its own agenda ahead of that of its alliance relationship with Japan.

The claim that the BRAVO shot was intentionally harmful to the Japanese is not sustainable. Lithium-deuteride rather than cobalt was the core fissile material, and given the exposure, not only of the Marshall islanders but of US naval vessels in the vicinity of the test area,[31] it is clear that the extensive environmental damage caused by the test was the result of miscalculation rather than an attempt to disperse radiation on the high-seas. By contrast, the argument that America should have apologized sooner is much more persuasive. It was only on March 30, two weeks after news of the disaster had emerged, that the United States decided to send a formal note to the Japanese government expressing its regret (albeit without admitting any legal responsibility),[32] and Allison subsequently observed in his memoirs, "As I look back on the tragic incident, I am inclined to believe that I should have made an apology at the very beginning."[33] However, this should not entirely overshadow the initial US efforts to respond promptly to the crisis. As of March 24, Robert McClurkin, the acting assistant secretary of state for northeast Asian affairs, chaired both the OCB working group on Japan and an ad hoc interdepartmental group, made up of representatives from the AEC and State and Defense departments, set up to deal with the *Lucky Dragon* incident. A summary of US government actions after March 16 reveals a series of responses of varying degrees of effectiveness: on the 16th, Dr. Morton's name had been passed on to the embassy in Tokyo as a technical consultant to examine the two fishermen in Tokyo University hospital; on the 17th, the embassy issued a statement indicating that the US government was prepared to provide fair compensation if the facts warranted; on the 18th, Washington instructed the embassy to inform the

Japanese government that the danger zone for future tests had been expanded; on the 23rd the embassy was authorized to inform the Japanese Foreign Ministry that the United States would reimburse Japan for any medical care for the crew members and relief for family members; on the 24th, US-Japan working-level meetings were held in Tokyo to try to improve joint co-ordination between the two governments, and Kōseishō (the Japanese Ministry of Health and Welfare) established an Atom Bomb Inquiry Investigating Committee which the Americans hoped would address the problem of a lack of Japanese internal co-ordination; and on the 28th, the US Far Eastern Command had flown the twenty-one fishermen still in Yaizu to Tokyo where they could receive more effective medical supervision.[34] The OCB, it was clear, recognized the need to respond, although it appears to have been divided or at least confused over the long-term implications of the incident. For example, two memoranda from March 24 present contrasting assessments of the urgency of the situation. One appeared relatively alarmed:

> The discussion recognised that the full facts in the situation had not been developed. However, a great deal of concern was expressed with respect to the reactions which have developed in Japan from the resulting injuries and damages.[35]

The second sounded overconfident and more preoccupied with the question of financial compensation than any need to allay Japanese concerns:

> Political effect in Japan will be short-range, particularly if there is no residual radiation hazard to Japanese fishing industry. US actions already taken would appear to be sufficient to satisfy requirements vis-à-vis the Japanese. Future actions should be weighed carefully against the hazard of encouraging the Japanese to overplay their hand.[36]

The charge that the Americans chose not to share technical information with the Japanese is easy to substantiate. In treating the crew of the *Lucky Dragon*, Japanese medical personnel understandably wished to know the composition of the ash which appeared to have caused the fishermen's illness. However, the Americans worried that any disclosure of either the content of the fallout or details of the design of the BRAVO bomb would reveal the unique character of the weapon—in particular, that it was a dry thermonuclear device based on a lithium core.[37] Such information, it was feared, would be beneficial to the Soviets and jeopardize the US lead in the nuclear arms race. While this reasoning might seem overly cautious, it was entirely consistent with existing policy. The timing of the CASTLE series had been deliberately concealed and the testing area made as expansive as possible in order to prevent any Soviet ship from obtaining samples of the fallout material, from which Soviet scientists might deduce the design of the new super-bomb.[38] Moreover, as early as 1952 Eisenhower had emphasized the importance of secrecy where the testing program as a whole was concerned, not only because of the obvious need to prevent important technical information from being disclosed to the enemy, but also to maintain a psychological edge over the Soviets. He calculated that it would be more of a blow to the Russians' morale to learn for themselves of America's testing successes than to have the information disclosed publicly.[39]

Washington's general preoccupation with maintaining the confidentiality of its nuclear technology was reinforced in its dealings with Tokyo by a deep-seated concern that the Japanese government had yet to develop its own reliable internal security and intelligence structure. An extensive report (based on a visit to East Asia by a government team headed by General James Van Fleet) highlighted the main shortcomings: the Diet had considered but refused to enact suitable legislation to protect classified military information, and since the ending of World War II the Japanese authorities had failed to take adequate measures to safeguard against Communist infiltration, whether in the form of North Korean and Communist Chinese agents or repatriated Japanese civilians and soldiers indoctrinated during their time, both during and after the war, in Communist-dominated areas on the Asian mainland. Moreover, in interrogating these repatriates, the Japanese government had shown only a limited willingness to share information with the US military and intelligence services, refusing to allow American personnel to question the repatriates from either the PRC or the USSR. The Japanese authorities had provided valuable political and economic information derived from their "own secret and small-scale interrogation reports," but, according to Van Fleet, these reports had "failed to produce enough of the data desired by the United States military, including information pertaining to United States citizens thought to be held by Communist countries."[40] Even with increased working-level cooperation between US and Japanese security personnel and the provision of American financial assistance to train Japanese officials in US intelligence techniques,[41] there was little evidence of any major progress on this issue, and in early 1955 officials in Washington still felt that the Japanese government had failed to adequately grapple with the problem of internal security.

William Leonhart, first secretary in the Tokyo embassy during 1954 and, from January 1955, a member of the Policy Planning Staff in Washington, summed up the situation in a lengthy analytical paper entitled simply "Japan":

> In the period from 1950 to 1952, it was generally assumed that conservative Japanese governments would deal adequately with internal security. The enthusiastic acceptance of the 1950 Occupation purges of Japanese communists, the formation of Sōhyō as an anti-communist labour federation, the passage of an Anti-Subversive Activities Prevention Law after the communist rioting on May Day, 1952, were all projected into a belief that communist influence would be satisfactorily controlled. Instead, Japan has yet to initiate or apply a systematic program to deal with the broad or the incisive problems of internal security. . . . More importantly, there is no law in Japan today which defines treason, espionage or state secrets or which provides for the political screening of public employees. . . . In the present period in Japan, the problem for the communists is not so much winning over a Japanese majority as it is the penetration of the Japanese government and society and the infiltration of its key positions. The prolonged failure of the Japanese to recognise or deal with this problem threatens Japanese stability and US national interest.[42]

Assessing the Communist Challenge

From the perspective of the Americans, there was little doubt that Communism in Japan represented a serious and persistent threat, not only to Japan's internal security but also to the development of a working alliance partnership between Washington and Tokyo. In July 1954, Samuel Berger, counselor at the embassy, drafted, in conjunction with his colleagues, William Leonhart and William Sherman, a detailed study of the capabilities of the Japanese Communist Party.[43] Endorsed by the ambassador, John Allison, it was dispatched to the State Department with recommendations that it be circulated to other branches of the government involved in Japan-related issues.

The report is significant in broadly reflecting the attitudes toward the JCP of American officials in Japan and back home in the United States,[44] and also in providing a chronological overview of the fluctuating fortunes of Japan's Communists from 1945 onwards. Communist activity could be divided, according to Berger, into four distinct periods: one of rapid growth and increasing popularity from 1945 to 1949; a sharp reversal of fortunes in 1949–50; a period of "retrenchment and revival" from 1951 to 1953; and finally, from 1953 onwards an increasing emphasis in JCP activities on subversion and the aggressive infiltration of other sectors of Japanese government and society—a strategy, in the words of the report, of "boring from within."[45]

The early period of growth from 1945 onwards was, according to Berger, the result of a combination of factors. The Occupation itself had provided Japan's Communists with a degree of respectability and legitimacy that they had hitherto lacked. Released from prison in October 1945 and freed from the persecution they had suffered under the authoritarian governments of the 1930s, the Communists had sufficient organization and discipline to capitalize on the 1946 purge of conservative politicians and develop an active presence in the country's emerging trades union movement. At the same time, they were able to appeal, albeit in a limited fashion, to a public opinion that at this stage remained partially receptive to a type of centralized state-planning that was consistent with Communist ideology and which seemed well suited to the immediate challenge of rebuilding the country after the war. The Communists' focus on the union movement found expression in the establishment of Sanbetsu (the Congress of Industrialised Unions) in August 1946. Ostensibly a broad church, Sanbetsu in time acquired a more radicalized character, designed to rival the more moderate Sōdōmei (the Japan Federation of Labor). Radicalization, in turn, encouraged the Occupation authorities to grow suspicious of Sanbetsu, fearing that the Communists were seeking to subvert and control the organization.[46]

MacArthur's cancellation of the General Strike of 1947 at one level put labor on the defensive. However, a deteriorating economy, a rash of strikes in late 1947 and early 1948, and the collapse of the Katayama cabinet in February 1948 strengthened the position of confrontational unionism and by extension bolstered the position of the Communists. In the words of the embassy report:

> By mid-1948 the communists were for all practical purposes in effective control of or exerting an overpowering influence on the whole Japanese trade union movement. Excluding over two million members of unions which had never affiliated with either of the two main trade union federations, nearly half of the three million affiliated union members were in Sanbetsu. These the communists controlled more or less openly. As for the more than million and a half members still in Sōdōmei, the communists by unity propaganda, by covert manipulation, and by making use of fellow travelers, sympathizers, or innocents were exerting ever-increasing influence on more and more Sōdōmei unions.[47]

The clearest expression of this rapidly growing strength was the lower house elections of 1949, which saw the Communists increase their share of the vote from 3.7 to 9.6 percent, significantly boosting their representation in the Diet from 4 to 35 seats.

Success, however, provoked a backlash. The onset of the Cold War meant that both SCAP and the US authorities in Washington were increasingly concerned about the threat posed by Communism worldwide. In May 1948, at the prompting of MacArthur, the Japanese government banned all strikes among public sector workers. Improvements in the economy, the provision of US financial assistance, and the easing of inflationary pressures moderated some of the domestic factors that had bolstered the Communists in the first instance, and with the gradual relaxation of some of the original 1946 purge restrictions, conservative politicians were able to begin making an electoral comeback. Equally important, the occurrence in 1949 of a series of high profile cases of industrial sabotage in the railway sector, including the murder of Shimoyama Sadanori, the president of the National Railway corporation in July 1949, led to growing public suspicion, if not active fear, of Communism. It was unclear who was behind the sabotage, but rumors of Communist involvement were enough to damage the JCP's standing in the public eye, a trend further reinforced by a parallel effort to wrest control away from the Communists in the labor movement through the establishment of Democratization Leagues, and by growing disillusionment with strikes as a means of exerting trade union influence.[48]

By 1951, Japan's Communists were experiencing significant reverses. The formation of Sōhyō in 1950—a new union organization that was Socialist in philosophy, anti-Communist in principle, and focused on economic goals rather than active political campaigning—signaled the marginalization of more radical groups in the union movement. The outbreak of the Korean War led MacArthur to crack down on the Communists, and encouraged by increasingly anti-Communist public and press opinion, the Yoshida government, with the active support of SCAP, launched a "red purge" in August 1950 that led to the suppression of *Akahata* ("Red Flag"), the Communists' newspaper, and the removal of some 11,000 Communist Party members and sympathizers from government and private sector employment.

Communist reversals at home prompted intervention from abroad through the dramatic publication by the Cominform in January 1950 of a six-point indictment of the JCP, criticizing Japan's Communists for, among other things, placing too much reliance on legal and parliamentary methods, for too great a willingness to compromise with the moderate Left in Japan, for a failure to view the Occupation authorities as the enemy, and for a general lack of revolutionary determination. The party responded to the criticism by attempting to strengthen its underground apparatus and to devote more energy to building up "front" organizations which might allow it to shield itself from public suspicions. In addition, the Communists shifted their overt attention away from the union movement and increasingly toward intellectuals, teachers, journalists, and students, as a way of cultivating a broader constituency of support and building a wider anti-Yoshida "popular front." Covertly, the JCP continued to focus on the unions, but now "tremendous emphasis was placed on secret infiltration of Sōhyō and its affiliated unions . . . in an effort to regain as much influence as possible in this decisive sector." On policy matters, the party sought to exploit emotive topics that might be calculated to resonate with the public, such as antinuclear issues and pacifist and anti-rearmament sentiment. Given the growing fear of Russia, it made sense for the party to tilt its propaganda toward China and to argue in favor of increased Sino-Japanese trade, while highlighting the worsening economic situation within Japan. Equally important, the JCP railed against the United States, seeking to stoke up a sense of grievance regarding the Peace and Security treaties and the Administrative Agreement, as well as criticizing the US troop presence in Japan and particularly in Okinawa and the Article III territories.[49]

This renewed and refocused activity did not have any appreciable impact in terms of the Communists' electoral fortunes. In the lower house elections of 1952, the Communist share of the vote dropped to 2.5 percent and the party failed to secure any seats. The following year the JCP was able to claw back a single seat in the lower house elections of 1953, but this was based on a further reduction of its overall share of the vote, down to 1.9 percent. The party's inability to make inroads electorally propelled it and its supporters to embrace more radical measures involving active subversion and infiltration of organizations, including trade unions, agricultural groups, and cultural and intellectual organizations. Securing influence and control over the unions involved the establishment of "fractions"—covert and overt organizations set up alongside and intended to dominate the bona fide "struggle committees" established by the wider labor movement to manage and coordinate industrial disputes.[50] In fomenting and directing industrial action, the Communists also, according to US intelligence reports, relied on covert attack corps (totsugeki-tai) and defense corps (bōei-tai) to spread propaganda and engage in espionage and acts of direct sabotage. Overt activities involved heavy use of agitation and propaganda (agitprop) and promotion of Communist views via party members and a much wider body of active sympathizers (shimpa). Sympathizers might be drawn from a wide variety of sources, such as the resident Korean community in Japan or the radical student movement, Zengakuren (the All Japan Federation of Student Self-government Associations). In 1950, there were some 600,000 legal and a further 400,000 illegal Korean residents in Japan. The majority of them, according to SCAP and State Department findings, were sympathetic to North Korea and included many individuals supportive of direct action. Likewise, of the 200 institutions and 150,000 individuals that made up Zengakuren in 1952, 20 percent were active Communists according to Japan's attorney general.[51]

Overall, the United States viewed Communist activity in Japan during the 1950s as a coordinated and systematic campaign of infiltration and subversion encouraged and in some instances directed by Moscow, alongside more legitimate, conventional parliamentary politics as practiced by the JCP.[52] The threat from the Communists was therefore unlikely to emerge through the ballot box, nor was there any immediate prospect of a revolution or a popular uprising against the state. Instead, the challenge was more insidious and long-term. Its purpose was:

> to sow dissension between Japan and the US; to get the US forces out of Japan; to keep Japan out of any alliance with the West; to keep Japan weak and defenseless in both economic and military terms; to discredit Yoshida; to confuse any and every issue; and to keep intact a ruthless hard-core revolutionary underground apparatus which would be called into action in the event of war or on "the day of revolution."

The Rastvorov Incident

The Communist Party's reliance on subversion and infiltration left Japan particularly vulnerable to Soviet-inspired espionage, and this weakness appears to have been acknowledged by the Japanese government. Certainly, officials in the Gaimushō, shortly after the *Lucky Dragon* incident, were quick to acknowledge that "in regard to the issue of maintaining secrecy . . . there is in our country, no appropriate legal foundation."[53] Moreover, 1954 also provided striking evidence of some of the shortcomings of Japan's domestic security system. On January 24, Yuri Rastvorov, third secretary in the Soviet mission in Japan, but in reality a lieutenant colonel in the Soviet security service, walked out of his office and unexpectedly disappeared into the snow-bound streets of Tokyo. Six months later, on August 14, the Gaimushō's Culture and Information Bureau, together with the Public Security Investigation Agency (Kōan chōsachō) unexpectedly announced that Rastvorov wished to seek refuge in the United States, a claim that Washington rapidly confirmed.[54] While Japan's press had speculated extensively following the third secretary's surprise disappearance and the Russians' reluctant admission that their official had gone missing, it turned out that, behind the scenes, Japanese and American officials had been cooperating to smuggle Rastvorov out of the country and to ensure that the details of his planned defection were not disclosed to the Japanese media. At one level, the incident revealed that Washington and Tokyo were, in particular instances, able to cooperate over security matters.[55] (Some thirty six Gaimushō officials had been assigned to the case.[56]) However, the information provided by Rastvorov following his defection revealed a more troubling general state of affairs. "Operation Earthworm" (as the debriefing exercise was known), and the extensive interrogation reports of the US Army's 441st Counter Intelligence Corps (CIC), documented in vivid and at times lurid detail the scale and character of the espionage campaign directed by the Russian mission.[57]

Rastvorov himself had managed and in some instances personally recruited a wide network of agents within Japan, including Japanese nationals working in both government and the private sector, former "White Russian" émigrés in Japan who either remained stateless Russians or who had renounced their former Czarist allegiances and become "New Soviet citizens," and various members of the US security forces in Japan. The latter provided intelligence of varying usefulness, mainly in return for financial compensation (rather than out of ideological conviction) and often connected with US Air Force deployments and basing arrangements in Japan.[58] In the case of the Russian émigrés, cooperation with the Soviet mission tended to be less explicitly linked to active espionage and included financial support (a number of the operatives had amassed considerable financial fortunes during their time in Japan), procurement of indigenous supplies for the Soviet mission, help in recruiting potential Soviet agents in Japan, and general pro-Soviet propaganda activities through the Society of Russians Residing in Japan.[59] Japanese nationals were generally the most valuable source of intelligence and were targeted in a variety of ways. Rastvorov's detailed debriefing statements revealed that some had been successfully recruited from among individuals attached to the Japanese embassy in Moscow at the end of the war; others were former Japanese prisoners of war who had been "turned" early on during their captivity, required to pledge loyalty oaths to the Soviet Union, and then planted as sleepers within the Japanese government or remarkably, in some cases, in US counter-intelligence in Tokyo, ready to be activated some years after their repatriation to Japan. Many other agents were recruited during the 1952 Japanese general elections when members of the Soviet mission traveled widely throughout Japan on the pretext of observing the voting.[60]

Rastvorov's detailed revelations blew the whistle on the activities of some fairly prominent officials in the Japanese government, including a number of mid-ranking bureaucrats in the Gaimushō, one of whom, Higure Nobunori, dramatically committed suicide by plunging from the fourth floor window of the Tokyo district prosecutor's office during his interrogation.[61] Others involved in the Soviet espionage net included Suzuki Masakata, a lieutenant colonel in the Japanese army who worked for the intelligence section of the US Far Eastern Air Force, Watanabe Zenichirō, the assistant chief of the Europe-America section of the *Mainichi Shinbun*, and former Major Shii Masaji. Shii had been an intelligent and highly regarded staff officer and had served in Mukden during the 1930s. Captured by the Soviets at the end of the war, he was recruited as an agent during his time in a POW camp. He returned to Japan in 1948 and was able, in part by posing as a potential double agent willing to betray his former recruiters, to secure a position first in the geographic section of the intelligence division of the US Far Eastern Command, and ultimately in the Asia Bureau of the Japanese Foreign office. In reality, Shii was functioning as a triple agent: having first made contact with Rastvorov in January 1951, he continued to serve as a particularly valuable source of intelligence information to the Soviets.[62]

Without a doubt Rastvorov's revelations constituted a major counter-espionage coup for the Americans.[63] At the time of his defection, Rastvorov was the highest ranking Soviet official to switch sides in the Cold War.[64] The full public disclosure of Rastvorov's revelations only occurred two years after his defection, when he testified in February 1956 to a US Senate subcommittee, but it was clear to US officials from the very early stages of his debriefing that he would be an unusually valuable source of information. His testimony confirmed that the Soviets had an active program of using Communist front organizations to disseminate Soviet propaganda throughout Japan and routinely liaised with the JCP, providing the party with not insignificant financial assistance.[65] It was also clear that the Soviets had developed a significant espionage presence in the Russian trade mission in Japan and especially in the Tokyo offices of TASS, the Soviet information agency. Much of Soviet espionage activity was concentrated on finding out about US military, especially Air Force installations in Japan. However, some was directed at encouraging organized criminal activity, with money from the Soviet mission used to support a large multinational money-laundering and narcotics ring centered on Kobe and Osaka.[66]

There were, it should be emphasized, limits to what the Russians could accomplish. The mission in Tokyo remained understaffed and poorly funded and with limited Japanese-language expertise; espionage activity was concentrated on collecting rather than analyzing and processing intelligence; and perhaps most important of all, the absence of full diplomatic relations between Moscow and Tokyo rendered the mission's status unclear and somewhat precarious, and the Soviets worried that US counter-intelligence might have had more success in establishing internal influence in many of the organizations and institutions that Moscow was attempting to capture.[67]

The Russian mission's weaknesses notwithstanding, the defection and its revelations were sufficient to prompt US officials at the embassy in Tokyo to write to the State Department in Washington warning that a country lacking a system for managing domestic security might be incapable of developing a modern military, and pointing out not only the shortcomings of the legal system but also the Japanese government's failure to give serious attention to ways of preventing industrial sabotage.

The weakness of intelligence safeguards in Japan helps to explain American reluctance to share sensitive information with their Japanese colleagues. Given the US insistence on maintaining nuclear secrecy, it is easy to appreciate why the Americans would have felt unable to reveal the precise composition of the ash from the BRAVO shot to the Japanese authorities. However, a policy of non-disclosure soon turned into a strategy of disinformation when, on March 31, Lewis Strauss, the Chairman of the AEC and in many respects the public face of the US reaction to the crisis, suggested at a press conference that the symptoms displayed by the ailing fishermen might be the due to the chemical composition of the coral dust from Bikini rather than the result of radiation exposure.[68] On the surface, Strauss's crude assessment seems absurd and hardly calculated to convince either public opinion or the scientific community in Japan, particularly given the country's firsthand experience of the effects of radiation-related illness. A more charitable interpretation might be that the Americans, confronted by the dilemma of not being able to reveal the composition of the dust while also not wishing to antagonize Japan by suggesting either publicly or privately that they could not trust the government to handle secret information, had settled necessarily on a poor compromise solution. Advancing a patently implausible explanation would allow the United States to avoid debating the radiation issue, while Japan's direct experience of caring for the victims of Hiroshima and Nagasaki would allow the Japanese to devise their own effective treatment regime for the *Lucky Dragon* crew-members. If the March 31 press conference were the only instance in which the coral argument was used, it might be simplest to characterize the remark as an off-hand, poorly judged statement. However, as late as April 22 the OCB was itself recommending that the United States "seek to attribute continued illness of Japanese patients to chemical effects of coral dusting rather than radioactivity per se,"[69] lending weight perhaps to the notion that this highly imperfect strategy was a calculated second-best solution.

Whatever the precise motivations behind such statements, it is clear why the Japanese should have been suspicious of American intentions. Yet, at the same time, US officials in Japan undoubtedly recognized that the issue risked running out of control and were conscious of the presentational and symbolic side to the bilateral relationship. Reports from Tokyo warned against taking Japan for granted as a strategic ally,[70] senior embassy officials attended Kuboyama's funeral,[71] and Allison, whatever his own regrets about not issuing an apology immediately, sought to convey the urgency of the situation to his superiors back home.[72] Moreover, there is little reason to question the sincerity and good intentions of the Americans sent out to examine the afflicted fishermen. A detailed Gaimushō report, commenting on the visit by Dr. Morton and the ABCC inspection team to Yaizu, noted that the US officials had behaved "extremely courteously" (*kiwamete shinshiteki de aru*), while other reports on the Yaizu visit pointed out that the Americans had offered to provide treatment for the fishermen only to have the offer rejected by the local doctors. This in turn generated the expression of displeasure from the Americans, prompting a hostile local Japanese response and some of the more critical and "inaccurate" (in the words of the Gaimushō report) press reports—all adding up to mutual US-Japanese misunderstanding which, although difficult to resolve quickly, the Japanese Foreign Ministry was taking pains to settle as smoothly as possible.[73]

The Gaimushō report is particularly relevant because, in general, it confirms the US perception that local conditions in Yaizu were a source of much of the original bilateral tension. On March 22, Merril Eisenbud, the director of the Health and Safety Laboratory of the AEC, had arrived in Japan, en route to Yaizu in order to inspect the hull of the *Lucky Dragon* for signs of radiation exposure. Commenting in general on Eisenbud's visit, the minutes of a joint meeting of the embassy and Far Eastern Command held in Tokyo to assess the state of the crisis noted:

> The Japanese, while accusing the US of desiring to use the injured as "guinea pigs," are in fact doing this themselves. Although it is generally agreed that the hospital in Yaizu is unable to provide adequate treatment for the crew members, professional jealousies and bickering by the local doctors have so far prevented their movement to Tokyo. . . . The press is continuing its emotional outbursts and otherwise responsible scientists and other prominent individuals are indulging in a similar vein.[74]

Moreover, almost a month later there were no signs of any improvement in the situation. At a meeting of the embassy-FEC consultative group, it was clear that the Americans were growing increasingly frustrated with continued inaccurate press reporting and the apparent refusal to acknowledge earlier US offers of assistance:

> Mr. Leonhart . . . summarized the happenings of the last two weeks. He stated that Drs. Eisenbud and Morton left a few days ago after three weeks of Japanese non-cooperation and refusal of US offers of assistance. He referred to stories appearing in the April 21 press stating that the patients were getting worse and *asking for assistance from any quarter.* Mr. Leonhart pointed out that we have been permitted to examine only two patients thoroughly, that we have never been given full information on the patients' condition, that the Japanese have failed to give us promised clinical data and that the offers of assistance by Drs. Morton and Eisenbud and more recently by Dr. Lewis, Chief of Medicine on the Atomic Bomb Casualty Commission, have been ignored. [Emphasis added][75]

US irritation with the local reaction quickly extended into a broader criticism of the Japanese government, based, not on a substantive disagreement with senior government officials, but rather on a sense of poor internal coordination in the Japanese administration[76] and a belief that the Yoshida government was not doing enough to correct the inaccurate and damaging press reports.[77] To what extent was this criticism justified? As far as public and press reaction to the nuclear issue was concerned, it seems fair to assume that much of the reporting was overly speculative, attributing the worst intentions to the Americans.[78] Certainly, post-war Japanese media commentary on the nuclear issue in US-Japanese relations is almost uniformly negative when analyzing US motivations—often in direct contravention of accepted empirical findings[79]—and it does not seem far-fetched to assume that this characteristic "Japan-as-victim" thesis would already have begun to take root by 1954, especially since no consensus had been reached either during or after the Occupation on the vexed question of Japan's responsibility for the Pacific War.

There is some evidence to suggest that the Japanese authorities compounded the crisis and that some senior figures in the government, out of domestic political considerations rather than any particular concern for the well-being of the fishermen, may have deliberately sought to exploit the tension with the United States. In general, the Yoshida government's response appeared to be slow, unfocused, and at times contradictory. Shortly after the crisis broke, a Japanese inter-ministerial committee made up of the principal civil servants from six ministries was established to coordinate the government's response, and in the Diet, the administration maintained a united position, with the foreign minister, Okazaki Katsuo, refusing to condemn the US tests.[80] Yet these early Japanese efforts took place in March. As the American files reveal, by April the government had still failed to counter the spate of damaging press reports. This problem continued throughout the remainder of the year. Senior officials in Washington, while apparently able to reassure their counterparts in Tokyo, were losing the public relations battle with Japan as a whole— a shortcoming the Americans attributed in part to the absence of strong Japanese leadership. As one US report in October noted:

> The complex emotional reactions of the Japanese, particularly as sensationally represented in their press, to United States actions and policies, the threat of nuclear warfare, and the growth of Communist power in Asia have tended more and more to prejudice United States–Japanese relationships. . . . While the Japanese Government has demonstrated a sense of trust and confidence in the willingness and determination of the United States to assist in the realization of Japan's legitimate national aspirations, the failure of the Japanese Government to exert strong leadership, to resolve intra-conservative factionalism and to combat intellectual and neutralist tendencies affords a latent threat to Japan's political stability and consequently to its ability to cooperate effectively with the United States and the free world.[81]

The Japanese government's inability or reluctance to manage the problem might simply have been due to institutional inertia—a shortcoming exacerbated by a tendency to send confusing signals to the Americans. For example, Japanese press reports in late March highlighted internal ministerial tensions in the Japanese government as Foreign Ministry officials struggled unsuccessfully to persuade their Education and Health and Welfare Ministry colleagues to encourage Japan's doctors and scientists to work with US officials in a joint treatment program for the crew of the *Lucky Dragon*.[82] Similar tensions surfaced the following month when the Kyodo wire service leaked news of a forthcoming report from the Ministry of Health and Welfare criticizing American medical personnel for failing to provide treatment for the crew members despite alleged repeated requests from Japan for assistance. Given past US offers of help, it is no surprise that Allison responded immediately to this news, contacting Okazaki, the foreign minister, to protest against the criticism in the strongest possible terms. For their part, the Gaimushō responded quickly, admitting that the report was irresponsible and damaging to bilateral relations, while noting that it would be held back from publication for revision and that in future Foreign Ministry officials would assist the Health and Welfare Ministry in its press briefings.[83]

Notwithstanding the Foreign Ministry's damage control, other issues continued to expose serious internal divisions on the Japanese side. By late May the problem of financial compensation had emerged as a source of disagreement between the two governments. Bilateral negotiations revolved around Japanese pressure for indirect (but at the same time unquantifiable) damages and US irritation at Japan's refusal to agree to a rapid settlement[84]—differences which can in part be attributed to the hard-line position of Andō Masazumi, the minister of state heading Japan's inter-ministerial committee, who, as a former purgee, may have "had personal political motives for publicly rejecting" US offers of compensation and whose combative approach was popular with the Japanese public.[85] Andō's stance was, as Sakamoto Kazuya has pointed out, one among several different views within the government. Although senior Foreign Ministry officials privately informed US embassy personnel that they disagreed with the tactics over compensation,[86] the issue continued to exacerbate an already tense relationship throughout 1954. When Allison was finally able to persuade his superiors in Washington to agree to an increased settlement of $1 million, some on the Japanese side ratcheted up the tension by demanding an additional $1 million in payment, citing as justification the additional time that had elapsed since the start of the compensation talks. Even though both Yoshida and Okazaki privately informed Allison that the increased demand was excessive and not in Japan's long-term interests,[87] the Japanese government appeared powerless to resist pressure from both interest groups (mainly fishermen) and individual ministers (Andō and Hori, the minister of agriculture) for the additional payment and eventually (in January 1955) the United States agreed to a $2 million settlement.

Andō, it should be stressed, was not the only senior Japanese official willing to play to the public gallery. On August 9 and 10, Ikeda Hayato, on two separate occasions—a press conference and a national meeting of all the local branches of the Liberal Party—claimed in off-the-record remarks, critical in tone, that the Geneva conference of June–July had demonstrated the failure of America's "roll-back strategy" (makikaeshi seisaku) of resisting Communism in Vietnam, and that in light of this failure Japan should distance itself from the United States and move closer toward the Soviet Union.[88] The remarks generated little interest in Japan, but were picked up by startled US embassy personnel. A shocked Allison wrote to Washington, noting that Ikeda's remarks suggested that Japan was an unreliable ally, unprincipled and willing to sell itself to the highest bidder.[89] What prompted Ikeda's remarks is not immediately clear. Ishii Osamu (whose work focuses on the US-Japan relationship during the 1950s) has suggested four competing explanations. The remarks may have been internally directed and a way of deflecting criticism of the Yoshida administration from both the Japanese Left and Right, by ostensibly distancing the government from the United States. Less plausibly, the reference may have been merely a slip of the tongue, as Iguchi Sadao (the Japanese ambassador in Washington) suggested to Robert Murphy the US undersecretary of state. Alternatively, Ikeda may have been motivated by purely personal considerations. Yoshida, at this stage, was politically beleaguered and there was widespread speculation that he would soon be eclipsed by rival conservative politicians. Ikeda, as a senior figure in the Liberal Party close to the prime minister, may have been attempting to distance himself from his political mentor while also appealing to other conservative factions. Finally, the critical remarks may have been externally focused. By implying that Japan's commitment to its partnership with the United States was vulnerable, Ikeda may have been angling for further economic assistance from the Americans—an interpretation which would be consistent with Allison's analysis.[90]

Whatever the reason behind Ikeda's comments, there is little doubt that many Japanese conservatives believed that criticizing the United

States was politically advantageous and a way of boosting their electoral chances. By December 7, 1954, Yoshida had resigned as prime minister in the face of steadily declining support for the government and, most important, following the disintegration of the already fragmented conservative forces supporting the Liberal Party. In late November, Hatoyama Ichirō, leader of a splinter group of anti-Yoshida Liberals established in April 1953, had (partly at the prompting of Kishi Nobusuke) formed an alliance with the main conservative opposition group, the Progressive Party, led by Shigemitsu Mamoru. The Hatoyama-Shigemitsu alliance, renamed the Democratic Party, commanded 121 seats in the Diet compared with 185 seats for the Liberals, now formally under the leadership of Ogata Taketora. Yoshida's decision to stand down had opened the way for a general election of the lower house in February 1955 in which the Liberals and Democrats would be fighting not only one another but also the principal left-wing forces represented by the formally separate Left and Right Socialist parties.[91] Anticipating a close electoral contest, a number of leading Japanese conservative politicians, mainly from the Democratic Party, suggested privately to US embassy officials, and with surprising frankness, that in their public pronouncements they might have to sound more critical of the United States than they genuinely felt in order to garner public support. This "last-chance" or "Ichimada thesis" (named after the governor of the Bank of Japan), was, according to the Japanese politicians, based on a belief that the coming election would be the final opportunity for conservative forces to secure a Diet majority sufficiently strong to allow revision of the Occupation-drafted Constitution (a policy favored by the Democratic Party)—a claim which both Dulles and Allison suspected was disingenuous, intended instead to extract politically advantageous concessions from the United States.[92] The implication, in this and earlier incidents, that some of Japan's politicians were willing to treat the alliance in a cavalier fashion for immediate electoral and personal gain, would clearly have done little to strengthen bilateral relations against an already volatile and tension-fraught background.

Scientific Shortcomings

It is important to keep in mind that Japan was not alone in registering intense alarm following the Bikini test. Even before the full circumstances of the *Lucky Dragon* incident had become known, the simple magnitude of the new super-bomb had raised fears worldwide. In Britain, Churchill faced considerable pressure in the Commons from a Labour opposition demanding to be informed of the details of the test and calling for a ban on further testing, and the prime minister himself was deeply disturbed by the weapon, worrying that a single comparable device detonated off the coast of Britain might saturate the country with radioactive fallout. By April, Pope Pius XII and Albert Schweitzer had expressed grave concern and prime minister Nehru of India had joined the chorus of voices advocating a moratorium on testing.[93] However, there were particular elements of the Japanese experience which made the reaction in Japan more pronounced than elsewhere. The bombing of Hiroshima and Nagasaki was obviously a critical factor, but so too was the process of interaction with American authorities, particularly representatives of the ABCC, in the years after 1945. This experience had given the Japanese powerful reasons to discount the findings and advice of the United States in matters relating to radiation exposure.

The critical controversy was the debate over the effects of residual radiation. While it was accepted that massive, instantaneous radiation exposure following the detonation of an atomic bomb would have lethal results for humans, there was no such certainty about the biomedical and genetic effects associated with living in an environment in which background levels of radiation may have increased markedly as a result of an explosion. Shortly after the end of the war, a number of Japanese scientists, some with experience in researching radiobiology, had begun to explore this question, increasingly skeptical (on the basis of their own fieldwork) of US reassurances in 1945 that residual radiation was not harmful. Their efforts were reinforced when the Japanese Welfare Ministry organized a long-range study of the genetic effects of the Hiroshima and Nagasaki bombings. The study led to a series of findings, but because of Occupation censorship these were not published at the time.[94]

Frustrations and suspicions over censorship were aggravated by the approach adopted by US researchers exploring the issue of residual radiation. In 1947, the AEC had launched its own program to examine the long-term effects of the atomic bombing, to be carried out by ABCC officials in Japan.[95] However, as Sue Rabbitt Roff has pointed out in her detailed study, the project was crucially flawed from the very start because of suspect methodology and the distorting professional ambitions of the US scientists engaged in the project, as well as economic pressures and the desire by the federal government to persuade American public opinion of the safety of the emerging nuclear power industry in the United

States—factors which limited the scope of the inquiry. US officials were anxious to avoid any suggestion that background radiation might be in any way harmful—a finding which, it was feared, would encourage a rash of claims for compensation from individuals living close to nuclear power plants.[96] A related reason was a general desire by the American authorities to allay public fears that a possible future conflict involving nuclear weapons would be catastrophic. In the early years of the nuclear era, as part of the developing civil defense program and in order to support claims that a nuclear war was winnable, the US government sought to persuade the American public of the survivability of an atomic attack by detailing practical steps for guarding against the dangers of radiation.[97]

In light of these serious shortcomings, it is understandable why both in 1954 and subsequently, the ABCC was viewed with suspicion by some in Japan. Bound up in this distrust were a set of emotional issues that almost inevitably ensured that the American scientists would receive a cool reception. From the perspective of the ABCC, examining the survivors of the atomic bombings was purely a scientific exercise—it had no humanitarian dimension. For the affected civilians, by contrast, there was the much more immediate and personal need to receive treatment and care from the informed and technologically sophisticated Americans. Since the US government had designed, built, and deployed the bomb, surely it would be fair to assume that it could, if not should, help those who had been exposed to its effects.

Over time, State Department officials (including Allison) did recognize the need to provide assistance to the Japanese, but the assistance appears to have been motivated largely by a desire to reduce antagonism toward the ABCC and also to encourage more individuals to participate in the biomedical research program. Moreover, the initiative came late in the day.[98] In 1954, the ABCC had no adequate facilities for examining patients other than a small and understaffed diagnostic clinic,[99] and the first serious efforts to cooperate with the Japanese government occurred only in November 1955, involving mainly the provision of ABCC data, the offer of medical consultations for A-bomb survivors, and the creation of a Japanese Advisory Council (JAC) to the ABCC.[100] Cooperation increased gradually as the Japanese, in conjunction with the development of their own health care program, agreed in 1957 to refer increasing numbers of patients to the ABCC.[101] However, the degree of common effort should not be exaggerated. It was only in the early 1960s that a joint document (endorsed by both the ABCC and the Japanese government) was issued—one of the earliest cases of the publication of results simultaneously in Japanese and English—but even in this instance, the study employed the same flawed assumptions as the initial American studies.[102]

From the perspective of Japanese public opinion, it would be easy to conclude that the unhelpful and misleading American approach on the residual radiation issue was directed at Japan—proof, in effect, that US interest in a cooperative alliance relationship was synthetic rather than genuine. Yet this would be to misinterpret a general weakness in American policy as a specific failing in the bilateral relationship. It is important to recognize that much of the US nuclear program—both testing and the development of nuclear power—placed the concerns of the federal government and the demands associated with the Cold War ahead of the interests of individuals and communities, both within and outside the United States. American civilians as much as foreign nationals were caught in the literal and broader environmental fallout associated with the intense political and strategic pressures to develop the power of the atom, and it is worth emphasizing that nuclear tests continued within the continental United States after the CASTLE series, often involving cases where the AEC deliberately minimized or distorted the health risks associated with testing.[103] Japan had not been singled out for special treatment, whatever Japanese popular fears and press reports may have suggested. Naturally, this raises the larger question of how much of the US nuclear program was based on self-deception and a refusal to scrutinize inconvenient scientific findings and how much rested on a willful disregard of the dangers associated with nuclear testing in general. The problem is a complex one and cannot be resolved here. However, setting the events of 1954 in this context helps to clarify the motivations and reactions of the Japanese and American participants. State Department officials in Tokyo, for example, confronted by the pressures of daily diplomacy, were unlikely to have had any reason to question the advice they were receiving from their scientific advisors in Washington, nor would they have been privy to the wider detailed debate taking place between physicists and radiobiologists—a controversy which, after all, would take more than a decade to resolve.[104] Under these circumstances, it is perhaps reasonable to argue that the *Lucky Dragon* crisis was virtually unavoidable. Contrary to the suggestion of some commentators at the time that the United States could have side-stepped much of the controversy if it had acted in a more straightforward fashion,[105] a combination of chance events and conflicting global pressures and local sensibilities inevitably triggered a major diplomatic incident.

Individual Attitudes

The importance of context should not overshadow the role of individuals in either exacerbating or moderating the crisis. On the US side, Lewis Strauss, the head of the AEC, can be singled out for censure. A number of his public remarks (in addition to his suggestion that coral rather than radiation was the cause of the fishermen's symptoms), including the claim that the *Lucky Dragon* was well within the danger zone at the time of the explosion, together with a manner of presentation that was unsympathetic and "tended to belittle the implications of fallout on . . . the Japanese," particularly antagonized opinion in Japan.[106] In private conversations with US administration officials, Strauss showed no inclination to appreciate the Japanese position, and in certain instances he may even have intentionally misled his colleagues. To Jim Hagerty, Eisenhower's press secretary, he argued that the *Lucky Dragon* was a "Red spy ship" (repeating a claim made by Congressman W. Sterling Cole which had already provoked an angry response within Japan),[107] while in a telephone conversation with Dulles, on March 29, he painted an overly positive picture of the test result, arguing, "Nothing was out of control. Nothing devastated"—an assessment which prompted a quick rebuttal from the secretary of state, who observed blandly that "that was not correct from our point of view. Japan and England are upset."[108] Strauss also pointed out to Dulles that the fishing vessel was within the warning range—a curious statement (especially since he repeated it in a press conference two days later) in light of the March 30 OCB report that the ship had been fourteen miles outside the test zone.[109]

Strauss was firmly committed to the development of all aspects of America's nuclear program and, it has been argued, also "an accomplished twister of truth with a passionate interest in securing the outcome he did."[110] His penchant for deception was evident in a number of instances. Dr. Eugene Cronkite, for example, the head of a US medical team sent to the Marshall Islands to treat the local population following the BRAVO shot, recalls raising with Strauss his concern that the *New York Times* was deliberately publishing falsehoods in underplaying in its reports the severity of the exposure experienced by the islanders. Strauss, in a statement which strongly suggests knowledge of this deception, merely responded, "Young man, you have to remember that nobody reads yesterday's newspapers."[111] Similarly, Strauss appears to have worked behind the scenes to oppose "Operation Candor"—the Eisenhower administration's policy of partially releasing information relating to nuclear issues and designed to allay public fears in the United States. In the process, indirectly and subtly, Strauss was challenging the President's own position.[112]

Strauss's behavior, while reprehensible, is perhaps not especially surprising. The AEC as a whole showed little compassion for the Japanese fishermen[113]—and certainly none of the concern expressed by Allison and the State Department personnel in Japan. Strauss's role in the crisis was undoubtedly harmful and represents an instance when Eisenhower's distinctive leadership style, in particular the reliance he placed on selecting effective and trusted subordinates, had broken down.[114] As happened in the Oppenheimer controversy—when J. Robert Oppenheimer, a leading scientist, government advisor, and in many respects the father of the US nuclear program, had his security clearance revoked and reputation unjustly and perhaps irrevocably undermined because of unfounded claims (encouraged by Strauss) that he was a Communist sympathizer—Eisenhower had been "decisively misled."[115] The President erred in not overruling or reigning in the head of the AEC, and his memoirs repeat the mistaken assertion that the *Lucky Dragon* was inside the test area when the Bikini bomb was detonated.[116]

Judging from his public responses, Eisenhower either had not been especially troubled by the *Lucky Dragon* incident or was deliberately adopting a cautious attitude. In two press conferences held on March 17 and 24, shortly after news of the accident had been publicized, the President said very little, declining, in the first instance, to comment before he had received further information and, in the second, referring journalists to earlier comments by Strauss.[117] However, in private Eisenhower displayed considerable concern, clearly troubled by the risks associated with the new, powerful generation of nuclear weapons. Responding to a letter from Churchill, the President noted on March 19:

> You are quite right in your estimate of my grave concern at the steady increase in methods of mass destruction. Whether or not the specific possibilities of devastation that you mentioned are indeed demonstrated capabilities, the prospects are truly appalling. Ways of lessening or, if possible, of eliminating the danger must be found. That has been my principal preoccupation throughout the last year.[118]

Eisenhower was also not alone in recognizing the dramatic and destabilizing repercussions from the massive explosion in the Pacific. Dulles, in conversation with Strauss, warned the AEC chairman to bear in mind

> the tremendous repercussions these things have. It should be kept under control. The general impression around the world is we are appropriating a vast area of the ocean for our use depriving other people of its use. . . . [I]t would be a good thing if something could be said to moderate the wave of hysteria. It is driving our Allies away from us. They think we are getting ready for a war of this kind. We could survive but some of them would be obliterated within a few minutes. It could lead to a policy of neutrality or appeasement.[119]

Resolving the Crisis

Any balanced assessment of America's handling of the *Lucky Dragon* incident needs to consider what more the Eisenhower administration could, or should, have done to dampen bilateral tensions. Senior US government figures, including the President, were well aware of the delicate state of relations with Japan in 1954, but to some extent their hands were tied. The very weakness of the Yoshida administration and the confused state of Japanese domestic politics acted as a constraint, preventing a rapid solution. A stronger government in Tokyo, it could be argued, would have been better placed to defuse some of the more strident press criticism of the United States, as well as to take firmer action to ensure a speedier resolution of the compensation issue than eventually occurred.[120]

Yoshida's problems, in part, simply reflected the continued decline in popularity of the Liberal Party—a steady trend since 1949.[121] April 1953 saw the start of the fifth Yoshida cabinet—the previous premier had been Ashida Hitoshi who had served in that capacity for only six months, from March to October 1948—and by the beginning of 1954, the administration appeared to be nearing the end of its natural life.[122] By the spring, a damaging "shipbuilding scandal" (zōsen gigoku) had been exposed, in which two of Yoshida's senior faction members, Satō Eisaku and Ikeda Hayato, were implicated. By the end of April, it seemed inevitable that Satō would be arrested, but at the last minute the Justice Ministry, citing executive privilege, intervene and prevented the Public Prosecutor's Office from carrying out the arrest. Satō's political career was saved, but the reputation of the government was seriously tarnished.[123] The government's poor public image was further undermined in a political fight over its attempt to introduce legislation limiting the autonomy of local police forces and creating a National Public Safety Commission. The legislation was bitterly opposed by Socialist politicians, and the controversy erupted into physical scuffles in the Diet and the forced detention of the Speaker of the lower house in an effort by the Socialists to prevent an extension of the Diet session—needed to pass the legislation. The new measures were only enacted following police intervention and a Socialist boycott of the Diet proceedings.[124] Amidst all this controversy, Yoshida had been forced to postpone until November a visit to Europe and the United States which he had been hoping to make during the summer.

It would be tempting to explain Yoshida's problems and the absence of stable government in Japan as simply a reflection of the prime minister's personal unpopularity. "One-man" Yoshida was perceived as arrogant and was a popular target for critics on both the Right and the Left—either for appearing too dependent on the United States or for attempting to introduce legislative measures which the Socialist and Communists viewed as illiberal and anti-democratic. However, Yoshida's difficulties reflected a deeper set of problems. As the intense conflict over the new police legislation revealed, much of the polarization between the forces of the Left and Right during 1954 revolved around the question of the Constitution and the legacy of the Occupation. To the Right, MacArthur's Constitution was seen as an alien document, imposed from outside and at odds with Japanese culture and tradition, and a broad swathe of conservative politicians (not only Yoshida but also, most notably, Hatoyama Ichirō and Kishi Nobusuke) were strongly in favor of constitutional revision. For the Left, by contrast, the Constitution represented a bulwark against the past, preventing any return to the militarism and reactionary trends of the 1930s while safeguarding the values of freedom and democratic government.

Under these conditions, one might have imagined a US government inclined to support moderate left-of-center political opinion—individuals committed to the democratic process but also critical of the autocratic character of Soviet or Chinese Communism. Yet such forces did not exist (at least not in a prominent, influential capacity), and the Left-Right split in Japan never resembled such a neat, analytically convenient dichotomy. The Japan Communist Party, weakened by doctrinal differences and Japanese public opinion's distrust of its radicalism, had experienced a massive decline in political influence—between 1949 and 1953, JCP Lower House Diet seats dropped from 35 to one.[125] The Socialists, on the other hand, had seen their electoral fortunes steadily improve after 1949, and while Liberal support had fallen consistently over this period, it was off-set by the increase in the popularity of the non-Liberal conservative parties.[126] Moreover, Left and Right continued to be fiercely divided over ideological issues and there was no sign of a consensus on the structures and institutions which should govern Japanese political life.[127] As the OCB observed in October: "The instability now being displayed in Japan is in essence the result of the nation's attempt to adjust traditional values and practices to the new laws and ideas stemming from defeat in war and occupation."[128] Indeed, a dramatic illustration of the increasingly controversial legacy of the Occupation was the marked decline in the reputation of General MacArthur. In March, press reports had suggested that the former Supreme Commander of the Allied Powers might be planning a visit to Japan, and Allison, following an unexpected conversation with Aso Kazuko (Yoshida's daughter and confidante) as well as with a senior Foreign Ministry official, had written swiftly to Dulles to recommend that the visit not go ahead. Aso, Allison observed, had been, "horrified" at the news and had said that the visit would "certainly give father some more grey hairs." It was clear, according to the ambassador, that any mystique the Occupation may have had had long since disappeared:

> Contrary to the general impression in the United States, at least among certain members of Congress as reported yesterday by United Press, General MacArthur's name in Japan does not remain "magic." If he should come, I am afraid he would not find it as pleasant as he might anticipate. There would be considerable press criticism and while the government would undoubtedly put on a big show for him and be perfectly correct, there would be but little enthusiasm for it. Since the General's departure, there has been an increasing amount of public and private criticism of his action while here and there is no longer any pretence in the Japanese press or public discussion that the present Japanese Constitution was not "made in America" or rather in SCAP Headquarters.[129]

Under these conditions there was little, if anything, that Washington could do overtly to promote political stability within Japan.[130] However, behind the scenes, the United States employed a range of measures designed to strengthen Japanese ties with America as well as counterbalance the appeal of the Left and the alleged effects of Soviet-directed propaganda initiatives. The Fulbright and Smith-Mundt exchange programs brought Japanese teachers and researchers to the United States; the United States Information Agency (USIA) established information centers in Japan's major cities which were widely used by Japanese citizens (four-

teen centers existed in 1954); Voice of America broadcasts were frequently relayed over the domestic network; indirect support was provided
for the translation and publication of English-language material in Japanese; prominent Japanese were contacted in an effort to promote the US
position; USIA funding subsidized anti-Communist periodicals and films;
and unattributed written material was provided to Japanese writers and
editors in an effort to encourage favorable commentary in the media.[131]

Many of these initiatives reflected the legacy of the Psychological
Strategy Board (PSB), set up during the Truman administration and the
forerunner of the Operations Coordinating Board. In April 1952, planners from the CIA and the State and Defense departments had begun
work on designing a psychological strategy directed at Japan which by
early January 1953 led to the approval of PSB D-27.[132] The precise content of this plan remains unclear, since the document has yet to be declassified. However, by 1954, senior figures in the administration recognized
the limits of America's own propaganda machinery, and in October Walter Robertson wrote to Allison bemoaning the "diminishing objectivity in
Japanese vernacular press reporting," while arguing that PSB D-27 was
insufficiently detailed and would, therefore, be reassessed by the OCB.[133]

Despite the shortcomings of the early PSB initiative, there was one area
in which a concerted public relations campaign might work in America's
favor. Ever since Eisenhower's "Atoms for Peace" speech before the
United Nations in December 1953, in which the President had proposed
that the nuclear powers provide fissile material for peaceful purposes to a
new International Atomic Energy Agency, the United States had been well
placed to promote the non-offensive merits of nuclear energy.[134] In terms
of the relationship with Japan, this campaign could take the form of
working with the Japanese government to develop a civilian nuclear
power program. Early in the post-war period, the Japanese scientific community was ready to pursue research into nuclear issues,[135] and by 1954,
shortly after news of the *Lucky Dragon* incident came out, US officials
recognized that sharing nuclear technology with Japan might help contain
the resulting crisis. An OCB report of March 22, for example, recommended that the United States should offer to build an experimental nuclear reactor in Japan, pointing out that "a vigorous offensive on the non-
war uses of atomic energy would appear to be a timely and effective way
of countering the expected Russian [propaganda] effort and minimizing
the harm already done in Japan."[136]

During 1954, the US embassy in Japan launched a series of initiatives promoting the virtues of nuclear energy which appeared to be positively received by the Japanese public. A small atomic energy exhibition in Tokyo, for example, attracted large crowds,[137] while a similar display in Toyama, between April and June, also passed off peacefully—"no hostility and no incidents resulted"—attracting more than 800,000 visitors.[138] Seminars, lectures, films, and displays were organized in Tokyo and "attracted very favorable response and hearty participation by responsible Japanese scientists and intellectual and civic leaders. Over 100,000 people have been directly reached by these activities, which included ward by ward showing of atomic energy films and insertion of these films in a mass 'peace' rally in Tokyo."[139] USIA and embassy officials in Japan were quick to stress the benefits of promoting peaceful nuclear power, arguing that "the great majority of Japanese are receptive to US information on the peaceful uses of atomic energy, provided that it is presented creditably and with due respect for Japanese sensibilities."[140] Moreover, US efforts were well received by both official and public opinion. In October, the Japanese government made clear to the United States that it would respond positively to a planned proposal to establish a small experimental reactor in Japan for educational purposes,[141] and by early 1955 it was clear to the Americans that the Japanese authorities were focused on developing, with US support, their own nuclear power program. As a State Department intelligence report noted, "the Japanese reacted most favorably to hints that the United States might assist in a reactor development program in Japan and have appropriated funds and dispatched experts to this country and Europe in an effort to further their atomic energy development."[142]

In general, the Americans recognized the importance of working in close cooperation with the Japanese authorities in the area of peaceful development of nuclear energy, and by late 1955 there were signs that the distrust that had been so prominent during 1954 had begun to abate. Promoting nuclear energy was a sustained initiative in which US officials took pains to provide reliable information, and as a USIA report from Tokyo observed:

> The Agency's largest and best exhibit on atomic energy opened in Tokyo, November 1, under joint sponsorship with Yomiuri newspaper and with opening messages from the President and other high US and Japanese officials. This exhibit is complete, accurate and clear enough to satisfy a discriminating scientist. It will tour Japan for at least a year and should make a lasting impression on intellectuals and public alike.[143]

Extolling the virtues of nuclear energy was, it should be stressed, only a partial means of tackling Japan's nuclear allergy. Testing remained a controversial issue (both in Japan and worldwide), and in August 1955 some 30 million Japanese signed a petition calling for a total ban on nuclear testing.[144] Yet the United States remained committed to developing its nuclear arsenal and in early 1956 announced plans to carry out a new series of thermonuclear tests in the Pacific. Surprisingly, the American announcement provoked little immediate press commentary in Japan, partly because Washington leaked the news of the tests gradually (the embassy in Tokyo had informed the Japanese Foreign Ministry well in advance), and also because the Diet was out of session, ensuring that the Socialists and groups most strongly opposed to testing were poorly placed to respond swiftly. Also, America was not alone. The Russians had recently carried out nuclear tests and the British had publicized their own plans to carry out tests in Australian waters. Moreover, two years of association with the development of the peaceful uses of nuclear power may have encouraged the Japanese public to feel less isolated and singled out in terms of exposure to the harmful effects of testing. As Allison noted in a cable to Dulles, "Japan has been brought into international 'atomic community' as participant—no longer stands on outside as unwilling observer or 'innocent victim.'"[145]

Nevertheless, US officials were taking no chances in preparing for the tests. The experience of 1954 had clearly impressed on them the need to give special consideration to Japanese sensibilities. Jeff Parsons wrote to Washington from Tokyo to recommend a series of precautionary measures including: providing funding to cover the expenses of Japanese ships forced to make detours to avoid the test site; acknowledging that the United States was willing to provide ex-gratia compensation if any damage should result from the test; and inviting the Japanese government to participate in a scientific survey to check for the possible contamination of fish in the region of the tests. Even with such measures, Parsons feared that reaction in Japan would almost certainly be negative. State Department personnel were well aware of the risk of a repetition of the events of 1954 and displayed an almost fatalistic expectation that events might spiral out of control again. In Parsons's words:

> It now appears inevitable that test series will create in Japan serious political and propaganda problems even without repetition of the Fukuryu Maru incident. . . . Probably needless to point out that should unforeseen incident occur as a result of tests (e.g. contamination of fish or injury to fishing craft) reac-

tion here would be immediate and explosive and our efforts to counteract after the fact would very likely be almost completely unsuccessful.[146]

Washington appeared to take the State Department's advice seriously and sought to defuse the crisis in advance. An official note was issued to the Japanese authorities, incorporating some of Parsons's suggestions as well as highlighting past international initiatives by the Eisenhower administration to limit the spread of nuclear weapons and monitor the effects of radiation.[147] In the end, the embassy's fears were not confirmed, and in general the Japanese response to the tests was relatively muted, or at least mixed. While politicians and press reports criticized the United States, there was no wave of critical editorials and front-page attention comparable to that in 1954, and some papers, such as *Yomiuri Shinbun*, even highlighted the "over-nervousness" of some Japanese to the issue of radioactivity.[148] Moreover, the Japanese government, although opposed to the tests in principle, attempted to allay fears in advance and went out of its way to head off any damaging political repercussions. For example, prior to the tests, the Japanese authorities announced publicly that they would seek to coordinate test arrangements with the United States. Similarly, the Health and Welfare Ministry was careful to point out that the radioactivity ingested in the Bikini tests of 1954 had not been sufficient to warrant destroying fish stocks, and a Japanese survey vessel, staffed by scientists, was sent to the test area to monitor the results of the explosion.[149]

In the wake of the *Lucky Dragon* incident, it is difficult to determine precisely the extent to which US actions alone averted further crises over the nuclear issue, either in 1956 or subsequently. Both governments, it seemed, had learned valuable lessons from the events of 1954 and were concerned to avoid exposing the bilateral relationship to unnecessary strain. At the same time, testing remained a contentious issue during the second half of the decade. For example, the administration of Kishi Nobusuke (prime minister after February 1957) was concerned about the global risks associated with nuclear fallout and publicly pushed for an end to, or at the very least a suspension of, testing, both in the Pacific and the continental United States,[150] and the Diet periodically issued resolutions calling for an end to testing and in favor of nuclear disarmament. In response, the United States tended to discount the wider health hazards while restating the importance of strategic readiness and technological sophistication.[151] However, senior American policy-makers remained well aware of the sensitivity of the nuclear issue in Japan. Eisenhower, at the suggestion of his secretary of state, was careful to write publicly to Kishi setting out the US position in favor of continued testing,[152] while Dulles himself took pains on occasion to demonstrate American appreciation of the Japanese position.[153]

Remarkably, in 1958 there was a near repeat performance of the 1954 disaster. During nuclear tests near Eniwetok in the Marshall Islands, two Japanese Maritime Safety Bureau ships, despite being well outside the test zone, were exposed to radiation levels sufficiently high to cause a considerable drop in the white blood-cell counts of some of the crew members.[154] At the time, US officials—including the ambassador in Tokyo, Douglas MacArthur II—were all too conscious of the risk this posed to bilateral relations. Yet, remarkably, "the tests were concluded without arousing serious Japanese opposition or creating serious friction between the United States and Japan."[155] The absence of tension was noteworthy not only because of the irradiation of the Japanese sailors, but also in light of the Soviet Union's announcement of its unilateral suspension of testing and the publication by the United Nations Scientific Community of a report analyzing the effects of radiation—two events which, one imagines, might also have swung public opinion against the United States. Yet, while the Japanese remained "opposed to nuclear testing, their opposition [was] . . . now largely passive in character."[156]

Part of the reason for the lack of a Japanese reaction may have been the altered international political context in which testing was taking place. Since 1957, Eisenhower had publicly become much more actively committed to seeking a solution to the question of testing. In April 1958, he had proposed setting up an international committee of experts to explore ways of monitoring and enforcing a possible international test ban, and by August he had announced that the United States would temporarily halt testing for a year if the Soviets agreed to do the same.[157] In April 1959, Eisenhower went one step further and proposed to Khrushchev a limited ban on atmospheric testing. Agreement between Moscow and Washington on a partial test ban treaty would eventually be reached in 1963 during the Kennedy administration. It is conceivable that Japanese opinion in 1958 was influenced by the earlier US initiatives, although they were surely not the only reason for the subdued Japanese reaction to the Eniwetok test. It seems reasonable to conclude that the US initiative to encourage the development of a peaceful nuclear power industry, as well as American efforts to inform Japanese public and official opinion of future tests, while taking precautions to guard against future disasters, may have removed some of the tension and distrust that was prominent in 1954. None of this, of course, excuses the very real failings of the United States in handling the *Lucky Dragon* incident initially. However, these earlier shortcomings were linked to issues that went beyond the bilateral relationship—most notably, Cold War strategic priorities, institutional hubris, scientific shortcomings, and the blinkered approach to testing in general as well as the pressure to develop the nuclear industry within the United States. Additional crucial ingredients were weak leadership and domestic political instability in Japan, caused in part by the ideological tension associated with MacArthur's Constitution. Responsibility for the crisis therefore rests with the governments of both Japan and the United States, and in certain important respects predates the decisions of the Eisenhower administration. Consequently, although it is legitimate to attack particular American actions in 1954, Washington's handling of the bilateral relationship, when viewed in a wider context, should be interpreted less critically.

CHAPTER SIX

Rearmament, Security, and Domestic Politics, 1953–60

Retrospective assessments of US-Japan relations in the 1950s have frequently focused on the debate over rearmament as a sign of the fundamentally unequal character of the bilateral relationship and in particular the American government's tendency to propose policy options at odds with the national interests of Japan—a formally sovereign but, in practical terms, junior and dependent East Asian partner. Undoubtedly, the Security Treaty of 1952 was favorable to the United States, principally in allowing Washington to station troops in Japan without a formal commitment to defend Japan or a definite time frame for the treaty. However, Japanese disaffection with the security relationship developed only gradually during the decade, and the Security Treaty itself (as chapter two has demonstrated) was very much a response to immediate conditions rather than an effort to prescribe a long-term bilateral defense relationship. A gap certainly existed during the 1950s between the US Joint Chiefs of Staff's rearmament projections for the Japanese military and the preferences of Japan's leading conservative politicians, for whom economic and political constraints at home and an ostensibly less pessimistic assessment of the strategic situation in East Asia justified a more modest defense build-up.

However, it would be a mistake to view this difference in outlook as proof of a major and monolithic clash of interests between the two governments. Senior US officials, mainly State Department officials (in Japan and Washington), cautioned against pressuring Japan to rearm, although public statements by Dulles sometimes suggested a more pronounced difference of opinion between the two governments than that revealed by the private record. Moreover, the difficulty in fostering effective bilateral security cooperation was very much the result of serious divisions among the Japanese political leadership and bureaucracy, whose multiplicity of views seriously complicated the process of devising coherent Japanese proposals not only over the rearmament question but also in defining national security policy more broadly—a problem which arguably continued to affect Japan's defense policy in the 1990s. In addition to the general debate over rearmament (most notably the mutual security assistance talks of 1953–54), these shortcomings are particularly strikingly reflected in a number of incidents and negotiations, namely Foreign Minister Shigemitsu's efforts in 1955 to initiate bilateral negotiations on a new Security Treaty; the Soviet-Japanese normalization talks of 1956 and their impact on relations between Washington and Tokyo; and the extended process of Security Treaty revision beginning in 1957 and culminating in the ratification of a new US-Japan Mutual Security Treaty in the spring of 1960. These events highlight why, despite the best efforts of ambassadors Allison and MacArthur, the bilateral relationship continued to encounter difficulties during the 1950s, many of which reflected the negative legacy of the reforms of the Occupation and the ideological schism in Japanese politics over the question of constitutional revision. Domestic political tension throughout the decade and the personal ambitions and confusing signals given by individual Japanese politicians, as much as conflicting national policies, created obstacles to building a purposeful and energetic alliance partnership in East Asia.

Debating Rearmament and the Creation of Japan's Self-Defense Forces

In agreeing to a Security Treaty with the United States in September 1951, the Japanese government acknowledged, in the words of the treaty, an "expectation" that Japan would increase its defense capabilities once sovereignty had been restored.[1] From America's perspective, the Cold War and the continuing Korean conflict required not only a logistical and strategic base in the Far East but also an allied partner willing to contribute militarily to the containment of international Communism. As early as May 1951, the Truman administration approved recommendations by the JCS for a ten-division National Police Reserve (NPR—Japan's fledgling military forces), and in Tokyo, General Matthew Ridgway (MacArthur's replacement as SCAP) argued that the Japanese authorities could increase their existing manpower from 75,000 to between 150,000 and 180,000 during 1952–53, conceivably reaching 300,000 to 325,000 by the end of Japan's 1953 fiscal year.[2] The Yoshida government, while not officially accepting these figures, agreed informally to increase the NPR to approximately 110,000 during June or July of 1952, and representatives of the prime minister apparently "accepted as logical" a US-proposed troop level of 180,000 by March 31, 1953.[3] Initially, at least, there seemed to be scope for effective military cooperation between America and Japan. Ridgway, while well aware of the substantial economic and political obstacles in the way of rapid Japanese rearmament, approved of the prime minister's willingness to work with the United States, pointing out that Yoshida was "cooperating as much as possible in expanding and otherwise developing the NPRJ."[4] Moreover, in August 1952, Yoshida authorized the transformation of the NPR into the National Safety Agency (NSA or Hoanchō), and in late October the prime minister assured Ambassador Murphy that he intended to revise Article 9 of the Japanese Constitution (limiting Japan's explicit right to maintain armed forces) and confidently declared that "such revision would occur in the comparatively near future."[5]

By early 1953, the optimism of the previous year had begun to fade. In Washington, the Joint Chiefs, in submitting recommendations for the US government's Mutual Defense Assistance Program of 1954, had already drafted more ambitious goals for Japan, suggesting a ground force complement of 300,000 troops arranged in ten divisions, the provision of 75 naval vessels, and the establishment of a 27-squadron air force.[6] In Tokyo, General Mark Clark (Ridgway's successor as CinCFE) sounded notably less positive than his predecessor, expressing concern (both in discussions with the Japanese authorities and in his cables to his military superiors at home) at the long delays in increasing Japan's ground forces to the previously agreed level of 110,000 troops.[7]

Within the State Department, John Allison (serving as assistant secretary of state prior to his appointment as ambassador to Japan) recognized the difficulties in developing Japan's defenses but was quick to caution against exerting too much pressure on the Japanese authorities[8]—a position consistent with earlier State Department policy during the Peace and Security Treaty negotiations and also endorsed by Dulles. As the secretary of state noted in early March:

> The Department is concerned over the failure of the Japanese Government to take a more positive approach on defence questions, but appreciates the limi-

tations imposed by the present political climate and wishes to avoid any pressure on the Yoshida Government which may jeopardize its position and result in longer delays in the defence buildup.[9]

Dulles's problems in relation to the rearmament question were twofold. His first challenge was to avoid any initiatives which might appear overly interventionist or likely to jeopardize the position of a Liberal government vulnerable to criticism from both the Japanese Left and rival conservative groups, most notably Shigemitsu Mamoru's Progressive Party and Hatoyama's anti-Yoshida Liberal splinter group. This was especially important given the forthcoming Lower House elections scheduled for April 1953. The State Department's sensitivity over the issue, as well as its relative bureaucratic weight within the new Eisenhower administration, was in some measure reflected in NSC 125/6, approved in June 1953. The document largely reaffirmed the Japan-policy prescriptions of NSC 125/2 (formally agreed in August 1952), but it added the important proviso that continuing US "efforts to encourage the Japanese to develop defense forces [should be] consistent with the economic capability of Japan."[10] The State Department, with (it should be noted) the important backing of the President,[11] had successfully resisted the more uncompromising position of the Pentagon, which had starkly recommended an accelerated Japanese defense build-up with no allowance for Japan's poor economic conditions.

Dulles's concern not to intervene in Japanese domestic politics was also reflected in his care to avoid any public suggestion that the United States might favor constitutional revision by Japan. In Autumn 1953, Vice-President Nixon, while on a visit to Japan as part of a larger Far Eastern tour, had unexpectedly announced publicly that it had been a mistake during the Occupation for the United States to seek a permanently demilitarized Japan—a suggestion positively received by conservative Japanese political opinion but, since it also implied US endorsement of constitutional change, criticized by the Left and by the media.[12] Although a revision of Article 9 might have aided US rearmament plans, Dulles preferred to justify Japan's right to self-defense in terms of Article 51 of the UN Charter and was insistent that the State Department would "never say a word about amending the Japanese Constitution"—a position consistent with Japanese political realities in 1953.[13]

Dulles's second challenge was to persuade Congress to approve adequate financial appropriations to support Japan's rearmament efforts. There was little doubt that Japan was suffering economically. Foreign trade in April 1953 was well below pre-war levels, with imports at about one-half and exports one-third of the 1938 volume, and in 1952 Japan had experienced a commercial trade deficit of approximately $750 million. Continued US military expenditure in both South Korea and Japan was expected to counterbalance this trade deficit, but precious few resources would remain for military expansion.[14] Some $525 million was available under existing US Army appropriations for the 1953 fiscal year (enough to assist in the creation of a six-division, 180,000-man ground force), but further funding would require new legislative approval, and under the provisions of the Mutual Security Act of 1951, governing overseas military assistance, a separate bilateral agreement between the Japanese and US governments would need to be negotiated and signed before aid, equipment, or services could be provided to Japan during fiscal 1954.[15] Although the Eisenhower administration was eager to limit its defense spending (a goal that found logical expression in the New Look's emphasis on nuclear deterrence and the conscious effort to persuade America's allies to assume some of the burdens associated with conventional military preparedness), foreign military aid had increased in the first year of the new Republican government. In fiscal 1951, spending on military assistance stood at $5.2 billion. In fiscal 1952, it had risen to $5.3 billion, and even though it declined to $3.2 billion in 1954, only in 1955 did it begin to be overtaken by spending on economic and other assistance.[16] The Mutual Security Act (MSA) was an extension of the Mutual Defense Assistance Act of 1949 and symbolized the transition from primarily economic aid (expressed in Western Europe via the Marshall Plan and, in the case of Occupied Japan, by the "Government and Relief in Occupied Area"—or GARIOA—fund) to military assistance, following the outbreak of the Korean War. Providing aid to Japan under MSA was in no sense a novel development. The United States had already reached a series of comparable agreements with countries in both Europe and Latin America. However, the Japanese case was distinctive in two important respects, namely the constraints associated with Article 9 of Japan's Constitution and the Japanese government's reluctance to participate in collective security initiatives. Section 511 of the Mutual Security Act required that signatory states agree to six principal conditions, including a willingness to develop and maintain the defense capabilities of individual countries and the free world as a whole.[17] The latter condition might be construed as obliging Japan to violate its constitutional principles and was an important focus for negotiations between America and Japan beginning in the summer of 1953.

In March 1953, the JCS authorized General Clark and Ambassador Allison to begin talks with the Japanese government to establish a bilateral military assistance agreement.[18] Once the Lower House elections were safely concluded, the Gaimushō was eager to begin discussions, and negotiations opened in Tokyo in July. The US authorities had hoped that some agreement might have been reached on force goals prior to discussions on military aid, but matters remained unresolved and the State Department allowed Allison and Clark discretion to seek a commitment from the Japanese, either formally or verbally, to build up their defenses.[19] The prospects for rapid progress (from an American perspective) were not especially promising. John Steeves, the first secretary in the embassy in Tokyo, pointed out that a number of the leading Japanese newspapers, in particular *Asahi Shinbun*, were opposed to MSA, while a US Army intelligence report of July 7 emphasized that political opposition, both conservative and left-wing, to Yoshida's leadership (especially the prime minister's tendency to make decisions without full Diet discussion) significantly hindered an agreement on rearmament or military assistance. Yoshida's Liberals[20] held only 202 of 466 seats in the Lower House, and had to contend not only with a Left Socialist Party (vehemently opposed to rearmament of any kind) and a Right Socialist Party (in favor of a reduction in Japan's forces from 110,000 to 75,000 troops), but also with resistance from 77 Progressive Party Lower House representatives and the 35 members of Hatoyama's Liberal group.[21] Although these rival conservative groups favored a faster rate of rearmament than that publicly endorsed by Yoshida, they remained critical of the prime minister and were in a position, for political if not principled reasons, to scupper any US initiative by denying support to the government. In the words of the US Army report:

> Even if the Yoshida Government, under pressure by the United States, should agree to a substantial build-up of defence forces, it appears doubtful that Yoshida would be able to obtain Diet support to implement such a build-up in the near future in the face of his minority position in the Diet, general public opposition to rearmament, and the growing anti-American sentiment in Japan.[22]

Japanese public resistance to rearmament was also heightened by the perception that the United States was making excessive demands of Japan. Despite the State Department's agreed position of avoiding pressure on the Japanese government, Dulles on a number of occasions issued public statements on defense matters that risked provoking a hostile reaction in Japan, at least on the part of the Japanese media. On July 10, he was reported as having informed the Senate Appropriations Committee that Japan had agreed to make provision in its budget for the immediate creation of a ten-division defense force of some 350,000 men.[23] Similarly, in mid-August, Dulles's comments in an interview with an *Asahi* journalist were seen in Japan as clear US pressure for Japanese rearmament,[24] while in a September 3 press conference, the secretary of state reiterated the call for greater Japanese defense spending, pointing out that

> it is the hope of the United States that the Japanese Government will take more vigorous measures than they have taken to provide for their own internal security. We feel that too much of a burden is being thrown in that respect upon the United States and that Japan with its population of 85 million could make a greater contribution toward its own security than it is now doing.[25]

Allison responded with puzzlement and some irritation to these statements, pointing out their conflict with the agreed State Department policy of not publicly pressuring Japan to rearm, and the risk of undermining the Yoshida government and jeopardizing US long-term goals:

> Political situation in Japan is so delicate that in my opinion there should be no public statements by American officials regarding desire for rearmament no matter how carefully phrased. . . . [A]ny public statement by United States officials is only taken as interference and is used by opposition and by Communists as stick with which to beat government. I am convinced that steady, quiet pressure on Japanese government will bring desired result, that constant public pressure will only result in putting up backs of Japanese Government and requiring them in public to take even more negative attitude than at present.[26]

Dulles's approach might have been focused on persuading congressional opinion that Japan was serious about defense cooperation and was therefore a worthy recipient of US military assistance. However, Allison's concerned reaction suggests that the secretary of state may have miscalculated. Although it would be rash to interpret these public remarks as an expression of administration policy and private thinking,[27] Dulles's judgment in this instance was questionable and security relations with Japan might have been better served if the secretary of state had heeded the advice of his psychologically astute ambassador in Tokyo.

Despite US concern over the difficulties in promoting the expansion of Japan's defense capabilities, the Japanese government had already begun to consider the possibility of a more active rearmament strategy. In September 1952, following the establishment of the NSA, Yoshida had instructed the director of the new agency to set up an internal panel to investigate and make recommendations on Japan's defense structure.[28] By

March 1953, the panel—known as the "Systems Research Committee" (Seido chōsa iinkai)—had devised an ambitious thirteen-year defense plan recommending the ultimate establishment of ground forces totaling 300,000 troops, a 450,000-ton navy, and an air force of 6,744 aircraft.[29] This early plan envisaged an overly long period of expansion and in an effort to minimize uncertainty was soon replaced by a shorter five-year program, announced publicly by Kimura Tokutarō, the head of the NSA, in June 1953. This new plan was more modest in its goals, calling for a ground force of 200,000, a navy of 143,000 tons, and 1,536 aircraft by the end of fiscal 1958.[30] Although there was still a sizable gap between American and Japanese planning projections, some senior officials in Japan did wish to develop a more extensive Japanese defense capability.[31]

The views of Japan's military planners were paralleled by proposals from the Japanese business community. In May 1953, Keidanren (The Federation of Economic Organisations), the leading representative association of major businesses in Japan, had invited Ogata Taketora, the deputy prime minister, together with Kimura Tokutarō, to a meeting in Tokyo at which it presented its own defense proposal and urged the government to participate in the proposed MSA program with the United States. The Keidanren plan, like the NSA proposal, set ambitious targets—ground forces of 300,000, a 290,000-ton navy, and an air force of 2,700 aircraft, all to be achieved by 1960.[32] Japanese business was concerned to maintain the benefits of "special procurements"—the valuable revenue and foreign currency derived from US military expenditure in the Far East (an increasingly vulnerable and less dependable resource following the Korean armistice of July 1953)—and hoped through a concrete defense plan to maintain the profitable link with the United States.[33] In addition, leading industrialists, together with some (but by no means all) conservative politicians, were eager during the early 1950s to boost Japan's defense production as a means of strengthening Japan and establishing a secure foundation for key industries such as aerospace and shipbuilding.[34]

Despite these ambitious proposals, internal opposition within the Yoshida government, principally from a fiscally conservative Ministry of Finance, threatened to limit severely the proposed expansion of Japan's defense capabilities. By September, plans had been agreed, with the prime minister's approval, for Ikeda Hayato (Yoshida's loyal associate and a senior figure in the Liberal Party) to travel to Washington to negotiate with the Americans—a decision which Allison interpreted as an attempt to extract loans and economic assistance from the United States.[35] While some issues had been resolved during the MSA talks in Tokyo—the Japanese, for example, had persuaded the United States not to include any reference to collective defense in the final agreement—there had been no agreement on a Japanese defense plan and the US negotiators remained concerned that Japan was emphasizing the economic over the military advantage of bilateral cooperation.[36] Ikeda's mission to Washington represented an opportunity to present a trial military proposal, but one which was substantially smaller than the original five-year NSA plan released in June. The Ikeda plan envisaged a ground force of 180,000 troops at the end of three years, a navy of 210 vessels after five years, and a 518-plane air force. Financial outlays were also much reduced—¥620 billion and ¥280 billion respectively for Japan and the United States, in comparison with ¥800 billion and ¥550 billion in the case of the NSA proposals.[37]

Much significance has been attached to the Ikeda mission to Washington, and in particular to the talks with Walter Robertson, the assistant secretary of state for far eastern affairs, which took place in the middle of October. Miyazawa Kiichi, a member of the mission and a House of Councilors representative (later to serve as prime minister during the early 1990s), described the Washington negotiations in his own account written three years after the event, as "the most important post-war US-Japan meeting dealing with defence problems."[38] The talks have been represented as a series of tough negotiations in which the Japanese side successfully resisted strong pressure from the Americans to accelerate their defense program and won the right to substantially define the character of subsequent negotiations on rearmament.

Without a doubt, US officials were quick to point out the pressing strategic factors that required, in their judgment, an increase in Japanese military spending. On October 9, the Japanese delegation was given a detailed presentation on the threat posed by Soviet and Chinese forces in the Far East. Soviet ground troops alone, based in Eastern Siberia, numbered some 500,000 and, equipped with airborne and amphibious capabilities and supported by 5,000 to 6,000 war planes, were well placed to launch an attack on Hokkaido and northern Honshu. Under these circumstances, not to mention a possible two-front attack involving PRC troops, it was imperative for the United States that Japan eventually develop a ten-division ground force made up of 325,000 troops.[39] The Americans made little effort to conceal their "serious disappointment" at the modest Japanese proposals, emphasizing that without an adequate commitment by Japan to increase defense spending, Congress was unlikely to approve a military assistance program.[40]

Yet, despite these differences, the talks were neither an unambiguous diplomatic victory for the Japanese side nor a decisive turning-point in the defense negotiations. The Americans, before October, were well aware of the difficulty of securing a major rearmament commitment from Japan, and far from resolving the defense question, the negotiations concluded on an open-ended note, with both sides agreeing to a joint communiqué that avoided mentioning specific figures for military spending or defense expansion. Moreover, Ikeda's plan had no official status, was vague in its financial details, and could be interpreted as the expression of sectional interests rather than the views of the Japanese government as a whole.[41] Indeed, during the pre-departure policy sessions in Tokyo for the drafting of the Ikeda plan, the NSA, despite its involvement in defense policy since autumn 1952, had been, in effect, muzzled and purposely excluded from discussions between Ikeda, Miyazawa, and representatives from the Diet and the Ministry of Finance.[42] Nevertheless, there were still opportunities for negotiation on the basis of earlier assumptions. On September 25, General Clark and Ambassador Allison met with Okazaki and Kimura and were presented with a defense proposal similar to the earlier five-year NSA plan. Although Clark highlighted the United States ultimate goal of a roughly 300,000-strong Japanese ground force, he also stressed that the Japanese plan's naval and air projections were more in line with US thinking, and the overall tone of the discussions had been "friendly."[43] The Japanese authorities were not, it seems, speaking with one voice.

A September 27 agreement between Yoshida and Shigemitsu—not the Ikeda mission to Washington—was the critical event in the development of Japan's early post-war defense policy. The two conservative leaders, meeting in Shigemitsu's private residence, reached an explicit understanding that Japan's defense forces would be required not only to address the risk of internal subversion but also to repel external aggression, and that to this end the structure of the NSA would be reformed and strengthened. As a joint statement released to the Japanese press following the meeting made clear:

> In light of the current international situation and the growing spirit of national independence at home, we are on this occasion making clear our plan to strengthen Japan's self-defense power and to establish a long-term defense plan that is in accordance with our national capabilities and [will take place]

along with the gradual reduction of foreign troops. As well as revising the NSA law and transforming the NSA into a Self-Defense Force (SDF), this represents an increased obligation by Japan to defend itself against direct invasion.[44]

The agreement represented a major step forward toward conservative unity on defense matters—a compromise between the light-armament, gradualist defense build-up favored by Yoshida and the Progressive preference for immediate constitutional revision and a major increase in defense spending. This breakthrough provided the basis for subsequent agreement with the United States over MSA issues, a point well made by Uemura Hideki, who has played down the significance of the Ikeda-Robertson talks (rejecting Miyazawa's stress on their importance as a "myth") and described the Washington discussions as merely "one comma in a series of US-Japan negotiations."[45]

By early December, there were signs that the United States and Japan might be close to an agreement. Allison, in keeping with his earlier advice, was recommending moderation and suggesting a graduated build-up of Japanese ground forces to 180,000 troops by April 1956 (with an initial increase in the coming year of 30,000), in return for a Japanese agreement to establish a system of combined defense planning and the institution of an active reserve system.[46] The JCS, for their part, had accepted that their force targets were unrealizable at this stage, and were willing to accept Allison's proposal as a means of initiating a concrete Japanese build-up as soon as possible, while leaving room for the future development of a more balanced force structure with additional resources devoted to Japan's naval and air forces.[47]

Dulles endorsed Allison's approach, granting full discretion to the ambassador, asking only to be kept informed of the progress of the negotiations. The secretary of state announced that he would avoid making any independent statements from Washington (perhaps conscious of the difficulties caused by his remarks earlier in the autumn). Nevertheless, Dulles was clearly frustrated by Japan's unwillingness to play a more active role in its security relationship with the United States. As he noted privately to Allison:

> I am frankly disappointed that Japan has fallen far behind Germany in recovery and willingness to contribute to security. I refer not only to lag in rearmament, which contrasts sharply with German readiness to rearm, but also to failure to exclude Communist influence in labor unions, intelligentsia and youth circles, and widespread Communist propaganda in Japan directed against the US which makes a very sharp contrast with the close and friendly

relations between West German people and the US. Also, the Japanese squandering of windfall from Korea rather than practice of austerity makes very bad impression. Japanese are constantly asking more and more from US without feeling any obligation themselves to do what is necessary to promote security in Asia. . . . I think it is time that the Japanese leaders realized that they cannot expect forever to be on the receiving end without any corresponding effort on their part.[48]

Allison, while acknowledging Japan's economic and defense deficiencies, was perhaps, more tempered in his criticism, favorably comparing Yoshida to Woodrow Wilson in 1917 to highlight the Japanese prime minister's domestic political difficulties and making clear that the anticipated changes in the NSA represented a significant step forward.[49]

The ambassador's views were vindicated following Japan's 1954 budget announcement. In sharp contrast to the previous year, when defense appropriations had been cut by ¥60 billion, the new figures represented a ¥20-billion increase in NSA-related expenditure. This was particularly significant given the general climate of fiscal austerity in Japan at the time. All other budget items had been either cut or frozen, and in the wake of flood and typhoon damage from the previous year, the Japanese government was facing considerable pressure to increase social security spending and support for small business. Such was the extent of popular disquiet that four Finance Ministry officials had been physically attacked by "irate mobs protesting against budget cuts," and State Department officials had no doubt that it had "taken considerable political courage" for Yoshida to approve the increase in defense spending.[50]

In addition to the increase in budget allocations, the Japanese authorities had agreed for the coming year, via an exchange of confidential letters between Allison and Foreign Minister Okazaki in January (subsequently reaffirmed in April), to increase Japan's overall defense strength by approximately 41,000 personnel (31,000 of them uniformed personnel), in the process expanding the number of ground force divisions from four to six.[51] Japan also indicated that it would provide appropriations of ¥78.8 billion for the National Safety Agency, together with ¥58.5 billion in direct financial support for US forces stationed in Japan (in keeping with Article XXV of the US-Japan Administrative Agreement).[52] These figures matched Allison's earlier proposal and, together with the Japanese government's authorization of legislation converting the NSA into a National Defense Agency and establishing Ground, Maritime and Air Self-Defense Forces, paved the way for the formal signing of a Mutual Defense Assistance Agreement between the United States and Japan on

March 8, 1954. The agreement entitled the US authorities to extend military assistance to Japan under the terms of the 1951 Mutual Security Act, and provisions were established for activating an American Military Assistance Advisory Group (MAAG) from May 1. The agreement also acknowledged the US intention (although not a formal commitment) to fund $100 million in offshore procurement expenditure in Japan, while providing information and training for employees of Japan's defense-related industries. Similarly, the United States proposed, under section 550 of the Mutual Security Act, to sell some $50 million worth of surplus agricultural commodities to Japan. Twenty percent of the proceeds of these sales (to be transacted in yen) would then be used to support the development of Japan's defense sector.[53]

Despite the progress achieved through the March agreement, the bilateral security relationship remained subject to potentially destabilizing tensions. Taken at face value, economic issues lay at the heart of disagreements between the two countries. In late July, senior officials in the recently created Defense Agency informed the United States that cuts were likely in the fiscal 1954 Japanese defense budget and that earlier plans to increase Japan's forces by 30,000 men would have to be sharply restricted. At the same time, Japanese government representatives were making uncoordinated requests to the United States for financial assistance, with the Ministry of International Trade and Industry (MITI) submitting a plan for $49 million in American aid for equipment funds and $350 million in offshore procurement.[54] Allison, confronted by what appeared to be a clear violation of the earlier Allison-Okazaki agreement, in the wake of the *Lucky Dragon* crisis and Ikeda's unexpected claim that America's "roll-back" strategy in Asia had failed,[55] became increasingly skeptical of Japan's commitment to a cooperative and mutually supportive relationship with the United States. Writing to Dulles in late August, the ambassador made little effort to conceal his frustration:

> We have been assuming that Japan is potentially a strong ally and that the Japanese want to assume this role as soon as their economic and political situation permits. The present government has given lip service to this idea but many of its actions prove otherwise. Their actions indicate that Japan does not consider itself an ally or partner of the United States but rather a nation which for the time being is forced by circumstances to cooperate with the United States but which intends while doing so to wring out of this relationship every possible advantage at the minimum cost.[56]

Allison suspected that the Japanese were overly ready to lean on their larger, more powerful American partner, at times at the risk of compromising national independence. Japanese foreign ministry officials in relaxed dinnertime conversations suggested to their US counterparts on one occasion that America might be acting too cautiously toward Japan, noting, for example, that "US policy toward Japan has fluctuated too widely. During the Occupation the US intervened too much. Since the Occupation, the US has not intervened enough. The US should not hesitate to attach conditions to its aid, but in doing so, it should make it clear that decision is up to Japan."[57] More dramatically, Ikeda, in conversation in mid-June with Frank Waring, economic counselor at the embassy in Tokyo, made it clear that Japan was content to play the role of international supplicant:

> In discussing the desire of the Japanese for basic assurances from the United States, Ikeda smiled and said, "You realize that Japan has been a modern state for less than 100 years. It has been traditional in Japanese life for the people to look for guidance, assistance and support to some wealthy, influential patron. The United States could exploit this attitude to our mutual advantage." He went on to explain that assumption of the role of protector and advisor need not be costly. What the Japanese so desperately desire is the assurance of someone strong enough to make it meaningful. As a nation they seek the security which such assurance would afford, just as individuals covet the support of an employer, a political mentor, or a wealthy friend. Ikeda observed that perhaps the United States was making a mistake to treat Japan as a sovereign nation equal in strength and importance to itself. Perhaps, he said, it would be better if the relationship were that of a teacher to his student.[58]

Here, in striking form, was evidence of a lack of mutuality—a sign that Japan was satisfied with a degree of passive dependence, as Dulles had claimed the previous year. Coupled with signs that the Japanese government was reluctant to tackle its domestic economic problems energetically,[59] such passivity explains in part why American officials were finding it difficult to work with their Japanese partners.

Criticisms of the bilateral relationship at this stage were not limited to one side. In mid-August, Takeuchi Ryūji, the chief of the Bureau of European and American Affairs in the Gaimushō, in a private meeting with embassy officials, sharply attacked the Americans for allegedly reneging on an earlier "commitment" to provide $100 million of offshore procurement (OSP) funds.[60] A month later, he reiterated his claims in even more uncompromising terms, accusing the Americans of "sharp practices" and of making commitments which they had "no intention of keeping"—in effect deliberately hoodwinking the "naive" Japanese negotiators during the Ikeda-Robertson talks.[61] US OSP figures had indeed fallen, from $100 to $70 million (in part because of the competing need to provide military assistance to Vietnam and Southeast Asia), but US officials were shocked by Takeuchi's accusation—a criticism they felt represented "fantastic charges."[62] The claim of bad faith seems difficult to substantiate in light of Dulles's earlier instructions to Allison that it was "imperative" that no financial guarantee, either expressed or implied, be offered to Japan,[63] and especially given the earlier Allison-Okazaki notes making clear that no commitment had been agreed to. Moreover, while the United States was not supporting a formal economic aid program to Japan, it would be a mistake to underemphasize the substantial financial resources which the United States had supplied to support the development of Japan's defense-industrial base. Between 1945 and September 1953, the United States had, in part through the GARIOA scheme, provided $2,045.6 million to Japan,[64] and as US officials made clear in 1954, the total American contribution to troop support went far beyond OSP alone and amounted to more than $275 million.[65] Conceivably, Takeuchi adopted such an aggressive tone to extract more financial support from the Americans (a tactic which would have accounted for Allison's disillusionment and frustration). Alternatively, the rift may have been the result of a genuine misunderstanding or failure of communication between the two countries. At the very least, it is important to note that Takeuchi was not acting in isolation. In late autumn 1954, MITI minister Aichi Kiichi, accompanied by Miyazawa, traveled to Washington to lay the groundwork for the forthcoming visit by Prime Minister Yoshida in November. During his meeting with Walter Robertson, Aichi opened the discussion by stressing that Japanese public opinion was disturbed by the actions of the US government and felt America was "presumptuous" and overly inclined to give orders to Japan and that failure to respond to these developments would threaten US-Japan relations.[66]

Aichi's advice and the strain on bilateral relations prompted a quick response from the Americans. In early September 1954, Allison was suggesting in cables to Dulles that it might be sensible to consider a change of tack in the administration's Japan policy, de-emphasizing rearmament as a means of meeting external security challenges, in favor of enhancing Japan's internal security, primarily by focusing on the country's economic development. Such an approach would be more of a wait-and-see position than the existing effort to encourage Japan to build up its defenses and would, according to Allison, be more in accordance with current realities. It would acknowledge growing neutralism in Japan, as well as the Japanese public's perception that Cold War tensions were abating and that rearmament would foster militarism and heighten the likelihood of thermonuclear war—a trend which was discouraging the necessary Japanese "national spirit and purpose" for establishing a reliable alliance partnership.[67] Allison's advice was echoed by others in the State Department. Dulles, in meetings of the NSC, recommended that the United States "lower [its] sights on Japanese rearmament,"[68] while in the embassy in Tokyo, senior Foreign Service officers began to draft their own "New Look" for Japan which proposed similar changes. By October 25, William Leonhart, the first secretary, was calling for a shift away from rearmament in favor of fostering political stability in Japan, and was suggesting that the United States might, on its own initiative, suggest replacing the existing Security Treaty with a new "reciprocal and mutual defense treaty" as well as revising the Administrative Agreement.[69] The Eisenhower administration accepted a much less ambitious agenda as far as Japan was concerned, recognizing that there were real limits to what might be achieved in the short term. Despite some resistance from the Joint Chiefs, who argued that reduced Japanese defense spending would seriously undermine the US military position in the Pacific, these changes eventually came to fruition in NSC 5516/1 (agreed in April 1955) and the executive decision to de-emphasize the importance of rapid rearmament.[70]

It would be a mistake to assume that placing less emphasis on rearmament restricted opportunities for defense cooperation. The Military Advisory Group provided training and guidance to the Japanese military and was especially important in the establishment of the JDA's Technical Research Institute—a body which would come to play a critical role in the post-war expansion of Japan's indigenous defense industry.[71] In February and March 1954, representatives from the Defense Department visited Japan to review and make recommendations on the establishment of a coordinated US-Japan defense program; in April, Japanese technicians made a return visit to the United States to tour American military and commercial plants producing small arms and explosives.[72] By July, the Pentagon had drafted a plan for the initial assembly and later construction of US F-86 fighter planes in Japan within two years.[73] However, these signs of cooperation need to be balanced against what was not being achieved. Little scope remained for the establishment of an East Asian collective security framework including Japan,[74] and cultural and ideological disagreements within Japan—the legacy of the Occupation period—continued to stand in the way of a clear expression of an active defense policy that appealed to a broad consensus of public and official Japanese opinion. In the words of one detailed US government report:

> The instability now being displayed in Japan is the result of the nation's attempt to adjust traditional values and practices to the new laws and ideas stemming from defeat in war and occupation. Japan's dominant conservative forces are trying to facilitate this adjustment by grouping together in opposition to Socialists and leftist forces and by legalizing certain pre-war practices, such as central police, stronger control over education and economic concentration.[75]

At one level, the re-admission of Hatoyama's Liberals into the Liberal Party in November 1953 (in return for which a Constitutional Research Committee was established) signified this growing conservative unity. Yet cooperation was based on partisan considerations, and disagreements between the major parties persisted, preventing, for example, the establishment of a working National Defense Council (NDC) until 1956. The new SDF legislation had made provision for the NDC, but disagreements between Liberal and Progressive representatives over whether civilians should participate in the Council delayed the setting up of the organization by two years.[76]

Hatoyama's (Un)Diplomatic Departures, 1955–56

With the transition from a Yoshida to a Hatoyama-led administration in December 1954 and particularly following conservative (both Liberal and Democratic) successes in the Lower House election of February 1955,[77] one might have anticipated a more active pattern of defense cooperation between the United States and Japan. Yet, there was no change in the quality or tempo of Japan's defense buildup. William Sebald, the deputy assistant secretary of state for far eastern affairs, noted:

> Hatoyama will follow Yoshida's go-slow policy, will refuse to increase defense spending other than as permitted by reduction of Japan's contribution to the United States forces, and will argue that Japan must acquire political and economic strength before it can build up its defense. Revision of the Constitution will be studied but no effective efforts towards revision appear possible for at least a year.[78]

Bilateral defense discussions in the first half of 1955 were mainly focused on agreeing to a figure for Japan's contribution to US forces based in Japan, in accordance with Article XXV of the US-Japan Administrative Agreement. The article in question had originally stipulated an annual contribution of $155 million, but in practice the agreed amount had been significantly and steadily reduced, although there had been no formal modification of the original figure. Consequently, the contribution had become a subject for annual bilateral haggling, with the talks in 1955 proving especially awkward and at times acrimonious. Behind the scenes, the US negotiating position continued to stress moderation. Ambassador Allison (at times supported by General John Hull, the CinCFE) sought to deflect pressure from the JCS in Washington for an ambitious spending figure for Japan's own forces of approximately ¥90 billion. To US negotiators in the field, military planners at home seemed disturbingly out of touch with local conditions. Highlighting this problem to State Department officials at the beginning of 1955, Jeff Parsons, deputy chief of mission in Tokyo, noted with some exasperation:

> I hope that you and your colleagues will continue the fight to instil a more reasonable attitude into people who are far away from the situation and, apparently, impervious to any considerations except those which emerge from their military drawing boards. We will give you as much ammunition as we can but those fellows should either listen to you or go take the National War College course![79]

Eventually, a settlement was reached which in many respects represented a victory for Japan. On April 19, the United States and Japan agreed that the Hatoyama government's defense budget for the 1955 fiscal year would be a total of ¥132.8 billion. Of this, ¥86.8 billion would be devoted to Japan's forces (an ¥8 billion increase on the previous year), while the United States agreed to a ¥17.8 billion reduction in Japan's support for US forces—producing a new, reduced figure for Article XXV contributions of ¥38 billion. In addition, Japan agreed to pay ¥8 billion to the United States to support the construction and extension of air base runways in Japan. To all intents and purposes, Japan's additional spending commitments had been counterbalanced by the reduction in Japan's Article XXV contribution.[80]

America's compromise over defense spending was an acknowledgment of the weak state of the Japanese government. Hatoyama, in conversations with US officials, was quick to stress the vulnerability of his administration arguing that a modest defense budget was necessary to ensure the survival of his cabinet.[81] The prime minister himself was hardly a dynamic figure, having assumed the premiership at 71 and experienced a debilitating stroke in 1951.[82] It was clear also that the government suffered from internal divisions as well as confused leadership, at least where the defense question was concerned.[83] The domestic political environment in Japan in the first half of 1955 remained unstable and somewhat unpredictable, with one US analysis referring dramatically to a "Weimar Japan."[84] Against this background, US policy-makers felt frustrated in their efforts to establish an effective alliance relationship. Political disorder was exacerbated by economic confusion. Joseph Dodge, who had played such an important role in promoting the economic austerity measures of the Occupation and who now chaired the Eisenhower administration's US Council on Foreign Economic Policy, took a largely negative view of Japan's efforts to put its house in order, criticizing the emphasis placed on political expediency, the failure to stimulate exports, and the continued dependent state of a Japanese economy largely reliant on the revival of world demand for recent improvements in its financial and business health.[85] Some sense of the validity of US concerns also emerges if one analyzes Japan's spending plans for defense in a historical context. In 1955, Japan's defense spending was approximately 1.6 percent of national income (by comparison with the 15.5 percent spent by the United States in the same year). In the early 1930s, the share of Japan's national income allocated to defense was 7.1 percent, rising under the increasing pressures of the Pacific War to 27 percent in 1939 and 49 percent in 1944. A more dramatic illustration of the relatively low priority assigned by the Japanese government to defense expenditure can be gleaned from the figures for relative consumption in Japan in 1954. While the budget for 1954 allocated some ¥132.7 billion to defense, in the same year Japanese consumers spent ¥270 billion on sake, ¥240 billion on pachinko, and ¥210 billion on tobacco.[86]

Japan's cautious attitude toward defense spending did not imply complete neglect of military preparedness. In March 1955, the JDA had begun drafting a new six-year defense plan to take the place of the earlier five-year outlook which had formed the basis of the MSA talks. The plan came to fruition in August, but never acquired official status—in part a reflection of the weak bureaucratic power of the JDA.[87] Nevertheless, it did demonstrate the commitment to defense matters of some in Japan, and was analyzed closely by State Department and US military officials. The proposed build-up schedule for ground, air, and naval forces remained modest (envisaging 180,000 ground troops by 1960), and was far below what the United States believed Japan was capable of in terms of manpower and the overall capacity of the Japanese economy. However, the Eisenhower administration was not about to overlook such initiatives and by August acknowledged privately (in internal position papers) that Hatoyama and his foreign minister, Shigemitsu, were "making a serious effort to rearm Japan against considerable popular opposition," as well as arguing that it was "important that the United States do what it can to help them."[88]

Notwithstanding the positive exhortations of officials in Washington, it remained difficult to generate much sustainable momentum behind bilateral defense cooperation during 1955 and 1956. State Department representatives continued privately to express to the Japanese their disappointment at Japan's low defense spending,[89] and while officials from both countries sought constructively to minimize tensions,[90] such initiatives could not easily be translated into a new spirit of common endeavor and mutual support. Increasingly, in late 1955 and 1956, the defense debate focused on the question of the US troop presence in Japan, with the Pentagon, in keeping with the tenets of the "New Look," arguing for a withdrawal of US ground troops from both Japan and the Far East as a whole. In August 1955, officials in Washington had already formulated plans to cut by half the number of ground forces stationed in Japan—a reduction from 66,500 to 29,000 troops over a period of twelve months. This would entail a drop in the total number of US military personnel in Japan from 113,000 to 76,000 and would be a step toward meeting Japanese wishes to see all US ground forces withdrawn from Japan by July 1959, assuming that Japan's own forces had been increased to 180,000.[91] Almost a year later, Pentagon efforts to lower the US troop presence had gone one step further, and Secretary of Defense Charles Wilson informed the National Security Council in July 1956 of a new plan to reorganize the American military presence in the Pacific, redeploying the UN Command from Japan to Korea and creating a new, single Pacific Command located in Hawaii. This change would help, according to the Pentagon, to minimize Japanese feelings that Japan was still suffering the effects of occupation[92] and encourage Japan to build up its own defense capabilities, and it would also, one imagines, allow for more coherent and integrated US regional defense planning.

Troop redeployment, while in the long run a useful means of defusing bilateral tensions, was not a cost-free exercise from Japan's point of view. A reduced physical presence limited the scope for tension between Japanese civilians and culturally and diplomatically unsophisticated GIs, but it also removed a valuable source of revenue from the local Japanese economy—a point which was emphasized during the withdrawal of US forces from Hokkaido in September 1954.[93] Coupled with a general decline in US procurement orders in 1955, this trend exposed the United States to increasing criticism, frequently from local interests in Japan, for neglecting Japanese economic concerns. America was confronted with unpalatable choices[94] that would inevitably provoke opposition from some quarters in Japan, and US military planners could perhaps be forgiven for feeling that Japanese objections were at times inconsistent.[95]

Although rearmament and the stationing of US troops in Japan were important issues during 1955 and 1956, a key element in the debate over US-Japan policy at this time was the question of Security Treaty revision. The impetus for a reconsideration of the treaty developed in April 1955, with a proposal from Shigemitsu to visit Washington for talks with the Eisenhower administration. The Japanese foreign minister's proposal caught the Americans very much by surprise. Little attempt had been made to broach the issue via the usual diplomatic channels in order to determine the substance of any likely discussions and to see whether a meeting would be mutually convenient. In fact, the details of Shigemitsu's itinerary were simply leaked to the Japanese press as if the visit were a fait accompli—a decision which greatly irritated embassy officials, who felt that they were being bounced unreasonably into a commitment to a meeting. As Allison noted:

> Despite solemn caution against premature publicity re. Shigemitsu's proposed trip all morning papers today carry lead stories stating Foreign Minister's plan to leave for Washington during next week, to be gone week or ten days. This completely irresponsible action on part of Japanese Government places US in most awkward position. If we now consent to receive Shigemitsu, Japanese will gain impression they can act toward US with impunity in any manner they see fit. If we refuse to receive Foreign Minister we will be charged with "insincerity," with applying undue pressure (although in fact pressure is being applied by Japanese) and we can expect great upsurge of anti-Americanism.[96]

Allison advised Dulles to reject a meeting—a recommendation which the secretary of state followed— while taking pains to impress on the Japanese government that he was not in any way unwilling to enter discussions and noting that time constraints and competing schedules stood in the way of sufficient preparation for a meaningful exchange of views.[97]

There seems little reason to question US motives in canceling the meeting. Certainly, Dulles and the State Department believed that the behavior of the Japanese authorities had been "irresponsible"—a view which was confirmed by none other than the prime minister, albeit indirectly. In a remarkable meeting with Jeff Parsons on April 6, Matsumoto Takezō (Hatoyama's close confidant and interpreter)[98] made clear that Shigemitsu's decision to go to the United States had conflicted with the prime minister's wishes. Hatoyama had, according to Matsumoto, been eager to establish closer ties with the United States following his election and with this in mind the cabinet on April 1 had discussed the possibility of sending an envoy to Washington. Hatoyama had hoped to send Matsumoto, but Shigemitsu had opposed the decision, arguing instead in his own favor. Although internal cabinet disagreements are not unusual in a parliamentary system and among ambitious politicians, Matsumoto's remarks strikingly exposed to the Americans the Japanese government's internal divisions. Matsumoto himself used the conversation with Parsons to make arrangements for a forthcoming meeting between Hatoyama and General Maxwell Taylor,[99] "pointedly" indicating that the Japanese foreign minister was unaware of the planned meeting and hinting "broadly that it would be better for the Ambassador not to tell Shigemitsu when he saw him later in the afternoon"—in Parsons's judgment, "an extraordinary request!"[100] Matsumoto appears to have had no compunction in revealing the difference of views between Shigemitsu and Hatoyama and freely admitting that the confusion over the abortive Washington visit was entirely the responsibility of the Japanese government—an admission couched in terms designed to discredit the foreign minister. In the words of Parsons's cable: "Mr. Matsumoto regretted very much what had happened subsequently, including the publicity before we could get an answer back from Washington and Mr. Hatoyama regretted it too. No one blamed the United States for what had occurred and it was just too bad that the matter had not been handled better here."[101] Such evidence of conservative disunity was to become increasingly commonplace in discussions with US officials during 1955 and 1956.

Despite his setback in April, Shigemitsu was able to travel to the United States in late August. The foreign minister hoped to use his visit to discuss security issues, but even before he arrived in Washington, it was clear to the Americans that personal political ambition rather than substantive policy proposals provided the main motivation for the trip. Although Liberal and Democratic politicians were discussing the possibility of merger in 1955, Japan's conservatives remained sharply divided along personal, factional lines. Shigemitsu's mission reflected these divisions and he was accompanied by two of his main political rivals—Kōno Ichirō (the minister of agriculture), and Kishi Nobusuke (secretary general of the Democratic Party). For the foreign minister, closer security ties with the United States were primarily designed to enhance his reputation at home and to offset the influence of his more powerful conservative colleagues. As a US internal position paper, prepared for the August meeting, commented:

> Shigemitsu has strong political ambitions and would like to be Prime Minister when Hatoyama retires. As former President of the Progressive Party, Shigemitsu has some independent political strength but is evidently a poor politician who does not have the respect and loyalty of any large group of conservatives. It is obvious that Shigemitsu hopes to become a leading proponent of United States–Japan cooperation and largely on this platform to enhance his political prestige.[102]

The foreign minister's relative isolation in the Hatoyama cabinet was all too clear to the State Department, thanks to Matsumoto Takezō's willingness to reveal internal Japanese government rivalries with "embarrassing frankness." In another meeting with Parsons, this time in early August, Matsumoto made clear that he too would be traveling to Washington, explaining:

> Friction between Kishi and Shigemitsu still existed and Shigemitsu liked Kono even less. It was right for Shigemitsu to head the delegation but the Prime Minister wished us to know that he hoped Kishi and Kono could be present at important meetings in Washington. According to Matsumoto, there was some danger that they would overshadow Shigemitsu (who was referred to always as the Foreign Minister, not Deputy Prime Minister) because both were politically so much more influential than Shigemitsu was. One of the Prime Minister's reasons for wishing them and Matsumoto included was to make sure that he heard what went on as he did not always get full reports from Shigemitsu. Furthermore, Kishi and Kono could really tell us about the complexities of the political situation here and the merger problem which should be advanced by the visit.[103]

In the face of such blatant divisions, Dulles was reluctant to contemplate serious discussions on security matters during Shigemitsu's visit. Telephoning Bernard Baruch (President Truman's former advisor and envoy to the UN Atomic Energy Commission) on August 30, prior to a dinner that Baruch was hosting for Shigemitsu and other members of the Japanese delegation, Dulles expressed his concerns:

> The Secretary said this mission here is primarily concerned with domestic politics rather than international diplomacy and these people are all mixed up and fighting each other. It is a terrible political mess and various people are

trying to get credit they can use at home. We are not disposed to do much until they consolidate their own position and get their house in order. The big
thing to emphasize is that the conservative right wing elements need to merge
and present a united front against the Commies and Socialists. Today they are
all divided. They are getting nowhere and are not responsible to deal with.[104]

Shigemitsu's difficulties were not limited to his rivalry with fellow politicians. The Japanese Foreign Ministry was largely shut out of preparations for the Washington mission, with Shigemitsu and one or two select
advisors monopolizing the process of drafting position papers for the
talks. Annoyed to have been marginalized in this way, the Gaimushō officials made their discontent known to their American colleagues—another sign of the fragmentation of the Japanese government's administrative machinery. Yasukawa Takeuchi, head of the second section of the
European and American Affairs Bureau, complained quite freely about
the situation to Windsor Hackler, first secretary of the embassy in Tokyo:

> Yasukawa said he felt a certain grim pleasure in hearing officers at the Japa-
> nese Embassy in Washington complain about the way Shigemitsu was treating
> them—that is, leaving them completely out of the planning as well as opera-
> tions he was conducting. In explanation, Yasukawa said it was only human
> for him to take some pleasure in saying to his Embassy colleagues, "Now you
> know what we have been putting up with in the Foreign Ministry all these
> months."[105]

Dulles was cautious but not dismissive of the Japanese proposals. As
early as July 1955, Walter Robertson had raised with the secretary the
likelihood of a Japanese proposal regarding a new Mutual Defense
Treaty and Dulles had indicated that he was willing to actively consider
the matter.[106] During Shigemitsu's visit to Washington, the Japanese foreign minister as expected pushed energetically and insistently for a new
treaty, arguing that it would help challenge Japanese popular criticism
that the bilateral relationship was unequal while also, most importantly,
combating Japan's most pressing security problem—the risk of internal
subversion and the threat from Communism at home.[107] However, in
Dulles's view Shigemitsu was putting the cart before the horse and the
secretary remained skeptical that domestic conditions in Japan were sufficiently stable to provide the political and popular backing for a new
treaty, pointing out that the question of a new treaty was one of "timing"
rather than of "fundamental policy." America would agree to a new
arrangement once the Japanese government had developed the country's
defense capacities and no longer faced obstacles to such a policy in the
form of a "very confused" domestic political situation and "unfriendly

elements in the Diet."[108] Perhaps as a means of testing Shigemitsu's resolve (and no doubt anticipating a negative response), Dulles inquired
whether Japan would be able and willing to send forces abroad to assist
the United States. Surprisingly, the Japanese foreign minister assured the
secretary of state that Japan would have no problems providing such assistance, even going so far as to indicate that Japan's Self-Defense Forces
could conceivably, in the event of a security crisis, be dispatched to Guam
to support US forces.[109]

Shigemitsu's unqualified positive response surprised not only Dulles.
The other members of the mission—Kishi and Kōno in particular—were
also taken aback, as they made clear in a subsequent meeting on August
31 with Allison and Sebald (another instance in which the rivalry and divisions on the Japanese side were starkly highlighted). This later meeting
was an opportunity for some straightforward discussion, a chance for the
Japanese participants to, in their own words, "take off their coats and
speak with Mr. Sebald somewhat more frankly on an unofficial basis."[110]
As Kishi made clear, emphasizing that Hatoyama had specifically requested him to travel to Washington, the current mission was an opportunity to exchange views with the United States, not to request a new
treaty. Moreover, Shigemitsu's depiction of the internal Japanese Communist threat was, in Kishi's analysis, exaggerated, and while conservative union was a necessary goal in Japan, the principal problem was the
absence of economic stability, without which it made little sense to talk
of fighting Communism at home or developing a new alliance relationship with the United States.[111] Kōno was similarly critical of his cabinet
colleague, pointing out that he "had found that the Secretary's presentation was much more logical and reasonable than that of the Foreign Minister" and that "he was confident that the formula proposed by the Secretary would be agreeable to Prime Minister Hatoyama."[112] The minister
for agriculture made clear to the Americans that Shigemitsu's political influence and authority were minimal and that "when problems of major
importance arose it would be well to take them up directly with Mr.
Kishi, Bukichi Miki, or himself. They were the three men who presently
control the Japanese Government and they all had Prime Minister Hatoyama's full confidence."[113] At the end of the meeting, this picture of an
isolated and unpopular foreign minister was reinforced by Matsumoto
Takezō, who took pains to point out to the State Department officials

that Mr. Kono, Mr. Kishi and himself had been greatly disturbed at the Foreign Minister's presentation in his discussion with the Secretary on August 30.

The Foreign Minister's approach, his exaggeration of the Communist threat, had been all wrong; it had certainly not been worthy of a professional diplomat. Mr. Matsumoto said his colleagues were at a loss to know why the Foreign Minister had taken this approach, concerning which they had no knowledge.[114]

Shigemitsu's outspoken and unexpected remarks provoked a reaction back in Japan as well as among the members of the mission. Public opinion and press reports were critical of the foreign minister for endorsing the notion of overseas deployment of the SDF without cabinet or popular backing for an inherently controversial decision. However, criticism of Shigemitsu and the inconclusive Washington talks appear not to have been translated into specific bilateral tension. Although privately members of the Japanese negotiating team had been somewhat offended by the manner of Dulles's rejection of Shigemitsu's proposal for treaty revision—an approach which they apparently found "rude and blunt"[115]—substantively the two sides were not especially far apart, and the secretary should only be faulted for his plain speaking, a shortcoming which reflected perhaps his relatively limited understanding of the Japanese preference for indirect language. The Joint Communiqué from the Washington meeting had clearly endorsed plans to replace the existing treaty with a more mutual arrangement once appropriate conditions had been established,[116] and a number of conservative Japanese politicians at the time were quick to point out publicly and privately the shortcomings of Shigemitsu's approach.[117]

Shigemitsu's isolated position within the Hatoyama cabinet and the persistent divisions within the Japanese government also had an impact on the Soviet-Japan normalization talks of 1955 to 1956. During the general election campaign of 1955, Hatoyama had emphasized his intention of re-establishing diplomatic relations with Moscow and Beijing as a means of creating a distinctive political identity for himself in the eyes of the Japanese electorate, while distancing himself from the previous Yoshida administration. In the context of East-West bipolar rivalry, this new direction also implied a shift away from a United States–centered diplomacy in favor of a more self-consciously independent Japanese foreign policy. Not surprisingly, it encouraged both contemporary and later commentators to focus on points of friction and disagreement between decision-makers in Washington and Tokyo. However, on closer examination (and as was the case with similar "conflicts" during the late 1940s and throughout the 1950s), the difference between the two governments was more superficial than substantive, exaggerated by press reports and the failure to distinguish between the public and private motivations of key decision-makers.

The first signs of a possible warming of relations between Japan and the USSR appear in late 1954 in two statements from Molotov, the Soviet foreign minister, calling for the normalization of relations between two countries. By January 1955, Moscow had formally proposed holding bilateral discussions, and on June 1 the first round of discussions opened in London between Japanese and Soviet officials. Differences between the two countries included fishing rights in the northern Pacific and adjacent waters, the status of Japanese prisoners of war detained in Siberia, and Japan's application for membership in the United Nations. However, the key stumbling block involved territorial matters. Since the closing days of World War II, the Soviet Union had occupied the Kurile Islands, an extended archipelago to the north of Japan, stretching in an arc from Hokkaido to Russia's Kamchatka peninsula. In addition, Soviet troops had seized control over Shikotan and the Habomais, two smaller island groupings not formally included in the Kurile chain and situated very close to Hokkaido.

During the San Francisco conference of 1951, Japan had renounced (in keeping with the Potsdam declaration of July 1945) any past claim to the Kuriles and recognized as a consequence that its formal sovereignty was limited to the four principal islands of Japan—namely, Kyushu, Hokkaido, Honshu, and Shikoku—as well as the Article III territories of Okinawa and the Ogasawara islands (albeit under Dulles's residual formula). This decision was significant since Japan had previously enjoyed a well-established historical claim over the Kuriles, based on late nineteenth- and early twentieth-century treaties with Russia (in particular the Treaty of St. Petersburg of 1875 and the Portsmouth Treaty of 1905). Japan's decision in 1951 reflected the reality of conditions on the ground—Soviet troops had occupied the northern territories during August and September of 1945—as well as, implicitly, an earlier understanding between the United States and the USSR. At Yalta, in February 1945, President Roosevelt had secretly agreed with Stalin that in return for a Soviet commitment to enter the war against Japan, Russia would be entitled to claim the Kuriles as its own territory.

By 1955, from Japan's perspective, these territorial arrangements were open to question on a number of grounds. First, and perhaps most simply, Japan rejected the Soviet claim over Shikotan and the Habomais since these islands had never officially been recognized internationally as belonging to the Kuriles chain. Second, Soviet retention of the Kuriles was itself open to challenge since, although Japan had formally waived its right over these territories, it had not ceded the islands to Moscow's jurisdiction. The Soviet Union had chosen not to sign the San Francisco Peace Treaty and therefore had no firm legal basis, other than the Yalta agreement, on which to promote its claim over the Kuriles. Moreover, in the eyes of the Eisenhower administration, the Yalta accords had at best a dubious status. Roosevelt's compact had not been ratified by the American Senate and therefore was constitutionally invalid, and the US executive early on made it clear that it would not accept the legitimacy of such secret agreements. However, rejecting the Soviet claim did not extend into an easily supportable Japanese case for territorial reversion. The problem was mainly one of definitions. In addition to the Habomais and Shikotan, the Japanese government desired to regain sovereignty over Etorofu and Kunashiri—the two southernmost islands in the Kurile chain. Yet, in San Francisco, Yoshida had made no effort to distinguish between these islands and the rest of the Kuriles and had unambiguously acknowledged that Japan was giving up its claim over the entire archipelago[118]—a decision which was reconfirmed in October 1951 by a statement in the Diet by Nishimura Kumao, the head of the Treaties Bureau in the Japanese Foreign Ministry.[119]

The Hatoyama government discounted these earlier admissions and pursued (at least initially) an ambitious agenda on the territorial question. In February 1956 Matsumoto Shunichi, the Japanese negotiator, demanded the reversion of all four islands (Etorofu, Kunashiri, Shikotan, and the Habomais) from the Soviets[120] as a precondition for normalization and the signing of a peace treaty between the two counties. The Soviets offered to return only Shikotan and the Habomais, and negotiations remained deadlocked until August 1956, when Shigemitsu (having assumed responsibility for the talks from Matsumoto) suggested publicly in Moscow that it would be advisable to accept the Soviets' two-island proposal. The foreign minister's tactics appeared to be a surprisingly frank admission of diplomatic weakness. Back in Tokyo, the cabinet unanimously rejected Shigemitsu's proposal.[121] To the Americans, accepting Soviet terms seemed a mistake and unlikely to advance either Western or Japanese interests. Meeting Shigemitsu in London shortly after the Moscow talks, Dulles informed him that accepting Soviet claims of sovereignty over the southern Kuriles could potentially jeopardize other Japanese territorial interests. Under the terms of Article XXVI of the San Francisco Peace Treaty, Japan, in reaching an accommodation with its former wartime opponents, was obliged to extend to signatory states any provisions or terms subsequently agreed to with other non-signatory powers. In this instance, a territorial accommodation with the Soviet Union would require a similar concession to the United States in the form of an admission by Japan that it was renouncing its residual sovereignty over the Ryukyu and Bonin Islands. Dulles's remarks were made privately to Shigemitsu but were leaked to the press, generating considerable controversy in Japan. To contemporary observers, and also to a number of later diplomatic historians, the US secretary appeared to be attempting to limit Japan's room for diplomatic maneuver. Suggesting a linkage with the Article III territories was, according to this interpretation, a means of undercutting Shigemitsu's strategy, a basis for preventing a rapprochement between Moscow and Tokyo and also, importantly, a clever device by which the United States might reinforce its hold over strategically valuable islands in the western Pacific.[122] However, a close examination of Japanese and American decision-making processes at this time raises the possibility that Dulles may have been more interested in supporting than undermining the Japanese negotiating position with the USSR.

The Americans had little immediate reason to be concerned about Japan's alignment with the USSR, or to worry that an agreement with the Soviets would seriously threaten US interests. Frequently during the London and Moscow talks, Japanese officials privately impressed on the Americans that an agreement between Moscow and Tokyo would not conflict with existing Japanese-American relations[123]—a position which was bolstered by US intelligence reports indicating that a Japanese tilt toward Moscow and neutralism was unlikely to jeopardize Japan's alignment with the West.[124] Moreover, although Dulles suspected that formal diplomatic links between Moscow and Tokyo might allow the Soviets to widen their espionage activities within Japan, the United States was not in principle opposed to closer ties between the USSR and Japan.[125] Early in 1955, the Americans had recognized that the emergence of a new administration in Japan presaged the development of new ties with the Soviet Union and that it was in US interests to avoid any suggestion that they might be opposed to or interfering in such developments. As Dulles observed in a cable to the embassy in Tokyo, "US does not want to be put position suffering major public defeat prejudicial basic US-Japan security alignment if Japan essentially takes steps develop diplomatic relations

USSR or Communist China."[126] Similarly, the State Department, follow-ing the reporting of Dulles's August conversation with Shigemitsu, was concerned to avoid compromising Japan's decision-making autonomy, noting that the United States ought to "permit the Japanese to make up their own minds as to what course they will take [with the Soviet Union], rather than place on our shoulders the responsibility for a breaking off of the negotiations which they might decide upon in their own interests in any event."[127]

Where Japan's territorial ambitions were concerned, the United States found itself in an awkward position. Although the Eisenhower adminis-tration had rejected the Yalta provisions,[128] it could not on this basis sim-ply argue that Japan had a legitimate claim over the Kuriles. This would violate the terms of the San Francisco Peace Treaty and raise doubts over the legal status of Taiwan and the Pescadores (territories that Japan had renounced in 1951) while potentially jeopardizing the entire foundation of the US-Japan relationship as defined by the Peace and Security treaties.[129] The United States had already gone some way to supporting Japanese claims in 1955 by publicly announcing that Shikotan and the Habomais belonged to Japan and were not affected by the terms either of the Yalta Agreement or the 1951 Peace Treaty. In October 1952, the So-viets had shot down and seized the crew of a US B-29 aircraft flying off the coast of Hokkaido in Japanese airspace, and the State Department, in demanding damages from the Soviets, had emphasized that the territories were not part of the Kuriles and rightfully belonged to Japan.[130] However, a more energetic defense of Japan's territorial ambitions might conflict with US interests since, if the Soviets were to return the disputed Kuriles, America risked being obliged to withdraw from the Ryukyus—a point which Dulles and the State Department leadership were well aware of.[131] But these considerations did not necessarily entail a divergence between US and Japanese attitudes toward the USSR. Dulles, on August 24 (a few days after his meeting in London with Shigemitsu), instructed the State Department's historical division to determine if there might be any plau-sible basis for arguing that Etorofu and Kunashiri were not part of the Kuriles. Recognition of America's relatively insecure position in the Arti-cle III territories did not rule out efforts to support Japan, particularly if this was combined with a vigorous negotiating stance toward the Sovi-ets—an approach which the secretary of state considered more likely to produce concessions from Moscow, although not necessarily the return of the Kuriles. If the Soviets for strategic reasons were determined to hold onto Etorofu and Kunashiri, Dulles could recommend to the Japanese a hard-line (but low-risk) negotiating position, without jeopardizing US interests.

There is considerable evidence that this line of reasoning shaped Dulles's reference to Article XXVI in his conversation with Shigemitsu. Far from undercutting Japan, the secretary of state was attempting to provide the Japanese with negotiating ammunition with which to extract concessions from the Soviets. Dulles had already in December 1955 suggested to Shigemitsu in a confidential telegram that a firm position was likely to produce positive dividends. "I do not wish to comment on substantive issues raised by London talks," he wrote, "but believe that if Japanese Government persists steadfastly in seeking to achieve fair and reasonable agreement, chances are good Japan will come out well in negotiations."[132] When news of his reference to Article XXVI leaked to the press, Dulles quickly assured Japanese officials that he did not wish to put pressure on Japan,[133] a position he continued to stress more than a month after his original meeting with Shigemitsu:

> He explained that in London he had referred to Article XXVI of the Peace Treaty in his discussions with Foreign Minister Shigemitsu, explaining that if Japan conceded sovereignty by the USSR over the Southern Kuriles, that the United States would have the right to request sovereignty over the Ryūkyūs. The Secretary explained that he stated this only for the purpose of giving an argument to the Japanese in their discussions with the USSR and not as an expression of interest on the part of the United States.[134]

A skeptical observer might assume that Dulles's statements were merely an effort to save face. However, evidence from the British archives suggests a more complicated picture. On August 25, Arthur Ringwalt of the US embassy in London had briefed the Foreign Office on the Dulles-Shigemitsu discussions, assuring the British that the Article XXVI reference was "not meant as a statement of the US position but purely as an argument for the Japanese to use themselves and was put forward to stiffen them." Ringwalt's information was provided unofficially and "in confidence," independent of any prompting from Washington, and there is no particular reason to assume that he was trying to mislead his British colleagues.[135]

The public outcry which had greeted the publication of the Price Report on Okinawa in the summer of 1956 and the suggestion that a system of lump-sum payments might enable the United States to remain in the Ryukyus indefinitely had already demonstrated the sensitivity of territorial and sovereignty issues,[136] and it seems unlikely (as Sakamoto Kazuya has argued) that Dulles, who was conscious of the long-term requirements of the US-Japan relationship, would have risked provoking controversy so soon after this earlier upheaval.[137] Indeed, the controversy itself was triggered by Japanese rather than American actions, since it was Matsumoto Shunichi (the key Japanese negotiator during the London-stage of the Soviet-Japanese talks) who leaked to the Japanese press the details of the Article XXVI discussion, "with the intention of embarrassing not so much the Americans as Shigemitsu himself."[138] Matsumoto felt that ceding sovereignty over the Southern Kuriles to the Soviets was too high a price to pay for the return of Shikotan and the Habomais,[139] and it was clear to the US State Department that, through the disclosure, he was intentionally "knifing" his foreign minister, while "sending private reports to Kono in Tokyo that Shigemitsu was botching the negotiations."[140] State Department officials were made "exceedingly angry" by the leak of the conversation, and appear to have been focused on working cooperatively with their Japanese counterparts. As they complained to the British, "it is hard to do business with these fellows when they are all knifing each other to beat the band."[141]

On legal grounds, it is also doubtful that Dulles would have expected to achieve much by pressuring Japan. Under the terms of the 1951 Peace Treaty, Article XXVI retained binding force only for a period of three years, and even if it had remained valid in 1956 it is difficult to see how it might have been fairly applied among all the original signatory states. A Japanese territorial concession to the Soviet Union might have been "balanced" by a similar cession of sovereignty to the United States over the Article III territories, but it would surely not have been possible to extend similar territorial benefits to the other former wartime Allies. The State Department recognized the legal limitations of the original provision,[142] and Dulles, the former international lawyer, must have been fully aware of them.

Japanese Foreign Office officials also publicly denied that Dulles's remarks represented an effort by the United States to assert American territorial claims over Okinawa,[143] and maintained that privately Dulles was attempting to bolster the Japanese negotiating position. Writing to Allison in early September, the secretary outlined the importance of national resilience and standing firm in the face of Soviet pressure:

> Here is my personal thinking about the Russian Treaty situation: a solution is
> not to be found in ingenuity of formula, negotiating skill or persuasive ora-

tory. It is to be found in the nature of the Japanese nation's resistance to Soviet toughness. If the result of that toughness is to bring about increasing Japanese hostility toward Communism, both as regards the Soviet Union and mainland China, then I believe there is a fair chance that the Russians will take a compromise territorial formula the Japanese could live with. If, however, the result is to strengthen the hand of those within Japan who believe that they should be more conciliatory toward the Communists, then of course, the Russians will persist in their tough policies. The answer is then to be found not in any territorial conference or in any special form of negotiation, but with the hearts and minds of the Japanese people themselves. They and they alone can provide the answer.[144]

The United States did not need to threaten the loss of Okinawa to prevent the Japanese public from being seduced by Soviet blandishments. Historically there was little love lost between Japan and Russia, and the seizure in 1955 by the Soviets of some 125 Japanese fishing vessels and more than 1,000 Japanese fishermen had exacerbated a relationship already strained by mistrust and past territorial conflicts.[145] From an American perspective, the weak link in Japan's policy toward the Soviet Union was to be found within the country's political leadership and not in ordinary mass opinion. Despite their success in creating a unified Liberal Democratic Party in November 1955,[146] Japan's conservative politicians remained sharply divided along personal and policy lines. Misgivings remained over the health of Hatoyama, who periodically received electric shock treatment for his earlier stroke[147]—a restrictive medical condition that aptly seemed to symbolize the paralysis enveloping the Japanese government. Even though Hatoyama had been chosen as the new LDP president, from January 1956 onward internal party activity was dominated by the contest to choose a successor.[148] This rivalry spilled over into the debate over policy toward the Soviet Union, reinforcing for State Department officials the image of an administration beset by internal divisions.

Some months prior to the formation of the LDP, Ogata Taketora, a senior Liberal politician and widely tipped successor to Hatoyama, stressed to the Americans his disagreement with Hatoyama's efforts to promote closer relations with Moscow. In June 1955, Takase Seizan, an advisor to Ogata, in a meeting with US embassy personnel in Tokyo, relayed Ogata's belief "that Hatoyama's 'two-faced diplomacy' would seriously impair the Free World's confidence in Japan, and injure Japan's chance for regaining her place in international society."[149] Doubts regarding Hatoyama's current Soviet policy were not limited to the Liberals:

Mr Takase said that Democratic leaders such as Sunada, Kishi, and Bukichi Miki are no longer nearly so enthusiastic about continuing negotiations with the Soviet [sic] as they were during the election campaign. Then it was politically fashionable and profitable to be in favour of "normalizing relations." Actually these same leaders now hope that the negotiations will end in failure. They hope that the Soviets will take an attitude which will make it possible for Japan to blame them for the breakdown of the negotiations.[150]

Ogata's unexpected death in January 1956 provoked further domestic political instability, but many other prominent politicians continued to criticize official policy. Former Prime Minister Yoshida remained (in keeping with Japan's political traditions) a powerful figure behind the scenes as well as an outspoken critic. Shortly before Shigemitsu's departure for Moscow in 1956, he published an open letter to his protégé, Ikeda Hayato, sharply criticizing the foreign minister and warning that he and his supporters would break away from the LDP if Shigemitsu continued his negotiations with the Russians.[151]

Yoshida's threat was never realized but it highlighted the diversity of conservative views over dealings with the Soviets.[152] In May 1956, Kōno Ichirō, the minister of agriculture, suggested to Dulles that it might be appropriate to adopt the "Adenauer formula"—a reference to the September 1955 agreement between West Germany and the USSR providing for a resumption of diplomatic relations, without a formal peace treaty or agreement on territorial issues.[153] Prior to the Shigemitsu visit to Moscow, Kōno had informed Allison that Japan's minimum condition for its talks with the USSR was an acknowledgment by the Soviets that Japan was entitled to residual sovereignty over Kunashiri and Etorofu.[154] However, Shigemitsu's acceptance of the Soviet's two-island formula in August clearly revealed that different figures within the government were pursuing conflicting strategies. As had been the case during the talks in Washington in 1955, the foreign minister found himself out of step with his colleagues. He also faced opposition from senior Gaimushō officials who favored a firm, uncompromising stance toward the Soviets (as Matsumoto's disclosure of the Dulles-Shigemitsu talks had demonstrated). It is no wonder that, as an already vulnerable and isolated foreign minister, Shigemitsu appeared "worried and distraught"[155] following the cabinet's rejection of the Soviets' two-island proposal, and by the end of August any hope he may have had of using the talks in Moscow to bolster his political career had almost certainly evaporated. As Allison noted: "Fo[reig]n Office working level gossip yesterday was that Shigemitsu has so thoroughly lost face by the succession of denials and confirmations that Kōno faction intends use episode to push through Cabinet reshuffle, including ouster of Shigemitsu."[156] Once again, internal political ambitions appear to have taken precedence over coherent national policy objectives.[157]

The intensity of these factional tensions and Japanese public reluctance to offer concessions to the Soviets raises the interesting counter-factual question "What would have occurred if Dulles had not invoked Article XXVI?" It is difficult to imagine that a two-island solution, involving a Japanese acceptance of Soviet sovereignty over the Southern Kuriles, would have been viable.[158] Opposition at home, rather than US intervention, appears to have been the critical factor standing in the way of a peace treaty on these terms, and since the State Department was well aware of the splits within the conservative camp in Japan, it is unlikely that Dulles would have felt any need to undercut an already fatally weak foreign minister. Indeed, we now know, thanks to the recent declassification of a number of important US records, that the Japanese cabinet was firmly opposed to a territorial compromise and had hung the hapless Shigemitsu out to dry three days in advance of his London talks with Dulles. Dulles's staff notes again provide the critical revelation:

> The Deputy Secretary of the Japanese Cabinet has told Allison that the Cabinet is unanimous in its opposition to Shigemitsu's recommendations that Japan yield to Soviet demands. He said the Japanese leaders were amazed that Shigemitsu proposed to yield not only on the Southern Kuriles but also on the limitation of passage of the Japan Sea Straits, and they believe that somehow "Moscow has affected his mind." For this reason the Cabinet has decided to send Shigemitsu to London where he can see the Secretary, talk more freely with Bohlen, and get a briefing on Japanese government and party sentiment from the Transportation Minister who is on the Japanese Suez delegation.[159]

There seems, therefore, little if any reason to support the traditional interpretation that Dulles's actions were an attempt to thwart the national interests of the Japanese government. Rather, his interaction with the Japanese foreign minister was an attempt to lay out an alternative negotiating strategy and one which may have been calculated to bring Shigemitsu "on side" with his own government.

British embassy personnel in Tokyo were well aware of the decisive role played by personal rivalries and Hatoyama's weak leadership, and their reporting confirms the impression of deep divisions and contradictory positions within the Japanese government. Commenting on the Japanese cabinet's rejection of Shigemitsu's concessionary approach in early August, one report observed:

There is . . . no evidence that public opinion in Japan would have applauded such a performance even if Shigemitsu had been allowed to carry it through and the Government, has, of course, adduced this unchanging public demand for the return of the South Kuriles as the reason for the rather startling change of mind of so many of its own members previously noted for their advocacy of an early settlement at almost any price. It is, however, difficult to avoid the impression from the way the negotiations have been handled at the Tokyo end that an important section of the Cabinet is intent on destroying Shigemitsu's political position whatever the outcome of the Soviet negotiations is to be.[160]

Similarly, analyzing the entire course of Soviet-Japanese negotiations during 1955 and 1956, the British embassy in Tokyo noted:

The negotiations throughout their course have been bedevilled by Japanese internal political feuds. Opponents of Mr. Hatoyama within the Liberal-Democratic Party, making Mr. Shigemitsu their figurehead, have bitterly opposed the territorial concessions that would allow the Prime Minister to fulfil his election promise. Opponents of Mr. Shigemitsu led by Mr. Kono, were equally determined, when the Foreign Minister decided in Moscow that concessions were unavoidable, to keep him from gaining the credit of having made an agreement, and so reversed their own previous advocacy of an early settlement at almost any price. The uncertain and vacillating personality of Mr. Hatoyama served only to accentuate the differences within the ruling party which hamstrung the Japanese government.[161]

Differences within the Japanese government were eventually resolved (although only temporarily, given the nature of the final settlement) with the signing on October 19 of a Soviet-Japanese trade protocol and a Joint Declaration ending the war and restoring diplomatic relations. No formal peace treaty was agreed, and in effect the Adenauer formula was adopted. The Soviets agreed to support Japan's entry into the UN, to repatriate a number of Japanese "war criminals," and to hand over Shikotan and the Habomais to Japan once a peace treaty was signed by the two countries.[162]

Kishi, MacArthur, and Treaty Revision, 1957–60

The partial settlement with the Soviet Union was the Hatoyama administration's last major diplomatic achievement and one that occurred against a backdrop of continuing conservative factionalism and internal squabbling. Symptomatic of LDP difficulties had been the party's poor performance in the July 6 elections for the Upper House. While the government maintained its pre-election strength of 122 out of 250 seats, the

Socialists through an astute and focused election campaign boosted their representation by 12 seats from 68 to 80 seats. This was especially important since, by securing (together with their left-wing allies) the one-third threshold of seats needed to block a constitutional amendment, the Left could now stymie any major changes to the country's political makeup. With many prominent conservative politicians committed to the notion of constitutional change, the election represented a major disappointment and tactical setback, provoking in turn criticism of the government and calls for a change of leadership.[163]

By the end of 1956, ill-health had forced the prime minister to resign and a new administration had been formed under the leadership of Ishibashi Tanzan. However, Ishibashi's tenure was exceptionally brief, cut-short by a severe case of bronchial pneumonia, and in late February, Kishi took over as prime minister.[164] This development represented a turning-point in the US-Japan relationship, and early on, US officials recognized that the new leadership offered the prospect of a more decisive and proactive Japanese government. For the State Department, the Ishibashi cabinet had heralded the emergence of more stable and effective Japanese leadership,[165] and Kishi was seen as a reinforcement and extension of this process. Indeed, for Douglas MacArthur, namesake and nephew of General MacArthur and recently appointed successor to Allison as ambassador to Japan, the new prime minister was someone with whom the United States could "do business."[166] Kishi had made a favorable impression on American officials during his visit to Washington in 1955 with Shigemitsu, and his early actions as prime minister rapidly underlined this view. To MacArthur, Kishi represented, despite continuing factional rivalries within the Japanese government, "a steadily emerging picture of purposeful effectiveness at the helm of a powerful and resurgent nation," skilled in handling Diet interpolations and likely to head a cabinet which would prove "the strongest yet in post-war Japan."[167] The new leader was energetic and decisive, embarking on a series of demanding and extensive overseas tours shortly after becoming prime minister, including in June a visit to the United States to discuss security issues and general bilateral relations. In anticipating this Washington summit, it was clear to embassy officials in Tokyo that the new prime minister represented a sharp contrast with the earlier confused and infirm leadership, and it was "worth keeping in mind" that Kishi was "an extraordinarily well-informed person, with a quick and agile mind," someone who would "probably . . . be very well briefed" and "likely to have much greater familiarity with and understanding of matters to be discussed than was for instance the case with Shigemitsu in 1955."[168]

The State Department's positive assessment of Kishi was quickly confirmed. The prime minister's visit to Washington proved a success, promoting an atmosphere of close, bilateral cooperation and establishing, through an agreement to create a new Japanese-American Committee on Security, a context for discussions on possible Security Treaty revision and more extensive consultation on strategic and diplomatic issues.[169] Prior to the Washington visit, Kishi positioned the development of a firm alignment with the United States at the center of his administration's policies, instructing the Foreign Ministry in March to set up a working group on US-Japan relations.[170] Taken at face value, the prime minister's ideological and political sympathies were somewhat hard to categorize. Kishi had entered public life as a bureaucrat, and during the war had served as minister of commerce and industry in the cabinet of Tōjō Hideki—an experience which led to his indictment during the Occupation as a class A war criminal and a period of incarceration in Sugamo prison, as well as earning him the distrust of the Left in post-war Japan. Following the Occupation, Kishi had established a new political movement—the Japan Reconstruction Alliance (Nihon saiken renmei)—but the organization performed disastrously in the elections of April 1952. Chastened, Kishi contemplated joining the Right Socialist Party, but chose ultimately to align with conservative interests, playing a key role in the formation of the Democratic Party and eventually in the establishment of the LDP in late 1955.[171]

Kishi's political objectives included avoiding the excessive personalism that characterized factional politics while also enhancing Japan's independence and strengthening the country's ties with the United States—goals which he felt need not prove contradictory. In pursuing these aims, he focused on rearmament—as he was to admit subsequently, 70 percent of his time as prime minister was devoted to security issues[172]—precisely the response that Dulles had found lacking among Japan's earlier post-war leadership. As Kishi pointed out, early in 1952:

> Japan should be strong enough to defend herself. This is the right and obligation of an independent nation. That the Japanese nation seems to prefer relying, as long as possible, on the protection of the United States, is proof enough that this country, conditioned by Occupation policies, has lost its sense of self-reliance, and that the spirit of independence she once had has been paralysed.[173]

On May 20, 1957, early during his administration, Kishi initiated a cabinet-approved "Basic Plan for National Defense"—a program which covered the period from 1958 to 1960 and in substance corresponded to the final three years of the earlier JDA six-year defense plan.[174] Unlike the previous plan, the new policy had official status—an indication that the government was formally committed to building up the country's defenses. This high-profile approach typified Kishi's leadership style: a preference for direct and unambiguous statements, reinforced (according to Kitaoka Shin'ichi) by an outstanding ability to anticipate key political developments and an extensive network of personal connections from his time as a bureaucrat, as well as strong links with Japan's business community.[175] Perhaps most important, in terms of relations with the United States, Kishi benefited from a close and effective relationship with his foreign minister, Fujiyama Aiichirō. Fujiyama was a prominent businessman whose financial support had been especially helpful in rebuilding Kishi's political career following the Occupation, and the friendship between the two men was important in minimizing the factional strife and divided decision-making that had dogged foreign policy under Hatoyama.

Where US-Japanese relations were concerned, Kishi's tenure as prime minister (from 1957 to 1960) was dominated by the question of Security Treaty revision. Bilateral negotiations between Washington and Tokyo over the treaty were detailed and extensive, stretching from late 1958 to the end of 1959, while in Japan, the domestic political repercussions associated with the new treaty were enormous and dramatic, ultimately contributing to the prime minister's political downfall. The treaty crisis has already been examined extensively in other sources,[176] but a number of central themes are worth highlighting here. To begin with, personalities and key individuals on both sides were important in promoting close and mutually beneficial coordination between the American and Japanese governments. Kishi's focus on cooperative US-Japan relations was complemented by Douglas MacArthur's constant insistence on the need for an early accommodation of Japanese interests through the drafting of a new treaty. MacArthur had had no direct experience in Japan prior to his service as ambassador. However, his work in Washington had involved East Asian issues, and the substance and tone of his reports from Tokyo echoed the analysis of his predecessor. Shortly before leaving Japan, Allison had dispatched a lengthy report to Washington, entitled "A Fresh Start with Japan," in which he documented the grievances (both real and perceived) on both sides of the bilateral relationship, as well as warning that a failure to develop greater mutuality in the relationship and more extensive consultation between Washington and Tokyo might ultimately encourage Japan to drift away from the United States. For the United States, critical shortcomings could be traced to the domestic Japanese political environment:

> The crux of our discontent with Japan lies in her political weakness . . . This weakness expresses itself in every sphere, foreign and domestic, military and economic. In each it takes the form of timid, faltering government, afraid of its own shadow, groping at almost any means of shifting responsibility (especially onto the US), delaying decision, evading the problems with which Japan is confronted[177]

Kishi's emergence as prime minister helped to address this problem, but MacArthur regularly stressed to Washington the need to "knit Japan . . . thoroughly into the fabric of the free world" by cooperating closely on security matters, by expanding Japanese trading opportunities in the American market, and also by increasing US public and congressional awareness of Japan's importance.[178]

By September 1958, MacArthur's persistent lobbying for a new treaty relationship with Japan had paid off, encouraged in part by signs that the conservatives were regaining their feet politically. Elections in May 1958 had allowed the government to retain its top-heavy majority in the Lower House, and by adding 11 nominally independent Diet members to the LDP fold, it could count on 298 out of 467 seats, a one-seat increase on the 1955 result. Kishi's victory was not an unqualified success. The prime minister, despite his undoubted tactical skills, failed to generate a popular following among the electorate, and the Socialists continued to gain support in urban prefectures and big cities. Nonetheless, among the voters who particularly counted—mainly farmers and small businessmen—conservative support remained steady. Improved party organization, the continuing importance of personal loyalties to conservative politicians at the grass-roots level, the LDP's ability to paint the Socialists as a "class party" overly beholden to organized labor in the form of Sōhyō, and Kishi's success in undermining any impression that Japan might be overly subservient to the US, all helped to bolster the position of the government.[179]

Against this backdrop of emerging political stability, Dulles (previously cautious in committing the United States to the principle of treaty revision, and wanting reassurance that Japan was genuinely willing to support US security efforts and the maintenance of a "balance of power" in the Far East[180]) accepted the principle of treaty revision, opening the way for formal negotiations in Tokyo between the two countries. US military and Defense Department officials continued, not surprisingly, to adhere to their traditional practice of offering minimal concessions to Japan. Lyman Lemnitzer, CinCFE, although accepting the importance of greater consultation and MacArthur's assessment that a change in the security relationship was necessary, argued in favor of piecemeal modifications of the existing Security Treaty rather than the drafting of an entirely new agreement.[181] In general, the US military remained disappointed with Japan's defense efforts. Kishi's new defense plan was thought to be a step in the right direction, but overall Japanese defense spending was still low by comparison with that of other advanced countries, with the share of GNP allocated to defense actually declining steadily over the decade. JDA officials had a generally positive relationship with their Pentagon colleagues, but the agency remained weak relative to other bureaucratic actors in Japan, and Japanese force goals stayed well below JCS objectives. Moreover, a residue of distrust occasionally influenced the US military's view of Japan—unsurprisingly after the bitterness of the Pacific War, but clearly not helpful in promoting closer bilateral cooperation. In May 1957, for example, the CinCPAC warned that Japan could become "a dangerous military opponent if lost to the free world," while in September 1958, Lemnitzer argued privately that in a future military crisis the United States could rely on cooperation and support from allies such as Britain but not from Japan.[182]

Issues of trust and cooperation were central to the new treaty negotiations. Mutuality in the new Mutual Security Treaty was defined in a somewhat unorthodox manner. It was not to be guaranteed by a Japanese commitment to assist in protecting US territorial interests or to participate in joint military operations in the Far East—an important concession that reflected Japanese political and constitutional constraints. There was, in other words, no common defense concept along the lines of the NATO agreement of 1949 in which the participating powers acknowledged that an attack against one represented an attack against all. Instead, in return for a formal US commitment to defend Japan (lacking in the original Security Treaty), the Japanese government accepted that US forces based in Japan could be deployed in the Far East to meet challenges to regional security. Japanese acceptance of any future US deployment would be based on "consultation," but consultation itself was loosely defined. It was far from clear that Japan enjoyed anything approaching a formal veto over US actions—something which both Congress and the Pentagon would have been loath to accept—and even the notion of the "Far East" was left intentionally vague. This ambiguity was counterbalanced by precision in other areas. The duration of the new treaty was now formally set at a minimum of ten years, after which either signatory could withdraw from the agreement following one year's advance notice. The internal security clause of the 1951 Security Treaty, under which US forces could, at the wishes of the Japanese government, be requested to quell domestic Japanese disturbances (a provision which some in Japan felt was a mark of inequality) was eliminated.[183] Perhaps most important of all in light of earlier negotiations, the Article XXV provisions of the Administrative Agreement, stipulating a formal Japanese financial contribution to US forces in Japan, were excluded from the new agreement. The concept of mutual support remained, but it was no longer defined in quantitative terms.

Agreement over security matters, although it had involved detailed negotiation, had been reached relatively amicably. Japan had accepted US proposals without any major modifications, and in January 1960 Kishi had traveled to Washington for a signing ceremony that represented a diplomatic and political success for the leaders of both countries. Bilateral relations appeared to be entering a "new era," and with this in mind the OCB was considering plans for a new NSC policy paper on Japan. This success was particularly noteworthy in light of the stresses placed on the bilateral relationship at the beginning of Kishi's premiership. In January 1957, the US press had reported that a US soldier in Japan had shot and killed a Japanese woman, Naka Sakai. Sergeant William Girard had been guarding a gun emplacement on a firing-range used by US troops where local inhabitants had a habit of collecting for re-sale the spent brass cartridge cases used in firing-practice. Girard had allegedly deliberately thrown out a cartridge to encourage Sakai to approach the emplacement, then fired a blank cartridge hitting her in the back and killing her instantly.

The Girard incident generated major controversy in Japan and particularly in the United States, provoking "the greatest outburst of American public indignation involving US-Japan relations since World War II."[184] At issue was the question of jurisdiction over US personnel stationed in Japan. Under the terms of the Administrative Agreement (and in keeping with similar Status of Forces agreements between the United States and its allies), the Japanese and American governments had agreed in 1953 that US military personnel accused of crimes committed outside the context of their official duties should be tried by Japanese courts. Initially, the embassy in Japan agreed that Girard's actions warranted a Japanese trial. However, the decision was soon challenged both by Defense Department officials in Washington and by a number of prominent and outspoken individuals in Congress. Pressure quickly mounted for a reversal of the earlier decision, with the secretary of the Army recommending a court-martial in the United States, and the Republican Representative of Ohio, Frank Bow, proposing a congressional resolution providing for exclusive US jurisdiction in all Status of Forces Agreements.

To both Dulles and the President, these suggestions seemed impractical, unwise, and overly emotional. Dulles was fearful that any attempt to reverse the earlier agreement with Japan would jeopardize the entire bilateral relationship, particularly in light of insensitive and offensive US newspaper reports suggesting, inaccurately, that Girard would be unable to secure a fair trial in Japan. Congressional and press criticism stimulated narrow-minded and damaging xenophobic prejudices. Eisenhower, although inclined to agree that the initial decision to cede jurisdiction over Girard to the Japanese authorities may have been mistaken, recognized the crucial importance of honoring America's earlier commitment to Japan. Writing to his boyhood friend and long-term correspondent "Swede" Hazlett, the President made little attempt to conceal his irritation and frustration with Congress:

> I am repeatedly astonished, even astounded by the apparent ignorance of members of Congress in the general subject of our foreign affairs and relationships. I realize that by this time I should accept, as a matter of course, Congressional reaction that seemingly reflects either this abysmal ignorance or a far greater concern for local political sentiment than for the welfare of the United States. . . . [R]ight at this moment, lack of understanding of America's position and obligation accounts for the fact that we seem to be trying to make a national hero out of a man who shot a woman—in the back at some thing like ten to fifteen yards distance . . . We have even had a serious attempt made to force me to denounce our Status of Forces treaties. These treaties, as you know, are fair and just to Americans serving abroad and are the only means by which we retain jurisdiction in most offences committed. Because they establish a reasonable jurisdictional balance between ourselves and the host country, they are at the very foundation of our defensive alliances. To denounce them would make us completely isolationist and force us to abandon practically every base we have abroad.[185]

Eisenhower's irritation also extended to the Defense Department for acting inconsistently and for going "too far" in seeking a correction of the earlier agreement with Japan.[186]

The crisis was eventually settled through a gradual erosion of congressional opposition to the original decision. The President was careful to conceal his private discontent from the legislature and patiently wooed his critics by stressing the fairness of the Japanese judicial system and by pointing out that, of some 14,000 similar cases that had occurred in Japan since the Occupation, Japan had voluntarily ceded jurisdiction to the United States in no fewer than 13,642 instances.[187] Bow's resolution failed to pass the House in the face of a threatened presidential veto, and on July 11, the US Supreme Court ruled that there was nothing to prevent the United States from granting jurisdiction over the case to Japan. The Japanese, for their part, responded diplomatically and in keeping with past cases by imposing a three-year suspended sentence on Girard, who was then able to return to the United States, where he was promptly discharged from the Army.[188]

Settling the Girard controversy had eliminated a potentially serious obstacle to closer security cooperation and allowed the bilateral relationship to develop relatively smoothly over the next two to three years. John Foster Dulles's death from cancer in April 1959 had removed one of the key stewards of the bilateral relationship,[189] but the signing of the new Security Treaty in January 1960 (a hundred years after the first Japanese mission to America) appeared to herald a new period of stability in US-Japan relations. However, events in the first half of the year soon revealed, in dramatic fashion, that a number of important questions remained unresolved. Kishi returned from Washington to find that ratification of the new agreement, as well as his own position as prime minister and LDP president, were by no means guaranteed. In part Kishi's difficulties stemmed from tensions between public, in particular left-wing, opinion and the government. His direct leadership style and identification with pre-war traditionalism made him an unpopular figure, and an attempt (ultimately unsuccessful) in the autumn of 1958 to introduce new legislation substantially strengthening national police powers provoked accusations that the government was autocratic and predisposed to ignore democratic sensibilities. At the end of May 1960, Kishi's efforts to ratify the treaty reinforced this impression. In the face of a JSP attempt to barricade the speaker of the House of Representatives in his office to prevent a vote on the new treaty, the prime minister authorized the police to enter the Diet to free the speaker and eject forcibly any opposition members who attempted to physically obstruct the ratification process. A vote was promptly held, but with only LDP Diet members participating (the Opposition boycotted the proceedings), and the treaty was finally approved.[190] Kishi's decision had quickly ended the deadlock but was criticized by the opposition and by the press as undemocratic and a refusal to tolerate minority opinion, and it added fuel to left-wing and opposition complaints and ultimately encouraged greater radicalism. The JSP had suffered a damaging split in late 1959 when moderate, non-Marxist elements in the party split away to form a new Democratic Socialist Party (DSP) or Minshaō, under the leadership of Suehirō Nishio. Internal splits and the Socialists' inability to unseat the government electorally, along with the impressive economic progress achieved under conservative administrations, contributed to frustration within the JSP and made the party more willing to protest through force.[191] By June, discontent had metamorphosed into a major protest movement. A general strike on June 4 brought thousands of workers onto the streets protesting against both the Kishi administration and the security relationship with the United States. The protest was complemented by large-scale student demonstrations in Tokyo, spearheaded by Trotskyite radicals and left-wing activists from Zengakuren—the national federation of Japanese university students—campaigning vociferously and often violently against the government.[192]

It is debatable to what extent this protest movement reflected popular opinion nationally. There was no consensus, for example, on the number of participants in the general strike, with protest organizers claiming five and a half million took part and the government setting the figure much lower, at 750,000.[193] Moreover, the State Department and officials in the embassy in Tokyo believed that there was evidence of active Communist Chinese and Soviet involvement in fomenting unrest and opposition to the Security Treaty. Perhaps the most important indication of the diversity of Japanese opinion was the results from recent local and national elections. The LDP had not only performed well in the Upper House elections of June 1959 but also enjoyed outstanding results in the gubernatorial elections of April 1960. The election results may in part have reflected improved economic conditions in the country—1959 had been a year of unprecedented prosperity, with industrial production increasing 28 percent on the previous year, with real incomes rising steadily, and with the country enjoying its largest ever rice harvest[194]—but to commentators at the time they were also evidence of Japan's largely silent, conservative majority and the relatively restricted character of the protest movement. As Hessell Tiltman, an American correspondent well versed in Japanese affairs, noted in June 1960:

> The real Japan—the millions of conservatives, farmers, fishermen and small and medium employers and their workers which represent the political backbone of the country and decide its political pattern—has remained largely on the sidelines. . . . Anti-Americanism, while it has grown as the demonstration proceeded, is still largely confined to the leaders, the communists and students, and neutralist intellectuals.[195]

The protesters were possibly in part intoxicated by their ability to challenge the ruling orthodoxy and encouraged also by a media and intellectual climate that seemed reluctant to advocate clear policies and to assess the legitimacy and implications of the demonstrations. In the words of Edwin Reischauer:

> [M]ost Western observers are discouraged by the naiveté of the democratic opposition in its acceptance not only of Communist support but even of Communist leadership. One can even detect a dangerous tinge of élitism in the intellectuals' unwillingness to accept the conservative vote of rural Japan as a valid expression of majority opinion—an élitism that harks back to an old and most undemocratic tradition. . . . Few intellectuals seem to have given serious thought to the question whether Japan can maintain true neutrality and independence without first rearming. None seems to have pondered what the Japanese would do if the decisions on nasty international problems were left up to them. . . . In other words, Japanese intellectuals have not realistically faced the logical conclusions of the course they advocate.[196]

Popular and academic concerns also reflected genuine anxiety about the state of the world and emerging international tensions. The shooting down in May 1960 of an American U-2 spy plane and the resulting cancellation of the Paris summit meeting between Eisenhower and Khrushev signified a shift away from any possible East-West détente that some in Japan had been hoping for. Particularly troubling to Japanese public opinion was the knowledge that similar aircraft were stationed in Japan—a fact which the Left quickly exploited in attacking the government.[197] Soviet and Chinese propaganda had been aggressively targeting Japan, and following Khrushchev's threat of retaliation against US bases and Moscow's May 30 announcement that Soviet rocket forces had been ordered to strike against any base from which US planes intruded into Soviet air space, public anxiety in Japan increased sharply.[198]

Protest, it should be stressed, was much more a reaction against Kishi personally than against the United States[199] and was not limited to the opposition parties. Within the LDP, there was also significant factional resistance to the prime minister, reflected partly in criticism of specific aspects of the new treaty. For example, during the negotiations with the Americans, prominent party officials, including Ikeda, Kōno, and Miki Takeo, had argued for a full renegotiation of the existing Administrative Agreement—a process that would have been detailed, time-consuming, and resisted by the United States.[200] (Ultimately, adjustments in the agreement were made through a less complicated exchange of side-letters.) Such differences were frequently based more on personal rivalry and political ambition than on substantive policy disagreements or efforts to modify the terms of the treaty,[201] and at critical moments Kishi was able to exploit these ambitions in his own favor. For example, following the 1959 Upper House elections, the Prime Minster had persuaded Ikeda to join the cabinet as MITI minister—a decision which marginalized the opposition to Kishi, concentrating it among the supporters of Kōno and Miki, and also creating a consensus behind the government's policy of US-Japan security cooperation.[202]

Although Kishi had proved successful in garnering support from business groups and throughout the LDP as a whole, his success provoked envy and resistance from his rivals. Moreover, particularly toward the later stages of his premiership, Kishi showed little willingness to compromise or accommodate the views of his internal party opponents. He preferred to appoint his own followers rather than striving for balance among the diverse coalition of interests that constituted the LDP, and cabinet appointments were increasingly concentrated among the members of the Kishi and Satō Eisaku factions. Kishi also had a perfectionist's instinct, reflected in his commitment to the negotiation of a new treaty rather than piecemeal revision, and in his commitment to a high-profile celebration of the agreement through his invitation to Eisenhower to visit Japan in June, shortly after ratification.[203]

The prime minister's high-risk strategy, had it been successful, would have substantially enhanced his political position. However, it had already provoked considerable resistance from his party rivals, who were steadily attempting to undermine his authority.[204] Shortly after his return from Washington, Kishi had planned to dissolve the Diet and hold a general election, but his LDP opponents recognized that the result would almost certainly be a victory for the government at the polls, in turn smoothing the path to treaty ratification and further enhancing the reputation of the prime minister.[205] Placing personal ambitions ahead of party interests, foreign policy, and relations with the United States, Kishi's opponents resisted the dissolution initiative and prevented the general elec-

TABLE 2

Results of Japanese Lower House Elections, 1952–1960

	1952	1953	1955	1958	1960
Conservatives (LDP)					
Popular vote	23,367,671	22,717,348	23,377,432	22,976,830	22,740,265
Pct. of popular vote	67.2	65.7	63.2	57.8	57.6
Diet seats	325	310	297	287	296
Socialists (JSP & DSP)					
Popular vote	7,768,061	9,553,321	11,193,154	13,093,948	14,351,284
Pct. of popular vote	21.9	27.5	30.2	32.9	34.6
Diet seats	115	143	160	166	162
Communist (JCP)					
Popular vote	896,765	655,970	774,158	1,012,036	1,156,723
Pct. of Popular vote	2.6	1.9	2.0	2.6	2.9
Diet seats	0	1	2	1	3
Independents & Minor Parties					
Popular vote	3,304,208	1,675,786	1,661,685	2,688,786	1,260,849
Pct. of popular vote	8.3	4.9	4.0	6.7	3.2
Diet seats	26	12	8	13	6

SOURCE: "Japan: Recent Developments and Short-Run Prospects," Mar. 27, 1961, OIR Report, No. 8438, NA-II.

tion from taking place as planned.[206] Moreover, to the anti-Kishi elements within the LDP, the public protests and demonstrations in Tokyo were an asset rather than a liability. Matters came to a head on June 15 when student protesters broke through to the Diet compound and a Tokyo university student was trampled to death in the ensuing violent clash between police and demonstrators. Unable to guarantee public order and the safety of the President, Kishi, was forced, much to his regret, to rescind the invitation to Eisenhower, and on June 24, the prime minister, in the face of internal party and media criticism as well as another huge strike on June 22, announced his intention to resign.

Notwisthstanding this personal defeat, the prime minister could nevertherless take comfort from the successful completion of the new treaty. Internal LDP rivalry has often been represented as a clash between "mainstream" and "anti-mainstream" elements in the party—between former bureaucrats and career politicians (for example, Kishi and Ikeda versus Kōno and Miki), or between protégés and opponents of former Prime Minister Yoshida. Yet, as Kitaoka Shin'ichi has pointed out, the contest had a broader significance. Approval of the new treaty established, for the first time in the post-war period, a consensus within the

LDP in favor of bilateral security cooperation and a strategy of aligning Japan with the United States, and removed the perception that relations between the two countries were fundamentally unequal.[207] Internal rivalry would of course persist after Kishi, but the new treaty had insulated the US-Japan relationship from some of these pressures, and future prime ministers would be careful to maintain more of a factional balance within cabinet. Strikingly, despite the intensity of the protests of June, the shift to a new administration under Ikeda Hayato proceeded smoothly, with the LDP actually increasing its strength in the Lower House following the November 1960 general election. The party initially secured 296 seats in the contest, and with the addition of 5 independent candidates boosted the number to 301—a powerful illustration of the continuing strength of Japan's conservative majority. Thereafter, US-Japan relations entered a period of relative stability in which the Japanese government concentrated on economic growth, while avoiding the contentious issues of constitutional revision, anti-Communism, and rearmament which had been politically prominent during the 1950s. Defense spending and military issues continued to be controversial, both domestically (given the continuing debate over Article 9 and the constitutional legitimacy of rearmament), and also in terms of relations between Washington and Tokyo. US military planners continued to feel dissatisfied with Japan's low level of defense preparedness, but it was clear, with the agreement of NSC 6008 in May 1960, that the Eisenhower administration had accepted the realities of the status quo. The new policy paper extensively brought NSC 5516/1 up to date, but did not recommend any basic departure in current US policy toward Japan.[208] For the immediate future, at least, the weathering of the domestic crisis and the approval of the new treaty suggested that the security relationship could move forward, free from the shocks and partisan political rivalries that had proved so damaging during the previous decade.

Conclusion

Historical perspective, as scholars so frequently point out, is a luxury rarely enjoyed by policy-makers and journalists. Amid the Japanese domestic turmoil over the Security Treaty in 1960, it might have seemed to contemporary observers that US policy toward Japan had failed.[1] Certainly, with the shift to a new administration under John Kennedy in 1961 and the appointment of Edwin Reischauer as ambassador to Tokyo, there was room for a change of direction and an ostensibly more harmonious bilateral relationship, as some commentators would argue in later years.[2] Such an assessment was perhaps encouraged by the general political climate in the United States, where the "passing of the torch" of government to a younger, arguably more vigorous Democratic leadership raised expectations of a more involved and active style of policy. Implicit in the analysis of the situation in Tokyo was a criticism of the way both the Eisenhower and the Truman administrations had managed relations with Japan. However, as the analysis in these pages has attempted to demonstrate, this criticism has been overstated. It has, in a number of instances overlooked or minimized important internal debates within the US government, the motivations of key individuals in the State Department, factional tensions in Japan which complicated the process of developing a strong security alliance, and the wider Cold War strategic context.

Early post-war US policy toward Japan certainly demonstrated that many American government officials were conscious of the fragile character of the developing bilateral partnership. Dulles, Kennan, Rusk, and other senior State Department figures recognized that policies toward Japan would have to accommodate, where possible, Japanese government and popular wishes, particularly concern over issues of "face" and sovereignty. Frequently, the State Department faced obstacles to such an approach, from US defense planners concerned with overly narrowly defined security priorities and allied nations eager for a restrictive peace settlement in San Francisco. Dulles's achievement in resolving these tensions should not be underestimated.

In terms of the later security and political relationship with Japan, the US government faced a more fundamental obstacle in the form of MacArthur's 1947 Constitution. In this respect, US officials had tied their own hands. Article 9 and the demanding requirements for constitutional amendment created practical barriers to a more active security role for Japan, while the divisive debate over the legitimacy of the new document encouraged a polarized political domestic environment in Japan limiting the policy options of Japan's leaders, frequently in a manner that undercut US security objectives. While Yoshida's position on rearmament remains open to interpretation, there was (as chapter six suggests) a constituency in Japan, represented by JDA members and senior politicians, such as Hatoyama and Kishi, willing to push for more rapid rearmament but constrained by political and economic realities at home from advancing such policies.

State Department recognition of the importance of mutuality persisted throughout the decade, reflected in the Amami reversion agreement, efforts to modify administrative arrangements in Okinawa, cultural exchange initiatives[3] (in many respects the logical extension of the Rockefeller mission of 1951), the Tokyo embassy's "New Look" policy of 1954, the drafting of NSC 5516/1 in 1955, and Ambassador MacArthur's vigorous backing for a revision of the Security Treaty in the late 1950s. The value of these initiatives was, at the same time, limited by conditions on the ground. The practical challenge of maintaining large numbers of US military personnel in Japan inevitably generated friction with local Japanese opinion—something which Eisenhower was well aware of, and which accounts for the gradual withdrawal of ground forces from Japan in the late 1950s and the President's efforts to promote an "enclave strategy" in Okinawa. More generally, where security policy was concerned, the American military's largely unimaginative and inflexible approach to alliance relations (with the exception of the more responsive attitudes of individuals such as Matthew Ridgway and Mark Clark) frequently stood in the way of a more accommodating State Department position, as the US policy discussions over Okinawa so aptly reveal. In certain key instances, State Department intervention proved critical. John Allison's advice from Tokyo in 1955 that pushing for rearmament was counterproductive was important in encouraging a marked shift in US security policy toward Japan, as officials in Washington acknowledged that building up Japan's military would have to be a long-term rather than immediate priority.

Security was, as the archival records reveal, more than simply an issue of military preparedness. Just as US and Japanese officials agreed at times over external threats (as reflected, for example, in the decision to exclude Okinawa from the terms of the new 1960 Security Treaty), there was similarly room for cooperation where internal security was concerned. The presence of a clause in the 1951 Security Treaty permitting US intervention in Japan to quell domestic unrest (at the request of the Japanese government) may well have reflected Yoshida's concern over the risk of internal agitation. Similarly, the Gaimushō's response to the Rastvorov incident of 1955—its cooperation with the US embassy in spiriting the Soviet defector out of Japan—indicates that in certain instances the two countries were able to work constructively with one another. However, such cases were rare and there were real and critically important limits to what the two states could accomplish together. For the most part, internal security remained a point of tension between the United States and Japan—not necessarily over the nature and extent of particular threats to Japan, but over devising practical measures to counter such challenges. The lack of comprehensive legal or institutional provisions to ensure government confidentiality and secrecy was, as chapter five reveals, a source of frustration to US officials in both the State Departments and the Defense Department.

Active and extensive security cooperation between Japan and the United States—whether in addressing internal or external problems—were often undercut by domestic political tensions within Japan. Both Yoshida and Hatoyama cited popular and opposition opinion as obstacles to rapid rearmament, while the confusion associated with the *Lucky Dragon* incident revealed, at least in American eyes, the difficulty of cooperating with an internally divided administration. Moreover, such divisions influenced the wider bilateral relationship and account for some of the tensions and confusion that arose between both countries, whether during the MSA negotiations, Shigemitsu's visit to Washington in 1955, or the Russo-Japan normalization talks of 1956. Such incidents are important when assessing the degree to which the US government was seriously committed to maintaining the stress on mutuality that had featured so prominently in the San Francisco peace treaty process. They are particularly relevant since they are frequently cited in the literature as evidence of an arguably dismissive attitude by the US authorities toward Japan or a willingness to undercut independent Japanese policy initiatives. A close reading of the diplomatic record suggests that there are powerful grounds for a reinterpretation of this critical view. A reading that highlights the sharp disagreements within the Japanese government and the sometimes confused and contradictory Japanese policies presented to the Eisenhower administration reveals that the image of heavy-handed US diplomacy is too one-sided and needs to be balanced by a more comprehensive picture of events.

It would be a mistake to suggest that the US government maintained throughout the 1950s the same awareness of and degree of responsiveness to Japanese interests which it had demonstrated in the San Francisco Peace Treaty negotiations. International crises, rival alliances relations, and domestic political interests competed for the attention of senior US policy-makers. Dulles, for example, in his public announcements on Japanese rearmament in 1954, seemed clumsily unaware of the damaging impact of his statements in Japan. Similarly, during the Soviet-Japanese normalization talks, Eisenhower appeared curiously absent from high-level policy discussions on Japan—at least as suggested by the existing archival material—perhaps a consequence, in 1956, of the crises over Suez and Hungary and the presidential election campaign in the United States. Moreover, in particular cases, wider US strategic priorities took precedence over a policy of accommodating Japanese interests. The US presence in Okinawa—the product of America's perimeter defense strategy in Asia—clearly generated opposition within Japan, although as chapter four reveals, senior Japanese politicians were also at times privately ready to play down the significance of the issue. Similarly, nuclear testing in the Pacific, driven largely by the deterrence philosophy that underpinned Eisenhower's "New Look," led to major tension in the bilateral relationship—perhaps the most exacting crisis for the two countries during the 1950s. In addressing the incident, there were a number of glaring shortcomings on the US side, complemented by internal weaknesses and inadequate crisis management within the Japanese government.

A close examination of these issues is also a basis for assessing the positive, revisionist views of both Eisenhower and Dulles. In many respects the conclusion is a mixed one. In Eisenhower's case, the President's relatively limited involvement during the *Lucky Dragon* incident and his endorsement of the conclusions of Lewis Strauss (the AEC Chairman) are a sign of poor judgment. This is offset by the evidence of his active involvement in resolving the Okinawa currency crisis, his support for the return of Amami, his desire to lower the US troop presence in Japan, and his support for a speedy resolution of the Girard incident. The President remained engaged in security policy as it affected Japan and sensitive to Japanese concerns, although rarely, if at all, in a high-profile or public fashion. In the case of Dulles, the record is perhaps somewhat more ambiguous. Dulles's undoubted achievements in San Francisco were, it should be stressed, part of a combined State Department effort. Nevertheless, his emphasis on the importance of the cultural dimension to the bilateral relationship suggests an understanding of the importance of issues of identity and national self-definition in Japan at the time. As secretary of state, Dulles did interact brusquely with Japanese government officials, although the extent to which this reflected insensitivity to Japanese concerns, rather than the secretary's own personal style, is debatable. At the very least, the evidence relating to the Russo-Japanese talks indicates that one should keep an open mind on the issue and avoid confusing the surface dimension of diplomatic initiatives with their underlying reality.

Finally, what light does the empirical evidence shed on the wider theoretical questions so frequently discussed by international relations specialists and raised in the introductory chapter? The Japanese government's willingness to participate in the security relationship with the United States clearly reflected a number of competing interests. Protection from external attack remained important to Japan's leaders throughout the 1950s, and the conventional and nuclear capabilities of the United States provided a valuable and cost-effective guarantee of Japan's territorial integrity, even if public opinion and the charged political nature of the issue prevented Japanese politicians from enthusiastically and openly endorsing the security partnership. The issue of internal security was also important, given Yoshida's preoccupation with domestic subversion. However, by the mid-1950s, judging from the lack of adequate anti-espionage legislation, and the different assessments of Kishi and Shigemitsu of Japan's internal vulnerability (documented in chapter six), there was no clear consensus among Japan's leaders on the issue. Nevertheless, the attention given to internal security suggests that Robert Osgood was correct in highlighting its importance in explaining some of the motivation behind alliance formation.

Walt's "balance of threat" realist argument provides at best a limited insight into the behavior and choices of policy-makers on both sides of the US-Japan alliance relationship. Although it can, in part, explain why consciousness of the Soviet threat encouraged Japan to turn to the United States for protection, it is of no help in explaining the State Department's efforts to accommodate Japanese concerns over sovereignty and national independence, particularly during the early 1950s. A strict materialist calculus of rational self-interest, in line with neo-realist theory, implies that such issues are relatively unimportant. However, they clearly influenced the thinking of American policy-makers in both Tokyo and Washington. Moreover, without some awareness of the intensity of the debates in Japan over constitutional reform and the sensitivity of Japanese public opinion to nationally and historically charged issues—such as the role of the Emperor or the question of nuclear weapons—Walt's approach is of little value in understanding the tensions which affected the US-Japan relationship during the 1940s and 1950s. Assessing the degree to which State Department policies provided a foundation for the development of a durable alliance relationship is largely a question of historical judgment, but there seems little reason to doubt that leading policy-makers in the United States believed that a degree of mutuality and recognition of Japanese interests was a necessary requirement for an effective partnership with Japan.[4]

Formally incorporating notions of "culture" into a diplomatic history is, as explained in the introduction, an ambitious task and beyond the scope of this study. However, Dulles's concern with cultural issues in 1951 and the Japanese debate over constitutional legitimacy suggests some observations that may be of value in understanding alliance relations. It is perhaps reasonable to argue that the absence of a consensus within Japan over the country's political structure and national self-definition influenced its foreign relations, and risked preventing it from developing an active partnership with the United States. Certainly, there were those in the State Department, both before, during, and long after the Occupation, who assumed that without a stable domestic environment in Japan it would be difficult to work effectively with Japan over the long term. Charles Spinks's analytical reporting from Tokyo is one example of such thinking, and both Kennan and Dulles appear to have reached similar conclusions, albeit independently. If domestic stability was a key ingredient for effective alliance cooperation and could be best secured (as some in the United States government had suggested) by allowing the Japanese to reappropriate or reconnect with their legitimate cultural and political heritage, then there is some basis for the stress on cultural factors in understanding alliance relations—a view advanced by writers such as Risse-Kappen and Katzenstein.[5] However, in the particular context of the US-Japan relationship, the importance of cultural factors perhaps lay less in members of an alliance being part of a community of common cultural and political values (as some constructivists have argued), and more in each of them having a distinct sense of national identity expressed in cultural terms. An active and extensive bilateral partnership perhaps requires both countries to have a clear sense of their own national priorities defined in both material and non-material terms and linked to a coherent (even if mythologized) awareness of their past. This is not a proposition which can be adequately addressed here, although it is interesting to speculate, in light of Japan's current debate over constitutional reform, whether a more well-defined and commonly accepted sense of the nation in Japan during the 1950s might have resulted in a stronger and less tension-fraught bilateral relationship.[6] Further work on alliance relations might profitably explore the links between culture, identity, and policy-making, although in order to have explanatory weight it would need to be genuinely comparative and historically wide-ranging. Such a major task might best be accomplished by collaborative work across disciplines and between scholars from different countries. In the process, one might achieve valuable insights into (although not precise predictive theories concerning) not only the origins of alliances but also their weaknesses and strengths.

That the benefits of this process are anything but academic can be readily appreciated by considering the experience of the Republican administration of George W. Bush. The US government's management of foreign policy in the wake of the 9/11 terrorist attack has been widely criticized as unilateralist, ideologically obsessive rather than pragmatic, and (judging from the post-war reconstruction process in Iraq) ill-suited to the challenges of nation-building.[7] If such criticisms are justified, then the United States's post-1945 experience in Japan might well offer some salutary lessons—including at a minimum the importance of advance planning, informed cultural awareness, and sensitivity to the sensibilities of a defeated nation. Paradoxically, the contemporary US-Japan relationship itself seems to have weathered post 9/11 tensions reasonably well. In fact, to many the alliance appears to have grown stronger, acquiring an unprecedented flexibility and resilience comparable to another long-lasting twentieth-century partnership—the Anglo-American alliance.[8] To what extent this is the consequence of new regional and international challenges, a growth of national assertiveness in post–Cold War Japan,[9] or judicious alliance management by experienced policy-makers in Washington and Tokyo is open to debate. At the very least, it suggests that the recommendations of the Nye-Armitage 2000 report (and indirectly the early post-war vision of Dulles, Kennan, Rusk, and Allison) have been taken to heart. At a time of much uncertainty, it suggests also perhaps a comforting thought on which to end—namely, that the lessons of history have not been entirely forgotten, at least where one particularly significant bilateral relationship is concerned.

REFERENCE MATTER

Notes

In addition to the abbreviations listed on page xiii, the following abbreviations are used in the Notes:

CNO	Chief of Naval Operations
EL	Dwight D. Eisenhower Presidential Library, Abilene, KS
FRUS	*Foreign Relations of the United States*
GA	Gaimushō Archives
IRR	Investigative Records Repository
JFD-OH	John Foster Dulles Oral History Project
JFD-P	John Foster Dulles papers
ML	Seeley G. Mudd Manuscript Library, Princeton, NJ
NA	National Archives, Washington, DC
NA-II	National Archives, MD
OCL	Office of Intelligence Coordination and Liaison
OIR	Office of Intelligence Research
ONEAA	Office of North East Asian Affairs
OSANSA	Office of the Special Assistant for National Security Affairs
PRO	Public Record Office, UK
WHO	White House Office

Introduction

1. For examples of such retrospective assessments, see Iriye and Wampler (2001), Hosoya (2001), Sotooka (2001).

2. See, for example, Johnson and Keehn (1995).

3. For an interesting Japanese exception to this pattern, see Sakamoto (1997).

4. John Lewis Gaddis has illustrated this point revealingly in his discussion of US policy toward the Soviet Union in the closing stages of the Cold War. See Gaddis (1992), pp. vii–viii.

5. Armitage went on to become deputy secretary of state in the Bush administration.

6. Bipartisan Study Group (2000).

7. For an extended analysis of these changes, see Green (2001).

8. See Ward (1967; 1987); Reischauer (1957).

9. Johnson, for example, argues provocatively that US post-war interaction with Japan was equivalent to the coercive relationship that existed between the former Soviet Union and the satellite states of Eastern Europe. Johnson (2000), pp. 22–25.

10. See, for example, Cohen (1990); McGlothlen (1993); Tucker (1983).

11. See Dingman (1990); Hellman (1969); Packard (1966); Watanabe (1970).

12. Auer (1973); Barnet (1983); Drifte (1986); Harries and Harries (1987); Weinstein (1971). Among notable recent studies, Michael Green's work examines in detail the links between industrial and defense policy in post-war Japan, focusing on Japanese efforts to develop an autonomous military production capability. His study concentrates on the Japanese side of the bilateral security relationship and does not explore American policy from the viewpoint of US diplomatic records. See Green (1995). Similarly, Peter Katzenstein has written at length about Japan's post-war national security policy from a perspective that relies heavily on the analytical tools of political science and international relations. See Katzenstein (1996a).

13. Kataoka and Myers (1989); Olsen (1985). For a recent edited volume on the bilateral relationship that usefully weaves together analysis of both historical and contemporary issues, see Vogel (2002).

14. Buckley (1992).

15. LaFeber (1997a).

16. Schaller (1997).

17. Schaller (1985; 1989).

18. However, unlike LaFeber, Schaller makes very little explicit reference to Japanese secondary sources, and in certain instances he is reliant on the observations of a very limited number of Japanese scholars. For example, chapters four and seven, dealing with Japanese domestic politics during the 1950s, are very heavily reliant on the work of Kataoka Tetsuya for an understanding of the Japanese side to the relationship, even though other researchers in Japan have advanced interpretations which are strikingly different from Kataoka's views.

19. Nick Sarantakes's monograph on post-war Okinawa is one of the few recent works that begin to grapple with some of these important security issues. See Sarantakes (2000).

20. Gallicchio (1988); Gallicchio (1990). Indeed, studies of US security policy regarding the East Asian region as a whole during the 1950s are few in number. As one specialist noted in the early 1990s, there is a "pressing need for more studies . . . on the role of the military in America's relations with East Asia." Barnhart (1992).

21. Ronald Dore has discussed this in illuminating detail in Dore (1997), pp. ix–xxi.

22. Leffler (1992).

23. See chapter five.

24. Ibid.

25. See especially chapter one for a more extensive description of these views.

26. Richard Neustadt's earlier work on Anglo-American relations, Neustadt (1970), in its focus on the internal bureaucratic decisions shaping US security policy, is a model for this approach.

27. Concepts of culture and national identity have recently become the focus of considerable interest from international relations specialists.

28. Security is interpreted here in traditional terms (protection against armed attack and internal subversion) and does not include the more recent broader definitions of challenges to national security—for example, environmental, population, and narcotics-related threats. See Ullman (1983).

29. For example, the papers of John Foster Dulles housed at Princeton—many of which were only declassified at the end of the 1990s. Other files of note include the CIA Murphy Papers and the records of the State Department's Office of Intelligence Research, both collections held at the National Archives in Maryland.

30. For example, Hosoya (1982; 1986); Iokibe (1989).

31. Tanaka Takahiko, for example, has drawn heavily on British Foreign Office records in analyzing Russo-Japanese relations in the mid-1950s, while Kōno Yasuko has made a detailed study of Okinawa's role in US-Japan relations, based on documents in the US National Archives. See Tanaka (1993) and Kōno (1994). Similarly, Kitaoka Shin'ichi has written in detail about Yoshida Shigeru, in part using his personal letters, while Hara Yoshihisa's work on the Security Treaty negotiations of the late 1950s is based both on archival work in the United States and on extensive interviews with Japanese politicians and bureaucrats. See Kitaoka (1994) and Hara (1991).

32. The range of contrasting views on Dulles is well documented in Richard Immerman's concluding chapter in Immerman (1990), pp. 263–83. Revisionist and post-revisionist scholarship on Eisenhower, particularly the more positive assessments of his leadership style, are discussed in Bischof and Ambrose (1995).

33. Michael Schaller's latest work devotes considerable space to both the China and the Southeast Asia questions, mainly from the perspective of economic relations, but with limited detailed attention to the importance of China in Japanese domestic politics.

34. According to Wolfers, "the term 'alliance' signifies a promise of mutual military assistance between two or more sovereign states." See Sills (1968).

35. Osgood (1968), pp. 21–22.

36. Walt (1987), p. 265.

37. Ibid., p. 5.

38. Since the advent of Walt's idea, there have been efforts by a number of neorealist thinkers to modify and refine the balance of threat argument. Thomas Christensen and Jack Snyder, for instance, have stressed the importance of individual decision-makers' perceptions of the relative advantages of offensive and defensive military strategies when making their alliance decisions. See, for example, Christensen (1997). Similarly, Glenn Snyder, using a variety of approaches drawn from game-theory, microeconomics, and "sociological coalition theory," has attempted to go beyond simple structural descriptions by explicitly incorpo-

rating in his analysis measurements of the interests, capabilities, alignments, and degree of interdependence of individual states. Snyder (1997). Such approaches share with Walt's argument an assumption that decision-making is essentially rational in character, as well as a preference for system-level "parsimonious" explanations and a heavy stress on quantitative analysis.

39. The term "long-term forces" is associated with the recent methodological work of the historian John Lewis Gaddis and his critique of international relations theory, summarized here. Gaddis has stressed the advantages of a historical approach over much international relations theory, and has highlighted the shortcomings of many in the international relations community in failing to anticipate the ending of the Cold War. For an early example of his criticism, see Gaddis (1992/93); for discussion of the differences and similarities between historians and international relations specialists, see the series of articles entitled "Symposium: History and Theory," *International Security* (22, no. 1, Summer, 1997). For Gaddis's most recent, extended discussion of historical method, see Gaddis (2002).

40. Gaddis (1992/93), p. 58.

41. I have discussed this debate (prompted by a series of seminars held by John Gaddis at Oxford University during 1993) in a paper entitled "Archetypes and Historical Change: Long-Term Forces and the Collective Unconscious." The paper attempts to combine Gaddis's approach with concepts from analytical psychology and Japanese intellectual history and is available (in Japanese only) as Swenson-Wright (1997).

42. Huntington (1998), p. 20. It is worth emphasizing that a number of historians have long stressed the importance of cultural factors in understanding international relations. See, for instance, the work of the Harvard historian Akira Iriye—Iriye (1981)—or the Annales tradition in France, exemplified by the writings of Ferdinand Braudel and Marc Bloch.

43. Wendt (1996); Pasic (1996).

44. One illustration is the claim that *ideas* function as "road-maps" in shaping the decisions of policy-makers, or the suggestion that *interpretation* needs to be part of "systematic social science." See Goldstein and Keohane (1993b).

45. It should be stressed that not all past theoretical work on alliances has ignored culture. At times, as for example in the work of George Liska, it has simply suggested that the concept is relatively unimportant. According to Liska: "The growing number of actors with highly varied cultural backgrounds is no more likely to reshape international politics fundamentally. It is probably true that differences in cultural norms like those in ideological beliefs, aggravate relations by facilitating misperceptions of the different parties' motives, objectives and actions. But, in the past, culturally diverse communities did not find it impossible to relate themselves to each other." See Liska (1962), p. 10.

46. Barnett (1996); Risse-Kappen (1996). Similarly, Dan Reiter, although not explicitly addressing the issue of culture, has challenged the rigidity of much neo-realist theorizing by proposing a new theory of alliance formation stressing the importance of uncertainty and historical learning, based on the "formative events" of policy-makers and public opinion. He also criticizes the "band wag-

oning" versus "balancing" option as too limited a description of policy-makers' choices—one which fails to consider the possibility of neutrality or non-alignment. His analysis, drawing both on case studies and on quantitative work, combines approaches from social psychology (particularly the importance of analogical reasoning), organization theory and decision-making analysis. Most important of all, in this context, is his explicit recognition of the limitations of assumptions of rationality and his emphasis on the importance of historical experience in interpreting alliance choices. Reiter (1996).

47. Walt (1997).

48. Katzenstein (1996a), pp. 3–16, 107, 148.

49. Ōtake (1997), pp. 518–23.

50. For a useful and persuasive discussion of these themes, see Gluck (1993); Hein (1996); and Hammond and Hein (1992). For an approach (similar to Katzenstein's and equally open to criticism) which suggests that post-war Japanese identity has been coherent—although, in this instance, defined less in terms of anti-militarism and more in terms of a commitment to a distinctive Japanese model of economic development—see Morris (1994).

51. For an illustration of the debate over contemporary security policy in Japan, see Etō (1996).

52. McSweeney (1996), pp. 86–90.

53. Berger (1996), p. 325.

54. Iriye (1997), pp. 178–81.

55. The notion of manufactured identity is well described in Anderson (1983).

56. For example, the concept of the "Yoshida Doctrine," frequently cited as a central component in Japan's post-1945 security policy, or the suggestion that Yoshida was opposed to constitutional revision, are both open to reinterpretation. See, respectively, chapters two and five for a discussion of these points. For an illustration of the Yoshida Doctrine thesis, see Chai (1997).

57. Rothstein (1968), pp. 26–27.

58. For a fuller account of "satisficing," see Koutsoyiannis (1979), pp. 388–90. Economics, it should be stressed, has been a source for many of the rationally based international relations theories of alliance behavior. For example, some writers have drawn on the concept of "public goods" to argue that small states in a bipolar system have an incentive to "free-ride," spending relatively little on defense and relying instead on the collective and mutually beneficial security resources provided by their more powerful alliance partner. For a critical analysis of this argument, see Goldstein (1995).

59. See, for example, Inoguchi (1991), pp. 9–37.

60. Kōsaka Masataka's writing has perhaps been most influential in this regard and has contributed to the "Yoshida Doctrine" argument referred to in note 56 above.

Chapter 1

1. Truman (1951), p. 708.

2. See, for example, Dower (1993b), p. 11; Cumings (1993), p. 34, and, more

recently, Dower (1999), p. 23. Similarly, Reinhard Drifte, in his avowedly "revisionist" account of the early security relationship between Japan and the US, has argued that America was disinclined to listen to Japanese views, intent instead on securing a position of "hegemony" in Japan. See Drifte (1983), p. 135. Among Japanese writers, Kataoka Tetsuya, in a controversial work, has denied that there was any genuine "mutuality" in the alliance—see Kataoka (1991), p. 8—while the left-wing writer Iwanaga Kenkichirō has criticized the United States for forcing Japan to participate in the US security system—see Iwanaga (1985), p. 31.

3. For example, Finn (1992).

4. For example, Miyasato (1990).

5. Dale Hellegers, in her recently published study of wartime and early postwar planning on Japan, provides a rich and detailed analysis of these competing interests that adds substantially to our understanding of this important period. See Hellegers (2001), pp. xii, 11, 33, 58, and passim.

6. Hata (1976), p. 9.

7. Hornbeck had in fact headed the Office previously between 1928 and 1937 and was brought back in briefly in 1944. See Hellegers (2001), p. 369.

8. Nakamura (1992), p. 7. Rivalry between the State Department's Japan and China hands, and in particular between Grew and Hornbeck, can be traced back to 1940 when the two men disagreed over the merits of imposing an economic embargo against Japan. See Borton (2002), p. 75.

9. Hellegers (2001), p. 58.

10. Nakamura (1992), p. 79.

11. Hata (1976), pp. 21–22. Assessing the significance of this implicit guarantee and the motivation of those who proffered it is difficult. Senior US government opinion was sharply divided on the merits of offering any political concessions to the Japanese, with Acheson and MacLeish strongly opposed to the Japanese throne and Byrnes and President Truman himself seemingly skeptical that the monarchy needed to be maintained in the post-war period. See Hellegers (2001), pp. 124–25. Public opinion in the United States remained, not surprisingly, after nearly four years of bitter and bloody fighting in the Pacific, vehemently opposed to conciliation. Consequently, the August 11 letter was intentionally drafted as a model of "studied ambiguity" that would preserve bureaucratic unity at home while offering an interpretive escape hatch to the Japanese government. Japan's foreign office officials seized this opportunity, optimistically convincing themselves that surrender while ushering in political and administrative change, would not threaten the fundamental integrity of the national political ethos or "kokutai." See Hellegers (2001), pp. 151–52.

12. Max Bishop, for example, a young Foreign Service officer had argued in 1942—see Hellegers (2001), p. 172—that the Emperor system functioned as a symbol of national unity and could help to stave off domestic unrest and the risk of Communist subversion—a view that was echoed in the reports he sent back from Tokyo in 1946 while serving in the office of the political advisor (POLAD) to MacArthur. Similar views were expressed by the Quaker Hugh Borton, another young Japan-specialist, who first traveled to Japan in 1928 as the representative of the America Friends Service Committee and subsequently studied Japa-

nese at Columbia, Harvard, and Leyden, before entering the State Department in 1942. Borton's views on the Emperor had been heavily influenced by the ideas of his mentor, Sir George Sansom, the former British diplomat and distinguished scholar of Japan, who argued strongly against forcibly deposing the Emperor and stressed the need to allow the Japanese to chart their own political destiny in the post-war period. See Borton (2002), p. 97.

13. Quoted in Weinstein (1971), p. 9.
14. Nakamura (1992), pp. 81–82.
15. Igarashi (1993), p. 135.
16. Sebald (1965), p. 43.
17. Finn (1992), p. 71.

18. As Dower dramatically notes, "However high minded they may have been, General MacArthur and his command ruled their new domain as neocolonial overlords, beyond challenge or criticism, as inviolate as the emperor and his officials had ever been." Dower (1999), p. 27.

19. Finn (1992), p. 82. Recent Japanese and American scholarship on the origins of Japan's post-war Constitution has revealed a somewhat more complicated picture of the development of the new, post-1945 political framework, one which acknowledges a vigorous and serious effort by Japanese politicians and legal and constitutional specialists across the political spectrum to anticipate the Occupation changes and devise their own blueprints for political reform. For example, academics such as Yabe Teiji, of Tokyo University, and Sasaki Sōichi, formerly of Kyoto University, worked with the prominent aristocratic politician and former wartime prime minister Konoe Fumimaro to devise appropriate drafts, acting on their own initiative and separately from SCAP. Such efforts were ultimately unsuccessful and did not directly affect the SCAP-orchestrated process, although in some instances the proposals had a progressive quality that would not necessarily have conflicted with the final document—providing for, in Sasaki's case, civil liberties, constitutional amendments, popular referendum, academic and artistic rights, and the beginnings of genuine local government. Sasaki's work was eclipsed by the far more traditional proposals of the Kenpō Mondai Chōsa Iinkai (the Committee for the Investigation of Constitutional Problems), headed by the deeply conservative legal scholar and former government minister Matsumoto Jōji, and these helped shape the position of the Shidehara cabinet in deliberating in private with SCAP's government section over the terms of the SCAP drafted Constitution in late February, early March 1946. Yet the SCAP final draft bore all the hallmarks of a rehearsed script with little room, if any, for Japanese divergence from the Occupying authority's blueprint. MacArthur had hoped to allow the Japanese considerable freedom in shaping their post-war political future, but he rapidly shelved any devolutionary idealism he may have had when it conflicted with more pressing issues, particularly political ones. Perhaps the most that can be said is that Japanese and Occupation proposals proceeded in parallel, rarely intersecting and with limited mutual impact, but occasionally emboldening and encouraging those SCAP reformers who discerned in some Japanese drafts a true commitment to genuine, radical political reform. For detailed and fascinating discussion of this issue, see Hellegers (2001), pp. 495, 502–5, 541; Koseki (1998).

The latest English-language study of the Constitution, by Ray Moore and Donald ,Robinson, builds on this theme, but also extends the analytical and historical framework beyond SCAP's March 6 publication of a draft Constitution, to include the important Japanese parliamentary (or Diet) debates and, critically, the Japanese translation of the original draft, culminating in Diet approval in August 1946. In doing so, the writers suggest a more nuanced pattern of interaction between SCAP and the Japanese political establishment in developing Japan's postwar political framework, assigning greater significance to Japanese contributions as well as providing a clue into the Constitution's relative durability over the postwar period. See Moore and Robinson (2002), pp. 329–38.

20. Sebald (1965), p. 66. The de facto subordinate status of POLAD became all too apparent from the very first days of the Occupation. As Borton noted in his memoirs: "Although General MacArthur had agreed to the establishment of a special Political Advisor's Office to which State Department personnel were assigned, it was not set up as a regular section of SCAP under the chief of staff, and so its members were not necessarily kept informed of other SCAP activities. It was also slow in getting organized. For example, John K. Emmerson, the first member of that office, arrived in Japan three weeks after its surrender. For the next three weeks he had no specific assignment, and no one in SCAP knew what his duties were. . . . The Department of State's ability to receive accurate, up-to-date information and critical analyses of the activities of SCAP and current events within Japan was greatly restricted by the fact that all telecommunications from any section of SCAP headquarters to Washington, and all telecommunications from Washington to SCAP, regardless of their origin, had to be channeled through the Joint Chiefs of Staff. The disadvantages of this arrangement soon became apparent, but the State Department was powerless to do anything about it." Borton (2002), p. 158.

21. Colonel Charles Kades, for example, the Harvard-trained lawyer, who played the critical role in managing the constitutional revision process "knew almost nothing about Japan, its language, or legal traditions" and what knowledge he did have was heavily distorted by wartime American stereotypes of the Japanese as feudalistic, "prone to militarism and imperialism, imitative and mystical." Moore and Robinson (2002), p. 7. Admittedly, there were some in the Occupation—particularly those working within or advising the Government Section—who had had prior exposure to Japan. These included Harry Emerson Wildes (a former journalist and academic who had lectured at Keiō University in 1924–25), Beate Sirota (a 22-year-old who had spent ten years in Japan from the age of five and who became involved in helping draft some of the human rights' provisions of the new SCAP Constitution), and three US academics—Kenneth Colgrove, T. A. Bisson, and Cyrus Peake—with knowledge and practical experience of Japan who acted as advisors to Kades. The insights of these last three were potentially important, but should not be exaggerated. As Kades himself noted: "I accepted their advice only in those cases when they agreed, and reported to General Whitney. The reason was that Colgrove was very conservative, Bisson was a member of the IPR (Institute of Pacific Relations), that is, left wing, and Peake was in the

middle, and so their views tended to be at odds with each other. Their views did carry some weight, but as a group, not as individual opinions." Koseki (1998), p. 153. Similarly, Sirota faced the frustration of seeing her culturally informed efforts to include in the draft Constitution social provisions guaranteeing the well-being of Japanese mothers and their children stymied by the opposition of her SCAP military superiors. Moore and Robinson (2002), p. 104.

22. William Sebald (the second POLAD in Tokyo following George Atcheson's death in an air crash in August 1947) described SCAP's ostrich-like tendency to avoid mixing with the Japanese—an attitude that Sebald felt might unnecessarily complicate future US-Japan relations. See Sebald (1965), p. 69.

23. From the autumn of 1945, the Office of Far Eastern Affairs had been giving serious thought to Japan's political and institutional future. Hugh Borton was responsible for drafting, in consultation with his colleagues, a document entitled "The Reform of the Japanese Government System" that eventually acquired official status as SWNCC 228 on January 4, 1946. The document envisaged a constitutional monarchy in which full executive and legislative powers would be assigned to the cabinet and the Diet. In this respect, and in allowing for the continuation of a constitutionally constrained Emperor, it prefigured the SCAP provisions that eventually emerged in 1947. SWNCC 228's overall impact, however, was marginal at best. The document was sent to MacArthur for his guidance rather than as a directive and had no binding force. Moreover, the General relied on State's inability to consider Japanese potential opposition to political change or the practical challenge of promoting reform in the context of a continuing Occupation to justify to himself his policy of ignoring Washington's advice. State had, in effect, an optimistic (and arguably unrealistic) faith in a gradualist approach in which the Japanese would play an initiating role under Allied supervision. Critically also, the foreign service officers in Washington in early 1946 were "completely ignorant" of MacArthur's independent drive to have SCAP's government section create a draft Constitution "in strictest secrecy." Borton (2002), pp. 163–67; Hellegers (2001), pp. 246, 545–48.

24. Leffler (1992), p. 127.

25. Leffler (1992), p. 84. See also Alperovitz (1965) for a revisionist argument that Truman's decision to use the atomic bomb was influenced more by a desire to impress the Soviets than to end the war with Japan. For a more balanced assessment, see Sherwin (1994), pp. 77–94. J. Samuel Walker's short but comprehensive synthesis of the scholarly arguments on this issue reinforces the view that differences with the Soviet Union were one but not the critical factor in the decision to use the bomb. Walker (1997), pp. 94–95, 104–6. Richard B. Frank's recent path-breaking research has added weight to the contentious claim that nuclear weapons played a vital and justifiable role in accelerating Japan's surrender. See Frank (1999), pp. 343, 359.

26. Finn (1992), p. 70. New revelations prompted by the opening of former Soviet archives following the ending of the Cold War have demonstrated that these contemporary assessments were too sanguine. Stalin's East Asian ambitions did, in fact, extend to Japan, and in the closing stages of the war, the Russians

were planning to invade Hokkaido, in an effort to secure "a springboard for attacks on Honshu and a right to participate in the occupation of Japan." Frank
(1999), pp. 322–23.

27. Leffler (1992), p. 105.
28. Gaddis (1982), pp. 22–23.
29. Pollard (1989), p. 209.
30. Finn (1992), p. 124.
31. James Hilgenberg claims that even from the earliest days of the Occupation, US policy-makers were consistently attempting to establish an Alliance partnership with Japan. However, his argument suffers from its excessive reliance on
a single body of source material (the opinions of the American business press) and
his unwillingness to scrutinize the policy debate within the Truman administration. See Hilgenberg (1993), pp. 157–59 and passim.
32. Schaller (1986), passim. For a less critical view of MacArthur, see Sodei
(1991).
33. Hosoya (1986), p. 5.
34. Kennan (1968), p. 374.
35. Dunn (1963), p. 58.
36. Miscamble (1992), pp. 250–52.
37. Kennan (1968), pp. 375–76. Kennan's concerns were shared by the Japan
specialists in SCAP's Government Section whose reports were routinely for-
warded by POLAD to the State Department. Harry Wildes, for example, warned
in 1946 that "shortage of food, accelerated inflation, ineffective policy of the government and other unsettled conditions have presented a very favorable ground
for aggressive activity of the communists in Japan." This included a campaign of
press intimidation and efforts to infiltrate newspaper unions and editorial officers, capitalizing in part on the relative political inexperience of a general public,
which, thanks to the authoritarian wartime regime, was unfamiliar with the tactical realities of open political competition. "During the period of 15 years since
the Manchurian incident it was a taboo for the Japanese people to openly study
and discuss true democracy or liberalism. Needless to say, it was prohibited to
study or discuss socialism, communism and general social sciences. Thus handi-
capped during best years of life, not a small number of young men who consist of
members of the employees union misunderstood the meaning of 'Liberty' and
'Freedom' and are apt to confuse democracy with selfishness. And many of them
cannot distinguish between democracy, socialism and communism. As they are ignorant or not conscious of evils and harm that communism causes to the political, economic and social structure of the country, they cannot see through designs
and conspiracies cleverly set by the Communist Party." H. E. Wildes, "Communist Activities in Press Circles in Japan," May 27, 1946, RG273, CIA Murphy Papers, Box 94, NA-II.
38. "Political Events in Japan during 1946," Nov. 26, 1947, OCL, No.
3436.76, OIR files, NA-II. The purge, as a means of disqualifying individuals
from participation in public life, affected no fewer than 330 of the 440 members
of the previous Diet, ensuring that of the 1,931 candidates contesting the April

1946 election, 90 percent were political neophytes. Max Bishop to State, Feb. 15, 1946, RG273, CIA Murphy Papers, Box 94, NA-II.

39. Yoshida was a former career diplomat who had served previously in Britain and the United States. "Proud, stubborn, and uncompromisingly conservative," he was outspokenly pro-British in the run-up to the Pacific War. This attitude, coupled with close family ties to the liberal Japanese statesman Count Makino Nobuaki, earned him the suspicion of Japan's wartime government and he was arrested in 1945 for participation in efforts to secure a peaceful settlement to the war. This, more than anything, ensured that he escaped the 1946 "white purge" of conservative leaders and allowed him to assume the leadership of the Liberal Party from Hatoyama Ichirō, who had been disqualified. His political success in heading no fewer than five cabinets between 1946 and 1954 established him, arguably, as Japan's most high profile and successful early post-war premier. "Biographic Reports on the Members of the Third Yoshida Cabinet," Feb. 23, 1949, OIR Report, No. 4902, OIR files, NA-II.

40. "Situation Report, Japan," Dec. 7, 1947, OCL, No. 3479.41, OIR files, NA-II.

41. Yamazaki Takeshi, the Speaker of the House of Representatives, reflected such concerns in March 1947 in conversation with Hugh Borton, who noted subsequently that Yamazaki had stated "in a very simple but convincing manner . . . that democracy in Japan, in spite of the new Constitution and the apparent increase in responsibility assumed by the Diet, was not understood or appreciated by the masses of Japanese. It was questionable whether persons of his generation would ever understand the real meaning of democracy. A whole new language and way of thinking must develop and at least ten or fifteen years would be necessary before democracy was finally accepted. It was his view that while political thought in Japan contained some elements of democracy, it would have to undergo radical change in order for real democracy to be understood." Borton (2002), p. 196.

42. Kennan (1968), p. 382.

43. Dunn (1963), p. 58.

44. Kennan (1968), pp. 388–90. Hugh Borton, in a visit to Japan in the spring of 1947, made similar observations, noting that the "reservoir of Japanese friendliness toward the United States was rapidly being drained" by the illogical censorship, the widespread application of the purge, [and] the housing program for dependents of SCAP personnel." Borton (2002), p. 201.

45. Ibid., pp. 391–92.

46. "Recommendations with Respect to US Policy toward Japan," NSC 13/2, RG59, PPS, Country and Area Files "Japan," 1947–53, Box 19, NA.

47. Gaddis (1982), p. 28.

48. Ibid., p. 35; Thompson (1987), p. 34.

49. Quoted in Gaddis (1982), p. 35.

50. Kennan (1968), p. 394.

51. See, for example, Nakamura (1994b). For a description of the "reverse course" debate, see Gluck (1983), pp. 199–203. Recently, Takemae Eiji, one of

Japan's leading authorities on the Occupation period, has moderated his earlier observations, remaining critical of the Americans but characterizing the reverse course as a "change in emphasis" rather than a complete "volte-face." See Takemae (2002), pp. 457–515.

52. Finn (1992), pp. 142–43.

53. The State Department's intelligence analysts noted, for example, that the growing support in 1948 for Yoshida and the Democratic Liberals was largely "derived from the prospect that a strong and stable government led by a party more devoted to economic recovery than to reform would be the best representative of the nation in the coming period." "An Interpretation of the Japanese Lower House Election of January 1949," Feb. 4, 1949, OIR Report, No. 4894, NA-II. Similarly, as one observer pointed out a few years after the Occupation, Japanese popular frustration with low living standards in the summer of 1948 was being replaced by a greater focus on issues of political independence. See Brown (1955), p. 258.

54. NSC 13/2, p. 3.

55. Pollard (1989), p. 214.

56. Leffler (1992), p. 210.

57. Pollard (1989), p. 220.

58. Gaddis (1982), p. 42.

59. Watanabe (1986), p. 37.

60. Finn (1992), p. 248. Miyasato Seigen has accused Kennan (largely, it seems, on the basis of his proposal to maintain US forces in Okinawa) of being arrogant, elitist, and insensitive to Japanese interests at this time. See Miyasato and Koseki (1992), pp. 296–97. However, as well as overlooking Kennan's criticism of the Occupation, this argument probably mistakes ignorance for insensitivity. Okinawa was geographically distant from the main Japanese islands, and Kennan, like many foreigners, may not have been aware of the degree to which the Japanese government regarded Okinawa as a legitimate part of Japan, especially since the issue of the revision of Okinawa had not yet become a point of contention in discussions between Washington and Tokyo. The Okinawa issue is examined in detail in chapter four.

61. McGlothlen (1993), pp. 27–28.

62. Nitze (1989), p. 58.

63. Some writers have argued that Acheson and company were promoting a grand regional recovery strategy, involving the creation of a "great crescent" of economic prosperity centered on Japan and reaching out to encompass non-Communist Asia and, especially, the markets of Southeast Asia. See Schaller (1982). Others have sounded a more skeptical note, arguing that this strategy was never fully developed. See Finn (1992), pp. 225–26. Schaller's more recent work somewhat modifies his earlier position, acknowledging that the earlier plan for a Marshall Plan in Asia was never realized. See Schaller (1997), p. 19.

64. McGlothlen (1993), p. 32.

65. Miscamble (1992), pp. 256–57. Interestingly, Nakamura Masanori reveals that Joseph Grew was honorary chairman of the Council—see Nakamura

(1992), p. xi—a sign perhaps of the continuing influence of Grew in shaping America's post-war Japan policy.

66. McGlothlen (1993), pp. 38–40.

67. Finn (1992), p. 216.

68. By contrast with popular opinion, Japan's Finance Ministry bureaucrats generally welcomed Dodge's reforms as an improvement on Occupation economic policy. See Masumi (1983), p. 348.

69. "Biographic Reports on the Members of the Third Yoshida Cabinet," Feb. 23, 1949, OIR Report, No. 4902, OIR files, NA-II.

70. "An Interpretation of the Japanese Lower House Election of January 1949," Feb. 4, 1949, OIR Report, No. 4894, NA-II.

71. Sir Hoyer Millar to Foreign Office, "Attitude of the Far Eastern Commission to Japan 'Building Up' policy of the United States Administration," Feb. 3, 1950, FO371/83081, FJ1015/9, PRO.

72. Leffler (1992), p. 334; Sebald (1965), p. 247.

73. Rotter (1987), p. 116.

74. Leffler (1992), p. 333; Rotter (1987), p. 107.

75. Dunn (1963), p. 83.

76. NSC 60, Dec. 27, 1949, RG59, PPS Country and Area Files "Japan," 1947–53, NA.

77. Howard to Butterworth, "Papers for Secretary on Japanese Peace Treaty," Jan. 10, 1950, RG59, State Dept. decimal files, 694.001/1–1050, NA.

78. Butterworth, judging from his later recollections, shared Howard's assessment. "I used to say to General Bradley, if five or six dozen highly placed Japanese got together in one room and decided one night that the Occupation must cease, by the next morning no Japanese would drive a streetcar if an American was in it, unload a ship, or allow water to go into our barracks and compounds, that we would stand there naked and ashamed with our bayonets in our hands completely impotent. Therefore, there was no time to lose, because we would not have half-way measures from the responsible elements in Japan, we would have one moment thorough cooperation, and the next moment they would turn their backs on us." Butterworth, Oral History, Sept. 8, 1965, JFD-OH, ML.

79. Ibid.

80. Kennan to Marshall, Mar. 14, 1948, RG59 PPS Country and Area Files "Japan," 1947–53, NA.

81. Ibid.

82. Roger Dingman, in analyzing US security policy in the late 1940s, has argued that institutional and budgetary conflicts, the existence of competing military plans (other than those emanating from the JCS), and most importantly the lack of clear political guidance to America's military planners all contributed to this pattern of inertia and the JCS tendency to vacillate between offensive and defensive strategies—between a continental and maritime view of US interests in Asia. See Dingman (1979).

83. Chancery, Tokyo to Far Eastern (FE) Dept., Dec. 26, 1950, FO371/84032, FJ1661/3, PRO.

84. See, for example, Acheson's National Press Club speech of Jan. 1950.

85. Hosoya (n.d.), p. 86.

86. Leffler (1992), p. 345; Umemoto (1986), p. 150.

87. The role of China, especially the recognition issue, in influencing US-Japan relations, is dealt with more extensively in chapter three.

88. Cohen (1980a), p. 49.

89. The suggestion that the Sino-Soviet accord accelerated progress on the Peace Treaty was made by Sir Oliver Franks, the British ambassador to Washington. See Franks to Foreign Office (FO), Mar. 3, 1950, FO371/83013, F1022/10, PRO.

90. McGlothlen (1993), pp. 44–45.

91. Recent scholarship has confirmed that Washington's view was well justified. Moscow was fully involved in and supportive of North Korea's attack on the South, although the pressure and lobbying for invasion came clearly from Kim Il-sung, the North Korean leader. See Stueck (1995), pp. 4, 31. Later in the decade, the Americans were to receive confirmation of their suspicions from an unusual source, following the defection in early 1954 of Yuri Rastvorov, 3rd secretary in the Soviet liaison mission in Tokyo. Rastvorov was a lieutenant colonel in the Soviet intelligence services and during his debriefing with US officials revealed a past conversation with a Soviet colleague (previously posted to the Soviet mission in Pyongyang) who, in a moment of alcohol-fueled candidness, claimed to have seen the formal written order from Stalin "directing Kim Il Sung to commence the invasion of South Korea." Report of Investigation, Yuriy [sic] A. Rastvorov, Jan. 26, 1954, IRR files, NA-II. The Rastvorov incident and its wider implications for US-Japan relations are treated in greater detail in chapter five.

92. Foot (1985), p. 60.

93. Finn (1992), p. 263.

94. Allison, like so many of the State Department's Japan hands, had experienced Japan in the prewar period, first visiting in 1927 as a high-school teacher after he had finished university. Allison, Oral History, Apr. 20, 1969, JFD-OH, ML.

95. Allison to Rusk, July 12, 1950 (microfilm, LM90 Roll 16), 794.5/7–1250, NA.

96. As Allison pointed out in a briefing paper for Dulles, MacArthur had "consistently refused to give effect to any of the organizational changes recommended by the State and Army departments." Allison to Merchant, "Briefing papers on Japan," Apr. 20, 1950, RG59, State Dept. decimal files, 694.001/4–2850, NA.

97. Untitled top secret paper, July 7, 1950, State Dept. decimal files, 694.001/7–650, NA.

98. Gaddis (1982), pp. 108–9.

99. NSC 68, *FRUS* I, 1950, p. 279.

100. NSC Consultants' Meeting, June 29, 1950, *FRUS* I, 1950, pp. 325.

101. NSC 73, July 1, 1950, *FRUS* 1, 1950, p. 332 and 338.

102. Rotter (1987), pp. 204–5.

103. NSC 73/4, "The Position and Actions of the United States with Respect

to possible further Soviet moves in the light of the Korean situation," Aug. 25, 1950, *FRUS* I, 1950, p. 383.

104. See, for example, his memo to Acheson highlighting the risk of Soviet subversion in Japan, "Memorandum by the Counsellor to the Sec. of State," Aug. 8, 1950, *FRUS* I, 1950, pp. 363–66.

105. Hamilton and Allison to Dulles, July 10, 1950, *FRUS* VI, 1950, p. 1238; Kennan to Dulles, July 20, 1950, State Dept. decimal files, 694.001/7–250, NA.

106. Ibid.

107. Dulles to Acheson, July 19, 1950, *FRUS* VI, 1950, pp. 1243–44.

108. See, for example, Hosoya (n.d.) p. 96; Miyasato (1986), p. 126; Finn (1992), p. 289.

109. Schaller (1989), pp. 179–80; Unsigned State Dept. memo, Aug. 14, 1950, *FRUS* VI, 1950, p. 1274.

110. The comment was by Dean Rusk, quoted in Schoenbaum (1988), p. 194.

111. McGlothlen (1993), p. 46.

Chapter 2

1. Dingman (1993), p. 34.

2. Watanabe (1986), pp. 19–26; Amakawa (1986), p. 60. Such was the Gaimushō's confidence in its rearmament strategy that in early 1947 a Japanese official approached W. Macmahon Ball, the Commonwealth representative on the Allied Council for Japan, and proposed the creation of a 100,000-strong Japanese armed force. See Amakawa (1986), p. 83.

3. Yamaguchi (1989), p. 14.

4. Watanabe (1986), p. 28.

5. Ibid., p. 33.

6. Drifte (1983), p. 69; Watanabe (1986), pp. 33–35.

7. Finn (1992), p. 116. The amended, finally agreed-upon clause reads as follows: "Aspiring sincerely to an international peace based on justice and order, the Japanese people forever renounce war as a sovereign right of the nation and the threat or use of force as a means of settling international disputes. In order to accomplish the aim of the preceding paragraph, land, sea, and air forces, as well as other war potential, will never be maintained. The right of belligerency of the state will not be recognized." Recent Japanese scholarship has cast doubt on the critical importance of Ashida's role in this important interpretive shift by revealing, dramatically, that the personal diary entries of the former foreign minister and prime minister on which this long-standing view has been based were in fact a journalistic forgery. The evidence now indicates that Minister of State Kanamori Tokujirō (together with perhaps three or four members of the cabinet's influential Legislation Bureau) had first proposed the more flexible interpretation of the clause during the Diet subcommittee deliberations, albeit somewhat cautiously and without securing an unambiguous endorsement of this notion from other members of the committee. Indeed, American intelligence analysts were, as long as three years after the Diet deliberations, still uncertain how best to view Article 9, noting that Prime Minister Yoshida had himself "in his testimony be-

fore this committee argued that there should be no attempt to distinguish between offensive and defensive war." Publicly, the Japanese government, both in
1946 and in 1949, appears to have intentionally embraced ambiguity, with "Foreign Ministry officials . . . join[ing] Yoshida in agreeing that Article 9 denies Japan the right of defensive as well as offensive war, although Nishimura Kumao,
Chief of the Treaty Bureau, on one occasion remarked that in an emergency Japan might have the right to resort to force to dispel an unjustly inflicted critical
danger." (Ironically, only the Japan Communist Party argued publicly in 1949
that Article 9 entitled Japan to maintain a defensive force.) By early 1950, however, the prime minister appeared to be shifting his position subtly, while still
seeking refuge in characteristically vague public pronouncements. "Government
spokesmen, although agreeing that Article 9 of the Japanese Constitution denies
Japan the right of defensive war, have been unwilling to discuss security issues.
Premier Yoshida has recently stated that renunciation of war does *not* mean
abandonment of self-defense, but he has thus far failed to clarify his meaning and
has refused to discuss the possibility of the establishment of US bases in post-
treaty Japan" (emphasis added). The evidence suggests, therefore, that the interpretive flexibility on the self-defense question emerged gradually and probably in
response to changing external events (not the least of which was the intensifying
Cold War). Subsequent attempts to assign Ashida a decisive role in this process
may reflect an understandable, but historically questionable, wish by official
opinion in Japan to shore up the constitutional foundations of post-war Japan's
vitally important non-offensive defense policy. See Koseki (1998), pp. 195–201;
"Japanese Attitudes toward the Peace Treaty," June 7, 1949, OIR Report, No.
4981; "Japanese Attitudes Toward Peace Treaty Problems," Dec. 22, 1949, and
Feb. 28, 1950, OIR Reports, No. 5136 and 5136A, both in OIR files, NA-II.

8. Drifte (1983), pp. 76–78.

9. Watanabe (1986), p. 41.

10. "Kokusai jōsei no mitōshi to tainichi kōwa" [Forecast of the international
situation and the Japanese Peace Treaty], Dec. 23, 1949, Section 7, B'0008/5/
0020–27, GA.

11. "Majoriti pīsu taisaku kenkyv sagyō" [Draft research on the majority
peace proposal], Dec. 3, 1949, Sect. 7, B'0008/5/0047–50, GA.

12. "Saikin no kokusai jōsei nitsuite" [Details on recent international condi-
tions], May 1, 1950, Sect. 7, B'0008/6/0225–0245, GA; "Anzenhoshō nikansuru
kihonteki tachiba" [Basic position on security guarantee], May 31, 1950, Sect. 7,
B'008/6/0247–0258, GA.

13. Watanabe (1986), p. 44.

14. Kōsaka (1968), p. 51.

15. Masumi (1983), p. 355.

16. Kōsaka (1968), p. 12.

17. "Beigawa e shukōshita 'Wagakata kenkai'" ["Our Opinion"—memorandum handed to the American side], Jan. 30, 1951, Sect. 7, B'0009/2/0049–57,
GA.

18. The plan in question reflected the views of former Japanese naval officers
and ambitiously envisaged a gradual process of rearmament over eight years lead-

ing to a standing army of 96,000, an air force comprising 1,789 aircraft and 39,000 personnel, and a 260,000-ton navy made up of 329 vessels. The plan also called for the creation of a new Ministry of Defense (or Ministry of National Security if international sensitivities called for a less conventional nomenclature), a lifting of all purge restrictions, and the creation of a civil defense organization composed of youths between 18 and 20. See Niles Bond to State, "Views of Former Japanese Ambassador Kichisaburō Nomura on Japanese Rearmament," Feb. 21, 1951, 794.5/2–2151, Records of the US Dept. of State Relating to the Internal Affairs of Japan, 1950–54, Reel 15 (microfilm), NA.

19. The Shirasu and Nomura incidents are covered in Drifte (1983), pp. 119 and 104 respectively; for Ichimada's conversation see "Conversation with Ichimada," Jan. 25, 1951, RG59, State Dept. decimal files, 694.001/1–2551, NA. The following account by a member of State's Office of Northeast Asian affairs, was also typical of the indirect reassurances on rearmament that the Americans received from different sources within the Japanese government. Citing a letter from Mr. Chuhei Matsuo, "an interpreter in the [US] Foreign Service since 1917 and . . . at present on duty at USPOLAD, Tokyo," the State Department official observed that "the most interesting comment is that 'Prime Minister Yoshida is actually in favour of rearmament but refrains from saying so for fear of repercussions from Australian and the Philippines.' This information was furnished by former Admiral Hasegawa, who was Governor General of Taiwan when the war started in 1941." Warner to Johnson, Jan. 29, 1951. 794.5/1–2951, NA. This and other evidence suggests that it was highly unlikely that Yoshida saw Japan, in the long term, as pursuing a low-profile foreign policy that eschewed the use of military force. Ambassador Chiba Kazuo, who entered the Gaimushō in September 1948, remembers as a freshman diplomat an inspection visit by Yoshida to the diplomatic training school where he was a student. In addressing the trainees, Yoshida made clear that in the future Japan would regain an active diplomatic role—a remark which Chiba cites (together with Yoshida's realpolitik, European-school style of diplomacy) as evidence that the prime minister envisaged Japan recovering, at some point, its Great Power status. Personal interview with Ambassador Chiba, June 1994. Further evidence that the prime minister saw postwar Japan adopting an active diplomatic role has emerged recently following the Japanese Foreign Ministry's dramatic declassification in April 2003 of a government policy review produced for Yoshida in April, 1951. While the review focused on understanding the historical factors and the policy errors that had led to Japan's war involvement in the Pacific War, it also sought to provide practical lessons for how Japan might engage in post-war international relations. See Ogura (2003).

20. Yamaguchi (1989), p. 3; Hiwatari (1990), pp. 1–3.

21. Public support for rearmament ranged from 38.9 percent in August 1950 to 54 percent in September 1950, reaching 63 percent in February 1951. See Masumi (1983), p. 365.

22. Maruyama (1963), pp. 149–50. The importance of native traditions as a source of identity in Japan is well illustrated by the failure of the Christian missionary movement in post-war Japan. Despite a major proselytizing campaign after 1945, the Church failed "to fill the moral vacuum" in Japan, and by 1955

only about one percent of the population identified with Christianity. Brown (1955), p. 272.

23. Iwanaga (1985), p. 11.

24. Kōsaka (1968), p. 41.

25. Many commentators have argued that Japanese popular opinion was favorably inclined toward MacArthur and the Occupation. However, Occupation censorship concealed Japanese discontent which was therefore often expressed indirectly—sometimes in plays or in popular literature. As one American observer noted: "Although the Allied occupation of Japan was benign, benignity is in the eyes of the beholder, and it is not patent that all Japanese found SCAP a non-intrusive government. While there was only a limited number of acceptable forms of self-expression, the theatre was usually exempt from overly strict censorship. As a result, the Occupation and the mannerisms and physical appearances of the occupiers were often the good humoured but nonetheless pointed butts of many jokes." See Schull (1990), p. 110. The most comprehensive and revealing study of the "kaleidoscopic " variety of Japanese responses to the Occupation can be found in Dower (1999), p. 25 and passim, while Sodei Rinjirō has provided a fascinating insight into the personalized, individual reactions to SCAP by publishing a selection of letters from ordinary Japanese to MacArthur. See Sodei (2001). For a literary example of Japanese discontent, see Abe Kōbō's short story "Chinnyusha" (Intruders), a thinly veiled satirical attack on the Occupation expressed in the account of a man who has his apartment and ultimately his entire life taken over by a gum-chewing family sanctimoniously preaching the virtues of democracy and majority decision-making. Abe (1991), pp. 101–35.

26. Kyoko Inoue has demonstrated via a detailed linguistic analysis how Japanese politicians in translating the American draft Constitution were able to preserve a number of Japan's distinctive cultural and political traditions. Inoue (1991), pp. 269–70 and passim. For a similar discussion, see also Koseki (1998), pp. 173–77.

27. Large (1992), p. 143; for a Gaimushō endorsement of the Emperor, see "Tennōsei nitsuite" [Details on the Emperor System], Mar. 13, 1950, Sect. 7, B'0008/6/0247–0258, GA.

28. Amakawa (1986), pp. 75, 86.

29. "Japanese Conservative Forces and the Future United States Position," report enclosed in McClurkin to Nitze, Oct. 18, 1951, RG59, PPS, Country and Area Files, Japan, 1947–8 [sic], NA. Spinks's analysis was clearly considered important by the State Department. McClurkin pointed out to Nitze that "this despatch and its enclosure is the most significant writing to come out of Tokyo in recent months," and William Sebald, in a covering note for the report, stressed, "Notwithstanding the length of the enclosed memorandum, it is believed essential that it be read in its entirety in order that there may be a complete understanding of the problems posed." Spinks, a former Stanford University political science Ph.D. who in the autumn of 1951 was First Secretary in the Embassy, had already demonstrated a keen interest in and detailed understanding of the complex political environment in post-war Japan. In late 1949, he completed an exhaustive 25-page study of the Konoe Memorial of 1945 in which Prince Konoe,

the former wartime prime minister, had warned of the dangerous and growing attraction of Communism within Japan and had sought, unsuccessfully, to persuade the Emperor to surrender to the United States in an effort to avoid strengthening the position of the "reformist," "control faction" (tōsei ha) within the Army. Spinks stressed the importance of this memorial in highlighting the ability of Communism, with its anti-capitalist message and stress on internal discipline and a pattern of centralized, authoritarian rule, to appeal to extremist sentiment on both the Left and the Right of the Japanese political divide. Imaginatively modifying the conventional metaphor of a spectrum of Left-Right political alignment, Spinks noted: "In actual practice . . . the line which extended across the ideological field in pre-war Japan was not a straight line. Rather it should be regarded as a semi-circle, one end-point of which represented the 'fascist' extreme right and the other end point, the communist extreme left. The ideological distance which separated extreme left from extreme right was not, therefore, the long course extending around the circle, which passed through various ideological hues from liberalism to conservatism, but the exceedingly narrow gap at each end of the semi-circle, which, if bridged, would complete the circle. Regardless of how much extreme rightists and leftists would decry such an interpretation of their respective positions, the political history of Japan since World War I has been marked by frequent examples of the remarkable identity of interests of leftists and rightists." See Charles Spinks, "The Konoe Memorial of February 14, 1945," Sept. 1, 1949, RG273, CIA Murphy Papers, Box 96, NA-II.

30. "Japanese Conservative Forces and the Future United States Position," NA.

31. Ibid.

32. This trend has been examined in considerable detail by J. Victor Koschmann in work dealing, in part, with the ideas of Takeuchi Yoshimi, an early post-war prominent Japanese sinologist. See Koschmann (1996). As Koschmann has noted, "in the environment of the end of Occupation in the early 1950s, the category of the nation again became a major focal point for subjective identification alongside class and humanity, a process in which the sinologist Takeuchi Yoshimi played an important role." Ibid., p. 4. Similarly, see Koseki (1998), p. 234, and Ruoff (2001), pp. 158–201, for confirmation of populist Japanese sentiment favoring identification with some of the traditional elements of the Emperor system and Japan's mythologized cultural and national identity, such as support for the preservation of the traditional National Founding Day (kigensetsu). Interestingly, this support was present both immediately after the promulgation of the new Constitution and well into the 1960s and 1970s.

33. For a discussion of the role of nationalism in influencing Japanese neutralism, see Stockwin (1968), pp. 15–16.

34. Ibid.

35. "Daresu kaidan no tame no junbisagyo kankei" [Preparatory draft documents for Dulles talks], Dec. 1950, Sect. 7, B'0009/1/0220–0231, GA.

36. Yoshida (1961), p. 4.

37. Yamaguchi (1989), p. 191.

38. Hiwatari (1990), p. 15.

39. "Daresu misshon kaidan rokushv" [Collected record of Dulles mission talks], Jan. 29, 1951, Sect. 7, B'0009/3/0078–0080, GA.

40. Sebald (1965), pp. 198–99; Finn (1992), p. 266. For an alternative interpretation which argues that Yoshida saw Japan's future foreign policy as centered on Asia rather than on alignment with the United States, see Welfield (1988).

41. Kōsaka (1986), p. 54. In the words of one US intelligence report, "Yoshida is noted . . . for his lack of personal popularity and his dislike of personal contacts. He is a poor speaker and heartily dislikes to speak in public, especially before the Diet." "Biographic Reports on the Members of Third Yoshida Cabinet," Feb. 23, 1949, OIR Report, No. 4902, OIR files, NA-II.

42. O'Neill (1981), p. 116.

43. Foot (1985), pp. 95–103.

44. Igarashi (1993), pp. 148–49; JCS 2180/2, "Memorandum for the Secretary of Defense," undated, RG 218, JCS Geographical files "Japan," 1951–53, NA.

45. Leffler (1992), p. 429.

46. Miyasato and Koseki (1992), p. 257; Yamagiwa (1994), p. 216.

47. Dulles to Acheson, Dec. 8, 1950, *FRUS VI*, 1950, p. 1359.

48. "Annual Report on Japan for 1950," Jan. 24, 1951, FO371/92518, FJ1011/1, PRO.

49. Fearey to Johnson, Dec. 5, 1950 (microfilm, LM90 Roll 16), 794.5/12–550, NA. Dulles, as he pointed out to New Zealand representatives in mid-January, favored only "modest" rearmament for Japan of a maximum of 5 to 10 divisions. UK High Commissioner, New Zealand to FO, Jan. 31, 1951, FO371/92648, FJ1191/4, PRO. Similarly, in conversation with Gascoigne in Tokyo, the US envoy indicated that he was against requiring Japan to rearm via a future security arrangement. Instead, America, he hoped, would "guide Japan's rearmament efforts" by contributing substantial amounts of military aid—in the form of (in Gascoigne's words) "strategic and heavy naval support." Gascoigne to FO, Feb. 2, 1951, FO371/92530, FJ1022/45, PRO. This American aid would have been important in light of economic conditions in Japan. Dodge's reforms and Korean War–related procurements (tokuju) had, it is true, boosted the economy. Industrial output was up by 70 percent over the three-year period from 1949, wages, employment, and investment were all increasing, and companies were shifting to higher value-added lines of production. However, despite an extra $592 million of demand in the economy and a narrowing of the gap between exports and imports, the country's balance of trade still recorded a deficit of $640 million. Japan's persistent dollar shortage is likely to have made the Americans wary of imposing new strains on the still fragile Japanese economy. Figures quoted in Finn (1992), pp. 267–68; Nakamura (1993), p. 440.

50. Foot (1985), p. 96; the Democrats majority fell from 12 to 2 in the Senate and from 17 to 12 in the House. See McCullough (1992), p. 814.

51. Leffler (1992), p. 409.

52. Pruessen (1982), pp. 433–38.

53. Dean Rusk, Oral History, Jan. 9, 1965, JFD-OH, ML.

54. It is worth emphasizing that the January–February talks in Tokyo pro-

duced no specific agreement by Japan to rearm in terms of troop numbers and military capabilities. The Japanese side did, apparently, propose a variety of concrete measures, including the addition of 50,000 men to the National Police Reserve (NPR) and the establishment of a General Staff and a Ministry of National Security. However, there is no evidence to suggest that Dulles accepted the Japanese plan. Moreover, details of this proposal come largely from a series of newspaper articles published in Japan in the 1970s, and none has yet been uncovered in either the American or the Japanese archives. Of course, it is conceivable that both governments have decided, for political reasons, to keep this information classified, but for the moment at least, the balance of evidence suggests that the nature of the security understanding was general rather than specific. See Finn (1992), pp. 280–83.

55. "Iguchi jikan, Arison kōshi no inishiaru shita bunsho" [Documents initialed by Vice-Minister Iguchi and Secretary Allison], Feb. 8, 1951, Sect. 7, B'0009/3/0061–2, GA.

56. Fearey (1991), p. 51.

57. Murakawa (1991b), p. 13.

58. "Summary Report by the Consultant to the Secretary," July 3, 1950, *FRUS* VI, 1950, pp. 1235–36.

59. "Japanese Peace Treaty Problems," Oct. 23, 1950, Council on Foreign Relations, Study Group Reports, JFD-P, Box 48, ML.

60. Ibid.

61. Ibid.

62. Ibid.

63. Ibid. For an alternative view which claims that the Americans, influenced by a "tacit racism," sought to strip Japan of its Asian identity and tie it explicitly to the US, see Koshiro (1999), pp. 15–48.

64. "Japanese Peace Treaty Problems," Oct. 23, 1950, Council on Foreign Relations, Study Group Reports, JFD-P, Box 48, ML.

65. Dulles's involvement in cultural relations with Japan preceded his role as President Truman's special consultant. In October 1949, for example, Joseph Grew had written to him asking him to serve as a member of the Campaign Sponsoring Committee seeking support for a new International Christian University. Established in June 1949 by a board of trustees including both prominent Japanese and Americans, and with Princess Chichibu, sister-in-law of the Emperor, serving as an honorary member of the University council, ICU gradually developed into a major institution, with a long and distinguished history of promoting liberal arts education in Japan. Grew to Dulles, Oct. 17, 1949, JFD-P, Box 41, ML. Dulles's belief in the importance of the cultural dimension to the US-Japan relationship is also tellingly reflected in a letter of September 1951 to Paul Hoffman, the President of the Ford Foundation, in which Dulles noted, "You already know my feeling as to the importance of Japan in relation to the future of the Far East which in turn vitally affects the total world picture. The people of Japan are both intelligent and hard-working, and their country is highly industrialized. They want to be part of the free world. It is essential from our point of view that they attain this objective. We can do much to help. One of the most important

factors is that they realize that we have a long-range interest in them, going beyond immediate strategic expediency. In my judgment a most effective way to bring this to their attention is through non-political, non-controversial channels. I have particularly in mind the cultural. I feel so strongly as to the importance of the cultural in international relations that I asked John Rockefeller, 3rd, to serve as an adviser to my mission to Japan and to make a study for me as to the long-range possibilities between the United States and Japan. The report was very favorably received by the Department of State." Dulles to Hoffman, Sept. 11, 1951, John Foster Dulles Papers, General Correspondence and Memoranda Series, EL.

66. Clutton to FO, Feb. 13, 1951, FO371/92701, FJ 1752/1, PRO. Rockefeller himself was well aware that Dulles's vision went far beyond the Peace Treaty itself, noting, "My assignment was not to join with him [Dulles] in working on the terms of the treaty. My assignment was to study US-Japanese relations to determine what, if anything, constructive or meaningful, could be done in strengthening them. My understanding of his position was that a treaty, in the long run, is only as important, as meaningful, as the relationship between the parties, is sound and constructive. In other words, he realized that unless US-Japanese relations were positive—were moving constructively forward—that the Peace Treaty would, to a large extent, be offset or vitiated in terms of what he hoped might be accomplished by it." John D. Rockefeller, III, Oral History, June 25, 1965, JFD-OH, ML.

67. Yoshida's assessment of Dulles is included in Murakawa (1991c), p. 113. Similarly, Yoshida claimed that Dulles's proposals "were of a far more generous nature than we had been led to expect and greatly heartened us." Yoshida (1961), pp. 250–51. Other US officials, such as Robert Murphy, the first post-war US ambassador to Japan, shared this impression, noting that "the Prime Minister, Yoshida . . . had great respect for Mr. Dulles—and the Foreign Minister, Mr. Okazaki, who was there at that time. In fact, all the members of the [Japanese] government had a great deal of respect regarding him as a man of character and determination and courage. He had never been closely identified with Japan as such in the preceding years. I think they were inclined to feel that perhaps his knowledge, and background, and interests related more to Europe that they did to Asia. But I think they respected him for his conduct of the treaty negotiations, because he tried to be fair about it and they knew that." Robert Murphy, Oral History, 19 May and 18 June, 1965, JFD-OH, ML.

68. "Prime Minister Shigeru Yoshida's statement on the occasion of the departure of Ambassador Dulles from Japan," Feb. 11, 1951, JFD-P, Box 53, ML.

69. Sebald (1965), p. 298. For an example of Dulles's public emphasis on the importance of treating Japan as an equal, see Dulles's CBS radio broadcast of March 1, 1951, in "Pacific Peace," Mar. 1, 1951 FO371/92533, FJ1022/120, PRO. As Dulles noted, "if Japan's admission to a place in the free world is to be meaningful, it must be a free choice and not a choice made under the coercion of any threat or the inducement of any economic bribe. In our talks with Japanese leaders we always had these necessities in mind. Our goal is not to get a mere piece of paper beginning with the word 'peace' and ending with a red seal. We seek deeds which will in fact enlarge and envigorate the whole free world. . . . The

peace should restore Japan as an equal in the society of nations. This means that Japan should not be subjected to restrictions on her sovereignty of a kind which other sovereign nations do not accept for themselves. These if imposed on the Japanese would understandingly [sic] hurt their pride, as seemingly designed to make them forever a second class nation." In an address to Whittier College, Los Angeles on March 31, Dulles reiterated this theme: "The major objective of any Japanese peace treaty is to bring the Japanese people hereafter to live with others as good neighbours. That does not require that the Japanese people should be pampered. It does mean that the victors should not take advantage of Japan's recent helpless state to impose, for the future, unequal conditions. It means that the peace settlement should restore the vanquished to a position of dignity and equality among the nations." "Peace in the Pacific," F0371/92539, FJ1022/225, PRO.

70. Leffler (1992), p. 428.

71. Clutton to FO, Feb. 17, 1951, FO371/92532, FJ1022/95, PRO.

72. "Nigatsu kokonoka gaisō kantei shōen ni okeru" [Feb. 9 banquet at foreign minister's official residence], Sect. 7, B'0009/03/0174, GA.

73. For example, Igarashi Takeshi has argued that greater attention should be given to Acheson's role in promoting the peace process and has pointed out that the basic framework for the eventual settlement was already in place when Dulles joined the administration. See Igarashi (1993), pp. 133, 154. At the same time, Acheson tended to be relatively more attuned to European rather than Asian concerns. As Dean Rusk pointed out, he "overlooked the brown, black and yellow peoples of the world." Quoted in Schoenbaum (1988), p. 193. Consequently, there may have been limits to Acheson's awareness of and sympathy toward Japan's preoccupation with questions of equality and sovereignty. Nonetheless, the working relationship between Acheson and Dulles during the Peace Treaty process appears to have been an effective one. As Rusk observed, "I think the two were never close friends in any personal sense, but they were close and loyal colleagues during this period when the Peace Treaty was being worked upon. I think there were some obvious personal qualities on each side that did not mesh together completely. One was a very strong Democrat; one was a very strong Republican. I think that partisanship, outside of this period, played some role in keeping the two from becoming close friends. But nevertheless, they worked very closely during the two-year period between the spring of '50 and the summer of '52." Dean Rusk, Oral History, Jan. 9, 1965, JFD-OH, ML.

74. Sebald (1965), pp. 93–94.

75. Cohen (1980a), pp. 6, 15.

76. "The Strategy of Freedom in Asia," Feb. 9, 1951 in Chancery, DC to FO, Feb. 20, 1951, FO371/92067, F10345/11, PRO.

77. Rusk (1991), pp. 101–6, 132.

78. Schoenbaum (1988), p. 199.

79. Ibid., p. 234.

80. Ibid., p. 226.

81. W. W. Butterworth also claims to have had a role in lobbying for Dulles's appointment. W. Walton Butterworth, Oral History, Sept. 8, 1965, JFD-OH, ML.

82. Schoenbaum (1988), p. 200.

83. Rusk (1991), p. 155.
84. Schoenbaum (1988), pp. 194, 199; Cohen (1980a), p. 69.
85. Schoenbaum (1988), p. 228.
86. See chapter three.
87. McGlothlen (1993), p. 45.
88. See, for example, Ryan (1949), pp. 62–69; Sissons (1950), pp. 29–40.
89. Gascoigne to FO, "Visit of Mr. Menzies to Tokyo," Aug. 17, 1950, FO371/83014, F1022/28, PRO.
90. Commonwealth Relations Office, Aug. 19, 1950, FO371/83014, F1022/27, PRO.
91. Kikuchi (1986), p. 195.
92. Howard to Rusk, Feb. 1, 1950 (microfilm, LM 90 roll 16), 794.5/2-150, NA; "Memorandum of Conversation by the Special Assistant to the Secretary," Apr. 7, 1950, *FRUS* VI, 1950, p. 1165.
93. Commonwealth Relations Office (CRO), Jan. 31, 1951, FO371/92648, FJ1191/4, PRO.
94. Dening to Scott, Jan. 6, 1951, FO371/93014, FZ1022/22; CRO to UK High Commissioner, FO371/92072, F1072/20, PRO.
95. Kikuchi (1986), pp. 203–9.
96. Ibid., p. 220.
97. Dening to Strang, May 3, 1950, FO371/83008, F1022/15, PRO.
98. Jebb to FO, Sept. 25, 1950, FO371/83018, F1026/8, PRO.
99. Undated FO minute, FO371/92532, FJ1022/47, PRO.
100. A. J. Maddocks, FO371/92554, FJ1022/516, PRO.
101. Rotter (1987), p. 47.
102. "Discussion on points of substance in the Japanese Peace Treaty," Mar. 21, 1951, FO371/92533, FJ1022/121; C. P. Scott, FO Minute, FO371/92553, FJ1022/49, PRO.
103. Steel to FO, Mar. 7, 1951, FO371/92533, FJ1022/122, PRO.
104. Franks to FO, Apr. 3, 1951, FO371/92067, F10345/14; Franks to FO, Apr. 6, 1951, FO371/92539, FJ1022/227, PRO.
105. Franks to FO, May 16, 1951, FO 371/92549, FJ1022/406, PRO.
106. Franks to FO, May 16, 1951, FO371/92549, FJ1022/406, PRO.
107. Clutton to Johnston, Apr. 24, 1951, FO371/92544, FJ1022/330, PRO.
108. "Record of a meeting between the Secretary of State and Mr. Dulles on 4th June, 1951," FO371/92551, FJ1022/498, PRO.
109. "Dulles Talks," June 14, 1951, FO371/92557, FJ1022/563, PRO; John Allison relayed to the Japanese the substance of Dulles's London talks in "Arison kōshi to no kaidanroku" [Record of discussions with Secretary Allison], June 25, 1951, Sect. 7, B'0009/7/0031-54, GA.
110. Steel to Strang, June 18, 1951, FO371/92560, FJ1022/630; Franks to FO, July 18, 1951, FO371/92568, FJ1022/781, PRO.
111. Despite Britain's acceptance of the US position, Foreign Office officials such as Esler Dening remained highly critical of the Americans—a bitterness which is not solely explained by disagreements over the drafting of the Peace Treaty. The British were frustrated at being relegated to the periphery of the pol-

icy-making process, both during the Occupation—"five difficult years" according to Dening—and in developing strategic thinking in the Asian region. The JCS were unwilling, for example, to accept British Chiefs of Staffs proposals for the establishment of formal consultative arrangements and joint cooperation on Far Eastern security matters. "Report to the Sec. of State on a Tour in the Far East, South and SE Asia and Australia by Sir Esler Dening," F0371/93017, FZ1022/87; "Chief of Staff discussion on the conversations of the Chief of Staff with US Chiefs of Staff during the former's visit to Washington," Jan. 22, 1951, FO371/92067, F10345/9, PRO. Above all perhaps, London's annoyance is best explained by a combination of inflated self-confidence in Britain's ability to understand the Asian situation, wounded national pride, and intense irritation at the loss of empire. As one senior government official neatly summarized the problem: "We consider that American Far Eastern policy is wrong-headed, will necessarily add to the hostile forces ranged against us, and may precipitate a world war. There can be no doubt that we are right . . . [However], we should accept the disagreeable conclusion, in the end, that we must allow the US to take the lead and follow, or at least not break with them. It is difficult for us, after several centuries of leading others, to resign ourselves to the position of allowing another and greater Power to lead us." Sir Pierson Dixon, "Views on HMG's policy towards the United States on Far Eastern Matters," Jan. 28, 1951, FO371/92067, F10345/8, PRO.

112. Truman had recalled MacArthur ostensibly because of the Far Eastern general's indiscreet remarks in a letter to Republican Congressman Joseph W. Martin implying criticism of US policy in Asia and Europe. MacArthur's comments appeared to be part of a general pattern of high-profile, public dissent from Washington's policy. Equally important, however, were the fears on the part of both the JCS and America's allies that MacArthur might act impulsively and independently, engaging in retaliatory bombing against China and dramatically inflaming the East Asian conflict. Stueck (1995), pp. 178–82. MacArthur's recall prompted Dulles to fly immediately to Tokyo to reassure the Yoshida government that the change in leadership did not imply a change in US policy toward Japan. The consultant and the general passed in the air in opposite directions, trading messages but not actually meeting.

113. Rusk (1991), p. 155.

114. Masumi (1983), p. 334. Yoshida's satisfaction is evident in the warmth and gratitude of his handwritten letter to Dulles composed shortly before returning home to Japan. "My Dear Dulles, I cannot leave these shores of America without sending you a line to say how happy and grateful I am—grateful for the triumphant outcome of the Peace Conference. This simply means the fructification of your patient and painstaking efforts of the eleven months past and final dramatic efforts at the conference itself. Your blasting of the Soviet proposals by exposing the hypocrisy and trickery of the Russians was surely effective. That finished them, I think. I wish you a good, long rest which you need and more than deserve." Yoshida to Dulles, Sept. 10, 1951, JFD-P, ML.

115. Truman (1951), p. 708.

116. The critical wording in the Security Treaty was contained in Article 1,

which read in part: "Japan grants, and the United States of America accepts the right, upon the coming into force of the Treaty of Peace and of this Treaty, to dispose United States land, air and sea forces in and about Japan. Such forces may be utilized to contribute to the maintenance of the international peace and security in the Far East and to the security of Japan against armed attack from without." This, according to the Treaties Bureau memorandum, was "understood to mean actually that: 'Such forces *will* be utilized to contribute to the security of Japan against armed attack from without—and *may* be utilized to contribute to the maintenance of international peace and security in the Far East.'" The memorandum went on to note: "In that part of the sentence which says that 'Such forces *may* be utilized to contribute to the maintenance of international peace and security in the Far East,' the word 'may' is construed to mean that Japan would have no objection to the United States using its armed forces in Japan for the purpose of contributing to the maintenance of international peace and security in the Far East." (Emphasis in original.) See "Japanese Interpretation of Certain Points in Connection with the Proposed Bilateral Security Arrangement between the United States and Japan," Aug. 9, 1951, Records of the US Department of State relating to the internal affairs of Japan, 1950–54 (microfilm), Reel 16, 794.5/8–951, NA. In this way, both sides had reached an implicit, although not a formally constraining, security understanding. Without a standing army, navy, or air force, Japan was clearly in no position to enter into a formal collective security pact. Hence the need for this qualified cooperation.

117. The *Mainichi shinbun* recorded 79.9 percent in favor of the Security Treaty and only 6.8 percent opposed; 76.3 percent supported Japanese rearmament, but of these 51.4 percent favored waiting until Japan had rebuilt its economy as against 24. 9 percent who favored immediate rearmament. Sebald to State, Sept. 18, 1951, State Dept. decimal files, 794.5/9–1751, NA.

118. Kōsaka (1968), p. 70.

Chapter 3

1. Dower (1993a), p. 233, and, in particular, Chap. 6, "Yoshida in the Scales of History," pp. 210–38; Schonberger (1989), p. 237.

2. Hosoya (1982), pp. 75, 81.

3. Tucker (1983), pp. 8–10.

4. Ibid., p. 17.

5. Ibid., p. 204.

6. Blum (1982), p. 219. Acheson, in particular, favored a strategy of accommodation with the PRC—at least up until Communist China's large-scale intervention in the Korean War in late 1950. For a detailed description of the differences over China policy between the secretary of state and his government colleagues, see Cohen (1980b), pp. 13–52. For a detailed and persuasive account of US-PRC relations up to normalization in 1972 which stresses the persistent US assumption that Moscow and Beijing were anything but monolithically united, see Chang (1990).

7. Cohen (1980b), p. 22.

8. Yasuhara (1986), p. 77.

9. Mendl (1978), p. 4.

10. Tanaka (1991), p. 45; Sakeda (1986), p. 102.

11. Furukawa (1981), p. 29.

12. "Estimate of Effect on Japan of United States recognition of Chinese Communist Regime," Dec. 5, 1949, RG273, CIA Murphy Papers, Box 96, NA-II.

13. Ibid.

14. Ibid.

15. Ibid.

16. Ibid.

17. Tucker (1983), p. 202.

18. Cohen (1987), p. 76.

19. Yasuhara (1986), p. 85.

20. Dingman (1975), p. 123.

21. Buckley (1982), p. 175.

22. Schonberger (1989), p. 270.

23. The British, as Roger Dingman has pointed out, were also able, via a curiously inverted logic, to defend Japanese trade with Communist China on strategic grounds. Trade with the PRC would promote Japanese prosperity, thereby discouraging the revival of Japanese expansionism in Asia and promoting regional stability. See Dingman (1975), p. 124.

24. "Memo of Conversation by the Second Secretary of the Embassy in the U.K.," Mar. 21, 1951, *FRUS* VI, 1951, p. 940; "Memo of Conversation," Mar. 30, 1951, *FRUS* VI, 1951, p. 954.

25. Dulles, for example, early on in his tenure as the administration's Japan consultant argued that trade with Southeast Asia would enable Japan to avoid excessive reliance on economic ties with the Chinese mainland. In general, Dulles was unsympathetic to British fears of Japanese competition in Southeast Asia. See Buckley (1982), p. 172.

26. Allison to Dulles, Apr. 5, 1951, *FRUS* VI, 1951, pp. 963–64.

27. "Secretary's meeting with President," May 28, 1951, *FRUS* VI, 1951, p. 1051.

28. "Secretary of State to POLAD," May 16, 1951, *FRUS* VI, 1951, p. 1045.

29. British press commentary in the summer of 1951 opposed the exclusion of Communist China from the Peace Conference. *The Guardian* argued that the Peace Treaty should be postponed if the PRC were excluded, while the *New Statesman* warned that including the Nationalists would lead to the expansion of the Korean War throughout Asia. See Dingman (1975), p. 125.

30. Schonberger (1989), p. 271.

31. Dulles talks, June 8, 1951, FO371/92566, FJ1022/547, PRO.

32. Ibid.

33. Untitled minute, June 8, 1951, FO371/92577, FJ1022/572, PRO.

34. Schonberger (1989), p. 272.

35. Ishii (1986), p. 302. Ishii's article is especially valuable since it is based ex-

tensively on Taiwanese diplomatic records and therefore provides a perspective often absent from studies of the China issue in Japanese-American relations at this time.

36. Ibid., p. 302.

37. Cohen (1987), p. 80.

38. Sec. of State to Sebald, Aug. 2, 1951, *FRUS* VI, 1951, p. 1236.

39. Editorial note, *FRUS* VI, 1951, p. 1347.

40. Dingman (1975), p. 127; Dower (1993), p. 233.

41. Smith Papers, unsigned memo for the week of Sept. 3–8, 1951, *FRUS* VI, 1951, p. 1327.

42. Hosoya (1982), pp. 79–80; Ishii (1986), p. 306.

43. Dulles to Acheson, Nov. 7, 1951, *FRUS* VI, 1951, p. 1393.

44. Sebald to Sec. of State, *FRUS* VI, 1951, pp. 1437–38.

45. Dower (1993a), p. 234.

46. "Japan's Relations with Chinese Nationalist Government," *FRUS* VI, 1951, pp. 1444–45.

47. Dulles wrote to Acheson in late December 1951: "I am clearly of the opinion that what I did in Tokyo involves no violation of the letter or the spirit of my agreement of June 17 with Mr. Morrison. Also, when it was decided not to invite any representative of China to the San Francisco Conference but to leave China relations to future Japanese action, it was taken for granted by the British Government that Japan would in fact align itself with United States policy in this respect. The Morrison-Dulles memorandum of June 17 was never designed to prevent Japan independently acting in its own interests. It was designed merely to assure that SCAP's authority over the Japanese Government would not be exerted to influence Japan's foreign policy." "Memorandum for the Secretary," Dec. 26, 1951, State Dept. decimal files, 693.94/12–2651, NA.

48. Ibid., p. 1444.

49. Sec. of State to Sebald, Dec. 18, 1951, *FRUS* VI, 1951, p. 1450.

50. Dower (1993a), p. 236.

51. It is worth considering that Dulles's own position may not have been as well defined or as intransigent as has sometimes been assumed. While Dulles remained wary of Beijing, he may not yet have been firmly and irrevocably committed to a strategy of isolating the PRC. Dulles was eager to become secretary of state in the next administration and by late 1951 was very conscious of the forthcoming presidential elections. Part of his strategy of positioning himself for this contest involved winning the backing of Republicans in Congress and also distancing himself from the Democratic administration. In doing this, he occasionally indulged in rhetorical brinksmanship, suggestive of uncompromising anti-communism and unshakable support for the Chinese Nationalists. However, as H. W. Brands has pointed out, Dulles's public language was often based on narrow, political calculations and may not always have reflected his true private intentions. See Brands (1988b), pp. 18–19. Moreover, there is evidence to suggest that, as late as September 1951, some thought was being given in the State Department to the possibility of relaxing trade controls between Japan and main-

land China—although by late 1952 stringent controls had in fact been introduced on Sino-Japanese trade. See "Minutes of the Meeting of the Drafting Group of special committee on East-West Trade. Sub-committee on Japanese trade with Soviet bloc, particularly PRC and Manchuria." Sept. 8, 1951, P26 files, NA; Foot (1995), p. 57.

52. "Japan and China," Jan. 9, 1952, State Dept. decimal files (microfilm), no class mark (but follows immediately after 693.94/12–2651), NA.

53. Okazaki Katsuo, who served as Yoshida's foreign minister, put the matter even more strongly, underlining Japan's decision-making autonomy on this issue and agreeing that Dulles "had little or nothing to do with making up Japan's mind in this respect." Commenting on the situation in late 1951, early 1952, Okazaki noted: "Our people, or at least a majority of the Japanese people, did not like the Communistic doctrine. Oh yes, we had very friendly feelings toward Nationalist China, especially we were grateful to Generalissimo Chiang Kai-shek when he declared at the end of the war that Chinese people should not revenge [sic] the Japanese people on what Japan did in the past. And by his interference all our soldiers and residents in China could come back to Japan safely. Therefore, our sympathy—I mean, our people's sympathy—was altogether toward Nationalist China. And up to that time, we are [sic] not sure whether the Communist regime will establish itself and be secure like today all over Chinese continent. We thought or at least our people thought—Nationalist China, which governed, administered all China until a few years before, could again go back to the continent. So, people did not think, it was strange at that time that we would conclude a peace treaty between Nationalist China and Japan, and not with Communist China." Accepting that Dulles "had a better appreciation of the Japanese government's feelings, perhaps, than the British did," Okazaki added "on top of that, I should like to stress that it was a very natural way, at that time, for Japan to conclude a treaty with Nationalist China, and not with Communist China. Whether Mr. Dulles wanted that or not, if we are left free, we would surely make treaty." Okazaki Katsuo, Oral History, Oct. 2, 1964, JFD-OH, ML. Interestingly, John Sparkman, who had traveled out to Japan with Dulles and H. Alexander Smith and who met with Yoshida "almost every day" during his stay in Tokyo, echoes Okazaki's observation. Asked whether Yoshida had been "pressured" into agreeing to the Yoshida Letter, Sparkman noted, "No, I think he was perfectly willing. In other words, I think it represented his feeling. Now, you talk about pressuring. I got this impression from working with the Japanese—I have found them . . . I've been to Japan, by the way, a good many times since that, and I've talked with every Prime Minister they've had and every Foreign Minister, I believe; and I find them remarkably fine people to deal with. I admire the clarity of their thinking. The thing that utterly amazed me when I first went to Japan was to see how eager they were to cooperate and to do all they could to set things right. I've been impressed with that throughout the years, and I believe people who have visited Japan have been. Japan has been a wonderful ally of ours. And I think Mr. Yoshida wanted to do what we felt they ought to do, but at the same time I think, in his own thinking, he wanted nothing to do with the Communists

on the mainland. And he was probably glad that we had taken this attitude."
John Sparkman, Oral History, Mar. 19, 1966, JFD-OH, ML.

54. Kitaoka (1994).

55. Yoshida's emphasis on national morality and his desire to recreate a legitimate sense of patriotism in Japan was based, in part, on his belief that without these things the Japanese people would embrace Communism in the same self-destructive way that they had slavishly followed Japan's military leaders in the 1930s. See Ōtake (1988), pp. 19–20.

56. Kitaoka (1994), pp. 16, 19–20. For the traditional view of Yoshida which emphasizes his desire for an Asia-focused foreign policy, see Welfield (1988), p. 531.

57. Kitaoka (1994), pp. 16–17.

58. Ibid., p. 21.

59. Kern to Robertson, Dec. 11, 1958, State Dept. Decimal Files (Microfilm, US Political Relations with Japan, 1955–59, Roll 5), 611.94/12–1158, NA.

60. Yoshida, in fact, relied on his political allies to inform the Americans of the constraints preventing him from speaking out publicly on the China issue. In early December 1951, for example, Inukai Ken, a prominent Democratic Diet member, called on U. Alexis Johnson, deputy assistant secretary of state, in Washington. According to Johnson, Inukai's "purpose was to convey to the Department a message from Yoshida to counteract the effect of Yoshida's statements in a recent debate in the Japanese Diet on the Japanese Peace Treaty and Security Pact concerning Japanese rearmament and attitudes toward Communist China." Inukai stressed that "Prime Minister Yoshida's statements in the Diet with respect to Japanese relations with China had also been motivated by the tactical political situation in the Diet on the Treaty and not by any lack of recognition of the true nature of the Communist regime in China. The Prime Minister had received the impression from his conversation with Secretary Acheson at San Francisco that it would be well for Japan not to be precipitous in determining the question of Japanese relations with China, and it was the Prime Minister's view that the Japanese public position on this should remain equivocal until ratification of the Treaty had been carried out by such countries as the United Kingdom and Australia." "Japanese Rearmament and Japanese Attitudes toward Communist China," Dec. 7, 1951, State Department decimal files, 794.5/12–751, NA.

61. Iriye (1992), p. 97.

62. Furukawa (1981), p. 21.

63. Tanaka (1991), p. 43.

64. Furukawa (1981), p. 24.

65. Ibid., p. 41.

66. Sakeda (1986), p. 96.

67. Sebald to Rusk, Jan. 2, 1952, FRUS XIV, 1952–54, pp. 1065–66.

68. For example, Iguchi, in early November 1951, reassured Sebald that Yoshida's public suggestion that Japan might be prepared to open a trading office in Shanghai was entirely intended to offset potential hostile British and Commonwealth reactions to the earlier news that Japan was establishing an Overseas Agency in Taibei. See Sebald to Acheson, Nov. 7, 1951, FRUS VI, 1951, p. 1391.

69. For an extensive analysis of gaiatsu in the context of US-Japan relations in the 1980s and early 1990s, see Schoppa (1997).

70. Dower has argued that it was widely assumed in 1952 that the letter had been dictated by Dulles. See Dower (1993a), p. 234.

71. Memo of conversation, Aug. 9, 1951, *FRUS* VI, 1951, p. 1250.

72. Memo of conversation, Sept. 9, 1951, *FRUS* VI, 1951, pp. 1343–44.

73. Dingman (1975), p. 129.

74. Gifford to Sec. of State, Nov. 14, 1951, *FRUS* VI, 1951, pp. 1401–2.

75. Smith papers, Dec. 18, 1951, *FRUS* VI, 1951, p. 1447.

76. Merchant to Dulles, Nov. 26, 1951, *FRUS* VI, 1951, p. 1415.

77. Memo of conversation, Jan. 9, 1952, *FRUS* XIV, 1952–54, pp. 1075–76.

78. "Japan's relations with China," Jan. 10, 1952, *FRUS* XIV, 1952–54, p. 1080.

79. Acheson (1969), p. 604. Indeed, following the opening in 1994 of previously closed elements of Dean Rusk's 1965 oral history, the seriousness of the breakdown in communication between Whitehall and the British embassy in Washington can now for the first time be documented. As Rusk observed, "I think the real story has never been told, and perhaps should not be for quite some years. . . . The British had been here for consultation; and the public impression of the incident was that the Foreign Minister of Great Britain had arrived in Britain to be confronted with the Yoshida letter, which came as a surprise to him—that he felt he had been somehow let down by Mr. Dulles for not having had this explained to him when he was here in Washington. In *fact*, Mr. Dulles had showed the letter to the British Ambassador, had *read* him the letter, before the final talk between the Foreign Minister and Mr. Dulles here in Washington. Mr. Dulles, therefore, assumed that the British Ambassador had briefed his own Foreign Minister about this Yoshida letter. In fact, this had not occurred. The British Ambassador [Sir Oliver Franks], for some reason, had failed to brief his own Foreign Minister about this letter . . . Well, this was an embarrassing matter, because it could only be resolved by explanations that would have created very serious problems for the British government and between the British Ambassador and his own Foreign Minister. With some restraint the United States did not make this issue, this part of it, public. But there was a misunderstanding which Mr. Dulles did not deserve, because he felt that he had informed his British colleagues when he informed the British Ambassador. But that particular incident led to a sense of unreliability that I think was just not deserved and was unfair to Mr. Dulles" (emphasis in original). Dean Rusk, Oral History, Jan. 9, 1965, JFD-OH, ML.

80. Ishii (1986), p. 312.

81. Sebald to State, Mar. 4, 1952, *FRUS* XIV, 1952–54, p. 1212.

82. Bond to Department of State, Apr. 7, 1952, *FRUS* XIV, 1952–54, p. 1234.

83. Miyasato (1985), p. 135; "Dulles Mission Staff Meeting," Feb. 5, 1951, *FRUS* VI, 1951, p. 859.

84. Acting Sec. of Defense (Lovett) to Sec. of State, Aug. 22, 1951, *FRUS* VI, 1951, pp. 1282–86.

85. Allison to Rusk, Aug. 22, 1951, *FRUS* VI, 1951, p. 1287.

86. "Principles to be applied in stationing US forces in Japan," Aug. 29, 1951, *FRUS* VI, 1951, pp. 1307–9.

87. Rusk to Nash, Oct. 24, 1951, *FRUS* VI, 1951, p. 1382.

88. Memo of Undersecretaries' meeting, Nov. 14, 1951, *FRUS* VI, 1951, pp. 1403–4.

89. Memo of conversation, Jan. 30, 1952, *FRUS* XIV, 1952–54, p. 1125.

90. Sebald to State, Feb. 1, 1952, *FRUS* XIV, 1952–54, p. 1130; Sebald to State, Feb. 8, 1952, *FRUS* XIV, 1952–54, pp. 1141–43; Memo of conversation, Feb. 18, 1952, *FRUS* XIV, 1952–54, p. 1178.

91. Sebald to State, Feb. 1, 1952, *FRUS* XIV, 1952–54, p. 1129; Sebald to State, Feb. 19, 1952, *FRUS* XIV, 1952–54, p. 1183.

92. See chapter two.

93. Dulles to Webb, Sept. 10, 1951, *FRUS* VI, 1951, p. 1346; Miyasato (1985), p. 138.

94. Dulles was uncompromisingly clear on the importance of this issue and aware that the US stance on the Administrative Agreement was critical not only for America's bilateral relationship with Japan, but also in terms of its wider position in Asia as a whole:

> I consider it essential that the Security Treaty be implemented in a manner consistent with the Treaty of Peace itself. That implementation must treat Japan as a sovereign equal and in so far as compatible with security necessity— and "necessity" is not mere convenience or prestige—should respect the wishes and sensibilities of the Japanese people and their status as sovereign equals.
>
> To meet this test will be difficult but it is essential that it should be met. If we do not meet it, our position in Japan will become untenable and our position in all of Asia will have been undermined. We face in Japan a crucial test of whether or not it is possible for representatives of the West to deal on a basis of equality with Asiatics. If we meet that challenge, then we can look forward to increasing cooperation with other peoples of Asia. If we fail to meet it, then the communists will seem to be vindicated in their slogan of "Asia for the Asiatics" and all of Asia will be united under that slogan to drive out all Western influence from Asia.
>
> To meet that challenge in Japan it is peculiarly difficult because the challenge confronts soldiers who for over six years have looked upon the Japanese as inferiors, both because of their race and because of their defeat in battle. To alter that attitude will be tremendously difficult, but I repeat, it is extremely vital and no effort should be spared to accomplish it.
>
> The Security Treaty provides a basis for the exercise by the United States for very broad rights in Japan and the Administrative Agreement will, even in its most modern form, implement this in ways which cannot but be irksome and burdensome to the Japanese. There will be a tendency on the part of those who think in legalistic terms to attempt to obviate the danger of Japanese ill will by getting complete legal rights of an extraterritorial character.

Such legal rights read well on paper. But it must constantly be borne in mind that legal rights are totally ineffective unless good will goes with them. A United States military position in Japan is totally untenable and a liability rather than an asset if the Japanese people are resentful of it and want it to end and if it can only be preserved by a show of force. (Untitled memorandum, Oct. 17, 1951, John Foster Dulles Papers, JFD-JMA Chronological Series, Box 2, EL).

95. Dulles to Sec. of State, Oct. 3, 1951, *FRUS* VI, 1951, p. 1373.

96. Johnson to Nash, Feb. 11, 1952, *FRUS* XIV, 1952–54, pp. 1153–55.

97. Allison to Rusk, Nov. 8, 1951, *FRUS* VI, 1951, pp. 1394–95; CinCFE to JCS, Oct. 14, 1951, RG218, JCS Geographical Files (Japan), 1951–53, NA; CinCFE to JCS, Jan. 13, 1951, RG218, JCS Geog. Files (Japan), 1951–53, NA.

98. CinCFE to JCS, Apr. 19, 1952, RG218, JCS Geog. File (Japan), 1951–53, NA.

99. Johnson to Nash, Jan. 28, 1952, RG218, JCS Geog. Files (Japan), 1951–53, NA.

100. POLAD to State, Jan. 17, 1952, *FRUS* XIV, 1952–54, p. 1092.

101. Sebald to State, Feb. 19, 1952, *FRUS* XIV, 1952–54, p. 1183.

102. Ridgway (1956), p. 225.

103. See chapter six.

104. Ridgway to JCS, Nov. 18, 1951, RG218 JCS Geog. File (Japan), 1951–53, NA.

105. SCAP to Dept. Army, Jan. 27, 1952, RG218, JCS Geog. Files (Japan), 1951–53, NA. Indeed, press reports in early 1952 indicated that the Japanese government was committed to reorganizing the NPR into a "defense corps" in October of 1952 and expanding its strength in keeping with, and in some instances beyond, American military plans. In pursuing this strategy, the government moved cautiously. "Yoshida and his Cabinet colleagues have emphasized that the creation of the 'new defense corps' would not constitute rearmament and thus would not require a revision of the Constitution. . . . [T]he tactic of the government apparently is designed to counter the element of anti-rearmament sentiment present among the electorate and to avoid, if possible, the issue of an amendment of Article 9 of the Constitution." "Japanese Government and Press Debate Expansion and Reorganization of the National Police Reserve," Feb. 12, 1952, OIR Report, No. 5811, OIR files, NA-II.

106. Auer (1973), pp. 80–84.

107. Ibid., p. 89.

108. "Feasibility of Japanese Rearmament in Association with the United States," Apr. 20, 1951, *FRUS* VI, 1951, pp. 993–98.

109. Yoshida (1961), p. 272.

110. Sebald to Rusk, Jan. 2, 1952, *FRUS* XIV, 1952–54, p. 1066.

111. Steeves to State, Apr. 26, 1952, *FRUS* XIV, 1952–54, p. 1253.

112. See Kitaoka (1994).

113. See Richard Immerman's introduction in Immerman (1990), p. 20.

114. Tucker (1990), p. 262.

115. Schonberger and Dower, in criticizing American policy, have perhaps been too inclined to view American-Japanese relations through the distorting prism of Left versus Right revisionist diplomatic history. While it is legitimate to stress the self-serving nature of much post-war US foreign policy, this policy did not make a clash of interests between America and its allied partners inevitable. In the case of Japanese-American relations, a disinterestedly altruistic America was not a requirement for an efficient and mutually beneficial alliance relationship. The mutual and pressing concerns of the Cold War could compensate for differences, and perhaps in some cases (for example, by promoting cultural exchange) even encourage bilateral diversity.

116. Berding (1965), p. 136. Dean Rusk had similarly grasped the relevance of this fact of international life, noting in November 1951: "It will take Japan some time to discover from experience that no country, including the United States, is as 'sovereign' in the world community of the 1950s as was the case ten, twenty or fifty years ago. The more sophisticated countries of the West are aware of the requirements of cooperation but Japan, with little responsible experience in recent international politics, will require time to adjust to new world conditions." "Foreign Policy Considerations involved in the Administrative Agreement with Japan and related arrangements," Nov. 9, 1951, State department decimal files, 794.5/11–951, NA.

Chapter 4

1. "Japan. A Sovereign State," *Dallas Morning News*, Apr. 29, 1952.

2. For example, Henry Hayward, writing in the *Christian Science Monitor*, was convinced that the Occupation had had a positive, liberalizing effect, freeing the Japanese public from the scourge of oppressive militarism. Hayward (1952). By contrast, Lindesay Parrot of the *New York Times* was much more cautious in analyzing the degree of change that Japan had experienced, suggesting, "No responsible leader or observer of the six-year occupation of Japan has yet been bold enough to contend that a basic change in national character has been made." Parrot (1952). Whatever the merits of these contrasting views, it was clear to the US government that some in Japan at this stage had been contemplating—perhaps unrealistically—some fairly drastic change, including the possibility of the Emperor's abdication once the Peace Treaty had come into effect. "Upon investigation, we have found that this was considered as a possibility but had been discarded by the Government. Yoshida assured Ambassador Sebald that the Emperor will continue and this will be made clear to the Japanese people in the near future." Secretary's staff meeting, Mar. 27, 1952, JFD-P, ML.

3. Allison (1973), p. 199.

4. Brands (1988a), p. 9.

5. Dockrill (1996), p. 22; Donovan (1956), pp. 18–19.

6. Eisenhower (1963), p. 122.

7. See, for example, "Japan Is Done with Kow-Towing After Today," *Washington Post*, Apr. 27, 1952; "US Firing Ranges Stir Japanese Ire," *New York Times*, June 20, 1953; "Malicious Lies Stir Japanese Against US," *Washington*

Post, July 12, 1953; "Dulles Not Likely to Enjoy Trouble-Shooting in Japan," *New York Times*, Aug. 4, 1953.

8. Reischauer (1952); Sect. 9, A'0128/21/0124–139, GA (Gaimushō archives).

9. For the latest study on Okinawa during the Occupation, see Eldridge (2001). For coverage of the entire post-war period up until reversion in 1972, see Sarantakes (2000).

10. America suffered some 50,000 casualties in the battle for Okinawa, with 12,520 killed or missing in action and close to 37,000 wounded. Hellegers (2001), p. 27.

11. Kennan to Marshall, Mar. 14, 1948, RG59, PPS Country and Area Files, "Japan," 1947–53, NA.

12. NSC 13/1, "Recommendations with Respect to US Policy Toward Japan," Sept. 24, 1948, RG59, PPS Country and Area Files, "Japan," 1947–53, NA; Watanabe (1970), p. 23.

13. Kennan to Marshall, Mar. 14, 1948, NA.

14. "Staff Study on United States Long-Term Objectives with Respect to the Ryukyus Islands," Dec. 5, 1951, RG218, Geog. File (Japan), 1951–52, NA.

15. Watanabe (1970), pp. 12–13.

16. Dulles to Sebald, Aug. 8, 1951, John Foster Dulles Papers, JFD-JMA Chronological Series, EL.

17. Watanabe (1970), p. 30.

18. Allison (1973), p. 167.

19. MacArthur had, by contrast, adopted a far less enlightened position. As William Sebald noted in his diary entry of January 21, 1951: "Regarding the Ryukyus and the Bonins, the General said that he is unalterably opposed to leaving any vestige of sovereignty in the Japanese over these islands, and that they must be subject solely to the United States." Cited in William Sebald, Oral History, JFD-OH, ML.

20. "Staff Study on United States Long-Term Objectives with Respect to the Ryukyus Islands," Dec. 5, 1951, NA.

21. "Decision on JCS 1380/135," undated, RG218, Geog. File (Japan), 1951–53, NA.

22. "NSC Staff Study on 'United States Objectives and Courses of Actions with Respect to Japan,'" July 23, 1952, RG319 (Japan), Box 17, NA.

23. NIE-52, May 29, 1952, *FRUS* XIV, 1952–54, p. 1265.

24. Young to Allison, June 10, 1952, *FRUS* XIV, 1952–54, p. 1272.

25. Johnson to Acting Sec. of State, Aug. 5, 1952, *FRUS* XIV, 1952–54, p. 1298.

26. Kōno (1994), p. 10.

27. The Socialists had split into two separate parties in October 1951, with the Left Socialists opposing the Peace Treaty and rearmament and the Right Socialists adopting a more accommodating position, broadly in support of the peace settlement, but with mixed views on military alignment with Washington. Left and Right reunited again in October 1955 as the Japan Socialist Party (JSP). Stockwin (1986), pp. 88–89.

28. Yoshida' s decision not to sign the letter (a not uncommon pattern in his correspondence with US government officials) suggests, perhaps, that he was anxious to avoid the risk, should the letter leak, of providing electoral ammunition to his opponents at home who were criticizing him for being overly dependent on the United States. Whether he feared a leak within the Japanese or the US government is unclear. Certainly, his discretion was in keeping with his cautious handling of diplomatic material and his general reluctance to commit himself publicly on sensitive issues—something he had demonstrated both in Diet presentations and in earlier negotiations with the Americans.

29. Kōno (1994), pp. 85–86.

30. "Additional briefing material on Ryukyu and Bonin islands for NSC Planning Board meeting," June 3, 1953; "The Japanese Treaty Islands," June 15, 1953; Robertson to Dulles, June 16, 1953—all in RG59, PPS Country and Area Files, "Japan," 1949–53; "Military Requirements in the Amami Island Group," Aug. 22, 1953, RG218, Geog. File (Japan), 1951–53, NA.

31. "The Japanese Treaty Islands," June 15, 1953; "Additional briefing material on Ryukyu and Bonin islands for NSC Planning Board meeting," June 3, 1953.

32. "Memorandum of discussion at 151st meeting of NSC," June 25, 1953, *FRUS* XIV, 1952–54, p. 1441.

33. Ibid., pp. 1441–42.

34. Ibid., pp. 1442–44.

35. "Soviet Gestures to Japan," Aug. 12, 1953, C. D. Jackson Records, EL.

36. Allison to Embassy in Korea, Aug. 4, 1953, *FRUS* XIV, 1952–54, p. 1468.

37. Allison (1973), p. 242.

38. Ibid., p. 239.

39. Ibid., p. 242.

40. The debate over rearmament was a central issue in the US-Japan relationship in the 1950s, especially during the early part of the decade, and is dealt with extensively in chapter six.

41. Allison (1973), p. 243.

42. Ibid., p. 140.

43. Dulles, it is worth noting, was evidently both displeased and surprised by Reston's article and the repercussions in Japan. See Dulles to Allison, Aug. 14, 1953, Dulles Papers, Chronological Series, EL.

44. Allison to Dulles, Dec. 31, 1953, *FRUS* XIV, 1952–54, p. 1575.

45. Allison, op. cit. p. 209; Murphy to Allison, Aug. 11, 1952, *FRUS* XIV, 1952–54, p. 1312; Allison to Sec. of State, Mar. 18, 1953, *FRUS* XIV, 1952–54, p. 1399.

46. Ibid., p. 228. The various CinCFE's during Allison's period as ambassador in Japan were, in order of appointment, Mark Clark, John E. Hull, Maxwell Taylor, and Lyman Lemnitzer.

47. Allison (1973), pp. 41–42, 233.

48. Interestingly, both the PRC and Taiwan firmly opposed the reversion decision when it was announced, arguing that the territory belonged to China, and

claiming (in the case of the Nationalist Chinese) that the islanders had approached China for assistance and that historically Japan had no right over the territory, having acquired it from China without a formal treaty. "Amami guntō henkan keii" [Details on the return of the Amami islands], Jan. 1954, Sect. 11, A' 0146/14/0004–0067, GA. While these statements should clearly not be taken entirely at face value, they do reveal that there may indeed have been some basis for the assumption by certain US planners at the beginning of the post-war period that the inhabitants of the Ryukyus had been ambivalent about their relationship with Japan.

49. "Statement by Sec. of State John Foster Dulles," RG59, PPS Country and Area Files, "Japan," 1947–53, NA.

50. Halperin (1992).

51. "Memorandum of discussion at the 177th Meeting of the National Security Council," Dec. 23, 1953, *FRUS* XIV, 1952–54, pp. 1569–70.

52. "The Far East Command, Jan. 1, 1947–June 30, 1957," RG218, Central Decimal File, Box 43, 1957, NA.

53. "Report of a Special Subcommittee of the Armed Services Committee (Price Report), Oct. 14–Nov. 23, 1955," CCS 383.21 POA (1-12-47), NA.

54. Ibid.

55. Ma (1992), p. 441.

56. "OCBWorking Group on NSC 125/2 and 125/6," Third Meeting, Mar. 16, 1955, WHO, NSC Staff, OCB Central Files, EL.

57. Price Report, NA; Watanabe (1970), p. 37.

58. For details of the working of the NSC under Eisenhower, see Nelson (1995), pp. 111–26; Prados (1991), pp. 54–90.

59. "Working Group on NSC 125/2 and NSC 125/6," Jan. 24, 1955, WHO, NSC Staff, OCB Central Files, EL.

60. "The Far East Command," NA.

61. Watanabe (1970), p. 140.

62. Price Report, NA.

63. One in four Okinawans worked for the US military in 1956. Ibid., NA.

64. Ibid., NA.

65. See chapter five for a discussion of this issue.

66. Horsey to Hemmindinger, Aug. 27, 1956, RG59, ONEAA, Japan Subject Files, 1947–56, NA.

67. OCB "Intelligence Notes," June 25, 1956, WHO, NSC Staff, OCB Central Files, EL.

68. Watanabe (1970), p. 38. See also chapter six below. The Liberal Democratic Party (LDP) was created in November 1955 following the merger of the conservative Liberal and Democratic parties. This consolidation brought together Yoshida's Liberals and the Democrats under Hatoyama Ichiro and had been prompted in part by senior Japanese corporate anxieties following the establishment in October 1955 of a new Japan Socialist Party (JSP), uniting the Left and Right Socialists.

69. Kōno (1994), pp. 128–29.

70. Watanabe (1970), p. 142.

71. Ibid., pp. 40–41. As Higa Mikio has pointed out in his study of post-war Okinawan politics "the OPP does not have socialism or communism as its party ideology officially . . . but would appear to be under strong communist influence, if not a front organization of communists." Higa (1963), p. 72.

72. "Report on United States Foreign Assistance Programs," March 1957, US President's Citizen Advisors on the Mutual Security Program (Fairless Committee), EL.

73. "OCB Report on US Policy toward Japan (NSC 5516/1)," July 23, 1958, RG 59, PPS Office Files, NA.

74. Higa (1963), p. 56.

75. "OCB Report on US Policy toward Japan (NSC 5516/1)," Apr. 8, 1959, PPS Office Files, 1957, Lot File No. 66D487, NA; Watanabe (1970), p. 40.

76. The deputy governor also served as Commanding General of the Philippine and Ryukyus Command (Rycom). See Miyasato (1992), p. 4.

77. Watanabe (1970), p. 22. Okinawa's political parties often paralleled those on the Japanese mainland, although much of the political change that took place in Okinawa during the 1950s was separate from events within Japan proper and the local Okinawan parties remained for these ten years quite protective of their institutional independence. Kōno (1994), p. 136; Watanabe (1970), pp. 14, 130–32.

78. "NSC Draft Directive for US Civil Administration of Ryukyu Islands," Feb. 17, 1954, Dwight D. Eisenhower (DDE), Records as President, Confidential File, Subject Series, Box 21, EL.

79. 185th NSC meeting, Feb. 17, 1954, *FRUS* XIV, 1952–54, pp. 1607–8.

80. CinCFE to Dept. of the Army, June 28, 1954, CCS 383.21 POA (1-12-47); Hemmindinger to Robertson, Feb. 28, 1956, RG59, ONEAA, Japan Subject Files, 1947–56, NA.

81. Memorandum of Information for Sec. of the Navy, Mar. 26, 1957, CCS 0092 Japan (12-12-50), JCS Geographic File, 1954–56, NA.

82. Watanabe (1970), p. 35.

83. Higa (1963), p. 80.

84. Watanabe (1970), pp. 157–58.

85. Herter to Francis Case, July 16, 1957, Christian Herter Papers, EL; Watanabe (1970), p. 40.

86. NIE-41-54, "Probable Developments in Japan through 1957," *FRUS* XIV, 1952–54, p. 1697.

87. 210th NSC meeting, Aug. 13, 1954, DDE Papers, Papers as President, Ann Whitman File (AWF), EL.

88. Deputy Assistant Sec. of State for Far Eastern Affairs to Sec. of State, Oct. 12, 1954, *FRUS* XIV, 1952–54, pp. 1742–43.

89. Allison to State Dept., Oct. 18, 1954, *FRUS* XIV, 1952–54, pp. 1749–50.

90. John E. MacDonald to Elmer B. Staats, "Summary of NSC 5516/1," Apr. 14, 1955, WHO, NSC Staff, OCB Central Files, EL.

91. Donovan (1956), p. 345; Dockrill (1996), p. 142.

92. "Psychological Aspects of United States Strategy," Nov. 1955, WHO, NSC Staff, Executive Secretary's Subject File, Box 14, EL.

93. Ibid.

94. Paul M. A. Linebarger, "The Discrete Problems of the Far East," WHO, NSC Staff, Executive Secretary's Subject File, Box 14, EL.

95. "Psychological Aspects of United States Strategy."

96. F. S. Dunn, "Alliance and Coalition Problems," Quantico Vulnerabilities Panel, undated, DDE Papers, Records as President, Confidential File, Subject Series, Box 63, EL.

97. McClurkin to Parsons, undated, RG59, ONEAA, Japan Subject File, 1947–56, Box 2, NA. McGeorge Bundy, in analyzing the Eisenhower administration's national security policy, has suggested that the Quantico findings had little impact on high-level policy-making, pointing out that there is no direct evidence that Eisenhower read the final report and that Dulles actively discouraged his subordinates from taking any interest in the group's conclusions. However, at least where Japan policy was concerned, this seems at odds with McClurkin's comments and the close parallels with NSC 5516/1. See Bundy (1988), p. 298.

98. Kōno (1994), p. 120; "Highlights of Developments in Japan, 1952–55" (undated), RG218, CCS 092, Japan, NA.

99. Kōno (1994), p. 129; Watanabe (1970), p. 89.

100. Kōno (1994), p. 133.

101. Watanabe (1970), p. 123.

102. Kōno (1994), pp. 133–35.

103. Greenstein (1995), pp. 55–64.

104. "I always found Eisenhower business-like and even tempered. He was well-informed, wanting to know everything about the question before him, and an intent and intelligent listener. . . . Originally I had some doubts as to whether he was fully knowledgeable about what his administration was doing and whether he was in control of it. I realized my initial judgment was wrong, however, once I began to have direct contact with him." Bissell (1996), p. 114. For perhaps the most authoritative and persuasive revisionist accounts of Eisenhower's presidency and its relationship to national security policy, see Bowie and Immerman (1998).

105. Eisenhower to Dulles, June 4, 1958, *FRUS* XVIII, 1958–60, p. 31.

106. "Introduction of US Currency in the Ryukyu Islands," WHO, Office of the Staff Secretary, International Series, EL.

107. MacArthur to State, Aug. 15, 1958, DDE, Papers as President, AWF, International Series, Box 34, EL.

108. As the ambassador in Japan, Douglas MacArthur II (Allison's successor), noted: "There is no doubt that the President's handling of this problem has touched Kishi deeply and has led him to withdraw his original basic objections to currency conversion on assumption that his views on timing et cetera can be met." MacArthur to Sec. of State, June 19, 1958, WHO, Office of the Staff Secretary, International Series, EL.

109. Eisenhower (1963), p. 250.

110. However, Eisenhower's declaratory position on colonialism needs to be set against his overall policy toward the Third World and especially those instances when the actions of the Eisenhower administration seemed to violate the

notion of national sovereignty (most notably the campaign against Mossadeq in Iraq, the removal of the Arbenz regime in Guatemala, or US policy toward Cuba and the initial planning that crystallized as the Bay of Pigs operation under the Kennedy administration). Robert McMahon and Stephen Rabe, for example, are sharply critical of Eisenhower's handling of relations with the Third World. See McMahon (1986 and 1994); Rabe (1988); and Takeyh (2000), a study of Eisenhower's policy toward Egypt that reveals a US administration seeking to restore British power in the Middle East and relying on conservative Arab monarchies to contain radical nationalism. Acknowledging Eisenhower's antipathy toward colonialism and his conceptual preference for non-intervention nevertheless provides a useful context in which to assess his administration's policy toward Japan. An illuminating parallel to the cautious handling of US-Japanese relations in the 1950s is American policy toward Austria between 1953 and 1955 and the pragmatic willingness of both Eisenhower and Dulles to accept Austrian neutrality. See Bischof (1995), pp. 136–62. For Eisenhower's views on the importance of reducing the US military presence in Europe, see Winand (1997).

111. Adams (1961), p. 331.

112. "United States Overseas Military Bases" (Nash Report), Dec. 1957, MILL 191, NA.

113. Eisenhower to Dulles, Apr. 9, 1958, Dulles Papers, Telephone Conversation Series, Box 13, EL.

114. Dulles to Robertson, Mar. 23, 1958, Dulles Papers, Chronological Series, Box 15, EL.

115. Untitled, Apr. 17, 1958, Christian Herter Papers, Box 11, Telephone Calls, EL; "Memorandum of Telephone Conversation between Pres. Eisenhower and Sec. of State Dulles," Apr. 17, 1958, *FRUS* XVII, 1958–60, pp. 21–22.

116. Gordon Gray, "Memorandum of Meeting with the President," Apr. 18, 1959, WHO, OSANSA, Special Assistant Series, Presidential Subseries, Box 4, EL.

117. Eisenhower (1965), p. 135.

118. According to one account, the US government had moved atomic missiles to Okinawa in the spring of 1953. Donovan (1956), p. 116.

119. Hull to Dept. Army, Dec. 8, 1953, RG218, CCS 092 (Japan) (12-12-50), Geographic File, 1954–56, NA.

120. Price Report; "The Far East Command," NA.

121. George A. Morgan, Counselor of Embassy to Noel Hemmindinger, Acting Director, ONEAA, June 26, 1956, RG59, ONEAA, Japan Subject Files, 1947–56, NA.

122. Freedman (1989), p. 136.

123. Nash Report, 1957, NA.

124. Ibid.

125. "Joint Communiqué following Prime Minister Kishi's Visit to US," DDE, Papers as President, AWF, International Series, Box 33, EL.

126. Eisenhower had commissioned a second major analysis of US bases, produced in the spring of 1960 as a follow-up to the earlier Nash report of 1957. The declassified report includes a map detailing the dispersed deployment of me-

dium-bombers and tanker units supporting America's Strategic Air Command (SAC), and Okinawa is conspicuously not marked as a base for these forces. "Review of United States Overseas Military Bases," Apr. 1960, MILL 191, NA.

127. Ibid.

128. "CinCPAC Operation Plan No. 1–61 (General War Plan)," Jan. 26, 1961, RG218, Central Decimal File, Box 44, NA.

129. Ibid.

130. China detonated its first nuclear device in 1964.

131. "CinCPAC Operation Plan No. 1–61," NA.

132. Ibid.

133. It is worth noting that the base review of 1960 had concluded, in part, that future weapons development might ensure a declining role for overseas bases, after 1963, in the support of America's nuclear retaliatory forces. "Review of United States Overseas Military Bases." This provides further support for the suggestion that in 1958 both Dulles and Eisenhower believed that it might be feasible to return the Ryukyus fully to Japan within a period of three to five years.

134. "Military Assistance Advisory Group (MAAG), Monthly Activities Report for July 1955," RG319, 091 (Japan) 1955, Box 57, NA.

135. CinCFE to Dept. of the Army, May 20, 1957, RG218, JCS Geographic files, Japan, 1957, NA.

136. L. L. Lemnitzer to Arleigh Burke, Apr. 23, 1957, RG319, Japan 1957, Box 57, NA.

137. The full texts of the two treaties can be found in Buckley (1992), pp. 175–78. The background to the reversion of the Security Treaty is examined in more detail in chapter six.

138. Windsor G. Hackler, First Sec. of Embassy to the State Dept., June 28, 1955, RG319, G3 Records of the General Staff, Box 58, NA.

139. "OCB Report on 'US Policy Toward Japan (NSC5516/1),'" July 23, 1958, RG59, PPS files, NA.

140. "The Relationship of Japan to Nuclear Weapons and Warfare," Apr. 22, 1957, OIR Report, No. 7466, OIR files, NA-II.

141. CinCPAC to CNO, Feb. 22, 1958, RG218, CCS 092 (Japan), JCS Geog. file, 1957, NA.

142. "CinCPAC Staff Study on the revision of the Japanese Security Treaty," CinCPAC to CNO, July 1, 1958, RG218, CCS 092 (Japan), JCS Geog. file, 1957, NA.

143. "Report by the J-5 to the Joint Chiefs of Staff on Security Treaty—Japan," RG218, CCS 092 (Japan), JCS Geog. file, 1957, NA.

144. "OCB Report on 'US Policy Toward Japan (NSC5516/1),'" July 23, 1958, RG59, PPS files, NA.

145. Clark to State, June 24, 1958, State Dept. decimal files, 611.94/6–2458, NA.

146. Kishi changed his family name following his adoption (a common practice) into his uncle's family.

147. Wakaizumi (1994), p. 388. A shorter English-language edition of Wakaizumi's important memoir is now available. See Wakaizumi (2002).

148. In April 2000, the Japan Communist Party revealed that it had obtained declassified US documents suggesting that in June 1959 Kishi and Secretary of State Christian Herter had secretly agreed that US nuclear weapons–equipped vessels entering Japanese ports would be exempt from any requirement to consult with the Japanese government. The Japanese government has consistently maintained that no such agreement exists—precisely the same position it has adopted in response to Wakaizumi's revelation of a secret accord between Nixon and Satō.

149. "MAAG, Monthly Activities Report for August 1955," RG319, 091 (Japan) 1955, Box 57, NA.

150. "MAAG, Monthly Activities Report for September 1955," RG319, 091 (Japan) 1955, Box 57, NA.

151. "The Outlook for Nuclear Weapons Production in Japan," Aug. 2, 1957, OIR Report, No. 7553, OIR files, NA-II.

152. Ibid.

153. Kishi had been influenced in this regard by the thinking of individuals such as Nomura Kichisaburō, Ashida Hitoshi, and former admiral Hoshina Zenshirō. Hoshina was chair of the LDP'S subcommittee on defense problems and in 1957 had circulated a nuclear warfare study which asserted "that the effective defense of Japan [was] dependent upon the utilization of tactical nuclear weapons by forces in the home islands, and indirectly upon the possession by the US of a greater supply than the Soviet Union of strategic nuclear weapons." Ibid.

154. Satō had also in 1965, in private discussions with Ambassador Reischauer, expressed his "common sense" belief that Japan "should have nuclear weapons." Wakaizumi (2002), p. 9.

155. Harrison (1996), pp. 8–12. The most recent example of such interpretive flexibility occurred in May 2002 when, prompted by North Korea's unilateral abrogation of a series of important nonnuclear agreements, LDP Chief Cabinet Secretary Fukuda Yasuo hinted at a possible qualification (subsequently retracted) of Japan's long-standing ban on the possession of nuclear weapons. See International Institute for Strategic Studies (2003), p. 257.

156. Reischauer (1986), pp. 250–51, 346–47.

157. Shindō and Miyagi (1992), p. 210.

158. Hemmindinger to Robertson, Oct. 28, 1955, RG59, ONEAA, Japan Subject Files, 1947–56, Box 7, NA.

159. Nomura was a particularly outspoken exponent of the need for a more rigorous approach to security issues by Japan and the importance of nuclear weapons in protecting Japan—a point which America's military planners readily recognized. As one report noted, "Admiral Nomura, in his study, 'The Okinawa and Bonin Island Problem,' . . . concludes that unless Japan is prepared to recognise the existence of not only a US base on Okinawa after the return of administrative authority to Japan, *but also of nuclear weapons in the area,* and institute thorough measures . . . to control espionage, to prevent sabotage, and to prevent ideological struggles, Japan cannot even hope for planning for the return of administrative authority" (emphasis added). "CinCPAC Staff Study on the revision of the Japanese Security Treaty," CinCPAC to CNO, July 1, 1958, RG218, CCS 092 (Japan), JCS Geog. file, 1957, NA.

160. Embassy, Tokyo, to State Dept., Nov. 28, 1958, *FRUS* XVIII, 1958–60, pp. 100–102.

161. There is anecdotal evidence that Dulles in 1956 was seriously contemplating returning one or more of the other Article III islands to Japan. According to William Sherman, then a junior State Department official stationed in Japan, the secretary of state arrived in Tokyo for talks with the Hatoyama government quite prepared to return territory, but on discovering that the Japanese authorities had reservations about building up their armed forces, promptly changed his mind. Not only did he not make the offer, but he also clumsily informed his Japanese counterparts (who had formerly been unaware of the possible concession) of his change of mind and the reasons for his decision. Such an insensitive action seems at odds not only with the recommendations of the Psychological Strategy Board and the earlier Rockefeller report, but also with the example of cautious diplomacy so carefully practiced by Dulles during the San Francisco Peace Treaty negotiations of 1950–51. Personal interview, June 1995.

162. "Report on United States Foreign Assistance Programs," Mar. 1957, US President's Citizen Advisors on the Mutual Security Program (Fairless Committee), Box 2, EL.

163. WHO, Staff Research Group (Toner Notes), July 17, 1957, EL.

164. "Intelligence Report: The Bonin Islands Problem," July 13, 1956, PPS Office Files, 1957, Lot File No. 66D487, Box 109, NA.

165. "Ogasawara kyvjvmin no kitō mondai ni kansuru tai bei sesshō" [Negotiations with the United States regarding the problem of the return of former inhabitants of the Ogasawara Islands], Oct. 11, 1954, Sect. 11, A'0137/15/0270–0282, GA.

166. Ibid.

167. Ibid.

168. In the period between 1952 and 1956, the Japanese government approached the United States on the issue no fewer than fifteen times. "Intelligence Report: The Bonin Islands Problem," NA.

169. CinCPAC to CNO, May 20, 1957, RG218, CCS 092 (Japan), JCS Geog. files, 1957, NA.

170. The Japanese authorities requested compensation totaling $12.5 million. The US offered $5 million, reflecting the value of private land holdings at the ending of the Occupation, with an additional sum based on an annual rent of 5 percent interest on the land price in 1952. The two sides eventually agreed to a figure of $6 million. See editorial note, *FRUS* XVII, 1958–60, p. 83.

171. William Sherman, personal interview, June, 1995.

172. OCB Working Group on NSC 125/2, 125/6 and PSB D-27 (Japan), Third Meeting, Wednesday, Mar. 16, 1955, WHO, NSC Staff, OCB Central Files, EL; "OCB Report on 'US Policy Toward Japan (NSC5516/1),'" Apr. 8, 1959, RG59, PPS Files, NA.

173. Kōno (1994), p. 2.

174. Ibid., pp. 97–98. Matsuoka Hiroshi has, in analyzing the Eisenhower's administration's overall alliance policy, advanced a similar point of view, although without focusing Okinawa. He argues that from 1953 onward, both

Dulles and Eisenhower sought to define America's relations with its Asian allies in economic, social, and cultural terms and not merely on a military basis. See Matsuoka (1994).

175. Buckley (1992), p. 58.

176. Of Naha's population of 180,000, a crowd of some 100,000 to 150,000 welcomed Eisenhower. By contrast, the demonstrators, in their largest concentration, numbered 1,500. Naha to Sec. of State, June 3, 1960, James Hagerty Papers, Box 30, EL.

177. Okinawa to Washington, DC, June 9, 1960, Edward Beach and Evan Aurand Records, Box 8, EL.

178. Hagerty had been on an advance trip to Japan to make the arrangements for the President's visit.

179. Okinawa to White House, June 14, 1960, DDE Papers as President, AWF, International Series, Box 46, EL.

Chapter 5

1. Dingman (1990), p. 188.

2. Roger Buckley, for example, lays the blame for the disaster and subsequent tensions squarely with the United States. Buckley (1992), p. 58. Dingman (1990), by contrast, is less uncompromising in his criticism, acknowledging serious shortcomings on the Japanese side, as well as identifying constructive efforts by US officials, both in Washington and in Tokyo, to deal with the crisis.

3. "Perry Centennial," Feb. 24, 1954, WHO, NSC Staff, OCB Central Files, Box 8, EL.

4. Rhodes (1995), p. 542.

5. Lapp (1958), p. 4.

6. Ibid., p. 23.

7. "US Position with Respect to Injury and Damages resulting from Pacific Nuclear Test," Mar. 30, 1954, WHO, NSC Staff, OCB Central Files, Box 8, EL.

8. Dingman (1990), p. 188.

9. Rhodes (1995), p. 541.

10. Ibid., p. 542.

11. While the magnitude of the blast was the critical cause of the exposure of the *Lucky Dragon*, a second contributory factor was a shift in high altitude winds, shortly before the tests, in an easterly direction—the opposite direction to that initially planned for by the US scientists. Jonathan Weisgall has suggested that the Americans were fully aware of this change and proceeded with the test despite recognizing the risk that radioactive fallout from the explosion might be blown in the direction of the inhabited Marshall islands. Weisgall (1994), p. 306. If this is true, then the US can be rightly criticized for, at the very least, negligence, or, more seriously, a willful disregard for the interests and safety of the islanders. In the case of the Japanese fishermen, American ignorance of the presence of the *Lucky Dragon* and its location outside the safety zone makes any suggestion of malicious design much less sustainable.

12. Lapp (1958), pp. 43–49.

13. Ibid., p. 67.

14. Ibid., p. 75.

15. The ABCC was established in 1946 under the orders of President Truman, charged with undertaking a "long-range, continuing study of the biological and medical effects of the atomic bomb on man." Roff (1995), p. 59. While formally under the jurisdiction of the AEC in Washington, it operated as a field organization based in Japan, with offices in Hiroshima. A personal account of the work of the organization, from the perspective of one of its principal researchers, can be found in Schull (1990).

16. Hewlett and Holl (1989), pp. 175–76.

17. Lapp (1958), p. 108.

18. Ibid., pp. 76–86.

19. Ibid., p. 111.

20. While the cause of Kuboyama's death was a source of controversy at the time, subsequent accounts revealed that he died as a result of hepatitis contracted while apparently recovering from his radiation injuries in hospital in Tokyo. See Hewlett and Holl (1989), p. 624. However, from the vantage point of Japanese public opinion, there would presumably have seemed little point in emphasizing this distinction since Kuboyama would not have been hospitalized without the initial exposure to the radioactive fallout.

21. LaFeber (1997a), pp. 145–48.

22. Dockrill (1996), pp. 46–47; Ishii (1989), pp. 109–10. Kennan in fact was a key participant in the review process.

23. Hewlett and Holl (1989), p. 166.

24. Dockrill (1996), p. 4.

25. Ibid., p. 66. For a similar argument that stresses that Eisenhower rejected the notion that a war with the Soviet Union could be limited or contained, see Craig (1998), pp. 67–70. The President sought to avoid a nuclear conflict by demonstrating unequivocally to the enemy and to his colleagues—both civilian and military—that he would use America's nuclear weapons in the event of a conflict with the Russians, prompting in turn a retaliatory exchange that would be catastrophic. Paradoxically, therefore, the credibility of America's deterrence strategy rested on the President's ability to convince those around him that he would be willing in effect to commit the country to a strategy of collective national suicide.

26. Dockrill (1996), p. 93.

27. The evidence in support of the bomb's political usefulness is far from conclusive, but is discussed in Garson (1994), p. 61, and Bundy (1988), pp. 271–87. For an interesting analysis of the Clausewitzian "logic" which may have underpinned Eisenhower's commitment to a strategy of threatening total war as the best (albeit imperfect) means of ensuring survival in the nuclear age, see Gaddis (1997), pp. 233–34.

28. "Kojireta Nichibei kankei," *Asahi Shinbun* (Apr. 9, 1954), p. 1.

29. Hewlett and Holl, p. 176; "Bikini no hai—kidorui no sankabutsuka," *Asahi Shinbun* (Mar. 17, 1954), p. 3.

30. Lapp, p. 105.

31. Immediately after it became clear that the test had been much larger than

anticipated, the test officials ordered US naval vessels to head south fifty miles and begin emergency damage control. For more than four hours, all crew members were required to remain below decks, as extensive steps were taken to decontaminate the ships' surfaces. Hewlett and Holl (1989), p. 173.

32. "US Position with Respect to Injury and Damages Resulting from Pacific Nuclear Test," Mar. 30, 1954, WHO, NSC Staff, OCB Central Files, Box 8, EL.

33. Allison (1973), p. 265.

34. "US Position with Respect to Injury and Damages Resulting from Pacific Nuclear Test," EL.

35. Undated minute referring to Mar. 24 OCB meeting, WHO, NSC Staff, OCB Central Files, Box 8, EL.

36. "Japan and Atomic Tests," Mar. 24, 1954, WHO, NSC Staff, OCB Central Files, Box 8, EL.

37. Hewlett and Hull (1989), p. 176.

38. Ibid., p. 170.

39. Ibid., p. 14.

40. "Japan," undated section of draft report, Van Fleet Report, 1954, RG330, Box 11, NA.

41. Ibid.

42. "Japan," Feb. 9, 1955, RG59, Lot 66D70, PPS files, 1955, Box 5, NA.

43. "An Appraisal of the Capabilities of the Japanese Communist Party as they appear in June, 1954," July 16, 1954, CIA Murphy papers, Box 97, NA-II.

44. The extensive holdings of the CIA Murphy Papers on International Communism are especially revealing of US attitudes on this issue. A relatively underused archival source, the papers in this collection provide a fascinating insight into how Washington perceived and reacted to the Communist presence in Japan from the aftermath of surrender up until 1961. For the early part of the period, the files contain detailed analyses, debriefings, and surveillance reports from G-2, the intelligence arm of the Occupation authorities, as well as commentary from US embassy officials. G-2, not surprisingly, was predisposed to view skeptically any Communist activity in Japan whether overt or covert. Less expectedly perhaps, the State Department more often than not shared and reinforced these doubts and suspicions.

45. "An Appraisal of the Capabilities of the Japanese Communist Party as they appear in June, 1954," op. cit.

46. Ibid.

47. Ibid.

48. Ibid. "Japan Communist Party Comparative Political Strength," Dec. 3, 1949, CIA Murphy Papers, Box 96, NA-II.

49. "An Appraisal of the Capabilities of the Japanese Communist Party as they appear in June, 1954," op. cit.

50. "The Communist Potential in Japan," Sept. 24, 1948, CIA Murphy Papers, Box 95, NA-II.

51. "Evaluation of the Japan Communist Party," July 17, 1952, CIA Murphy Papers, Box 97, NA-II.

52. American attitudes toward Japan's Communists were not monolithic.

While SCAP routinely adopted a hard-line and skeptical approach, with some in-dividuals, such as Major-General Charles Willoughby, displaying an uncompro-misingly ultraconservative position, America's diplomats were more cautious in their judgments. For example, in December 1950, Niles Bond, counselor in the US mission in Tokyo, highlighted his concerns regarding the red purge that had taken place in August of that year. Neutral observers, he noted, had warned that the purge appeared to be in conflict with the Labor Standards Law of the Japa-nese Constitution; the purge may also have been unnecessary, since the country's moderate unions had already successfully blocked Communist influence; and most worrying of all, the crackdown might end up creating more problems than it solved by ensuring a new mass of disaffected, unemployed purgees liable to re-sort to covert action. See Niles Bond to State, "The Red Purge and its Political Implications," Dec. 26, 1950, CIA Murphy Papers, Box 96, NA-II.

53. "Ōbei ikka kankei hikitsugu jikkō" [Matters relating to the First Section of the European-American Affairs Bureau], Mar. 29, 1954, Sect. 11, A'0134/2/0335–342, GA.

54. Ishii (1989), p. 212.

55. Allison (1973), p. 263.

56. Ishii (1989), p. 212.

57. The files relating to the Rastvorov incident are part of the Records of the Investigative Records Repository (IRR) [class reference, XA546786], which are in turn part of RG319, Records of the Army Staff, Records of the Office of the Assistant Chief of Staff, G-3, Intelligence. To the best of my knowledge these files have not been the subject of previous academic study and the following repre-sents the first detailed account of the espionage case based on these remarkably revealing sources.

58. John Byington, a nineteen-year-old air policeman serving in the 35th Air Police Squadron in Japan, is one example of the sometimes laughably naïve meth-ods adopted by some of the Soviets' agents in Japan. Byington had enlisted the support of his Japanese girlfriend in approaching the Russian mission to offer his services as a paid informant. Byington was something of a fantasist, exaggerating his importance to the Soviets and trying, unsuccessfully, to pass himself off as a counter-intelligence officer to his American colleagues. Some astute Japanese po-lice-work led to his discovery, and after his arrest and confession he was returned in 1953 to the United States and presumably was swiftly discharged from military service. (There was, at the time, insufficient evidence at the time to take his case to trial.) Rastvorov, during his debriefing, was able to confirm Byington's role as a spy, albeit not an especially successful one. The full details on the Byington case can be found in IRR files, NA-II.

59. In some instances, the activities of Russian émigrés were somewhat more unorthodox in nature. Angelina Panarina, for example, a stateless Russian born in Manchuria who had arrived in Japan from China in May 1949, spent much of her time soliciting classified information from the large number of US military and civilian personnel whom she succeeded in seducing. This was a technique she appears to have perfected in her days in Tientsin and Tsingtao when she had worked as an informant for the Russians under the code name "muza." In the

colorful words of one intelligence report: "The general consensus is that SUB-JECT is a prostitute, a nymphomaniac and a possible dope addict." Report of Investigation, Angelina Panarina, 27 Jan. 1954, IRR files, NA-II.

60. "Activities of Soviet Mission in Japan," Feb. 10, 1954, IRR records, NA-II. The Soviets also sought, according to Rastvorov, to recruit as agents the sons of former prominent pre-war conservative politicians and military officials. These included the son of General Araki Sadao, Foreign Minister Matsuoka Yōsuke, and Prime Minister Konoe Fumimaro. Nothing in the files indicates whether or not these approaches were successful. See "Exploitation of DS-2072," Aug. 25, 1954, IRR records, NA-II.

61. "Ex-Official of Foreign Office Suicides During Spy Probe," Aug. 29, 1954, *The Mainichi*, IRR files, NA-II.

62. Agent report, Shii Masaji, Apr. 28, 1954, IRR files, NA-II. Shii was typical of many former Japanese conservative military officers who were able to reconcile their traditional nationalism with support for the Communists. In many ways, his example confirmed the observations of Konoe Fumimaro and Charles Spinks (see chapter two) who had stressed the possible convergence of left- and right-wing extremism. In Shii's own words: "Since the San Francisco Peace Treaty, Japan has been subjected to many untold humiliations and even today she is gradually being drawn into the path leading to another war. These thoughts are based upon my subjective analysis of the situation and I believe them to be entirely true. I have constantly been thinking of freeing Japan from her bondage, so that her people can live in genuine freedom and peace without the threat of war. Thus when I received my initial contact from the Soviets, I felt that I could place myself in a position whereby I could contribute toward the action of requiring the US forces to leave Japan through pressure applied by the Soviets." Ibid.

63. Ishii (1989), pp. 212–13. Ishii suggests that the Rastvorov affair ranks among the ten most important espionage incidents of the twentieth century—an interesting assessment given that there appears to be no authoritative and comprehensive English-language description of the affair, and Allison refers to the incident in his memoirs only very briefly.

64. The motives for Rastvorov's defection remain somewhat unclear. Ostensibly, his professional advancement had been relatively rapid up until 1954. Conscripted into the army in 1939 at 18, he had studied Japanese at the Military Faculty of Far Eastern Languages in Moscow. After a year spent supervising the physical transfer of minority groups from the Caucuses and the Crimea to Siberia, he was assigned in 1944 to the foreign intelligence section of the first bureau of the KGB, with responsibility for Germany, Japan, China, and Italy. In February 1946 he was sent to Tokyo, under a journalist's cover, to recruit agents. In November of the same year, he was suddenly recalled to Moscow for having failed to notify the Soviet authorities that his father—a military commissar—had been briefly expelled from the Communist Party in the 1930s. Eventually cleared of any wrongdoing, Rastvorov was reassigned to Japan in 1950, remaining there until his defection in 1954.

The defection may in part have been prompted by the perception that he had been unjustly discriminated against because of his father's past suspension from the party—a decision which was itself the result of malicious and unfair allegations. Similarly, Rastvorov's wife had also experienced state-sanctioned discrimination. Prior to her marriage, she had accepted a ride from a US serviceman and as a result was permanently viewed with suspicion by the Soviet authorities who chose to prevent her from joining her husband on his overseas postings. Rastvorov's decision to jump ship may also have been prompted by more immediate worries. In mid-January he had learned that he was due to be recalled to Moscow a second time and he worried that, in the wake of the July 1953 purge of Lavrenti Beria (the head of Soviet intelligence), he himself might be liquidated as part of a wider settling of old political scores in Moscow.

In planning his defection, Rastvorov had initially considered turning to the British for help and on the evening of January 23 had got as far as boarding a Royal Air Force plane at Tachikawa Air Force Base, intending to fly to Singapore. However, at the very last minute, taking advantage of poor weather conditions which had delayed his flight, he changed his mind and returned to Tokyo. The third secretary had been worried by what appeared to be unnecessary changes in his departure arrangements, and he suspected that the British ultimately planned to exchange him for several UK subjects who were being held by the Soviets. See Agent Report, Yuriy A. Rastvorov, Jan. 25, 1954; Colonel Richard Collins to Assistant Chief of Staff, G2, Feb. 4, 1954; DS-2072, 2nd Interim Report, Mar. 6, 1954; all in IRR files, NA-II.

65. Rastvorov revealed that the Soviet mission provided the JCP with $300,000 in 1952, $15,000 in April 1953, and a further $150,000 in September 1953. "CIC Exploitation of Rastvorov," Feb. 7, 1954, IRR files, NA-II.

66. "Rastborofu jiken sara ni kakudai" [Further Facts of Rastvorov Case Disclosed] *Yomiuri Shinbun*, Sept. 28, 1954.

67. "Activities of Soviet Mission in Japan," Feb. 5, 1954, IRR files, NA-II.

68. Lapp (1958), p. 127.

69. "Outline check list of US Government actions to offset unfavourable Japanese attitudes to the H-bomb and related developments," Apr. 22, 1954, WHO, NSC Staff, OCB Central Files, Box 8, EL.

70. OCB working group on NSC125/2 and NSC125/6, meeting minutes, Aug. 26, 1954, WHO, NSC Staff, OCB Central Files, Box 48, EL.

71. Dingman (1990), p. 202.

72. Ibid., p. 193. Hewlett and Holl, for example, in the official, but relatively balanced history of the AEC, assesses Allison's role in the crisis positively: "Both the State Department and John M. Allison, the American ambassador in Tokyo, at once sensed the full potential of the incident for damaging international relations. Allison had some success in conveying a deep personal concern and in reassuring the Japanese government. He may also have been instrumental in keeping public criticism focused almost entirely on nuclear weapons while surprisingly little hostility was expressed against the United States." Hewlett and Holl (1989), p. 177.

73. "Ōbei ikka kankei hikitsugu jikkō" [Matters relating to the First Section of the European-American Affairs Bureau], Mar. 29, 1954, Sect. 11, A'0134/2/0335–342, GA.

74. Minutes of 10th meeting of Embassy-FEC Consultative Group, Mar. 24, 1954, RG59, Lot 57D149, Records of the Bureau of Far Eastern Affairs, ONEAA, alpha-numeric file on Japan, 1941–53 [sic], NA.

75. Minutes of 12th meeting of Embassy-FEC Consultative Group, Apr. 21, 1954, RG59, Lot 57D149, Records of the Bureau of Far Eastern Affairs, ONEAA, alpha-numeric file on Japan, 1941–53 [sic], NA. Early on in the crisis, Japanese medical specialists at Tokyo University hospital were loath to allow US officials access to the afflicted *Lucky Dragon* crew members, arguing that, while the Americans should provide information on the explosion, the treatment and investigation of the victims would remain the exclusive preserve of the Japanese side. See "Shi no hai no shōtai o shiraseyo," *Asahi Shinbun* (Mar. 18, 1954), p. 7; "Bikini hisaisha o meguri—gakusha, jishusei o shuchō," *Asahi Shinbun* (Mar. 23, 1954), p. 7.

76. According to a report of April 14, "there is still no working level cooperation from the Japanese, although everything is fine at the high governmental level." John MacDonald to Elmer B. Staats, "Japanese Fishing Boat Incident," Apr. 14, 1954, WHO, NSC Staff, OCB Central Files, Box 8, NA.

77. Minutes of 12th meeting of Embassy-FEC Consultative Group, Apr. 21, 1954, NA.

78. The Americans were not alone in criticizing the Japanese media's response to the crisis. In London, Hugh Cortazzi (a relatively junior Foreign Office official dealing with Japan matters but in later years ambassador to Japan), in an internal minute on the Bikini crisis, noted the "Japanese hysteria over the death of Mr. Kuboyama and the anti-American tendencies of the Japanese press." "Bikini Atom Bomb Explosion," Oct. 2, 1954, F0371/110462, FJ1241/3, PRO. Similarly, some weeks earlier, Cortazzi had observed, again in connection with Bikini: "Waves of anti-American feeling have occurred periodically in Japan since the signing of the Peace Treaty. . . . These outbursts tend to be exaggerated by the press and in the Diet and do not reflect accurately the feelings of ordinary Japanese in the countryside. Nevertheless they are dangerous because they provide emotional material for extreme left and extreme right. . . . Japanese medicine and science generally tend to be out of touch with latest developments and the accuracy of the observations of Japanese Scientists is open to question. It seems clear that on many of the occasions on which tuna fish have been condemned as contaminated and accordingly destroyed, the scientific observations leading up to this decision have been unreliable. Reports of 'atomic rain,' 'atomic cows' and even 'atomic milk' have been caused more by emotional fears than real observations." "Bikini A-Bomb Explosion," Sept. 16, 1954, FO371/110462, FJ1241/2, PRO.

79. For example, as Asada Sadao has pointed out, there is widespread acceptance in Japan of the "revisionist" view that the atomic bomb was used against Japan, not to hasten the end of the war, but to advance America's larger geopolitical objectives vis-à-vis the Soviet Union. Similarly, the notion that racist motivations underlay the choice of Japan as a target for the bomb and the "guinea-pig" theory that the bomb was used against civilians primarily to test its destructive power carries considerable weight among contemporary Japanese university students. Asada (1995), pp. 107–12.

80. Dingman (1990), p. 194.
81. "OCB Progress Report on NSC 125/2 and NSC125/6," Oct. 27, 1954, EL.
82. "Bikini hisaisha o meguri—gakusha, jishusei o shuchōo," *Asahi Shinbun* (Mar. 23, 1954), p. 7.
83. Sakamoto (1994a), p. 250.
84. Dingman (1990), p. 197.
85. Ibid., p. 200.
86. Sakamoto (1994a), p. 255.
87. Ibid., p. 257.
88. Ishii (1989), p. 138.
89. Ibid., p. 139.
90. Ibid., p. 140.
91. Borton (1957b), pp. 10–19.
92. Allison to Dulles, Jan. 7, 1955 (Parts 1 and 2) 794.5/1–955; Dulles to American Embassy, 794.5/1–1755, all in State Department Decimal Files, NA.
93. Ibid., p. 274.
94. Roff (1995), p. 70.
95. Ibid., p. 63.
96. Ibid., p. 44.
97. Ibid., p. 47.
98. It is worth stressing that the Japanese authorities also dragged their feet on the issue. It was only in 1957 that the Japanese government, in response to pressure from survivors, enacted a Law Concerning Medical Care for A-bomb Victims. Yet, the level of support was minimal and followed some "twelve years of total neglect." See Tachibana (1995), p. 337.
99. Roff (1995), pp. 114–15.
100. Ibid., pp. 140–41.
101. Ibid., p. 172.
102. Ibid., pp. 191–92.
103. Hewlett and Holl (1989), pp. 154–58.
104. Roff (1995), p. 184.
105. See, for example, Lapp (1958), p. 129.
106. Hewlett and Holl (1989), 177.
107. Ibid., p. 177.
108. "Telephone conversation with Adm. Strauss," Mar. 29, 1954, Dulles Papers, Telephone Conversation Series, EL.
109. See above.
110. Bundy (1988), p. 316.
111. Advisory Committee on Human Radiation Experiments, *ACHRE Report*. Online. Internet. Aug. 20, 1997. http://www.ohre.doe.gov/roadmap/achre/chap12_3.html.
112. Hewlett and Holl (1989), pp. 56–57.
113. Ibid., p. 177.
114. This is in contrast to his handling of the Okinawa issue, where he intervened to question or alter relatively low-level policy decisions. (See chapter four.)

For an interesting study that examines Eisenhower's crisis management style and his generally tight control over the security and foreign-policy decision-making process, see Kingseed (1995).

115. Bundy (1988), p. 314.

116. Eisenhower (1965), p. 474.

117. Hewlett and Holl (1989), p. 178.

118. Eisenhower to Churchill, Mar. 19, 1954, Dulles Papers, Subject Series, Box 3, EL. As the crisis persisted, Eisenhower remained engaged with the issue. In late May, in response to a long cable from Allison in Japan explaining conditions there, the President wrote to Dulles, pointing out that he was "concerned about the Japanese situation" and requesting the secretary of state to have the State Department prepare an analysis of the event and its implications. "Memorandum for the Secretary of State," May 26, 1954, DDE Papers as President, AWF, International Series, Box 33, EL.

119. "Telephone conversation with Adm. Strauss," Mar. 29, 1954, Dulles Papers, Telephone Conversation Series, EL. It would have been surprising if Eisenhower had failed to grasp the full significance of the *Lucky Dragon* incident and of nuclear issues in general for US-Japanese relations. After all, long before becoming President, in 1945 General Eisenhower had written to the secretary of war, Henry Stimson, arguing that the atomic bomb should not be dropped on Japan, claiming that the United States should not be the first country to use the new weapon, and subsequently pointing out that it may have been unnecessary. See Ishii (1989), p. 109.

120. The United States and Japan agreed to the final settlement of $2 million in January 1955. By this stage, Shigemitsu had replaced Okazaki as foreign minister in a new Hatoyama cabinet, and Hatoyama, with his eye on the February elections, was eager to reach a speedy resolution of the problem. See Dingman (1990), pp. 204–5. Fewer doubts regarding the longevity of the Yoshida cabinet would also presumably have discouraged individuals such as Ikeda from courting popular opinion by criticizing the United States.

121. Borton (1957b), p. 10.

122. Ishii (1989), p. 204.

123. Ibid., p. 205.

124. Borton (1957b), pp. 15–16.

125. "OCB Progress Report on NSC 125/2 and NSC125/6," Oct. 27, 1954, WHO, NSC Staff, OCB Central Files, Box 47, EL.

126. Borton (1957b), pp. 10–11; Kōno M. (1997), pp. 65–66.

127. One indication of the continuing salience of the constitutional issue was the emphasis that Yoshida placed on revision in his visit to the United States in November—his last overseas visit as Japan's premier. In an English-language document drafted prior to his departure for Washington, Yoshida criticized the Occupation reforms, pointing out that "some of them unfortunately went too far" and adding, "The rectification of such excessive reforms is one of the most difficult tasks confronting Japanese politics today, as can be seen from the defense question, labor problems and the state of affairs in the educational system as well as the police system. The great majority of the Japanese people feel that modifi-

cations should be made in occupation instituted reforms which went too far."
"Ōkurashō nite Ikeda seichōkaichō no kōsō toshite Yoshida sōri tobeiyō ni junbi
seru mono" [Finance Ministry materials prepared for Prime Minister Yoshida's
visit to America—in accordance with the instructions of PARC Chairman Ikeda],
undated, Sect. 11, A'0135/1/0385–394, GA.

128. "OCB Progress Report on NSC 125/2 and NSC125/6," Oct. 27, 1954,
EL.

129. Allison to Dulles, Mar. 23, 1954, Dulles Papers, General Correspondence and Memoranda Series, EL.

130. Dingman has suggested that Dulles used the controversy over financial
compensation to undermine Yoshida politically and to influence the prime ministerial succession in Japan. See Dingman (1990), pp. 204, 207. However, the evidence is not especially persuasive. By the time of Yoshida's visit to Washington,
there were powerful signs that his political days were numbered. Immediately
prior to the prime minister's departure from Japan, anti–mainstream faction Liberal Party members had convened a preparatory conference focused on forming a
new political party—see, Ishii (1989), p. 205—and this opposition, together with
Yoshida's catalogue of existing domestic difficulties, meant that it was probably
not within the secretary of state's powers to determine Japan's leadership. Certainly, Dulles had (as the documents cited by Dingman reveal—see, *FRUS* XIV,
1952–54, pp. 1769, 1785) decided not to offer a settlement which would have enabled Yoshida to return to Tokyo and possibly seek to continue in office. Yet, in
making this decision, Dulles was, it seems, bowing to the inevitable, rather than
trying to shape domestic political events in Japan. Moreover, as Robert Murphy,
the undersecretary of state, had pointed out to Eisenhower as early as May, the
State Department was already anticipating a change of leadership in Japan and
was careful not to become involved in the succession contest. As Murphy said:
"We doubt that Yoshida will remain much longer as Prime Minister and he may
retire after his world trip in June and July. However, the trend in Japan is toward
a more powerful grouping of the dominant conservative forces and a more effective government. This is a problem which the Japanese must solve for themselves." *FRUS* XIV, 1952–54, pp. 1648–49.

131. "OCB Progress Report on NSC 125/2 and NSC125/6," Oct. 27, 1954,
EL. Such measures were consistent with the wider US effort to shape cultural and
intellectual life globally in a pro-Western, anti-Communist direction. For two fascinating accounts of this wider campaign which focus especially on the American
propaganda campaign in Europe, see Saunders (1999) and Hixson (1998). A
number of the intellectuals involved in this campaign also turned their attention
to Japan. Melvin Lasky, who had played a key role in establishing the Congress
for Cultural Freedom in Berlin in 1950, spent a month in Japan in 1953 considering the prospect for establishing an American-funded, Western-friendly
monthly intellectual journal. His observations reflected a critical view, shared by
a number of leading US Japan specialists such as Edwin Reischauer and Edward
Seidensticker, of Japanese intellectual life as rigidly doctrinaire and dominated by
Marxist analysis. As Lasky noted on his return from Japan, "I know of no other
Western-minded modern intelligentsia which, as a whole, is so confused on the

major issues of international politics, so dogmatic in its sociological conceptions, so dominated by antiquated notions of what constitutes 'capitalism,' 'socialism,' 'communism,' 'imperialism,' etc. Conversations in Tokyo in the year '53 of the cold war reminded me of the atmosphere in Germany in '46 and '47, in Paris and Rome in '47 and '48. In Western Europe there has been, by and large, a fundamental improvement. Intellectuals have more and more come to understand the nature of Soviet totalitarianism; publishers have been increasingly willing to put out material unfavorable to Marxism-Leninism and present Moscow policy; fewer Labor and Left publicists subscribe to simple naïve 19th century notions of 'American capitalism.' In Japan there has been a time-lag. This has left the Japanese intelligentsia in a state of what some of the Japanese themselves call 'backwardness.' This half-ignorance has enabled the Communist propaganda offensive—whether from the Japanese CP and its affiliated Peace Fronts, or from Mao's China and the Soviet Union—to create an atmosphere on the Japanese Left which, when it is not directly favorable to them, is at least unfavorable to the US." WHO, NSC Staff, PSB Central Files, Box 13 PSB 091 Japan, EL.

Writers such as Chalmers Johnson and Michael Schaller have argued that American efforts to influence the political debate in Japan went much further than cultural diplomacy and involved regular financial support from the CIA to shore up the position of Japan's conservatives and to distort the electoral process in favor of the LDP. See Johnson (1995); Schaller (1997), pp. 125, 135-37. Johnson points to the existence of a large fund of financial resources, known as the "M (or Marquat) fund," created from confiscated Japanese assets during MacArthur's Occupation and used up until the late 1950s by the US government, and subsequently by the LDP to bankroll individual conservative politicians throughout the post-war period. The evidence for this fund is suspect, however, originating largely in the testimony of Norbert Schlei, an American attorney who was convicted in 1995 of major securities fraud directed at the Japanese government and investors in both Japan and the United States. Schlei failed to have his conviction overturned in a lengthy appeals trial in which US officials categorically rejected his claims. Stanley Sporkin, general counsel for the CIA, testified for instance that the M-fund was "a crazy idea, preposterous," while Daniel Russel, a US diplomat and executive assistant in the mid-1980s to the US ambassador to Japan Mike Mansfield, informed the appeals court that it was "totally unbelievable that such a conspiracy could have been in progress for decades without becoming widely known," because "it involved such a massive conspiracy that would have entailed the connivance of virtually every senior politician in Japan." As part of the appeals process, the court also held extensive in-camera hearings with US government officials to investigate claims in an October 1994 *New York Times* article, based on Schlei's assertions, that the CIA "gave money to the Liberal Democratic Party and its members in the 1950's and the 1960's" according to "retired intelligence officials and former diplomats." The purpose of these hearings was to determine whether any archival evidence of such a conspiracy existed, and the court directed the government to carry out an extensive and comprehensive search of its official holdings. As the record of the appeal court ruling notes: "The government searched hundreds of files of CIA paper records dating back to 1948 in search of any documents that might indicate that payments made by the CIA to either the Japanese government, the Liberal Democratic Party, or individual party members. They also conducted computer searches for Marquat Fund, Marquet Fund, Marqeat Fund, MacArthur Fund, and fund generally. The district court then required the Government to search for all names and relevant information contained . . . in the *New York Times* article. . . . The court subsequently ordered numerous in camera ex parte proceedings involving the prosecutors and CIA representative, and directed many searches to cover every conceivable connection to Schlei's recitation of the history of the M Fund. We have reviewed the sealed record of the court's in camera proceedings. The search of the records of the CIA, the Secret Service, and the National Archives did not disclose any relevant or material documents or information that substantiated the report in the *New York Times* that the CIA gave money to employees or officials of the Japanese government, or any political party in Japan." US versus Norbert Schlei appeal (1997). It would be unwise to discount the possibility of periodic efforts by the US government to shore up Japanese conservative politicians financially. Indeed, given Rastvorov's revelations of Soviet subsidization of the JCP, it is almost certain that Washington would have actively considered such a course. Nonetheless, for now at least, the more lurid claims of a massive and systematic US effort to subvert the democratic process in post-war Japan seem exaggerated and unjustified.

132. Ishii (1989), pp. 113–17.

133. Robertson to Allison, Oct. 22, 1954, WHO, NSC Staff, OCB Central Files, EL.

134. Robert Donovan, writing in 1956, described Eisenhower's speech as "one of his best performances as President"—Donovan (1956), p. 190—although it is worth recognizing that the power of the proposal was more rhetorical than substantive and had, as McGeorge Bundy has pointed out, little impact in checking the growth in the number of nuclear weapons. See Bundy (1988), p. 294.

135. "Review of Policies Governing Japanese Research in Nuclear Physics and Related Fields and Stockpiles of Radioactive Materials in Japan," Feb. 28, 1950, RG319, G-3, Operations, 1950–51, Box 118, NA.

136. "Japan and Atomic Tests," Mar. 22, 1954, WHO, NSC Staff, OCB Central Files, Box 8, EL.

137. Working Group on NSC125/1 and 125/6, May 5, 1954, WHO, NSC Staff, OCB Central Files, Box 8, EL.

138. "Tokyo Trade Fair," Nov. 5, 1954, WHO, NSC Staff, OCB Central Files, Box 8, EL.

139. Ibid.

140. Ibid.

141. Working Group on NSC 125/2 and NSC 125/6, Oct. 6, 1954, WHO, NSC Staff, OCB Central Files, Box 48, EL.

142. "Recent Effects of Increasing Nuclear Capabilities on US Allies," Intelligence estimate, No. 72, Feb. 16, 1955, WHO, Office of the Special Assistant for Disarmament (Harold Stassen), Records, 1955–58, Box 5, EL. Contemporary Japanese sources confirm that the Japanese government was actively promoting a

Japanese nuclear power industry, earmarking sections of the 1955 fiscal budget for this purpose and establishing sections within the Economic Planning Agency and MITI to develop long-range plans for nuclear energy generation. See "Gutaika shita genshiryoku dō'nyv no shōtai," *Ekonomisuto* 33, no. 18 (1955); "Amerika no genshiryoku enjo to Nihon," *Heiwa* 33 (1955).

143. "USIA Contribution to OCB Working Group Paper on Japanese Intellectuals," Nov. 4, 1955, WHO, NSC Staff, OCB Central Files, Box 48, EL.

144. Weisgall (1994), p. 304.

145. Allison to Sec. of State, Jan. 14, 1956, WHO, Stassen Records, 1955–58, EL.

146. *FRUS XX*, 1955–57, p. 343.

147. "Note to Japanese Government Concerning Pacific Nuclear Tests," Mar. 23, 1956, RG59, PPS Office Files, Lot File No. 66D487, NA.

148. "Press Coverage of the Nuclear Tests," June 27, 1956, WHO, Stassen Records, 1955–58, Box 5, EL. The detail here is based on an extensive Embassy summary and translation of Japanese articles dealing with nuclear testing.

149. Allison to Sec. of State, Mar. 6, 1956; Windsor Hackler to State Department, May 24, 1956; both in WHO, Stassen Records, 1955–58, Box 5, EL. Interestingly, the tests of 1956 never developed into a major issue between the Japanese and US governments. Dulles, as part of a Far Eastern trip, had been in Japan in March for meetings with the Hatoyama government. Anticipating a hostile reaction on testing, he had stressed in advance the importance of staying ahead of the Soviets in the development of nuclear weapons, but had been surprised to find that the Japanese officials "never once" raised the issue during his visit. 280th NSC meeting, Mar. 22, 1956, DDE Papers, Papers as President, Ann Whitman File (AWF), NSC Series, Box 7, EL.

150. Horsey to Sec. of State, Sept. 17, 1957, WHO, Stassen Records, 1955–58, Box 7, EL.

151. "Memorandum for the President—Reply to Prime Minister Kishi's Telegram on Nuclear Tests," Sept. 28, 1957, DDE Papers as President, AWF, Dulles-Herter Series, EL.

152. Ibid.

153. For example, in April 1957, Dulles met Dr. Matsushita Masatoshi, a personal envoy of Prime Minister Kishi who had recently traveled to London to lobby against forthcoming British tests in the Pacific. Dulles appears to have handled the meeting well, and shortly afterward reports in the Japanese press "gave extensive play to 'great sympathy' shown by Secretary for Japanese viewpoint and to his desire for Japanese understanding of US responsibility in defending free world. Matsushita quoted to effect he was deeply impressed with Secretary's sincerity and that meeting was very profitable. . . . While editorial comment has not yet been developed, press reports have so far been favorable. Impression has been given, Secretary, despite his busy schedule went out of his way to meet with Matsushita, even on Easter Sunday, and that serious and full discussion was held on problem which most Japanese feel is important." MacArthur to Sec. of State, Apr. 23, 1957, WHO, Stassen Records, 1955–58, Box 6, EL.

154. Staff Notes, No. 397, July 25, 1958, WHO, Staff Research Group, EL.

155. OCB Report on US Policy Toward Japan (NSC 5516/1), Apr. 8, 1959, NSC 5516, RG273, NSC files, 1948-60, NA.

156. Ibid.

157. Bundy (1988), p. 332.

Chapter 6

1. Cited in Buckley (1992), p. 175.

2. CinCFE to JCS, Apr. 19, 1952, RG218, JCS Geog. File (Japan), 1951–53, NA.

3. Ibid.

4. Ibid.

5. CinCFE to JCS, Oct. 31, 1952, RG319, Army Operations (Japan), 1952, Box 17, NA.

6. Watson (1986), p. 268.

7. CinCFE to JCS, Jan. 14, 1953, RG218, JCS Geog. File (Japan), 1951–53, NA.

8. Allison to Sec. of State, Mar. 12, 1953, *FRUS XIV*, 1952–54, p. 1393.

9. Sec. of State to Embassy, Tokyo, Mar. 12, 1953, *FRUS* XIV, 1952–54, p. 1394.

10. Note by acting Executive Secretary to NSC, June 29, 1953, *FRUS* XIV, 1952–54, p. 1451.

11. Dickinson (1987), p. 105.

12. Allison to Sec. of State, Nov. 26, 1953, DDE Papers as President, Ann Whitman File (AWF), International Series, Box 33, EL.

13. Telephone Conversation with Mr. Robertson, Oct. 12, 1953, Dulles Papers, Chronological Series, Box 5, EL; Tōkyō kaidan to bōei sesshō," *Jitsugyō Tenbō* 25, no. 12 (1953), p. 17.

14. Progress report on NSC 125/2, Apr. 28, 1953, *FRUS* XIV, 1952–54, p. 1413.

15. Allison to Sec. of State, Mar. 12, 1953, *FRUS* XIV, 1952–54, p. 1393.

16. Kaufman (1982), p. 58.

17. Katō (1994), pp. 132–33.

18. JCS to CinCFE, Mar. 10, 1953, *FRUS* XIV, 1952–54, p. 1391.

19. Johnson to Sec. of State, July 10, 1953, *FRUS* XIV, 1952–54, p. 1458.

20. The Democratic Liberal Party had repackaged itself as the Liberal Party in 1950. Such frequent, but often superficial, rebranding exercises among Japan's political parties were all too common in the 1950s. A similar trend took place in the 1990s following the defection of young conservative politicians from the LDP in 1992, and particularly after 1993 and the LDP's dramatic and unprecedented loss of power to a short-lived anti-LDP coalition led by Hosokawa Morihiro.

21. G2 Memorandum for the Chief of Staff, July 7, 1953, RG319, Army Operations, General Decimal Files, 1953, Box 39, NA. Hatoyama had strong personal reasons for opposing the prime minister. He had been purged during the Occupation and forced to cede his position as leader of the Liberal Party to

Yoshida. On returning to political life in 1952, he had expected to resume his leading role only to discover that Yoshida was no longer willing to honor an agreement to step down once the purge had been lifted.

22. Ibid.

23. Allison to State, July 10, 1953, *FRUS* XIV, 1952–54, p. 1459.

24. Allison to State, Aug. 14, 1953, *FRUS* XIV, 1952–54, pp. 1485–86.

25. Editorial Note, *FRUS* XIV, 1952–54, p. 1497.

26. Allison to State, Aug. 14, 1953, *FRUS* XIV, 1952–54, pp. 1485–86.

27. John Welfield's work, for example, although very extensive in its treatment of press reports and secondary Japanese-language material, tends to take the US position at face value and makes little attempt to explore American primary sources. Welfield (1988), pp. 98–99 and passim.

28. Uemura (1994), p. 185.

29. Muroyama (1992), p. 141.

30. Ibid., p. 142.

31. Former Japanese military officials were also actively involved in initiatives to rebuild Japan's military capabilities and, in some instances, were willing to challenge to principle of civilian control that in time became a hallmark of postwar Japanese defense policy. See Weste (1999), Shibayama (2001).

32. Dickinson (1987), p. 130.

33. Ibid., p. 114.

34. Green (1995), p. 10.

35. Allison to State, Sept. 7, 1953, *FRUS* XIV, 1952–54, p. 1497.

36. Katō (1994), pp. 135–37.

37. Uemura (1994), p. 185; Sec. of State to Embassy, Japan, Oct. 14, 1953, *FRUS* XIV, 1952–54, p. 1530.

38. Cited in Uemura (1994), p. 192.

39. Sec. of State to Embassy, Japan, Oct. 9, 1953, *FRUS* XIV, 1952–54, pp. 1523–25.

40. Sec. of State to Embassy, Japan, Oct. 22, 1953; Sec. of State to Embassy, Japan, Oct. 24, 1953; both in *FRUS* XIV, 1952–54, pp. 1538, 1540. Some months after the October talks, an article in a spring 1954 edition of *Ekonomisuto* (an influential weekly business and current affairs journal) had severely criticized Ikeda for the passive and disingenuous character of his defense proposals. See Uemura (1994), p. 182.

41. CinCFE to JCS, Oct. 26, 1953, RG319, Army Operations, General Decimal Files, Box 39, NA.

42. Uemura (1994), p. 185.

43. Allison to State, Sept. 25, 1953, *FRUS* XIV, 1952–54, pp. 1511–13.

44. My translation. Original Japanese text cited in Dickinson (1987), p. 117.

45. Uemura (1994), p. 192.

46. Allison to State, Dec. 7, 1953, *FRUS* XIV, 1952–54, pp. 1558–59.

47. JCS to Wilson, Dec. 21, 1953, *FRUS* XIV, 1952–54, pp. 1561–62.

48. Sec. of State to Embassy, Japan, Dec. 28, 1953, *FRUS* XIV, 1952–54, p. 1573.

49. Allison to Sec. of State, Dec. 31, 1953, *FRUS* XIV, 1952–54, pp. 1573–75.

50. Allison to State, Jan. 12, 1954, *FRUS* XIV, 1952–54, pp. 1596–97; Mc-Clurkin to Robertson, Jan. 13, 1954, *FRUS* XIV, 1952–54, p. 1598.

51. Progress Report on NSC125/2 and 125/6, Oct. 27, 1954, WHO, NSC Staff, OCB Central Files, Box 47, EL.

52. Allison to Okazaki, Apr. 6, 1954, *FRUS* XIV, 1952–54, p. 1629.

53. Dunning to McClurkin, Mar. 1, 1954, *FRUS* XIV, 1952–54, p. 1614.

54. Allison to State, July 30, 1954, *FRUS* XIV, 1952–54, p. 1691.

55. For further detail see chapter five.

56. Allison to State, Aug. 25, 1954, *FRUS* XIV, 1952–54, p. 1714.

57. Memorandum of Conversation, Oct. 15, 1953, *FRUS* XIV, 1952–54, p. 1533.

58. Memorandum of Conversation, June 16, 1954, *FRUS* XIV, 1952–54, pp. 1658–59.

59. Some three years of declining taxation in Japan had stoked inflationary pressures—a problem which was exacerbated by deficit financing, easy credit, and excessive bank lending. Officials in the US Commerce Department felt that the dollar receipts from US military procurement could have been used more effectively and argued that the Japanese authorities should pursue their austerity program more vigorously. "General Considerations Regarding Trade Agreement Negotiations with Japan," July 21, 1954, Neil Jacoby Papers, Box 6, EL.

60. Allison to State, Aug. 14, 1954, *FRUS* XIV, 1952–54, pp. 1703–4.

61. Parsons to McClurkin, Oct. 1, 1954, *FRUS* XIV, 1952–54, p. 1738.

62. Ibid.

63. Sec. of State to Embassy, Japan, Mar. 12, 1953, *FRUS* XIV, 1952–54, p. 1396.

64. Memorandum by the National Advisory Council, Staff Committee, Sept. 15, 1953, *FRUS* XIV, 1952–54, p. 1505.

65. Allison to State, Aug. 14, 1954, *FRUS* XIV, 1952–54, p. 1704.

66. Miyazawa (1954), p. 40.

67. Allison to Sec. of State, Sept. 9, 1954, *FRUS* XIV, 1952–54, pp. 1717–20.

68. 214th meeting of the NSC, Sept. 12, 1954, *FRUS* XIV, 1952–54, p. 1725.

69. "A Preliminary Reappraisal of United States Policy with Respect to Japan," Oct. 25, 1954, *FRUS* XIV, 1952–54, p. 1756. Leonhart's suggestion regarding the Security Treaty is interesting since it appears to be the first documented instance of US officials contemplating revision in security arrangements—some time before the Japanese government made a formal proposal on the matter.

70. See chapter four.

71. For a detailed account of the post-war development of Japan's defense-related industries, see Samuels (1994).

72. Progress Report on NSC125/2 and 125/6, Oct. 27, 1954, WHO, NSC Staff, OCB Central Files, Box 4, EL.

73. "Production of Military Aircraft in Japan," July 20, 1954, RG59, ONEAA, Japan subject files, 1947–56, lot 58D118, Box 2, NA.

74. In preparation for the Bermuda heads of government conference of December 1953, the United States had set out a position paper strongly endorsing the concept of "collective security," while also highlighting the difficulties in implementing such a proposal, key among which was the continuing antipathy of most Asian states toward Japan and a number of unresolved legal and/or economic issues associated with the Pacific War. See "Collective Security in the Pacific," Dec. 4–8, 1953, RG330, Box 15, NA.

75. Progress Report on NSC125/2 and 125/6, Oct. 27, 1954, WHO, NSC Staff, OCB Central Files, Box 47, EL.

76. Uemura (1994), p. 191; Muroyama (1992), p. 178.

77. In total, Liberals and Democrats secured 64 percent of seats in the House of Representatives, equivalent to 63 percent of the popular vote. Cited in editorial note, *FRUS* XXIII, Part I, 1955–57, p. 9.

78. Sebald to MacArthur, Mar. 15, 1955, RG59, ONEAA, Japan Subject File, 1947–56, Lot 58D118, Box 2, NA.

79. Parsons to Hemmendinger, Jan. 5, 1955, State Department decimal files, Internal Affairs of Japan, 1955–59, 794.5/4–2055 to 794.13/1–257, Roll 36, NA.

80. Watson (1986), p. 278; Memorandum for Secretary, JCS, "Highlights of Developments in Japan, 1952–55" (undated), RG319, G3 Records of the General Staff, 1955, Box 58, NA.

81. Allison to State, Apr. 8, 1955, *FRUS* XXIII, Part 1, 1955–57, p. 51.

82. Yamamuro (1995), p. 95.

83. Ichimada, the finance minister, had (according to Allison) actively sought to undermine the US-Japan defense talks in early 1955 by making budgetary commitments to housing and social welfare which required a cut in the defense budget. Allison to State, Apr. 26, 1955, *FRUS* XXIII, Part 1, 1955–57, p. 71.

84. William Leonhart, "Japan," Feb. 9, 1955, RG59, PPS files, Lot 66D70, Box 5, NA.

85. Dodge to Hemmendinger, Aug. 30, 1955, US Council on Foreign Economic Policy, Office of the Chairman, Dodge Series, Correspondence Subseries, EL.

86. Statistics cited in "Report on Review of the Military Assistance Program for Japan" (undated), US President's Committee to Study the US Military Assistance Program (Draper Committee), Box 17, EL; "Japan's Defense Budget—A Reasonable Goal for 1960," paper prepared by Frank Waring, economic counsellor, Embassy, May 9, 1955, Japan, RG319, G3 Records of the General Staff, Box 58, NA.

87. Hara (1991), p. 50.

88. Foreign Minister Shigemitsu's Visit, Position Papers, "Japanese Defense Issues," Aug. 23, 1955, Declassified Documents Microfilm Series 1840/1983.

89. Memorandum of conversation, Dec. 1, 1955, RG59, ONEAA, Japan Subject file, 1947–56, Lot 58D118, Box 2, NA.

90. Early in 1956, for example, Dulles approved a new formula, suggested by the Japanese authorities, allowing Japan to reduce its financial contributions to US forces stationed in Japan by an amount equivalent to half of any increase in Japanese defense appropriations for its own forces. The new approach was a way

of avoiding the tension associated with the debate over Article XXV contributions in 1955. See Hemmendinger to Robertson, Jan. 21, 1956, *FRUS* XXIII, Part 1, 1955–57, p. 155.

91. "Foreign Minister Shigemitsu's visit. August 25–Sept. 1, 1955. Summary of Position," Aug. 22, 1955, US Council on Foreign Economic Policy, Office of the Chairman, Dodge Series, Subject Subseries, EL.

92. Memorandum of discussion at 290th NSC meeting, July 12, 1956, *FRUS* XXIII, Part I, 1955–57, pp. 188–89.

93. Memorandum for Secretary, JCS, "Highlights of Developments in Japan, 1952–55" (undated), RG319, G3 Records of the General Staff, 1955, Box 58, NA. A comparable clash of political and economic interests has featured in the recent debate over the US troop presence in contemporary Okinawa.

94. The same point could also be made with regard to relations between Japan and South Korea. Personal and historical animosities, particularly the legacy of Japan's twentieth-century annexation of the Korean peninsula, had long separated Seoul from Tokyo and stood firmly in the way of a North East Asian Treaty Organization (NEATO) or anything resembling active trilateral security cooperation between Seoul, Tokyo, and Washington. For a detailed discussion of this issue, see Chiefs of Mission Conference, Tokyo, Mar. 19–21, 1956, JFD-P, Box 1, ML. Both Yoshida and Syngman Rhee, the Korean president, made little effort to conceal their personal and national prejudices. The United States, as the ally of both Korea and Japan, was caught in the middle of this bitter relationship and was frequently criticized by each side for failing to compel the other to capitulate over a range of diplomatically contentious issues, including war reparations, the position of some 600,000 Korean nationals resident in Japan, fishing rights and the "Rhee Line" (established in January 1952), and the ROK's tendency to routinely seize and detain Japanese fishing vessels and their crews. In such circumstances, a US desire to avoid unwarranted intervention in the affairs of an independent state could easily (but nonetheless unfairly) be represented as a weak or inadequate commitment to strong alliance relations. As a US intelligence report of September 1956 noted: "Japanese conservatives are . . . not willing to envisage participation in a general coalition of the anti-Communist powers in Northeast Asia. They object most vehemently to military collaboration with the Republic of Korea, at least while that government is controlled by President Syngman Rhee, who in a recent election campaign address described Japan as a greater menace than the Communists. Public opinion polls indicate that Rhee is more unpopular in Japan than any other national leader, even those of Communist states. The Chinese and North Korean Communists have rather successfully fed this animosity by relatively mild treatment of Japanese fishing interests in their respective waters, in contrast to the so-called Rhee Line fishing limitation stringently enforced by South Korea. . . . The Japanese also regard President Rhee as a dangerous ally, capable of involving nations associated with his administration in a new war, an eventuality which all Japanese would abhor." "The Recent and Prospective Foreign Relations of Japan (1956–61)," Sept. 12, 1956, OIR Report, No. 7331, OIR files, NA-II. It would take, in fact, the collapse of the Rhee government in April 1960, for the two governments to begin to inch toward some sort of accommo-

dation of interests. "The new Government under Prime Minister Chang Myon ceased anti-Japanese propaganda, released all captive Japanese fishermen, and adopted only token enforcement of the 'Rhee Line.' Korean seizures of Japanese fishing vessels dropped sharply, Japanese newsmen were admitted into Korea for the first time, and in early September [1960] Foreign Minister Kōsaka was received in Seoul on an official goodwill mission during which agreement was readily obtained to the opening of preliminary negotiations for the settlement of outstanding issues. "Japan: Recent Developments and Short-Run Prospects," Mar. 27, 1961, OIR Report, No. 8438, NA-II. Even allowing for such positive developments, it would take a further five years before full diplomatic relations were established between Tokyo and Seoul in 1965—a process driven by changing "regional geostrategic conditions and the domestic political needs of the parties involved" rather than any fundamental shift in the attitudes of leaders in the two countries. See Cha (1999), pp. 24–28 and passim, for a fascinating and detailed study of the importance of American action and involvement in shaping and conditioning relations between these two emotionally and historically polarized neighbors.

95. The charge of inconsistency was, it should be noted, in certain instances also directed at the United States. A rapid withdrawal of US forces before Japan's own ground forces had been built up might have left Japan dangerously exposed to foreign attack—a development which might be read as evidence of an inadequate US commitment to Japan's security. At the same time, some Japanese military planners in 1956 argued that the United States was placing too much stress on the development of Japan's ground strength, at the expense of its air and naval forces. Under these circumstances, a withdrawal of US forces might be viewed as inconsistent with earlier American strategic priorities. See "Ambassador's Program Review," Oct. 11, 1956, US President's Citizen Advisors on the Mutual Security Program (Fairless Committee), EL.

96. Allison to State, Apr. 2, 1955, *FRUS* XXIII, Part 1, 1955–57, pp. 34–35.

97. Memorandum of Conversation, the Secretary, Sadao Iguchi (Ambassador of Japan), William Sebald, Apr. 3, 1955, RG59, ONEAA, Japan Subject Files, lot 58D118, Box 2, NA.

98. Matsumoto was nominally deputy chief cabinet secretary to the prime minister, but appears, according to State Department reports, to have occupied a role comparable to chief of staff in the Hatoyama cabinet.

99. Taylor served briefly as CinCFE between the tours of duty of generals Mark Clark and John Hull.

100. Parsons to State, Apr. 6, 1955, RG59, ONEAA, Japan Subject File, 1947–56, lot 58D118, Box 2, NA.

101. Ibid.

102. "Foreign Minister Shigemitsu's visit. August 25–Sept. 1, 1955. Summary of Position," Aug. 22, 1955, US Council on Foreign Economic Policy, Office of the Chairman, Dodge Series, Subject Subseries, EL.

103. Memorandum of conversation, "Frank" (Takezō) Matsumoto, J. Graham Parsons, Aug. 11, 1955, RG59, ONEAA, Japan Subject File, 1947–56, lot

58D118, Box 2, NA. State Department officials were not solely reliant on Matsumoto's testimony for evidence of internal Japanese political divisions. Their discussions with journalists and media commentators revealed a similar picture.

104. Telephone call to Mr. Baruch, Aug. 30, 1955, John Foster Dulles Papers, Telephone Conversation series, Box 4, NA.

105. "Observations on Shigemitsu's Visit to Washington," Sept. 22, 1955, RG59, ONEAA, Japan Subject File, 1947–56, lot 58D118, Box 2, NA.

106. Robertson to Sec. of State, July 28, 1955, *FRUS* XXIII, Part 1, 1955–57, pp. 78–79.

107. Second meeting with Shigemitsu, Aug. 30, 1955, *FRUS* XXIII, Part 1, 1955–57, pp. 93–103. The language in Shigemitsu's position papers for this meeting is remarkably candid about the scale and scope of the Communist threat and, taken at face value, conveys the impression of a Japanese administration entirely incapable of addressing the challenge of internal subversion:

> We find it extremely difficult to deal effectively with our Communists under the Constitution promulgated under the occupation period. The abrogation of all laws relative to public peace and order has deprived us of the effective means of combating subversive activities. The Communist elements who have subtly and secretly wormed their way into all segments of society—political, social and cultural—are building up a formidable strength.
>
> By tying up covertly with the Socialist parties, the Communists have been exerting themselves with a view to preparing the ground for an eventual revolution. Seeing that the situation has turned in their favor as a result of the Communist global peace offensive, the Japan Communist Party announced recently the conversion of their underground activities into a legitimate movement. The party has now emerged into the open to wage a determined battle for political hegemony. The Communists apparently feel that the time is ripe and are sharply alert for any chance to precipitate a revolution by consolidating their position in and out of the Diet through collusion with the Socialist and other left-wing factions.
>
> The Communist Party, the Labor-Farmer Party and the Socialist Party . . . have joined forces in defeating the basic bills for national reconstruction. . . . [T]hey are opposed to all legislation designed to promote cooperation with the United States. . . . They attack the Government's policy of enhancing cooperation with the United States at every turn, while they support any move inspired by international Communism and advocate the alignment with Communist China. The "united front" of the leftists, as propounded by the Communist Party, is an accomplished fact where Japan's international relations are concerned. The Communist Party, in collusion with other leftist elements, is obstructing thus our efforts toward the fulfillment of the program of economic self-support and self-defense, and is vigorously intriguing in order to seize an opportunity of starting a revolution. ("General Statement," Aug. 29, 1955, JFD-P, Box 5, ML)

108. Ibid., p. 98.

109. Ibid., pp. 101–2.

110. "Purpose of Mission to Washington," Aug. 31, 1955, RG59, ONEAA, Japan Subject Files, 1947–56, lot 58D118, Box 2, NA.

111. Ibid.

112. Ibid.

113. Ibid.

114. Ibid.

115. Hara (1991), p. 42.

116. It is perhaps worth noting that some time before the August meeting in Washington, Japanese government officials privately confirmed in conversations with State Department personnel that Japan needed to bolster its security provisions at home. While Shigemitsu may have overstated his case regarding the risk of Communist subversion, US concern about Japanese internal security was not necessarily a product of McCarthyite paranoia, as it was shared by Japan's own security organizations. As the deputy chief cabinet secretary pointed out to Jeff Parsons: "Yesterday the Cabinet listened for 45 minutes to a briefing on subversion from the security agency (PSIA) [Japan's Public Security Investigation Agency]. Mr. Hatoyama sat right in front under the map designed to show the principal centers of communism in Japan as he wanted to be sure and catch everything said. Mr. Matsumoto remarked that the Cabinet found the report reassuring in that it showed that the Security Agency was on the job, had a mass of facts, and had identified communist cells in various industries, notably the Labor and Communications Ministries. They had, however, given the Japanese Foreign Office a clean bill of health. The Cabinet had agreed that quiet but more stringent measures were necessary and was resolved to control this situation." See Memorandum of Conversation, July 16, 1955, Matsumoto and Parsons, RG59, ONEAA, Japan Subject File, 1947–56, lot 58D118, Box 2, NA. Similarly, in February 1954, the PSIA had produced an internal government report highly critical of the activities of the Japan Communist Party, noting: "Although its membership is not very large the Party's prime objective is the overthrow of the existing system of government from its foundation by violent means. With this objective in view the Party will take advantage of every possible method without regard to the question of its legality or illegality." The British Foreign Office had obtained a copy of the document and, in London, Hugh Cortazzi noted approvingly: "The interest of this white paper lies not I think so much in the facts it contains which are mostly well known but in the light which it throws on the attitude of the authorities . . . [who are] alive to communist tactics. . . . The wider these tactics can be understood in Japan the better." "Japanese White Paper on Communism in Japan," FO371/110404, FJ1016/12, PRO.

117. Kishi, for example, was reportedly "immensely pleased" with the outcome of the Washington trip (see, Allison to State, Sept. 13, 1955, *FRUS XXIII*, Part 1, 1955–57, p. 121), and in an interview conducted many years later pointed out his agreement with Dulles's position and his own opposition to Shigemitsu's proposal. Hara (1991), p. 48. Similarly, Ōhira Masayoshi (at the time a young conservative politician and eventually prime minister from 1978 to 1980) echoed Kishi's position in a journal article, stressing the need for a new treaty, but em-

phasizing the importance of economic stability and a willingness to endorse the principle of rearmament actively, in a manner comparable to the approach followed by formally neutral states such as Sweden and Switzerland. See Ōhira (1955), p. 37. By contrast, John Welfield has suggested that the impetus for overseas deployment came exclusively from the United States and that Shigemitsu was not enthusiastic about the idea of a closer strategic relationship with the United States—conclusions which may have reinforced the traditional image of heavy-handed American diplomacy in past scholarly interpretations but clearly clash with the documentary record and highlight the danger of neglecting accessible primary sources. See Welfield (1988), p. 108.

118. Glaubitz (1995), p. 40.

119. Kimura (1993), pp. 122–23.

120. Ibid., p. 131.

121. Editorial note, *FRUS* XXIII, Part 1, 1955–57, p. 202.

122. For a recent example of this view among non-Japanese historians, see Hill (1995), p. 43. For similar Japanese interpretations which stress the coercive character of Dulles's diplomacy in this context, see Hasegawa (1998), Kimura (1993), p. 132, and also Tanaka Takahiko's critical assessment, Tanaka (1993), p. 255 and passim. For a recent analysis that echoes the revisionist view I have advanced here, see Elleman et al. (1999).

123. Memorandum of a conversation, Mar. 19, 1956; "Reaffirmation of Japan's Friendly Attitude and Policy toward the United States," both in *FRUS* XXIII, Part 1, 1955–57, pp. 168–69 and 184.

124. Sec. of State's Special Assistance for Intelligence to Acting Sec. of State, Oct. 10, 1955, *FRUS* XXIII, Part 1, 1955–57, p. 132; "Neutralism in the Far East," report enclosed in Murphy to Rockefeller, Aug. 19, 1955, WHO, Staff Planning Co-ordination Group Series, Box 2, EL.

125. Sakamoto (1994b), pp. 145–47. Ishhii Osamu cites both NSC 5516/1 and his personal interviews with Andrew Goodpaster (Eisenhower's staff secretary responsible for national security affairs) and Richard Finn (an influential State Department Japan specialist) to demonstrate that while the US government opposed the establishment of diplomatic relations between Japan and China, it did not object to a rapprochement between Moscow and Tokyo. Ishii (1989), pp. 223–25.

126. State to Embassy, Tokyo, Jan. 10, 1955, *FRUS* XXIII, Part 1, 1955–57, p. 5.

127. Notes prepared in the ONEAA, Aug. 27, 1956, *FRUS* XXIII, Part 1, 1955–57, p. 210.

128. Britain by contrast, as a co-signatory of Yalta, took the view that Kuriles should be ceded to the USSR even though the Soviets had not participated in the Peace Treaty. See Hill (1995), p. 21. From the perspective of Whitehall and the Foreign Office, Churchill's agreement to the Yalta accords had not required endorsement by parliament in order to acquire binding international, legal status.

129. Sakamoto (1994b), p. 150.

130. "Application by the Government of the United States of America to the International Court of Justice Instituting Proceedings against the Government of

the Union of Soviet Socialist Republics," May 26, 1955, RG59 ONEAA, Japan Subject Files, 1947–56, lot 58D118, Box 1, NA. Interestingly, this incident, little noted in the academic literature, did not alarm the Japanese public at large, although at the elite level the Yoshida administration recognized its seriousness. As the US embassy in Tokyo noted, Japanese government officials saw "clearly the inescapable logic of Japanese-American cooperation if Japan is to remain with the free world." See "Japanese Reactions to US-Soviet Air Clash," Feb. 25, 1953, JFD-P, Box 2, ML.

131. Memorandum of discussion, 244th NSC meeting, Apr. 7, 1955, *FRUS* XXIII, Part 1, 1955–57, p. 43.

132. For Allison from Sec., Dec. 12, 1955, Declassified Documents Microfilm Series, 1496/1987.

133. Memorandum of a conversation, Sept. 7, 1956, *FRUS* XXIII, Part 1, 1955–57, p. 228.

134. "Japanese Domestic Political Situation," Sept. 27, 1956, RG59, ONEAA, Japan Subject File, 1947–56, lot 58D637, Box 7, NA.

135. Crowe to Dening, Aug. 29, 1956, FO371/121040, FJ10338/47. Hill cites this cable in her analysis but curiously neglects to mention Ringwalt's account of Dulles's motives. In fact, Hill's critical assessment of the US position rests in part on her citation of a report from Arthur de la Mare in the British Embassy in Washington suggesting that the "US was indeed serious about invoking Article XXVI." Hill (1995), p. 38. However, a close reading of the same report reveals that de la Mare's interpretation was far from conclusive. As he admitted, "one can only *speculate* as to what the State Department may have in mind. . . . I would not be surprised, although *I have no firm evidence*, if the Pentagon were behind a move to use the threat of Article XXVI to bring the Japanese to heal on the Okinawa issue" (emphasis added). Moreover, covering minutes from the same cable reveal that de la Mare's colleagues in London were far from certain about US intentions and were conscious of the high risks associated with putative pressure tactics. "It would," the minutes note, "be interesting to know just what the State Department have in mind." Similarly: "If the Americans were to try to annex Okinawa under the terms of Article XXVI they would drive the Japanese into the arms of the Russians and undo all the harm the Russians have done themselves." De la Mare to Crowe, Sept. 7, 1956, FO371/121040, FJ10338/51, PRO. Indeed, newly released material in the US archives reinforces this image of a secretary of state looking for constructive and practical ways to support the Japanese government in its extended and demanding negotiations with the Russians. As the notes from Dulles's staff meeting on the morning of August 28 indicate: "Mr. Sebald reported that he had conferred with Japanese representatives yesterday afternoon about the course of Japanese-Soviet negotiations. He said he felt the Japanese needed help and were now turning to this Government for guidance. The Secretary alluded to his conversations with Foreign Minister Shigemitsu in London and stressed the need for extending help to a friendly government. He asked that Mr. Sebald's staff engage in some imaginative thinking and that he be provided with a recommended course of action." Secretary's Staff Meeting Notes, Aug. 28, 1956, JFD-P, Box 2, ML.

136. See chapter 4.

137. Sakamoto (1994b), p. 154.

138. De la Mare to Crowe, Sept. 7, 1956, F0371/121040, FJ10338/51, PRO.

139. Tanaka (1993), p. 247.

140. De la Mare to Crowe, Sept. 15, 1956, FO371/121041, FJ10338/56, PRO.

141. De la Mare to Crowe, Sept. 7, 1956, F0371/121040, FJ10338/51, PRO.

142. McClurkin to Snow, Feb. 16, 1955, *FRUS* XXIII, Part 1, p. 19.

143. "Nisso kōshō to Amerika no taido," *Sekai shvhō* (37, no. 27, 1956), p. 21.

144. For Ambassador from Secretary, Sept. 6, 1956, Declassified Documents Microfilm Series, 1497/1989.

145. Lemnitzer to Taylor, Mar. 30, 1956, RG218, JCS Geog. files (Japan), 1957 [sic], NA. When asked whether Japan should accept Soviet demands for continued control of the southern Kuriles and South Sakhalin in order to secure a peace treaty with the Soviet Union, 17 percent of Japanese respondents answered "yes," 48 percent "no," and 35 percent registered "no opinion." See "Japanese Public Opinion—Mid. 1956," Sept. 27, 1956, DDE Papers as President, AWF, International series, Box 33, EL. British Foreign Office reporting confirms the picture of a Japanese public opposed to territorial concessions as a basis for normalization of relations. As Giles Bullard in London noted on March 5, 1956: "Japanese public opinion in its present stage would require extensive persuasion to find such a treaty satisfactory. The Foreign Office, having whipped sentiment high for substantial gains in territory, could not as readily as in prewar days turn off such sentiment. Less than 6 percent in a recent Japanese opinion poll said they would be satisfied with a peace treaty returning only the Habomais and Shikotan." FO371/121039, FJ10338/13.

146. As a result of the merger of the Liberals and Democrats, the LDP held 300 of the 467 seats in the lower house of the Diet and 118 of 250 seats in the upper house. The Left and Right Socialist parties had unified in October 1955, creating a new Japan Socialist Party (JSP) with 155 lower house and 69 upper house seats. Figures cited in McClurkin to Robertson, Nov. 18, 1955, *FRUS* XXIII, Part 1, 1955–57, p. 140.

147. Memorandum of conversation, K. Hirazawa, Richard Sneider, Nov. 22, 1955, RG59, ONEAA, Japan Subject Files, 1947–56, lot 58D118, Box 2, NA.

148. Yamamuro (1995), pp. 102–3.

149. Memorandum of conversation, June 2, 1955, Takase Seizan, George Morgan, William Sherman, RG59, ONEAA, Japan Subject Files, 1947–56, lot 58D118, Box 2, NA. Ogata's opposition to a rapprochement with Moscow appears to have been deep-seated. The deputy prime minister was, in the words of a report from the British embassy in Tokyo, "one of the firmest opponents of concessions to the Soviet Union and the rallying point of all those forces in the Liberal Democratic Party which are opposed to concessions." Ledward to Crowe, Feb. 1, 1956, F0371/121039, FJ10338/9.

150. Ibid.

151. Kitaoka (1996), pp. 79–80.

152. Tanaka has suggested that Yoshida and his supporters sought, via Republican "go-betweens" in the US Senate (mainly William Knowland and Alexander Smith), to persuade the Eisenhower administration to prevent the development of Soviet-Japanese relations. Tanaka's argument is speculative—pointing out that the administration, in the run-up to the presidential elections of 1956, would have been unable to ignore powerful Republican interests. Tanaka (1993), p. 260. However, there does not appear to be any documentary evidence, either cited by Tanaka or in the US archives, to establish a link between Republican lobbying and US policy regarding the Soviet-Japan talks.

153. Memorandum of conversation, Secretary Dulles's residence, May 19, 1956, *FRUS* XXIII, Part 1, 1955–57, p. 177.

154. Sakamoto (1994b), p. 150.

155. Dulles to State, Aug. 22, 1956, *FRUS* XXIII, Part 1, 1955–57, p. 204.

156. Allison to State, Aug. 30, 1956, *FRUS* XXIII, Part 1, 1955–57, pp. 212–13.

157. One US report noted: "In the present competition many conservative Japanese leaders view important questions of government policy, such as the negotiations with the USSR, less in terms of the national interest than their own factional advantage. This narrowness of view can lead to startling reversals of position, and to disconcerting displays of disloyalty within the government, as for example the criticisms of Japan's foreign minister voiced in Moscow on two occasions by special Japanese delegates for negotiations with the USSR." "Domestic Political Developments in Japan, Current and Prospective," Sept. 12, 1956, OIR Report, No. 7332, OIR files, NA-II.

158. It is also important to note that the invoking of Article XXVI (irrespective of Dulles's motivations) need not have precluded a two-island solution which left the status of the Southern Kuriles unresolved and subject to later negotiation.

159. "Japanese Cabinet Opposes Yielding to Soviet Demands," Aug. 14, 1956, JFD-P, Box 4, folder 2, ML. Similarly, less than a week later, and after the London meeting, "Kishi, Secretary General of the Conservative Party, told Allison the Cabinet is still completely perplexed by Shigemitsu's views on Japanese-Soviet negotiations and remains determined to resist present Soviet demands with regard to the Southern Kuriles and passage through the Japan Sea Straits." "Japanese Considering New Approach to Soviets," Aug. 20, 1956, JFD-P, Box 4, folder 2, ML. A newly declassified US intelligence report reveals that throughout the Soviet-Japan talks of 1955–56, the Americans had detailed, day-by-day information on the substance of the talks—indicating either that the Japanese were providing their US partner with a near verbatim account of the proceedings (an unusual level of frankness even for an ally) or, more likely, that the United States had at its disposal remarkably effective intelligence, either human, electronic, or some combination of the two. See "Chronology of Events Related to Soviet-Japanese Peace Negotiations," Sept. 21, 1956, OIR Report, No. 7343, NA-II. Further confirmation of the extent to which Shigemitsu had become an isolated player may emerge in time thanks to an increasing willingness on the part of the Japanese government to open some of its post-war files. I am indebted to

Takeuchi Haruhisa, minister and consul-general in the Japanese embassy in London, for details on this important new declassification initiative.

160. Selby to Mayall, Aug. 18, 1956, FO371/121040, FJ10338/43, PRO.

161. Selby to Selwyn Lloyd, Oct. 31, 1956, FO371/121041, FJ10338/68, PRO. The UK perspective is also helpful in explaining how the incorrect assumption of a deliberately disruptive intervention by Dulles came to be so widely accepted. The British embassy in Moscow transmitted to London a copy of a *Pravda* article of September 13 indicating that the Americans were the true spoilers in the negotiations and claiming that Allison had summoned Shigemitsu to his Tokyo hotel room in order to derail the Soviet-Japan negotiations—an assertion that Whitehall viewed as "probably pure fabrication," and an example of how "Communist propaganda distorts things." Untitled minutes, FJ10338/55, FO371/121041, PRO. Schaller argues that "American demands made it nearly impossible for Japan to reach a comprehensive settlement with Moscow"— Schaller (1997), p. 122—but makes no reference to the domestic political effort to undercut Shigemitsu.

162. Allison to State, Oct. 23, 1956, *FRUS* XXIII, Part 1, 1955–57, p. 234.

163. "Japanese Politics: Recent Trends and Prospects," Mar. 12, 1956, OIR Report, No. 7094, NA-II. Such was the impact of this setback for Japan's conservatives that some US analysts warned that failure to make gains in reappropriating traditional conservative symbols and values might encourage some politicians to embrace a more extreme style of politics with less deference to post-war democratic norms.

164. In the earlier party contest to select a successor to Hatoyama, Kishi had initially been the leading contender. The election for LDP President had involved three candidates (Kishi, Ishibashi, and Ishii Mitsujirō), and Kishi at this stage had been the front-runner, receiving 223 votes, compared to 151 for Ishibashi and 137 for Ishii. Since Kishi had led by a simple plurality rather than a majority, a second ballot was held between the two leading candidates in which Ishibashi achieved a seven-vote victory over Kishi, winning by 258 votes to 251. See Kurzman (1960), p. 296.

165. Allison to Sec. of State, Jan. 10, 1957, State Department decimal files, Internal Affairs of Japan, 1955–59, 794.5/4–2055 to 794.13/1–257, Roll 36, NA.

166. MacArthur to State, Feb. 25, 1957, *FRUS* XXIII, Part 1, 1955–57, p. 271.

167. MacArthur's remarks are summarized in Wheeler to Deputy Chief of Staff for Military Operations, May 24, 1957, RG319, G3 Records of the General Staff, 1957, Box 19, NA.

168. Horsey to Parsons, Apr. 5, 1957, State Department decimal files, Relations with Japan, 1955–59, 611.94/11–2257 to 611.94/6–558, NA.

169. OCB Progress Report on NSC5516/1, Sept. 25, 1957, WHO, OSANSA, NSC Series, Policy Papers Subseries, Box 15, EL.

170. George Morgan to State Department, Mar. 19, 1957, State Department decimal files, Internal Affairs of Japan, 1955–59, 794.5/4–2055 to 794.13/1–257, Roll 36, NA.

171. Kitaoka (1995), pp. 129–30.

172. Ibid., p. 134. Southeast Asia also remained a focal point for Kishi. In keeping with his predecessors—most notably Hatoyama and Yoshida—he sought to enlist active US support (both political and economic) in developing a presence for Japan in the region at the center of a new, integrated trading community. The Eisenhower administration was reluctant, however, to commit its financial resources to such an undertaking and preferred to concentrate on bilateral initiatives, while worrying that lingering hostilities from the war would render such ambitious initiatives unworkable. For recent scholarship dealing with the economic aspects of US-Japanese relations during the 1950s, see Forsberg (2000), Shimizu (2001), and Yokoi and Resnick (2003).

173. Kurzman (1960), p. 268.

174. See above, pp. 232–33.

175. Kitaoka (1995), pp. 131–32.

176. The most detailed and authoritative English-language analysis of the Security Treaty crisis, with a particular emphasis on events within Japan, is Packard (1966). In Japan, the most exhaustive treatment of the topic is to be found in Hara (1989).

177. Allison to State, Sept. 21, 1956, "A Fresh Start with Japan," Declassified Documents Microfilm Series, 2680/1988.

178. MacArthur to Dulles, Nov. 15, 1957, Christian Herter Papers, Box 20, EL.

179. "The 1958 Lower House Elections in Japan: a post mortem," Dec. 24, 1958, OIR Report, No. 7907, OIR files, NA-II. For example, Kishi's policy toward mainland China—one which kept open the door to closer political and economic dialogue with the PRC (while also maintaining ties with Taiwan), and which backed firmly away from diplomatic recognition of the Communists—helped reinforce the impression of a government shrewdly and deliberately pursing its national interests in the context of the critically important bilateral relationship with America.

180. Dulles to Robertson, Mar. 23, 1958, *FRUS* XVIII, 1958–60, p. 14.

181. CinCFE to Dept. Army, May 20, 1957, RG218, JCS Geog. files (Japan), 1957, NA.

182. CinCPAC to Chief of Naval Operations, May 20, 1957, RG218, JCS Geog. files (Japan), 1957, NA; Memorandum of Conversation, Sept. 9, 1958, *FRUS* XVIII, 1958–60, p. 65.

183. As US military officials recognized during the discussions on security revision, Article I of the original Security Treaty did not confer any authority upon the United States to intervene uninvited in Japanese internal disturbances. Consequently, the claim that this measure was a source of inequality was based purely on perception rather than reality, and the clause had almost certainly been introduced in 1951 to accommodate Japanese worries about domestic security rather than out of any desire to limit the decision-making authority of the Japanese government in dealing with unrest at home. See "Japanese Assumption of Defense Responsibility," June 4, 1957, RG218, JCS Geog. files (Japan), CCS 092, Section 26, 1957, NA.

184. OCB progress report on NSC 5516/1, Sept. 25, 1957, WHO, OSANSA, NSC series, Policy Papers Subseries, Box 15, EL.

185. Eisenhower to Captain E. E. Hazlett, July 22, 1957, DDE Papers as President, AWF, DDE Diary Series, Box 25, EL.

186. Telephone call from President, May 21, 1957; Telephone call to President, May 21, 1957; both in Dulles Papers, Telephone Conversation Series, Box 12, EL.

187. Excerpt from DDE's Press Conference, June 5, 1957, Bryce Harlow records, Box 10, EL.

188. State to Embassy, July 11, 1957, *FRUS* XXIII, Part 1, 1955–57, pp. 425–26.

189. On September 8, 1959, over two and a half-thousand prominent Japanese attended a memorial ceremony in Tokyo. Kishi used the somber occasion to characterize the late secretary as the "man who best understood Japan and who remained a staunch friend all his life," while former Prime Minister Yoshida praised him for his "tireless labors in raising the foundation for the post-war friendship and cooperation between Japan and the United States which constitutes today the bulwark of peace and prosperity of the Far East." See "Japanese Memorial Service for the Late Secretary Dulles," Oct. 20, 1959, JFD-P, Box 141, ML. Dulles was succeeded as secretary of state by Christian Herter.

190. Embassy, Tokyo to State, May 20, 1960, *FRUS* XVIII, 1958–60, pp. 295–96. Significantly, 25 of the 273 LDP Diet representatives present, including two leaders of anti-Kishi factions, Kōno Ichirō and Miki Takeo, abstained from voting—a mark of the intensity of internal party divisions. See "Japan: Recent Developments and Short-Run Prospects," Mar. 27, 1961, OIR Report, No. 8438, NA-II.

191. Ibid.

192. The Left had begun to mobilize against the Security Treaty as early as March 1959 with the establishment of a Peoples' Council Against Revision of the Security Treaty (known as the Peoples' Council or Kokumin Kaigi). With the forced vote in the Diet, however, the polarization between proponents and opponents of the treaty reached an altogether new level of intensity.

193. Embassy, Tokyo to State, June 6, 1960, *FRUS* XVIII, 1958–60, p. 326.

194. Office of Research and Analysis, "Communist Propaganda Activities in the Far East during 1959," Feb. 10, 1960, US President's Committee on Information Activities Abroad (Sprague Committee): Records, 1959–61, Box 9, EL.

195. Tiltman (1960).

196. Reischauer (1960), pp. 24–25.

197. On July 11, Foreign Minister Fujiyama announced that the United States had voluntarily withdrawn its U-2 planes from Japan, depriving the Left at this late stage of some of their important rhetorical ammunition.

198. "Japan: Recent Developments and Short-Run Prospects," op. cit.

199. Packard (1966), p. 54.

200. Kitaoka (1995), p. 141.

201. Schaller (1997), p. 139.

202. Given the long-term significance of this personal realignment in terms of

solidifying US-Japan relations, Kitaoka has described Ikeda's decision as "a moment of extreme importance in [Japan's] post-war history." See Kitaoka (1995), p. 142.

203. Ibid., pp. 144–45.

204. Even Fujiyama turned against the prime minister when he learned that Kishi favored Ikeda over him as a possible successor as premier. In pique, the foreign minister sought to undermine his long-term friend by informing the Americans, in early 1960, that Kishi was unlikely to survive much longer politically as prime minister. See LaFeber (1997b), p. 319.

205. Kitaoka (1995), p. 143.

206. Kishi himself, it is worth noting, was not immune to the temptation of risking foreign relations for political advantage. For example, in early June 1960, James Hagerty, Eisenhower's press secretary, together with Thomas Stephens, the White House appointments secretary, had traveled in advance to Japan to make final preparations for the President's visit. En route from Haneda airport to downtown Tokyo, the Americans' car was attacked by angry demonstrators and the occupants spent more than a few uncomfortable minutes waiting for police support to arrive before being helicoptered to safety. The men escaped unscathed, and ultimately the incident was useful in provoking both embarrassment and a sobering realization among Japanese press and public opinion that irresponsible and unrestrained mob behavior might be jeopardizing both a valuable bilateral relationship and Japan's standing in the eyes of the rest of the world. In Hagerty's judgment, the government, presumably with Kishi's approval, had deliberately ordered the Japanese police not to be present during the initial stages of the unrest so that "they could sort of let [the attack] happen." Kishi's gambit paid off, in terms of providing support for the government, or at least in discrediting the protest movement in the eyes of popular opinion—but one cannot help wondering what would have happened if the police had not arrived in time. See Oral History Interview with James Hagerty, by Ed Edwin, Jan. 31, 1968, Columbia University Oral History Project. US intelligence analysts speculated that the problems surrounding the Security Treaty conflict might have been exacerbated by a deliberate policy of passive policing early on during the protest period. Reluctance to act decisively from the outset—either because of a failure to understand the tactics of the more extremist groups, or because of a desire to avoid martyring any of the protesters, or out of a more calculated intention to build up popular sympathy for more forceful police action later on—may have allowed events to run out of control. See "Japan: Recent Developments and Short-Run Prospects," op. cit.

207. Kitaoka (1995), p. 146. As Michael Schaller has pointed out, "Eisenhower and Kishi considered the new security pact a step toward institutionalizing a partnership of equality while preserving US military and base rights." Schaller (1997), p. 143.

208. Parsons to Herter, May 27, 1960, *FRUS* XVIII, 1958–60, p. 312.

Conclusion

1. Reischauer (1960).

2. For example, Buckley (1992).

3. See chapter five.

4. While Japanese public and media opinion (as the *Lucky Dragon* crisis revealed) were often critical of the United States for appearing to ignore Japanese interests, Japan's leaders were more mixed in their reactions. Ikeda Hayato's suggestion to Frank Waring in 1954 that Japan be treated as a junior partner, requiring financial and security support from a wealthy United States (see chapter six), reveals that the Japanese government was at times willing to adopt a subordinate role—a finding which casts doubt on Rothstein's claim—Rothstein (1968)—that small powers desire "formal equality in all situations."

5. See introduction.

6. For a discussion of the contemporary debate, see Hook and McCormack (2001).

7. For a selection of critical assessments of President Bush's foreign policy, see Clarke (2004), Prestowitz (2003), and Daalder and Lindsay (2003).

8. See "Japan: Dynamism Abroad and at Home," in IISS (2004), pp. 267–78.

9. For a thoughtful discussion of Japan's new nationalism, see Nathan (2004).

Bibliography

Primary Sources

British Foreign Office Records, FO 371, Public Record Office (Kew Gardens, UK)
Declassified Documents, Microfilm Series
Dwight D. Eisenhower Presidential Library (Abilene, KS)
    Edward Beach and Evan Aurand Records
    Joseph Dodge Papers
    John Foster Dulles Papers
    Dwight D. Eisenhower, Papers as President (Ann Whitman File)
    Dwight D. Eisenhower, Records as President (White House Central File)
    James Hagerty Papers
    Bryce Harlow Records
    Christian Herter Papers
    C. D. Jackson Papers
    C. D. Jackson Records
    Neil Jacoby Papers
    Joseph Rand Records
    Clarence Randall Journals
    US Council on Foreign Economic Policy
    US President's Citizen Advisors on the Mutual Security Program (Fairless Committee)
    US President's Commission on Foreign Economic Policy (Randall Commission)
    US President's Committee on Information Activities Abroad (Sprague Committee)
    US President's Committee on International Information (Jackson Committee)
    US President's Committee to Study the US Military Assistance Program (Draper Committee)
    White House Office, National Security Council Staff
    White House Office, Office of the Staff Secretary

White House Office, Office of the Special Assistant for Disarmament
White House Office, Office of the Special Assistant for National Security Affairs
White House Office, Staff Research Group
Oral Histories:

Winthrop Aldrich	Najeeb Halaby
Dillon Anderson	Karl Harr
Andrew Berding	John Hollister
Richard Bissell, Jr.	Walter Judd
Charles Bohlen	William Knowland
Robert Bowie	Lyman Lemnitzer
Mark Clark	John McCone
Robert Donovan	Neil McElroy
William Draper	Robert Murphy
Dwight D. Eisenhower	Walter Robertson
Thomas Gates, Jr.	Richard Rovere
Andrew Goodpaster	Mansfield Sprague
Gordon Gray	Harold Stassen
James Hagerty	Ann C. Whitman

Louis Galambos and Daren van Ee, eds. 1996. *The Papers of Dwight David Eisenhower*, vol. 14. Baltimore, MD: Johns Hopkins University Press.
Japanese Foreign Ministry Records, Diplomatic Record Office, Tokyo (Gaikōshiryōkan)
Seeley G. Mudd Manuscript Library (Princeton, NJ)
Oral Histories

John Allison	Robert Murphy
W. Walton Butterworth	Okazaki Katsuo
Fujiyama Aiichirō	Arthur Radford
Gordon Gray	Matthew B. Ridgway
U. Alexis Johnson	Walter Robertson
Walter H. Judd	John Rockefeller
George Kennan	Dean Rusk
Nobusuke Kishi	William Sebald
Kōno Ichirō	H. Alexander Smith
Douglas MacArthur, II	John Sparkman
John McCloy	Percy Spender
Livingston Merchant	Yoshida Shigeru

National Archives (Washington, DC, and College Park, MD)
Army Operations, General Decimal Files, RG 319
CIA Murphy Papers, Robert Murphy Collection on International Communism, 1918–61 (Japan series, boxes 94 to 97), RG 273
Department of Defense, International Security Affairs, RG 330
Joint Chiefs of Staff, RG 218
National Security Council Policy Papers, RG 273
Policy Planning Staff, RG 59
Records of the General Staff (G3), RG 319

Records of the Investigative Records Repository (IRR), included within
  Records of the Army Staff, Records of the Office of the Assistant Chief of
  Staff, G3, Intelligence, RG319
State Department Decimal Files, RG 59
State Department, Office of Intelligence Research Files
State Department, Office of Northeast Asian Affairs (Various Lot Files), RG
  59
State Department, Records of the Assistant Secretary of State for Far Eastern
  Affairs (John Moore Allison) RG 59
Van Fleet Report, RG 330
US Dept. of State, *Foreign Relations of the United States* (FRUS), Pittsburgh, PA:
  Government Printing Office. (Various volumes, 1945–1960. Publication
  date listed in parentheses):
Vol. I, 1950. *National Security Affairs; Foreign Economic Policy* (1977)
Vol. VI, 1950. *East Asia and the Pacific* (1976)
Vol. VI, 1951. *Asia and the Pacific* (1978)
Vol. XIV, 1952–54. *China and Japan* (1985)
Vol. XX, 1955–57. *Regulation of Armaments and Atomic Energy* (1990)
Vol. XXIII, 1955–57, Pt 1. *Japan* (1991)
Vol. XVIII, 1958–60. *Japan and Korea* (1994)

Secondary Sources (Books and Articles)

Abe, Kōbō. 1991. *Beyond the Curve*, trans. Juliet Winters Carpenter. Tokyo: Ko-
  dansha International.
Acheson, Dean. 1969. *Present at the Creation*. New York, NY: W. W. Norton.
Adams, Sherman. 1961. *First-Hand Report: The Inside Story of the Eisenhower
  Administration*. London: Hutchinson.
Allison, John M. 1973. *Ambassador from the Prairie, or Allison Wonderland*.
  Boston, MA: Houghton Mifflin.
Alperovitz, Gar. 1965. *Atomic Diplomacy: Hiroshima and Potsdam*. New York,
  NY: Vintage.
Amakawa, Akira. 1986. "Kōwa to kokunai tōchi taisei no saihen" [The Peace
  Treaty and the reorganization of domestic rule], in Watanabe and Miyasato
  (1986).
"Amerika no genshiryoku enjo to Nihon" [America's nuclear power aid and Ja-
  pan]. 1955. *Heiwa* 33.
Anderson, Benedict. 1983. *Imagined Communities*. London: Verso.
Asada, Sadao. 1995. "The Mushroom Cloud and National Psyches: Japanese and
  American Perceptions of the A-Bomb Decision, 1945–1995," *The Journal of
  American-East Asian Relations* 4, no. 2 (Summer).
Auer, James E. 1973. *The Postwar Rearmament Planning of Japanese Maritime
  Forces, 1945–1971*. New York, NY: Praeger.
Barnet, Richard J. 1983. *The Alliance: America-Europe-Japan: Makers of the
  Postwar World*. New York, NY: Simon and Schuster.
Barnett, Michael. 1996. "Identity and Alliances in the Middle East," in Katzen-
  stein (1996b).

Barnhart, Michael A. 1992. "Whose Asia?" *Diplomatic History* 16, no. 3 (Summer).

Berding, Andrew H. 1965. *Dulles on Diplomacy.* Princeton, NJ: D. Van Nostrand.

Berger, Thomas U. 1996. "Norms, Identity, and National Security in Germany and Japan," in Katzenstein (1996b).

"Bikini hisaisha o meguri—gakusha, jishusei o shuchō" [Regarding the Bikini victims—scholars emphasize their independence]. 1954. *Asahi Shinbun,* Mar. 23.

"Bikini no hai—kidorui no sankabutsuka" [Ashes of Bikini—possibly rare earth oxides]. 1954. *Asahi Shinbun,* Mar. 17.

Bipartisan Study Group on the U.S.-Japan Partnership. 2000. *The United States and Japan: Advancing Toward a Mature Partnership.* Institute for National Strategic Studies, National Defense University. Online at http://www.ndu.edu/ndu/sr_japan.html [accessed May 23, 2003].

Bischof, Günter. 1995. "Eisenhower, the Summit, and the Austrian Treaty, 1953–1955," in Bischof and Ambrose (1995).

Bischof, Günter, and Stephen E. Ambrose, eds. 1995. *Eisenhower: A Centenary Assessment.* Baton Rouge, LA: Louisiana State University Press.

Bissell, Richard M., Jr. (with Jonathan Lewis and Frances T. Pueblo). 1996. *Reflections of a Cold Warrior: From Yalta to the Bay of Pigs.* New Haven, CT: Yale University Press.

Blum, Robert M. 1982. *Drawing the Line: The Origin of the American Containment Policy in East Asia.* New York, NY: W. W. Norton.

Borden, William S. 1984. *The Pacific Alliance: United States Foreign Economic Policy and Japanese Trade Recovery, 1947–1955.* Madison, WI: University of Wisconsin Press.

Borg, Dorothy, and Waldo Heinrichs, eds. 1980. *Uncertain Years: Chinese-American Relations, 1947–1950.* New York, NY: Columbia University Press.

Borton, Hugh, ed. 1957a. *Japan Between East and West.* New York, NY: Harper and Brothers.

———. 1957b. "Politics and the Future of Democracy in Japan," in Borton (1957a).

———. 2002. *Spanning Japan's Modern Century: The Memoirs of Hugh Borton.* Lanham, MD: Lexington Books.

Bowie, Robert R., and Richard I. Immerman. 1998. *Waging Peace: How Eisenhower Shaped an Enduring Cold War Strategy.* Oxford: Oxford University Press.

Brands, H. W., Jr. 1988a. *Cold Warriors: Eisenhower's Generation and American Foreign Policy.* New York, NY: Columbia University Press.

———. 1988b. "John Foster Dulles: Speak Loudly and Carry a Soft Stick," in Brands (1988a).

Brinkley, Douglas, ed. 1993. *Dean Acheson and the Making of U.S. Foreign Policy.* London: Macmillan.

Brown, Delmer. 1955. *Nationalism in Japan: An Introductory Historical Analysis.* Berkeley, CA: University of California Press.

Buckley, Roger. 1982. *Occupation Diplomacy: Britain, the United States and Japan, 1945–1952.* Cambridge: Cambridge University Press.

————. 1992. *US-Japan Alliance Diplomacy, 1945–1990*. Cambridge: Cambridge University Press.

Bundy, McGeorge. 1988. *Danger and Survival: Choices about the Bomb in the First 50 Years*. New York, NY: Vintage Books.

Cha, Victor D. 1999. *Alignment despite Antagonism: The United States-Korea-Japan Security Triangle*. Stanford, CA: Stanford University Press.

Chai, Sun-Ki. 1997. "Entrenching the Yoshida Defense Doctrine: Three Techniques for Institutionalization," *International Organization* 51, no. 3 (Summer).

Chang, Gordon H. 1990. *Friends and Enemies: The United States, China, and the Soviet Union, 1948–1972*. Stanford, CA: Stanford University Press.

Christensen, Thomas J. 1997. "Perception and Alliances in Europe, 1865–1940," *International Organization* 51, no. 1 (Winter).

Clarke, Richard. 2004. *Against All Enemies: Inside America's War on Terrorism*. New York, NY: Free Press.

Cohen, Warren I. 1980a. *Dean Rusk*. Totowa, NJ: Cooper Square Publishers.

————. 1980b. "Acheson, His Advisers and China, 1949–1950," in Borg and Heinrichs (1980).

————, ed. 1983 *New Frontiers in American East Asian Relations*. New York, NY: Columbia University Press.

————. 1987. "Nichibei kankei no naka no Chūgoku" [China within US-Japan relations], in Hosoya and Aruga (1987).

————. 1990. *America's Response to China*. New York, NY: Columbia University Press.

Cohen, Warren I., and Akira Iriye, eds. 1990. *The Great Powers in East Asia: 1953–1960*. New York, NY: Columbia University Press.

Craig, Campbell. 1998. *Destroying the Village: Eisenhower and Thermonuclear War*. New York, NY: Columbia University Press.

Cumings, Bruce. 1993. "Japan's Position in the World System," in Gordon (1993).

Daalder, Ivo H., and James M. Lindsay. 2003. *America Unbound: The Bush Revolution in Foreign Policy*. Washington, DC: Brookings Institution Press.

Dickinson, Fred. 1987. "Nichibei anpo taisei no henyō—MSA kyōtei ni okeru saigunbi ni kansuru ryōkai" [Changes in the US-Japan security system: understandings on rearmament as part of the MSA Agreement], *Hōgaku Ronsō* 122, no. 3 (Dec.).

Dingman, Roger. 1975. "'Yoshida shokan' no kigen—Nihon o meguru Ei-Bei no kōsō" [The origins of the 'Yoshida letter'—Anglo-US plans for Japan], *Kokusai seiji* 53, no. 1.

————. 1979. "Strategic Planning and the Policy Process: American Plans for War in East Asia, 1945–1950," *Naval War College Review*, Nov.– Dec.

————. 1990. "Alliances in Crisis: The Lucky Dragon Incident and Japanese-American Relations," in Cohen and Iriye (1990).

————. 1993. "The Dagger and the Gift: The Impact of the Korean War on Japan," *The Journal of American-East Asian Relations* 2, no. 1 (Spring).

Divine, Robert A. 1981. *Eisenhower and the Cold War*. Oxford: Oxford University Press.

Dockrill, Saki. 1996. *Eisenhower's New Look National Security Policy, 1953–1961*. London: Macmillan.

Donovan, Robert J. 1956. *Eisenhower: The Inside Story*. New York, NY: Harper and Brothers.

Dore, Ronald. 1997. *Japan, Internationalism and the UN*. London: Routledge.

Dower, John. 1993a. *Japan in War and Peace*. New York, NY: New Press.

———. 1993b. "Peace and Democracy in Two Systems: External Policy and Internal Conflict," in Gordon (1993).

———. 1999. *Embracing Defeat: Japan in the Wake of World War II*. New York: W. W. Norton.

Drifte, Reinhard. 1983. *The Security Factor in Japan's Foreign Policy*. Ripe, East Sussex: Saltire.

———. 1986. *Arms Production in Japan*. London: Westview.

Dunn, Frederick S. 1963. *Peace-making and the Settlement with Japan*. Princeton, NJ: Princeton University Press.

Eisenhower, Dwight D. 1963. *Mandate for Change, 1953–1956*. Garden City, NY: Doubleday.

———. 1965 *Waging Peace: A Personal Account, 1956–61*. Garden City, NY: Doubleday.

Eldridge, Robert D. 2001. *The Origins of the Bilateral Okinawa Problem: Okinawa in Postwar US-Japan Relations, 1945–1952*. New York, NY: Routledge.

Elleman, Bruce, Michael R. Nichols, and Matthew J. Ouimet. 1999. "A Historical Reevaluation of America's Role in the Kuril Island Dispute," *Pacific Affairs* 71, no. 4.

Emmerson, John K. 1978. *The Japanese Thread: A Life in the US Foreign Service*. New York, NY: Rinehart and Winston.

Etō, Jun, ed. 1996. *Nichibei anpo de hontō ni Nihon o mamoreru ka* [Is Japan truly protected by the US-Japan Security Treaty?]. Tokyo: PHP Kenkyūjo.

Fearey, Robert. 1991. "Beikoku no tainichi kōwa jōyaku teiketsu niitaru kōshō no keika" [The conclusion of the US Peace Treaty with Japan: the course of the negotiations], in Murakawa (1991a).

Finn, Richard B. 1992. *Winners in Peace: MacArthur, Yoshida and Postwar Japan*. Berkeley, CA: University of California Press.

Foot, Rosemary. 1985. *The Wrong War: American Policy and the Dimensions of the Korean Conflict, 1950–53*. Ithaca, NY: Cornell University Press.

———. 1995. *The Practice of Power*. Oxford: Clarendon.

Forsberg, Aaron. 2000. *America and the Japanese Miracle: The Cold War Context of Japan's Postwar Economic Revival, 1950–1960*. Chapel Hill, NC: University of North Carolina Press.

Frank, Richard B. 1999. *Downfall: The End of the Imperial Japanese Empire*. New York, NY: Random House.

Freedman, Lawrence. 1989. *The Evolution of Nuclear Strategy*. New York, NY: St. Martin's.

Furukawa, Mantarō. 1981. *Nitchū sengo kankei shi* [A history of post-war Sino-Japanese relations]. Tokyo: Harashobo.

Gaddis, John Lewis. 1982. *Strategies of Containment: A Critical Appraisal of Postwar American Security Policy*. Oxford: Oxford University Press.

————. 1987. *The Long Peace: Inquiries into the History of the Cold War*. Oxford: Oxford University Press.

————. 1992. *The United States and the End of the Cold War: Implications, Reconsiderations, Provocations*. New York: Oxford University Press.

————. 1992/93. "International Relations Theory and the End of the Cold War," *International Security* 17, no. 3 (Winter).

————. 1997. *We Now Know: Rethinking Cold War History*. Oxford: Clarendon.

————. 2002. *The Landscape of History*. Oxford: Oxford University Press.

Gallicchio, Marc S. 1988. *The Cold War Begins in Asia: American East Asian Policy and the Fall of the Japanese Empire*. New York, NY: Columbia University Press.

Gallicchio, Marc S. 1990. "The Best Defense Is a Good Offense: Evolution of American Strategy in East Asia," in Cohen and Iriye (1990).

Garson, Robert. 1994. *The United States and China since 1949: A Troubled Affair*. Teaneck, NJ: Fairleigh Dickinson University Press.

Glaubitz, Joachim. 1995. *Between Tokyo and Moscow: The History of an Uneasy Relationship*. London: Hurst and Co.

Gluck, Carol. 1983. "Entangling Illusions—Japanese and American Views of the Occupation," in Cohen (1993).

————. 1993. "The Past in the Present," in Gordon (1993).

Goldstein, Avery. 1995. "Discounting the Free Ride in Alliances," *International Organization* 49, no. 1 (Winter).

Goldstein, Judith, and Robert O. Keohane, eds. 1993. *Ideas and Foreign Policy: Beliefs, Institutions, and Political Change*. Ithaca, NY: Cornell University Press.

————. 1993b. "Ideas and Foreign Policy: An Analytical Framework," in Goldstein and Keohane (1993).

Gordon, Andrew, ed. 1993. *Postwar Japan as History*. Berkeley, CA: University of California Press.

Green, Michael J. 1995. *Arming Japan: Defense Production, Alliance Politics and the Postwar Search for Autonomy*. New York, NY: Columbia University Press.

————. 2001. *Japan's Reluctant Realism: Foreign Policy Challenges in an Era of Uncertain Power*. New York, NY: Palgrave.

Greenstein, Fred. 1995. "Eisenhower's Leadership Style," in Bischof and Ambrose (1995).

"Gutaika shita genshiryoku dōnyū no shōtai" [Concrete details on the introduction of nuclear power]. 1955. *Ekonomisuto* 33, no. 18.

Halperin, Morton. 1992. "American Decision Making on Reversion of Okinawa: A Memoir," in *Okinawa 20* (Proceedings of a seminar on Okinawa reversion and its long-term significance in US-Japan Relations, Tokyo: May 13–14, 1992).

Hammond, Ellen, and Laura Hein. 1992. "Multicultralism in Japanese Perspective," *The Journal of American East Asian Relations* 1, no. 2 (Summer).

Hara, Yoshihisa. 1989. *Sengo Nihon no kokusai seiji—anpo kaitei no seiji rikigaku* [Postwar Japan and international politics: the political dynamics of the revision of the Japan-US Security Treaty]. Tokyo: Chūō Kōronsha.

————. 1991. *Nichibei kankei no kōzu—Anpo kaitei o kensho suru* [An outline of US-Japan relations—an investigation of the revision of the Security Treaty]. Tokyo: NHK Books.

Harries, Merion, and Suzie Harries. 1987. *Sheathing the Sword: The Demilitarization of Postwar Japan.* New York, NY: Macmillan.

Harrison, Selig S., ed. 1996. *Japan's Nuclear Future: The Plutonium Debate and East Asian Security.* Washington, DC: Carnegie Endowment for International Peace.

Hasegawa, Tsuyoshi. 1998. *The Northern Territories Dispute and Russo-Japanese Relations,* vol. 1: *Between War and Peace, 1697–1985.* Berkeley, CA: University of California at Berkeley Press.

Hata, Ikuhiko. 1976. *Shiroku—Nihon saigunbi* [Japan's rearmament—the historical record]. Tokyo: Bungei shunjū.

Hayward, Henry. 1952. "'New Japan' Faces Problems Uneasily as Occupation Ends," *Christian Science Monitor,* Apr. 28.

Hein, Laura E. 1996. "Free-Floating Anxieties on the Pacific: Japan and the West Revisited," *Diplomatic History* 20, no. 3 (Summer).

Hellegers, Dale M. 2001. *We the Japanese People: World War II and the Origins of the Japanese Constitution,* vols. 1 and 2. Stanford, CA: Stanford University Press.

Hellman, Donald C. 1969. *Japanese Domestic Politics and Foreign Policy: The Peace Agreement with the Soviet Union.* Berkeley, CA: University of California Press.

Hewlett, Richard G., and Jack M. Holl. 1989. *Atoms for Peace and War, 1953–1961: Eisenhower and the Atomic Energy Commission.* Berkeley, CA: University of California Press.

Higa, Mikio. 1963. *Politics and Parties in Postwar Okinawa.* Vancouver, Canada: University of British Columbia.

Hilgenberg, James F. 1993. *From Enemy to Ally: Japan, the American Business Press and the Early Cold War.* Lanham, MD: University Press of America.

Hill, Fiona. 1995. "A Disagreement between Allies: The United Kingdom, the United States, and the Soviet-Japanese Territorial Dispute, 1945–56," *Journal of Northeast Asian Studies* (Fall).

Hiwatari, Yumi. 1990. *Sengo seiji to nichibei kankei* [Post-war politics and US-Japan relations]. Tokyo: Tōkyō daigaku shuppankai.

Hixson, Walter L. 1998. *Parting the Curtain: Propaganda, Culture and the Cold War, 1945–1961.* Basingstoke, Hants.: Macmillan.

Hook, Glenn, and Gavan McCormack. 2001. *Japan's Contested Constitution.* London: Routledge.

Hosoya, Chihiro. n.d. "Amerika no tainichi kōwa seisaku no tenkai" [The development of America's Japanese peace treaty policy], *Kokusai seiji* 70.

————. 1982. "Yoshida Shokan to Bei-Ei-Chū no Kōzu" [The Yoshida letter and Sino-Anglo-American plans], *Chūō kōron,* Nov.

————. 1986. "San Furanshisuko kōwa jōyaku to kokusai kankyō" [The San Francisco Peace Treaty and the international environment], in Watanabe and Miyasato (1986).

——, ed. 2001. *Nihon to Amerika: Pātonāshippu no 50 nen* [America and Japan: 50 years of partnership]. Tokyo: The Japan Times.

Hosoya, Chihiro, and Tadashi Aruga, eds. 1987. *Kokusai kankyō no henyō to Nichibei kankei* [US-Japan relations and the transformation of the international environment]. Tokyo: Tōkyō daigaku shuppankai.

Huntington, Samuel P. 1998. *The Clash of Civilization and the Remaking of World Order*. New York, NY: Touchstone Books.

Igarashi, Takeshi. 1993. "Dean Acheson and the Japanese Peace Treaty," in Brinkley (1993).

Immerman, Richard, ed. 1990. *John Foster Dulles and the Diplomacy of the Cold War*. Princeton, NJ: Princeton University Press.

Inoguchi, Takashi. 1991. *Japan's International Relations*. Boulder, CO: Westview.

Inoue, Kyoko. 1991. *MacArthur's Japanese Constitution*. Chicago: University of Chicago Press.

International Institute for Strategic Studies (IISS). 2003. *Strategic Survey, 2002–3*. Oxford: Oxford University Press.

——. (2004). *Strategic Survey, 2003-4*. Oxford: Oxford University Press.

Iokibe, Makoto. 1989. *Nichibei sensō to sengo Nihon* [The US-Japan war and post-war Japan]. Osaka: Ōsaka shoseki.

Iriye, Akira. 1981. *Power and Culture: The Japanese-American War, 1941–1945*. Cambridge, MA: Harvard University Press.

——. 1992. *China and Japan in the Global Setting*. Cambridge, MA: Harvard University Press.

——. 1997. *Cultural Internationalism and World Order*. Baltimore, MD: Johns Hopkins University Press.

Iriye, Akira, and Robert A. Wampler. 2001. *Partnership: The United States and Japan, 1951–2001*. New York, NY: Kodansha International.

Ishii, Akira. 1986. "Chūgoku to tai Nichi kōwa—Chūkaminkoku seifu no tachiba o chūshin ni" [China and the Japanese Peace Treaty], in Watanabe and Miyasato (1986).

Ishii, Osamu. 1989. *Reisen to nichibei kankei—pātonāshippu no keisei* [The Cold War and US-Japan relations—forming a partnership]. Tokyo: Japan Times.

Iwanaga, Kenkichirō. 1985. *Sengo Nihon no seitō to gaikō* [Post-war Japan's political parties and diplomacy]. Tokyo: Tōkyō daigaku shuppankai.

Johnson, Chalmers. 1995. "The CIA and Japanese Politics," JPRI Working Paper no. 11, July 1995. Online at: http://www.jpri.org/WPapers/wp11.html [accessed May 25, 2003]

——. 2000. *Blowback: The Costs and Consequences of American Empire*. New York, NY: Metropolitan Books.

Johnson, Chalmers, and E. B. Keehn. 1995. "The Pentagon's ossified strategy," *Foreign Affairs* 74, no. 4 (July/Aug.).

Johnson, U. Alexis. 1984. *The Right Hand of Power*. Englewood Cliffs, NJ: Prentice-Hall.

Kataoka, Tetsuya, and Ramon H. Myers. 1989. *Defending an Economic Superpower: Reassessing the US-Japan Security Alliance*. Boulder, CO: Westview.

Kataoka, Tetsuya. 1991. *The Price of a Constitution*. New York, NY: Crane Russak.

Katō, Yōko. 1994. "Sōgo bōei enjo kyōtei ami no tenkai" [The expansion of the mutual-defense-assistance agreement network], *Kokusai Seiji* 105 (Jan.).

Katzenstein, Peter. 1996a. *Cultural Norms and National Security*. Ithaca, NY: Cornell University Press.

———, ed. 1996b. *The Culture of National Security: Norms and Identity in World Politics*. New York, NY: Columbia University Press.

Kaufman, Burton I. 1982. *Trade and Aid: Eisenhower's Foreign Economic Policy, 1953–61*. Baltimore, MD: Johns Hopkins University Press.

Kennan, George F. 1968. *Memoirs: 1925–1950*. London: Hutchinson.

Kikuchi, Tsutomu. 1986. "Osutoraria no tainichi kōwa gaikō" [Australia's Japanese peace treaty diplomacy], in Watanabe and Miyasato (1986).

Kimura, Hiroshi. 1993. *Nichiro kokkyō kōshōshi* [A history of Russo-Japanese border negotiations]. Tokyo: Chūō Kōronsha.

Kindai Nihon kenkyūkai [Contemporary Japan Research Association]. 1994. *Sengo gaikō no keisei* [The making of post-war diplomacy]. Tokyo: Yamakawa shuppankai.

Kingseed, Cole E. 1995. *Eisenhower and the Suez Crisis of 1956*. Baton Rouge, LA: Louisiana State University Press.

Kitaoka, Shin'ichi. 1994. "Yoshida Shigeru no gaikō—senzen to sengo" [Yoshida Shigeru's diplomacy—pre-war and post-war], *Gaikō shiryō kanpō* 7 (Mar.).

———. 1995. "Kishi Nobusuke—yashin to zasetsu" [Kishi Nobusuke—ambition and frustration], in Watanabe (1995).

———. 1996. "Yoshida Shigeru's Choices," *Acta Asiatica (Bulletin of the Institute of Eastern Culture)*, no. 71. Tokyo: Tōhō Gakkai.

"Kojireta Nichibei kankei" [Worsening U.S.-Japan relations]. 1954. *Asahi Shinbun*, Apr. 9.

Kōno, Masaru. 1997. *Japan's Postwar Party Politics*. Princeton, NJ: Princeton University Press.

Kōno, Yasuko. 1994. *Okinawa henkan o meguru seiji to gaikō—Nichibei kankeishi no bunmyaku* [The diplomacy and politics of Okinawa's reversion—within the context of US-Japan relations]. Tokyo: Tōkyō daigaku shuppankai.

Kōsaka, Masataka. 1968. *Saishō Yoshida Shigeru* [Premier Yoshida Shigeru]. Tokyo: Chūō Kōronsha.

———. 1986. "Nihon no kokusai shakai fukki ni okeru hitsuzen to guzen" [Chance and necessity in Japan's return to international society], *Hōgaku ronsō* 120, nos. 4, 5, and 6 (combined edition).

Koschmann, J. Victor. 1996. *Revolution and Subjectivity in Postwar Japan*. Chicago: University of Chicago Press.

Koseki, Shōichi. 1998. *The Birth of Japan's Postwar Constitution*. Boulder, CO: Westview.

Koshiro, Yukiko. 1991. *Trans-Pacific Racisms and the U.S. Occupation of Japan*. New York, NY: Columbia University Press.

Koutsoyiannis, A. 1979. *Modern Microeconomics*. London: Macmillan.

Kurzman, Dan. 1960. *Kishi and Japan*. New York, NY: Ivan Obolensky.

Lacey, Michael J. 1989. *The Truman Presidency*. New York, NY: Woodrow Wilson International Center for Scholars.

LaFeber, Walter. 1997a. *America, Russia and the Cold War, 1945–1996*. New York, NY: Alfred A. Knopf.

———. 1997b. *The Clash: US-Japanese Relations Throughout History*. New York, NY: Norton.

Lapid, Yosef, and Frederich Kratochwil, eds. 1996. *The Return of Culture and Identity in IR Theory*. Boulder, CO: Lynne Rienner.

Lapp, Ralph E. 1958. *The Voyage of the Lucky Dragon*. London: Frederick Muller.

Large, Stephen. 1992. *Emperor Hirohito and Showa Japan*. London: Routledge.

Leffler, Melvin P. 1984. "The American Conception of National Security and the Beginnings of the Cold War, 1945–48," *American Historical Review* 89 (Apr.).

———. 1992. *A Preponderance of Power: National Security, the Truman Administration and the Cold War*. Stanford, CA: Stanford University Press.

Leffler, Melvyn P., and David S. Painter, eds. 1994. *Origins of the Cold War*. London: Routledge.

Liska, George. 1962. *Nations in Alliance: The Limits of Interdependence*. Baltimore, MD: Johns Hopkins University Press.

McCullough, David. 1992. *Truman*. New York, NY: Simon and Schuster.

McGlothlen, Ronald. 1993. *Controlling the Waves: Dean Acheson and US Foreign Policy in Asia*. New York, NY: Norton.

McMahon, Robert J. 1986. "Eisenhower and Third World Nationalism: A Critique of the Revisionists," *Political Science Quarterly* 101, no. 3.

———. 1994. *The Cold War on the Periphery: The United States, India, and Pakistan, 1947–1965*. New York, NY: Columbia University Press.

McSweeney, Bill. 1996. "Identity and Security: Buzan and the Copenhagen School," *Review of International Studies* 22, no. 1 (Jan.).

Ma, L. Eve Armentrout. 1992. "The Explosive Nature of Okinawa's 'Land Issue' and 'Base Issue,' 1945–1977: A Dilemma of United States Military Policy," *The Journal of American East Asian Relations* 1, no. 4 (Winter).

Marks III., Frederick W. 1993. *Power and Peace: The Diplomacy of John Foster Dulles*. Westport, CT: Praeger.

Maruyama, Masao. 1963. *Thought and Behaviour in Modern Japanese Politics*. London: Oxford University Press.

Masumi, Junnosuke. 1983. *Sengo seiji: 1945–1955* (vol. 2) [Post-war politics, 1945–1955]. Tokyo: Tōkyō daigaku shuppansha.

Matsuoka, Hiroshi. 1994. "Gojū nendai Amerika no dōmei saihen senryaku" [America's alliance strategy in the 1950s: a quest for integration], *Kokusai Seiji* 105, pp. 85–86.

Melanson, Richard A., and David Mayers, eds. 1987. *Reevaluating Eisenhower: American Foreign Policy in the 1950s*. Chicago, IL: University of Illinois Press.

Mendl, Wolf. 1978. *Issues in Japan's China Policy*. London: Macmillan.

Miscamble, Wilson D. 1992. *George F. Kennan and the Making of American Foreign Policy, 1947–1950*. Princeton, NJ: Princeton University Press.

Miyasato, Seigen. 1985. "Gyōseikyō no sakusei katei" [The process of drafting the Administrative Agreement], *Kokusai seiji*, May.

———. 1986. "Amerika gasshūkoku seifu to tainichikōwa" [The government of the USA and the Peace Treaty with Japan], in Watanabe and Miyasato (1986).

———. 1990. "John Foster Dulles and the Peace Settlement with Japan," in Immerman (1990).

———. 1992. "USCAR Policies, 1964–1972," in *Okinawa 20*. Proceedings of a seminar on Okinawa reversion and its long-term significance in US-Japan Relations, Tokyo: May 13–14.

Miyasato, Seigen, and Koseki Shoichi. 1992. "Kōwa—Anpo: Senryō no shūryō to dokuritsu" [Peace and security treaties—independence and the end of the Occupation], in Takemae and Rinjirō (1992).

Miyazawa, Kiichi. 1954. "Nihon no kangaekata to Amerika no kangaekata—Nihon kōshō no uchimaku" [Japan and America's thinking—behind the scenes of Japan's negotiations], *Jitsugyō no Nihon* 57, no. 29.

Moore, Ray, and Donald Robinson. 2002. *Partners for Democracy: Crafting the New Japanese State under MacArthur.* Oxford: Oxford University Press.

Morris, David. 1994. *Japan: Beyond the End of History.* London: Routledge.

Murakawa, Ichirō. 1991a. *Daresu to Yoshida Shigeru—Purinsuton daigaku shozō Daresu bunsho o chūshin to shite* [Dulles and Yoshida—Princeton University's Dulles Papers]. Tokyo: Kokushokan Gyōkai.

———. 1991b. "Jon Fosuta Daresu shōden" [A brief biography of John Foster Dulles], in Murakawa (1991a).

———, et al. 1991. "Nihon no shidōteki seijika no Daresukan—Purinsuton daigaku rekishi projekuto chiimu no intabyu" [Japan's leading politicians' views of Dulles—interviews of the Princeton University History Project Team], in Murakawa (1991a).

Muroyama, Yoshimasa. 1992. *Nichibei Anpo Taisei* [The US-Japan Security System], vol. 1. Tokyo: Yūhikaku.

Nakamura, Masanori. 1992. *The Japanese Monarchy: Ambassador Joseph Grew and the Making of the "Symbol Emperor System," 1931–1991.* Armonk, NY: M. E. Sharpe.

———, ed. 1994a. *Kindai Nihon no kiseki: Senryō to sengo kaikaku* [Contemporary Japan's locus—occupation and post-war reform]. Tokyo: Yoshikawa kobunkan.

———. 1994b. "Sengo kaikaku to gendai" [Post-war reform and the present], in Nakamura (1994a).

Nakamura, Takafusa. 1993. *Shōwa Shi* (vol. 2: *1945–1989*) [A history of Showa]. Tokyo: Tōyō Keizai shinpōsha.

Nathan, John. 2004. *Japan Unbound. A Volatile Nation's Quest for Pride and Purpose.* New York, NY: Houghton Mifflin.

Nelson, Anna K. 1995. "The Importance of Foreign Policy Process: Eisenhower and the National Security Council," in Bischof and Ambrose (1995).

Neustadt, Richard. 1970. *Alliance Politics.* New York, NY: Columbia University Press.

"Nisso kōshō to Amerika no taido" [Japan-Soviet negotiations and America's attitude]. 1956. *Sekai shūhō* 37, no. 27.

Nitze, Paul H. 1989. *From Hiroshima to Glasnost: At the Centre of Decision.* London: Weidenfeld and Nicolson.

Ogura, Kazuo, ed. 2003. *Yoshida Shigeru no Jimon* [Yoshida Shigeru's reflections]. Tokyo: Fujiwara shōten.

Ōhira, Masayoshi. 1955. "Nichibei kaidan no hamon to taiso kōshō" [The repercussions of the US-Japan summit and the negotiations with the Soviet Union], *Keizai jidai,* 20, no. 10.

Olsen, Edward A. 1985. *US-Japan Strategic Reciprocity: A Neo-Isolationist View.* Stanford, CA: Hoover Institution Press.

O'Neill, Robert. 1981. *Australia in the Korean War, 1950–53,* vol. 1. Canberra: Australian Government Publishing Service.

———, ed. 1984. *Security in East Asia.* Aldershot, Hants.: Gower Publishing.

Orr, James J. 2001. *The Victim as Hero: Ideologies of Peace and National Identity in Postwar Japan.* Honolulu, HI: University of Hawai'i Press.

Osgood, Robert E. 1968. *Alliances and American Foreign Policy.* Baltimore, MD: Johns Hopkins University Press.

Ōtake, Hideo. 1988. *Saigunbi to nashionarizumu* [Rearmament and nationalism]. Tokyo: Chūkōshinsho.

———. 1997. Review of Katzenstein (1996b), in the *Journal of Japanese Studies* 23, no. 2 (Summer).

Pach, Chester J., and Elmo Richardson. 1991. *The Presidency of Dwight D. Eisenhower.* Lawrence, KS: University Press of Kansas.

Packard III, George R. 1966. *Protest in Tokyo: The Security Crisis of 1960.* Princeton, NJ: Princeton University Press.

Parrot, Lindesay. 1952. "Japan's Mood as a New Chapter Opens," *New York Times,* Apr. 27.

Pasic, Sujata Chakrabarti. 1996. "Culturing International Relations Theory: A Call for Extension," in Lapid and Kratochwil (1996).

Pollard, Robert A. 1989. "The National Security State Reconsidered: Truman and Economic Containment, 1945–1950," in Lacey (1989).

Poole, Walter S. 1980. *The History of the Joint Chiefs of Staff: The Joint Chiefs of Staff and National Policy,* vol. 4: *1950–52.* Wilmington, DE: Michael Glazier,.

Prados, John. 1991. *Keepers of the Keys: A History of the National Security Council from Truman to Bush.* New York, NY: William Morrow.

Prestowitz, Clyde. 2003. *Rogue Nation: American Unilateralism and the Failure of Good Intentions.* New York, NY: Basic Books.

Pruessen, Ronald W. 1982. *John Foster Dulles: The Road to Power.* New York, NY: Macmillan.

Rabe, Stephen G. 1988. *Eisenhower and Latin America: The Foreign Policy of Anticommunism.* Chapel Hill, NC: University of North Carolina Press.

Reischauer, Edwin O. 1952. "Some Problems in Japanese-American Relations," paper submitted for Princeton University Conference of Nov. 15/16.

————. 1957. *The United States and Japan.* Cambridge, MA: Harvard University Press.

————. 1960. "The Broken Dialogue with Japan," *Foreign Affairs* 39, no. 1 (Oct.).

————. 1986. *My Life Between Japan and America.* New York, NY: Harper and Row.

Reiter, Dan. 1996. *Crucible of Beliefs: Learning, Alliances, and World Wars.* Ithaca, NY: Cornell University Press.

Rhodes, Richard. 1995. *Dark Sun: The Making of the Hydrogen Bomb.* New York, NY: Simon and Schuster.

Ridgway, Matthew B. 1956. *Soldier: The Memoirs of Matthew B. Ridgway.* Westport, CT: Greenwood.

Risse-Kappen, Thomas, 1996. "Collective Identity in a Democratic Community. The Case of NATO," in Katzenstein (1996b).

Roff, Sue Rabbitt. 1995. *Hotspots: The Legacy of Hiroshima and Nagasaki.* London: Cassell.

Rothstein, Robert L. 1968. *Alliances and Small Powers.* New York, NY: Columbia University Press.

Rotter, Andrew J. 1987. *The Path to Vietnam: Origins of the American Commitment to Southeast Asia.* Ithaca, NY: Cornell University Press.

Ruoff, Kenneth J. 2001. *The People's Emperor: Democracy and the Japanese Monarch, 1945–1995.* Cambridge, MA: Harvard University Press.

Rusk, Dean. 1991. *As I Saw It: A Secretary of State's Memoirs.* London: I. B. Tauris.

Ryan, R. S. 1949. "Some Thoughts on Japan," *Australian Outlook*, Mar.

Sakamoto, Kazuya. 1994a. "Kakuheiki to Nichibei kankei—Bikini jiken no gaikō shori" [Nuclear weapons and the US-Japan relationship: the diplomatic settlement of the Bikini Incident], in Kindai Nihon kenkyūkai (1994).

————. 1994b. "Nisso kokkō kaifuku kōshō to Amerika—Daresu wa naze kainyū shitaka" [America and the Soviet-Japanese diplomatic restoration negotiations: why did Dulles intervene?], *Kokusai Seiji* 105 (Jan.).

————. 1997. "Nichibei anpo ni okeru sōgosei no katachi" [The pattern of mutuality in the US-Japan Security Guarantee], *Gaikō fōramu* 113 (Dec.).

Sakeda, Masetoshi. 1986. "Kōwa to kokunai seiji—Nitchū bōeki mondai to no kankei o chūshin ni" [The Peace Treaty and domestic politics and their relation to the Sino-Japanese trade problem], in Watanabe and Miyasato (1986).

Samuels, Richard. 1994. *"Rich Nation, Strong Army," National Security and the Technological Transformation of Japan.* Ithaca, NY: Cornell University Press.

Sarantakes, Nicholas Evan. 2000. *Keystone: The American Occupation of Okinawa and US-Japanese Relations.* College Station, TX: Texas A&M University Press.

Satō, Yukio. 1984. "The Evolution of Japanese Security Policy," in O'Neill (1984).

Saunders, Frances Stonor. 1999. *Who Paid the Piper? The CIA and the Cultural Cold War.* London: Granta Books.

Schaller, Michael. 1982. "Securing the Great Crescent: Occupied Japan and the

Origins of Containment in Southeast Asia," *Journal of American History* 69, no. 2 (Sept.).

———. 1985. *The American Occupation of Japan: The Origins of the Cold War in Asia*. New York, NY: Oxford University Press.

———. 1986. "MacArthur's Japan: The View from Washington," *Diplomatic History* 10, no. 1 (Winter).

———. 1989. *Douglas MacArthur: The Far Eastern General*. New York, NY: Oxford University Press.

——— 1997. *Altered States: The United States and Japan since the Occupation*. New York, NY: Oxford University Press.

Schoenbaum, Thomas J. 1988. *Waging Peace and War: Dean Rusk in the Truman, Kennedy and Johnson Years*. New York, NY: Simon and Schuster.

Schonberger, Howard B. 1989. *Aftermath of War: Americans and the Remaking of Japan, 1945–1952*. Kent, OH: Kent State University Press.

Schoppa, Leonard. 1997. *Bargaining with Japan: What American Pressure Can and Cannot Do*. New York, NY: Columbia University Press.

Schull, William J. 1990. *Song Among the Ruins*. Cambridge: MA: Harvard University Press.

Sebald, William J. 1965. *With MacArthur in Japan: A Personal History of the Occupation*. London: Crescent.

Sherwin, Martin. 1994. "The Atomic Bomb and the Origins of the Cold War," in Leffler and Painter (1994).

Shibayama, Futoshi. 2001. "Chōsen sensō no bunmyaku ni okeru bei-ei ni totte no Nihon saigunbi no imi henka" [The changing significance of Japan's rearmament for America and Britain in the context of the Korean War], *Dōshisha Amerika kenkyū*, Mar. 20.

"Shi no hai no shōtai o shiraseyo" [Disclose the character of the 'Ashes of Death']. 1954. *Asahi Shinbun*, Mar. 18.

Shimizu, Sayuri. 2001. *Creating People of Plenty: The United States and Japan's Economic Alternatives, 1950–1960*. Kent, OH: Kent State University Press.

Shindō Eiichi and Miyagi Etsujirō. 1992. "Reisen no naka no Okinawa" [Okinawa within the Cold War], in Takemae and Rinjirō (1992).

Sills, David L., ed. 1968. *International Encyclopedia of the Social Sciences*. New York, NY: Macmillan.

Sissons, D. C. S. 1950. "SCAP's Statements on the Occupation of Japan," *Australian Outlook*, Mar.

Snyder, Glenn H. 1997. *Alliance Politics*. Ithaca, NY: Cornell University Press.

Sodei, Rinjirō. 1991. "Janus-faced MacArthur," *Diplomatic History* 15, no. 4 (Fall).

———. 2001. *Dear General MacArthur: Letters from the Japanese during the American Occupation*. Lanham, MD: Rowman and Littlefield.

Sotooka, Hidetoshi, Honda Masaru, and Miura Toshiaki. 2001. *Nichibei dōmei han seiki* [Half a century of the US-Japan Alliance]. Tokyo: Asahi Shinbunsha.

Stockwin, J. A. A. 1968. *The Japanese Socialist Party and Neutralism*. London: Cambridge University Press.

———. 1986. "The Japan Socialist Party: A Politics of Permanent Opposition," in Ronald J. Hrebnar, *The Japanese Party System: From One-Party Rule to Coalition Government*. Boulder, CO: Westview.

Stueck, William. 1997. *The Korean War: An International History*. Princeton, NJ: Princeton University Press.

Swenson-Wright, John. 1997. "Yungu shinrigaku o rekishi dōsatsu ni" [A historical view of Jungian analytical psychology], *Asuteion* 45 (July).

"Symposium: History and Theory." 1997. *International Security* 22, no. 1 (Summer).

Tachibana, Seiitsu. 1995. "The Quest for a Peace Culture: The A-bomb Survivors' Long Struggle and the New Movement for Redressing Foreign Victims of Japan's War," *Diplomatic History* 19, no. 2 (Spring).

Takemae, Eiji. 2002. *Inside GHQ: The Allied Occupation of Japan and Its Legacy*. London: Continuum.

Takemae, Eiji, and Sodei Rinjirō, ed. 1992. *Sengo Nihon no genten: Senryōshi no genzai* [The origins of post-war Japan—a contemporary history of the Occupation]. Tokyo: Yūshisha.

Takeyh, Ray. 2000. *The Origins of the Eisenhower Doctrine: The US, Britain and Nasser's Egypt, 1953–57*. Basingstoke, Hants.: Macmillan.

Tanaka, Akihiko. 1991. *Nitchū kankei, 1945–1990* [Sino-Japanese relations, 1945–1990]. Tokyo: Tōkyō daigaku shuppankai.

Tanaka, Takahiko. 1993. *Nisso kokkō kaifuku kōshō no shiteki kenkyū* [A historical study of the Russo-Japan diplomatic normalisation negotiations]. Tokyo: Yūhikaku.

Thompson, Kenneth W. 1987. "The Strengths and Weaknesses of Eisenhower's Leadership," in Melanson and Mayers (1987).

Tiltman, Hessell. 1960. *Asahi Evening News*, June 7.

Tōkyō kaidan to bōei sesshō" [Defense negotiations and the Tokyo Conference]. 1953. *Jitsugyō Tenbō* 25, no. 12.

Tucker, Nancy Bernkopf. 1983. *Patterns in the Dust: Chinese-American Relations and the Recognition Controversy, 1949–1950*. New York, NY: Columbia University Press.

———. 1990. "John Foster Dulles and the Taiwan Roots of the "Two Chinas" Policy," in Immerman (1990).

Truman, Harry S. 1951. "A Treaty of Reconciliation," in *Vital Speeches of the Day* 17, no. 23 (Sept. 15).

Uemura, Hideki. 1994. "Ikeda-Robātoson kaidan to bōeiryoku zōkyo mondai" [Ikeda-Robertson talks and the development of Japanese defense forces], *Kokusai Seiji* 105 (Jan.).

Ullman, Richard H. 1983. "Redefining Security," *International Security* 8, no. 1 (Summer).

Umemoto Tetsuya. 1986. "Amerika gasshūkoku gikai to tainichi kōwa" [The US Congress and the Peace Treaty with Japan], in Watanabe and Miyasato (1986).

US v Norbert Schlei Appeal. 1997. United States of America, Plaintiff appellee v. Norbert Schlei, B. J. Bravender Ah Loo, Defendants-Appellants. Sept. 18, 1997. Online at http://pub17.ezboard.com/fdiligizerfrm6.showMessage?topicID =165.topic&index=2 [accessed May 25, 2003]

Vogel, Steven K., ed. 2002. *US-Japan Relations in a Changing World*. Washington, DC: Brookings Institution Press.

Wakaizumi, Kei. 1994. *Tasaku nakarishi o shinzemu to hossu* [I should like to think that this was the best course available]. Tokyo: Bungeishunjū.

———. 2002. *The Best Course Available: A Personal Account of the Secret US-Japan Okinawa Reversion Negotiations*, ed. John Swenson-Wright. Honolulu, HI: University of Hawai'i Press.

Walker, J. Samuel. 1997. *Prompt & Utter Destruction: Truman and the Use of Atomic Bombs against Japan*. Chapel Hill, NC: University of North Carolina Press.

Walt, Stephen M. 1987. *The Origins of Alliances*. Ithaca, NY: Cornell University Press.

———. 1997. "Why Alliances Endure or Collapse," *Survival* 39, no. 1 (Spring).

Ward, Robert E. 1967. *Japan's Political System*. Englewood Cliffs, NJ: Prentice-Hall.

Ward, Robert. 1987. "Presurrender Planning: Treatment of the Emperor and Constitutional Changes," in Robert Ward and Sakamoto Yoshikazu, eds., *Democratizing Japan: The Allied Occupation*. Honolulu, HI: University of Hawai'i Press.

Watanabe, Akio. 1970. *The Okinawa Problem: A Chapter in Japan-US Relations*. Carlton, Victoria: Melbourne University Press.

———. 1986. "Kōwa mondai to Nihon no sentaku" [The problem of the Peace Treaty and Japan's choices], in Watanabe and Miyasato (1986).

———, ed. 1995. *Sengo Nihon no saishōtachi* [Post-war Japan's prime ministers]. Tokyo: Chūō kōronsha.

Watanabe, Akio, and Seigen Miyasato, eds. 1986. *San Furanshisuko Kōwa* [The San Francisco Peace Treaty]. Tokyo: Tōkyō daigaku shuppankai.

Watson, Robert J. 1986. *The History of the Joint Chiefs of Staff*, vol. 5: *The Joint Chiefs of Staff and National Policy, 1953–54*. Washington, DC: US Government Printing Office.

Weinstein, Martin E. 1971. *Japan's Postwar Defense Policy, 1947–1968*. New York, NY: Columbia University Press.

Weisgall, Jonathan M. 1994. *Operation Crossroads: The Atomic Tests at Bikini Atoll*. Annapolis, MD: Naval Institute Press.

Welfield, John. 1988. *An Empire in Eclipse: Japan in the Postwar American Alliance System*. London: Athlone.

Wendt, Alexander. 1996. "Identity and Structural Change in International Politics," in Lapid and Kratochwil (1996).

Weste, John L. 1999. "Staging a Comeback: Rearmament Planning and Kyūgunjin in Occupied Japan, 1945–52," *Japan Forum* 11, no. 2.

Winand, Pascaline. 1997. *Eisenhower, Kennedy, and the United States of Europe*. Basingstoke, Hants.: Macmillan.

Yamagiwa, Akira. 1994. "Chōsen sensō to Sanfranshisuko Kōwa" [The Korean War and the San Francisco Peace Treaty], in Nakamura (1994a).

Yamaguchi, Tsuyoshi Michael. 1989. "The Making of an Alliance: Japan's Alliance Policy, 1945–1952." Ph.D. dissertation, Johns Hopkins University.

Yamamuro, Kentoku. 1995. "Hatoyama Ichirō—Nisso kokkō kaifuku to kenpō kaisei e no shūnen" [Hatoyama Ichirō—a commitment to constitutional revision and the restoration of Russo-Japanese diplomatic relations], in Watanabe (1995).

Yasuhara, Yōko. 1986. "Japan, Communist China, and Export Controls in Asia, 1948–52," *Diplomatic History* 10, no. 1 (Winter).

Yokoi, Noriko, and Stephen A. Resnick. 2003. *Japan's Postwar Economic Recovery and Anglo-Japanese Relations, 1948–1962*. New York, NY: Routledge.

Yoshida, Shigeru. 1961. *The Yoshida Memoirs*, trans. Yoshida Kenichi. London: Heinemann.

Index

In this index an "f" after a number indicates a separate reference on the next page, and an "ff" indicates separate references on the next two pages. A continuous discussion over two or more pages is indicated by a span of page numbers, e.g., "57–59." *Passim* is used for a cluster of references in close but not consecutive sequence.

Acheson, Dean, 36, 39, 67f, 72, 86, 93–96, 272n6; and peace and security talks with Japan, 23, 25, 42–45 *passim*, 58, 66, 269n73
Adenauer formula, 220, 222. *See also* Soviet-Japan normalization talks
Administrative Agreement, *see* US-Japan Administrative Agreement
Aichi, Kiichi, 201
Ailinginae, 153
Akahata, 161
Alliance relations, 5. *See also* US-Japan relations
Allied Council for Japan, 25
Allison, John, 44, 62, 68, 83–87, 103–7 *passim*, 159, 180, 244, 260n94; and alliance with Japan, 97, 113–18 *passim*, 127, 192, 196–200 *passim*; and rearmament of Japan, 116f, 189–93 *passim*, 197f, 201–4 *passim*, 239; and Shigemitsu, 139, 207, 220f; and Lucky Dragon incident, 167, 170–77 *passim*, 183, 295n72
Allison-Okazaki agreement, 199, 201
Alperovitz, Gar, 255n25
Alsop, Joseph, 79
Alsop, Stewart, 79
Amami Ōshima, 113–19, 132, 241, 282fn48

American Civil Liberties Union (ACLU), 121
American Council on Japan, 37
Andō, Masazumi, 170
Anglo-American alliance, 244
Anglo-Japanese alliance 56
Anglo-Japanese relations, *see* United Kingdom
Anglo-US relations, *see* United Kingdom
Anpō, *see* US-Japan Mutual Security Treaty
Anti-Subversive Activities Promotion Law, 159
ANZUS, 70
Appeasement, 43
Araki, Eikichi, 114
Archives, *see* Diplomatic records
Armitage, Richard 3, 247n5
Article 51, UN Charter, 75, 190
Article 9, 10, 45, 50, 52, 189, 235, 238, 261fn7, 279n105. *See also* Constitution of Japan (1947)
Article I, 316n183. *See also* US-Japan Security Treaty
Article III territories, 118, 123–27 *passim*, 136, 213–18 *passim. See also* Okinawa; San Francisco Peace Treaty
Article IV, 138. *See also* US-Japan Mutual Security Treaty